1750

BIODIVERSITY IN CANADA

BIODIVERSITY IN CANADA:

ECOLOGY, IDEAS, AND ACTION

edited by Stephen Bocking

broadview press

Canadian Cataloguing in Publication Data

Main entry under title:
   Biodiversity in Canada : ecology, ideas, and action

Includes bibliographical references and index.
ISBN 1-55111-238-8
1. Biological diversity conservation – Canada.   2. Biological diversity – Canada.
I. Bocking, Stephen Alexander, 1959-   .
QH77.C3B562 1999   333.95'0971   C99-931936-1

Broadview Press Ltd., is an independent, international publishing house, incorporated in 1985.

North America:
P.O. Box 1243, Peterborough, Ontario, Canada K9J 7H5
3576 California Road, Orchard Park, NY 14127
TEL: (705) 743-8990; FAX: (705) 743-8353;
E-MAIL: customerservice@broadviewpress.com

United Kingdom:
Turpin Distribution Services Ltd.,
Blackhorse Rd., Letchworth, Hertfordshire SG6 1HN
TEL: (1462) 672555; FAX (1462) 480947; E-MAIL: turpin@rsc.org

Australia:
St. Clair Press, P.O. Box 287, Rozelle, NSW 2039
TEL: (02) 818-1942; FAX: (02) 418-1923

www.broadviewpress.com

Broadview Press gratefully acknowledges the financial support of the Ministry of Canadian Heritage through the Book Publishing Industry Development Program.

Text design and composition by George Kirkpatrick

PRINTED IN CANADA

Contents

Part Four: Taking Action

Preface

Many recent events have focused attention on our relation to other species: decisions allocating Ontario's forests for parks or for industry through the "Lands for Life" process; conflicts over wilderness at Clayoquot Sound and elsewhere in British Columbia; environmentalists' criticism of proposed federal endangered species legislation as ineffective. These episodes all testify to a concern for and conflicts over biodiversity: the varieties of life in Canada, and the spaces they inhabit. These controversies are complex, ranging across science, politics, economics, ethics, and other arenas of human thought and action. The exploration of these arenas is the task of environmental studies. It is also the purpose of this book. Its contributors include scientists, historians, anthropologists, lawyers, political scientists, economists, and planners. Together, they provide an interdisciplinary perspective on biodiversity.

The first part introduces the book and provides two views on Canadians' past relationship with biodiversity: our national history and the history of Banff, our oldest national park. Part Two examines the ecology of biodiversity: its current status on land and water, the roles of species in ecological systems, and the implications of modern agriculture for biodiversity. Part Three considers our ideas about the natural world and how they reflect diverse perspectives, including those of indigenous peoples, scientists, planners, economists, and the general public. Together these chapters illustrate how our views of biodiversity reflect, at least in part, our own attitudes and values. Finally, we examine human actions relating to biodiversity: the politics of exploitation and protection, and the roles of diverse interests —

governments, environmental organizations, communities, resource industries – in determining the relation between humanity and the other species with which we share the Canadian landscape.

Biodiversity in Canada is a dynamic, rapidly evolving arena of environmental affairs. New environmental legislation, new parks, new forms of human impact, and a natural world itself continually changing mean that any book on the topic, however authoritative, can become dated. To help ensure that this book avoids this fate, it is accompanied by its own web site. This site, at **www.trentu.ca/biodiversity** provides a wide range of resources, including information on biodiversity news and events, links to an array of relevant web sites, and other materials of use to students, university instructors, and other readers. The site will be updated regularly, with new information and links that relate directly to the chapters of this book.

The first step towards this book was taken in 1997, when I edited a theme issue of *Alternatives Journal* devoted to biodiversity. (Three articles from that issue appear here, revised and updated.) Editing that issue was a wonderful experience, in part because of the people at *Alternatives*: Robert Gibson, Ray Tomalty, Mark Meisner, Marcie Ruby, Suzanne Galloway, and Janice Dickie. My thanks to all for their advice and collegiality. That experience also illuminated for me the significance of biodiversity to Canada's past, present, and future, and the opportunity that the issue presents for an interdisciplinary exploration of environmental studies. This exploration quickly became a collective enterprise. I am deeply grateful to all the contributors, for sharing their knowledge of biodiversity and for their patience in the face of innumerable editorial e-mails. Much thanks as well to Michael Harrison of Broadview Press for encouraging and advising me throughout this project and to Barbara Conolly for guiding it to publication. Trent University, as always, provided a superb environment in which to think about our relationship to the land. Best thanks of all to my partner: Rita Furgiuele, and our children, Paul and Emma, for keeping my compass aligned and our life endlessly diverse.

Peterborough, Ont.

Stephen Bocking

Encountering Biodiversity:

Ecology, Ideas, Action

BIODIVERSITY IS A RECENT ARRIVAL ON THE WORLD'S environmental agenda, prominent only in the last two decades, and especially after the 1992 UN Conference on Environment and Development (the Earth Summit). The Convention on Biological Diversity – one product of the summit – focused attention on our impacts on our living environment. Species are going extinct at a rate likely unequalled since the age of the dinosaurs; countless habitats, from coral reefs to forests, are being lost; we consume an ever-increasing fraction of the world's biological productivity. We are living a crisis in how we relate to other species.

Biodiversity is also attracting the attention of Canadians. Consider some of the events occurring even as I write this. In Alberta the Special Places 2000 program, intended to identify areas worth protecting, is being wound up, having become mired in acrimony and accusations of political manipulation. In Ontario the Lands for Life planning process, after sparking intense reaction by recommending opening all but scattered fragments of the province's forests to industrial use, has led to negotiation of a revised plan to expand protected areas. Meanwhile, off the coast of Nova Scotia the federal government has acted to protect The Gully, an area of the continental shelf especially rich in species, while across the country, environmentalists gear up to lobby Ottawa as plans for a national endangered species act take shape, once again.

These events suggest some of the dimensions of biodiversity issues in Canada. Their urgency reflects perceptions of the impacts already sustained by biodiversity: endangered species, lost or degraded habitats, depleted resources, and diminished wilderness across the nation.

Political conflicts in Alberta and Ontario (and in most other provinces) reflect differences in how biodiversity is valued – in economic, aesthetic, intrinsic, or other terms – as well as contrasting ideas about how biodiversity decisions should be made: by whom, and through what process. Wrapped up in discussions about an endangered species act are questions regarding the actions necessary to conserve biodiversity. Should the focus be on species, or on habitats? Are regulations or incentives most effective? Is conservation the responsibility of governments, resource users, or all citizens? How can scientific expertise be accessed in making political decisions?

Biodiversity is a complex, many-sided concept. This complexity poses a challenge. How can we make sense of the incredible diversity of life and its countless points of contact with human society? The approach taken in this book is to suggest that this complexity can be understood in terms of three dimensions.

The first dimension is *ecology*, the variety of life itself – the millions of species (each harbouring diversity within itself) that exist in every habitat, the product of four billion years of evolution, together creating our living environment. A second dimension of biodiversity is *ideas* regarding this diversity. This includes scientific knowledge about individual organisms and their genetic make-up, about species, and about the ecosystems within which species interact. This knowledge is provided in part by scientists; it encompasses as well other perspectives on nature, including those of indigenous peoples and of other groups in society. Ideas of biodiversity also include values: for example, that some species are more valuable than others, economically or intrinsically; that nature itself is worth exploiting, or protecting; and that different groups within society hold conflicting values, particularly concerning the balance between ecological and economic values. Together, these ideas form the lens through which we perceive, understand, and appreciate biodiversity. Finally, the biodiversity concept refers to *actions* – how we harvest certain species, and destroy habitats, even while protecting other species. Such actions are the product of many factors: policy decisions by every level of government; resource management activities; market forces; business investments; individual and group initiatives.

Through these three dimensions we can combine insights from

diverse perspectives to understand how and why Canadians use, abuse, and sometimes protect other species. The chapters in this book provide many such perspectives; their authors include scientists, activists, historians, anthropologists, lawyers, political scientists, economists, and planners.

Where We've Been

While the biodiversity concept may have only recently captured our attention, many of the issues it encompasses have a long history. As I describe in the next chapter, Canadians' attitudes towards their living environment have evolved over the last two centuries. Once something to be subdued and turned to human purpose, nature and biodiversity are now more often valued in their original state. This change has been expressed in many ways: for example, in changing ideas about how parks should be managed; in attitudes towards certain species once seen as "evil," such as wolves; and in evolving forestry practices. But sometimes change is slow: even a century ago some Canadians were trying to conserve certain species, and even today forestry and fisheries controversies attest to our continuing assault on other species.

Few places exemplify the impact of the past on our present as dramatically as does Banff National Park. The park contains spectacular scenery and wildlife habitat. But there are also the Trans-Canada Highway, a busy railway, and facilities for several million visitors each year. This uneasy juxtaposition of economy and ecology reflects decisions made during the last century, since the park's creation as an instrument of economic development. Since then some values have changed, but government policies and economic forces have not always kept pace. For example, while amendments to the 1988 National Parks Act made ecological integrity a top priority, development continued, permitted by provisions in many commercial leases as well as by a federal reluctance to act decisively. Banff, as Bob Page concludes in his chapter on this park, is "both a reflection of its history and a prisoner of its past." In 1996 the Banff-Bow Valley Study, chaired by Page, examined how we could move beyond this history, and restore the park's ecological integrity. This, as Page explains, will occur only through a new vision of the park grounded in ecological realities.

The Ecology of Biodiversity

When we think of biodiversity, species come most readily to mind: the variety of plants and animals within, say, old-growth forests or coastal tide pools, and their obvious contrast to the impoverished uniformity of manicured urban parks or prairie wheat fields. Our ignorance of essential aspects of biodiversity also is often expressed in terms of species: we don't even know how many there are in the world (estimates range between five and 100 million), or how many have become extinct in the last day, year, or century.

Biodiversity is about more than species. One common approach to understanding the concept is to identify four levels of biodiversity: genetic, species, ecosystem, and cultural. Individuals of the same species usually vary amongst themselves. These differences, if inherited, reflect genetic diversity, the raw material of evolution. Its continuing erosion may reduce the capacity of many species to adapt to changing environments. On another level, beyond species, the distinct ecological communities we see around us each composed of many interacting species – forests, open fields, or streams – are expressions of ecosystem diversity. Species would not be so numerous without the variety of habitats found within diverse ecosystems. Beyond serving as habitats, many ecosystems also exhibit distinctive properties, such as resilience (the capacity to recover from stress). A forest, for example, may readily recover from disturbances such as fire or wind. This ability to recover reflects the significance of species diversity: an ecosystem may only be resilient if many species are available to fulfill essential roles within that ecosystem. Finally, biodiversity encompasses cultural diversity. Over thousands of years humans have developed many ways of using, conserving, and modifying other species. In consequence, biodiversity, especially in the case of agricultural species, has been enhanced by, and is now at least partly dependent upon, these diverse practices.

The importance of biodiversity at each of these levels also becomes evident when we consider the impacts of our actions. While we tend to think of human impacts only in terms of extinct species, in fact, these impacts can be severe even when no extinctions occur. Distinct populations within species may be eliminated, reducing genetic diversity. Ecosystems also can be lost without affecting species diversity. For example, the original Carolinian forest has been almost entirely eliminated in southern Ontario, but most of the species originally found within it still survive in isolated pockets of habitat.

The four chapters in this section together provide an extensive account of biodiversity in Canada. Ted Mosquin begins, with an assessment of current status and trends. As he explains, Canadian biodiversity, at every level, is exhibiting the impacts of more than a century of industrial and agricultural activity. These impacts are especially evident if we compare the current state of biodiversity with its state in about 1750, before humans became a powerful presence across the land. The prognosis for the future of biodiversity also is not entirely hopeful. Activities engaged in by certain interests reduce our ability to conserve biodiversity. Among these are the tendency by governments and corporations to obscure the real consequences of their actions. There also is a continuing decline in support for scientific research on biodiversity.

Canada's lakes, rivers, and sea coasts contain a rich array of species, many of which are threatened by a range of human activities. Some threats are obvious, such as destructive fishing gear and inappropriate logging practices. Others are more subtle, but no less pervasive: widespread deformities in frogs may indicate the impacts of pesticides. Equally important, as Don McAllister notes, are the root causes: governments' failure to regulate harvesting effectively; the pressures of a global economy; and continuing growth in the world's human population. Limited scientific knowledge also impedes our ability to protect biodiversity, resulting in a continuing decline in both aquatic species and ecosystems. Almost one-third of Canada's freshwater species are at risk, and more than two-thirds of all wetland habitats have been lost.

Diverse ecological communities only exist because species perform the many functions that make life possible. Some functions are familiar: certain species are food for others, while some act as predators, and others as waste recyclers, ensuring that energy and nutrients are available for further growth. Other functions are less obvious. Vegetation moderates climate, enhancing the habitats of other species. Trees, and kelp, form three-dimensional ecosystem structures, creating more habitats. Within many ecosystems certain species contribute to stability, resilience, and harmony. As Ted Mosquin explains in his second chapter, these functions, more pervasive, diverse, and complex than generally realized, have enabled the ecosphere – the earth and all living things on it – to survive and flourish. They represent the ultimate, ecological value of biodiversity, far outweighing that of the commodities we harvest.

Natural and cultural diversity connect most closely in agriculture. Building on natural variation, generations of farmers have bred diverse strains of plants and animals and have used this diversity to help ensure resilience in the face of an uncertain environment. As Bob Wildfong describes, however, this diversity is being eroded, as modern agriculture becomes ever more dependent on a diminishing variety of seeds. And as genetic diversity erodes, so does the diversity of those who own these seeds. Thousands of farmers no longer select and save seeds year after year; this task is instead now concentrated amongst relatively few agricultural companies. And as Jy Chiperzak notes, the same pattern of diminished genetic diversity and corporate concentration is evident among livestock. But agricultural diversity can be conserved, if farmers, working with organizations such as Seeds of Diversity Canada, again choose to perpetuate diverse strains or breeds.

Ideas, Knowledge, and Values

Humans have developed many perspectives on the world. A scientist describes a forest in terms of flows of nutrients and energy and the distribution and abundance of species. A forest company manager sees the trees as a resource, whose growth can be predicted and modelled and eventually harvested. To an amateur naturalist the forest may be pristine wilderness; to the hunter, habitat for big game. These diverse perspectives, mirroring the qualities of nature, shape how we use, or choose not to use, the living environment.

Scientists, especially, have shaped our perspectives on biodiversity. Geneticists map inherited variation within species. Taxonomists catalogue species and evolutionary biologists explain how they originated.

Wildlife biologists show how grizzly bears and other species require large areas for survival, and demonstrate how salmon streams and other ecosystems have been damaged by logging. Both in Canada and internationally, scientists have helped define biodiversity conservation priorities.[1] Their influence tends to dominate our understanding of the environment, reflecting our tendency to defer to those deemed best able to provide authoritative, reliable facts about the world. As Mosquin and McAllister noted in Part Two, our ability to act effectively to protect biodiversity also is at risk as governments continue to reduce support for scientific research. It is risked, too, when decisions that should be based on scientific grounds, such as determining which species are close to extinction, become subject to political influence.

But science cannot be our sole guide. Scientists cannot now confidently evaluate the significance of many emerging threats to biodiversity, from ozone layer depletion to climate change. We still lack an effective scientific basis for managing fisheries (as recent experience with the east coast cod and west coast salmon indicates). Amphibian populations are declining and coral reefs are dying, and we are not sure why. The replacement of diverse forests with even-aged, single-species stands constitutes a massive experiment, with an outcome still to be determined. Across an array of biodiversity issues, uncertainty is pervasive.

These gaps in our knowledge of biodiversity represent, in part, unfinished business: difficult questions demanding only more time and money. (Although as Canadian science budgets continue to decline, some questions may never be answered.) But some questions may not even have answers. Complex ecosystems can behave chaotically, swayed by apparently insignificant events, rendering predictions unreliable, no matter how much information we gather. And in the meantime crucial decisions – about harvesting biodiversity, or managing parks, or about many other human activities – cannot wait.

While science is important, there are other ways of knowing the world. Experience has shown that better decisions tend to be made through processes open not only to experts, but to diverse perspectives that are more democratic and pluralistic. Therefore, while it is appropriate to draw on scientific knowledge, it is also necessary to be open to other ways of understanding the world. In practice this poses challenges: to translate public concerns into technical terms, to communicate complex scientific issues in ways that everyone can understand, and to encourage trust between experts and citizens. Scientists and those with other perspectives may be mutually sceptical about the other's insights.

Such challenges are being encountered more often, as indigenous knowledge becomes more prominent in Canadian environmental affairs. Much wisdom has been accumulated by people who have lived and relied upon the land and its resources for thousands of years. As Russel Barsh explains, this knowledge of biodiversity is more than just observations. It combines ecological explanations and ethical principles, emphasizing forecasting of local phenomena, rather than the universal theories often sought by scientists. It is often the only source of long-term information about changes in the environment. The indigenous perspective also can generate new insights, because its focus on animal behaviour is so different from the emphasis of conventional wildlife science on counting populations and other approaches that rely on numbers.

As Richard Baydack notes, science retains a central role in biodiversity conservation. Within the North American Waterfowl Management Program (NAWMP) – one of the largest conservation programs on the continent – managers must decide which waterfowl habitats should be improved, and where to devote their limited resources. In making such decisions they depend on scientific information about waterfowl populations and their habitat requirements. Much of this information, however, is incomplete. For example, it is not yet precisely known how important particular habitats are to maintaining waterfowl populations. One approach to dealing with uncertain or incomplete knowledge, applied within NAWMP and elsewhere, is adaptive management, in which management activities are designed as learning experiences, subject to modification as new information is gained.

This concept of adaptive management is becoming more influential as awareness grows of the challenges involved in using uncertain and incomplete knowledge as a basis for action. As Nina-Marie Lister and James Kay explain, adaptive management, along with strategies for helping diverse interest groups develop a common vision and learn collaboratively, can provide the best prospect for conserving natural areas. Through a case study of an area within an urban region, Lister and Kay demonstrate how such strategies are especially important because they provide novel ways of adapting to the persistent tendency of ecosystems to surprise – to change in ways that we do not expect.

Scientific knowledge is one dimension of our ideas about biodiversity. Another is the values we assign to the world. Of course, only a fine line divides knowledge and values. Among indigenous peoples the line is erased, as their knowledge of biodiversity encompasses moral values, assigned to all living and non-living things. Some of the most influential statements of environmental values also combine science and personal conviction. In *Silent Spring* Rachel Carson drew on her knowledge of ecology and toxic chemicals to formulate a powerful statement of our need for an ecological ethic.[2]

One distinction often made is between anthropocentric and biocentric values. Anthropocentric values emphasize the contribution of biodiversity to human well-being, both directly (providing food, fibre, medical materials, recreation) and in terms of those essential ecological services (nutrient cycling, climate regulation, pollination, and so on) that form our global life-support system. Biocentric values, in contrast, emphasize the intrinsic worth of biodiversity, independent of its contribution to human well-being. In practice, both perspectives can sometimes have similar implications: we may protect a region because of its intrinsic value, or because of its value for camping and canoeing; the difference will not be evident to a rare plant or grizzly bear.

But sometimes these contrasting values can have very different implications. When our values change, so, too, may our conduct. National parks, once merely another instrument by which resources could be turned towards human benefit, now have as their first official priority protection of ecological integrity. Our attitudes towards predators have changed: wolves are no longer condemned as blood-thirsty criminals. Wetlands or deserts, once considered wastelands requiring transformation into something useful, are now more often seen as distinctive habitats worth protecting. These changing values reflect the influence of such individuals as Carson, John Muir, and Henry David Thoreau. They may also be the product of scientific knowledge: ecological research has shown, for example, how certain species once viewed as "useless" in fact play important roles in nature. Changes in society, including greater economic well-being and wider interest in outdoor recreation, also have contributed to changes in values. And with changes in values have come some changes in how we behave towards nature.

Nevertheless, many argue that anthropocentric values continue to compel the elimination of Canada's biodiversity. The forest industry clearcuts the countryside to extract those few species it considers valuable. Plows convert prairie grasslands, once rich in species, into wheatfields. On the edge of our cities market forces and government subsidies hasten conversion of fields and forests into monotonous malls and subdivisions. Economic values, it is often asserted, drive extinction.

But as Peter Whiting explains, economic values and motivations, properly guided, can encourage us not to eliminate, but to conserve biodiversity. Parks draw tourists, and create jobs; this economic impact may outweigh other, more destructive uses of the landscape, justifying additional parks. Economic incentives can encourage businesses and individuals to conserve biodiversity. We must also, Whiting stresses, be aware of the loss we risk if we neglect the economic value of biodiversity, and we must realize that conserving biodiversity is an investment, not a cost. Demonstrating the value of this investment is a challenge for economists: to measure in dollars and cents the contributions of biodiversity to our well-being – regulating climate, pollinating crops, and a thousand other services – which we do not pay for, but nevertheless depend on.

Pollsters often portray Canadians as preoccupied with economic concerns. But as Loren Vanderlinden and John Eyles explain, public attitudes are actually more complex than this. In particular, attitudes towards biodiversity are grounded in various ideas about the natural world. These ideas emphasize the more engaging species – deer, bears, whales – but also encompass a view of nature as a system of interdependent parts, balanced, but fragile and unpredictable in the face of human interference. Such ideas are derived from many sources, including direct experience (through camping, hiking, bird-watching, and other outdoor activities), and science (communicated through both education and the media). These ideas, along with widely held cultural values, such as concern for children, help form widely-held attitudes that tend to be anthropocentric, but that also express concern for more than what is of only immediate use. Many Canadians wish to protect nature for future generations and they draw satisfaction from knowing that certain parts of the world are not yet dominated by humans.

Taking Action

Knowledge and values shape the politics of biodiversity. For example, scientific awareness of the importance of habitat has led to a focus on endangered ecosystems, not just species. Public interest in the broad diversity of species, and not just those that can be observed down a gun barrel, has led some provinces to replace Game Acts that mention only a few species with Wildlife Acts that refer to all species.

The relation between ideas and action is complex, raising many challenges. How are values – economic or otherwise – to be translated into policy? Who can best protect biodiversity or manage its use: governments, business, environmental organizations? Can biodiversity be protected within an economy based on industrial resource extraction? How do we set priorities when more species and habitats are at risk than can be protected? How can conflicting priorities – to protect, or to exploit biodiversity – be resolved? Such conflicts exist because there are many ways of understanding, and using, the world, and many ways of defining problems and their solutions. The essence of the politics of biodiversity lies in efforts to address these conflicts, whether equitably, or in ways that favour certain interests and values.

As Robert Paehlke explains, action on biodiversity protection faces many challenges. Short-term political perspectives and jurisdictional boundaries slice across the time and space of ecological habitats. Biodiversity loss is slow and undramatic: habitats are chipped away and species disappear without a murmur. Governments, in contrast, tend only to react to emergencies, making it easy for them to dismiss these losses. Inadequate scientific knowledge and lack of a consensus on biodiversity values also impede initiatives. Nevertheless, there are many opportunities for action. Attention to endangered species and their habitats is essential. But cities are also a crucial arena for biodiversity protection. While resources may be extracted from the wilderness, they are mostly consumed in cities, and reducing consumption offers the best prospect for protecting biodiversity. Appropriate taxes would encourage more efficient resource use. So would compact, liveable cities that Canadians would prefer to the dispersed and environmentally destructive suburbs that now dominate our cities.

Political promises regarding biodiversity sometimes seem disposable: national endangered species protection legislation is not yet a reality, nor have provincial commitments to expand protected areas been met. But once passed, laws do tend to focus our attention. As Ian Attridge notes, biodiversity laws set out what we can and can't do. But they do much more. Legal incentives and penalties encourage or discourage sustainable use of other species, and protection or exploitation of their habitats. Conflicts over resources, and disputes over jurisdiction between governments, can be settled through recourse to laws. Biodiversity law can provide tools for individuals and groups to influence government or industry decisions. Across a wide range of issues, the legal system shapes our impact on the living environment.

Biodiversity law provokes debate and controversy because it raises basic questions about the role of government in society. Much of Canada's biodiversity, particularly in more densely populated areas, is on private land. Governments usually have been reluctant to regulate private property, and notions of "property rights" are still invoked by opponents of the need to balance individual and community needs. But many property owners are committed to biodiversity protection. As a result, voluntary stewardship of private land is becoming more common, encouraged by national organizations like the Nature Conservancy, by local stewardship groups and land trusts, and through legal and economic incentives, such as conservation easements and tax incentives.

Biodiversity policy-making takes place at many levels. Agreements such as the Biodiversity Convention and the Convention on International Trade in Endangered Species set the international context. While not legally binding they at least carry moral authority: failure of governments to fulfill their obligations can be embarrassing. Within Canada, as Attridge outlines, jurisdiction over biodiversity is divided between the federal and provincial governments. This division is often marked by fractiousness. While the ecological integrity of Banff and other Rocky Mountain national parks may, as Page notes, require that land uses near their borders be compatible, in practice rivalry between Ottawa and Edmonton impedes the co-operation necessary to achieve this.

Canadian provinces are crucial players in biodiversity policy. They have jurisdiction over natural resources, crown land, hunting, fishing, and many parks. Provincial governments determine what municipal governments can do, while the federal government is unlikely to act strongly without provincial co-operation (indeed, the absence of a national endangered species act may reflect in part a long-standing reluctance to step on provincial toes). Jacques Prescott explores one provincial initiative, in his account of the development of a biodiversity policy in Quebec. In response to the 1992 Biodiversity Convention, Quebec has developed an action plan setting out how the province will meet the Convention commitments. A major challenge in implementing this plan is that of bringing together separate departments to implement a comprehensive approach to biodiversity conservation. This has been accomplished through a "global framework," organizing specific tasks undertaken by government departments and other sectors of Quebec society. A single policy framework for biodiversity, Prescott suggests, can encourage agencies accustomed to acting independently to co-ordinate and co-operate. The complexity of the plan, and the number of agencies involved, reflects the complexity of the biodiversity issue, involving, among other areas, wildlife, forestry, agriculture, mineral resources, the urban environment, and biotechnology.

But biodiversity politics in Canada now encompasses far more than government initiatives. Indeed, that governments have acted to protect biodiversity at all is to some extent because individuals and groups have insisted they do so. National organizations, such as the Canadian Parks and Wilderness Society, regional groups, such as the Manitoba Naturalists Society, and neighbourhood groups meeting around a kitchen table have identified areas of ecological interest, built support for their protection, even acted as stewards of some areas. As Jerry DeMarco and Anne Bell explain, these organizations employ limited resources in creative ways, evolving new roles, moving beyond nature appreciation, embracing advocacy. Some groups are highly visible, and confrontational, such as Greenpeace. Some emphasize habitat protection (the Endangered Spaces Program of the World Wildlife Fund and the Canadian Parks and Wilderness Society is one example). Others focus on particular species, such as whales, seals, or birds. Biodiversity advocacy groups sometimes act in concert with governments: the Committee on the Status of Endangered Wildlife in Canada (cosewic) is one example of long-standing co-operation with government by other organizations. These organizations are becoming ever more essential in the face of budget cuts, weakened environmental laws, and the perception that governments are unable or unwilling to respond effectively to public concerns.

The existence of these organizations demonstrates how the public is becoming more reluctant to defer to decisions made behind closed doors. Another consequence of this reluctance is increasing recourse to round tables and similar forms of public consultation in which representatives of different interests are brought together to agree on a plan of action. British Columbia's Commission on Resources and Environment was one example; the Lands for Life planning process in Ontario was another. Such processes are seen as attractive because they can potentially reduce conflict and ensure that eventual decisions are more widely acceptable. But they carry their own risks. The Lands for Life process illustrated both the concept (three round tables made recommendations concerning the future of much of Ontario's forests), and a major risk: when the round tables recommended in November 1998 that most forests, even within parks, be open to resource extraction, it became obvious that the process had adhered too closely to the interests of resource industries. In the face of thousands of letters, phone calls, and e-mails expressing opposition to these plans, the provincial government reopened negotiations with the forest industry and environmental organizations, hammering out by March 1999 an agreement to protect significantly more land within parks. While this outcome has been acclaimed by both industry and environmentalists, it is nevertheless ironic: a flawed system of public consultation led to crucial decisions over protected areas once again being made through secret negotiations.

In Alberta the Special Places 2000 program has encountered even

greater difficulties. Initiated in 1992, Special Places was intended to identify areas deserving protected status. But the program has had a troubled history, and several environmental groups have pulled out. As
Lorna Stefanick and Kathleen Wells demonstrate in their analysis of
Special Places in Alberta's Castle-Crown Wilderness Area, participatory processes risk collapse if they fail to ensure that all interests are represented, if some interests are perceived as having undue influence, or
if decisions are not seen as balanced, fair, and legitimate.

The Special Places program was intended to balance diverse interests, defusing conflict. In fact, the process (as also occurred in Ontario)
has itself generated conflict, because of doubts that all interests were
represented, that those facilitating the process were truly neutral, and
that the process was autonomous from government. Instead, it
appeared to be subject to political interference – a thinly disguised
effort to manipulate the public agenda to achieve the goals of particular interests. Attention to process, as Stefanick and Wells show, is crucial, if decisions are to be seen as legitimate.

But can conflicts over biodiversity protection or exploitation be
resolved at all, given the economic importance of industrial resource
extraction? Can biodiversity be protected in Alberta, where a powerful
petroleum industry seeks to maintain access to almost the entire
province? Can Ontarians agree on protected areas, when several communities remain dependent on timber and mining, even as recreational interests become increasingly influential?

These conundrums might be soluble, if we are open to new ways of
thinking. In Ontario a coalition of environmental organizations, working with forestry experts, presented to the Lands for Life process a proposal, "Planning for Prosperity," that outlined how 20 per cent of
forested land could be protected, while maintaining timber production, and creating several thousand new jobs in northern Ontario.[3]
Such a plan demonstrates how the supposed conflict between economic and environmental priorities can be resolved, if we are willing
to re-think how we use biodiversity resources.

But as Michael M'Gonigle argues, failure to do this rethinking, and
to move beyond the conventional model of industrial forestry, is
ensuring that British Columbia will neither protect enough of the
province's biodiversity nor maintain a sustainable forest economy. In

recent years a provincial Forest Practices Code, funds for "forest renewal," and innovative management schemes have appeared, intended to balance protection and industry needs. But the benefits of these innovations are largely an illusion. Real change and genuine sustainability will come about only by reshaping the industry beyond the current structure in which authority is held by large corporations and by the provincial forest ministry and in which the chief priority is timber production. Most crucial, M'Gonigle suggests, is greater local control over forests. Communities, not corporations, should be allocated long-term access to forests with the authority to manage and harvest them so as to meet community goals. The province would remain an essential player in forest management, but it would support, not displace, community authority by monitoring and reporting on the state of the environment, and by ensuring transparency and access to government decisions and information.

Understanding Biodiversity

Biodiversity is an issue today because it is now accepted that many topics once viewed as separate – protection of endangered species; management of renewable resources, such as trees or fish; design of parks; sustainable agriculture – are in fact aspects of a single challenge: to learn to co-exist with other species. This book is intended to reflect this singular nature of biodiversity. I believe that the dimensions of ecology, ideas, and action can be the basis for a synthetic perspective on biodiversity, transcending the disciplines more often used to organize our understanding of the environment.

Biodiversity issues usually encompass all three dimensions. Consider again the recent Lands for Life process in Ontario. The role of *ecology* can be seen in concerns that the proposed parks and reserves were too small to protect the habitats required by many species and in predictions that forests would not be able to meet the future demands of the Ontario wood industry. *Ideas* about biodiversity have been expressed throughout the process, as in debates over how much land should be opened for development and how much should be maintained for tourism or wilderness protection. The significance of *action* can be seen in controversies regarding how the public has been consulted, in the ways that diverse interest groups have participated, in how conflicts over the future of Ontario's forests were exacerbated, and in the evident political impact of public concerns, compelling the provincial government to seek a plan that would protect more land.

Biodiversity, like many environmental issues, can be fully understood by applying an interdisciplinary perspective. Similarly, achieving environmental sustainability depends on change in many spheres of human thought and action. Conserving biodiversity is not just a matter of getting the science right, or adopting the right system of values, or ensuring that certain interests prevail in political debate.

Each year I am impressed by how many of my students choose environmental studies because they want to find solutions to environmental problems – they want to create change. In that spirit, many of the authors in this book present innovative ways of coexisting with other species. By examining all the dimensions of biodiversity we can better understand the prospects for coexistence.

Notes

1. See, for example, Environment Canada, *Biodiversity in Canada: A Science Assessment for Environment Canada* (Ottawa: Canada Communication Group, 1994); V.H. Heywood, ed., *Global Biodiversity Assessment* (Cambridge: Cambridge University Press, 1995).
2. Rachel Carson, *Silent Spring* (Boston: Houghton Mifflin, 1962).
3. This plan, prepared in 1998 by the Partnership for Public Lands, is available at: http://www.web.net/wild/planfor1.htm

Part One: Where We've Been

Stephen Bocking

The Background of
Biodiversity: A Brief History
of Canadians and Their Living
Environment

"BIODIVERSITY" SEEMS A WORD WITHOUT A HISTORY, appearing only in the last decade, pushing its way into our ideas about the living environment. What we now define as biodiversity issues have long been with us: in debates about new national parks; or in controversies about resource development; or in the history of scientific studies of Canada's environment.

Biodiversity issues today often exhibit the effects of decisions made long ago. In Ontario's Algonquin Park debate continues over forest industry activities in the park's interior – a relic of a century ago, when logging within the new park was seen as entirely appropriate. In British Columbia logging controversies reflect that province's economic history, when dozens of communities became dependent on an industry only now encountering a finite forest. In the Arctic, efforts to build a sustainable future for communities continue a long-standing debate concerning reliance on non-renewable or renewable resources, and between the imperatives of southern market demands and northern realities.

Donald Worster, an American historian, has suggested that our past relationship with nature can be understood in terms of three levels. The first is that of nature itself: the natural environments of the past and their significance in shaping human activities. The second level is that of our work in nature: how humans have pumped, harvested, or experienced the world's resources, and the structures – from oil companies to family farms to national parks – that have developed to obtain and distribute these resources. The third level is that of ideas: the meanings, myths, and knowledge that shape our understanding of how the world works and our notions of appropriate conduct within it.[1] Change within all these levels is the subject matter of environmental history. These levels are evident also in Canadians' contemporary relationship with their living environment and in how this relationship has evolved.

Canadians have been using, studying, thinking about their living environment for centuries. The story began with the inseparability of the lives and identity of indigenous people and their environment. It continued with European colonization and the foundation of colonial development on the exploitation of living resources: cod, beaver, timber. This account will not survey this entire history; instead, it will focus on events and ideas of the last 150 years.[2]

Confronting the Continent

Farmers on the edge of settled areas in colonial Canada tended to distrust, even fear, the wilderness: a cold, vast, hostile place, requiring sturdy response from axe, shovel, and rifle, and replacement by orderly arrays of domesticated crops. In 1876 Stephen Leacock emigrated with his family to Canada and a farm north of Toronto, just south of Lake Simcoe. He later described the attitudes of the time towards the forest:

> For the earlier settlers trees, to a great extent, were the enemy. The Upper Canada forest was slaughtered by the lumber companies without regard for the future, which in any case they could neither foresee nor control.... That was the early settler's idea of the bush, get rid of it where he could, and where it lay too low, too sunken, too marshy to clear it. Then cut out the big trees and haul them out, leave the rest of the bushes there and let farm clearings and roads get round it as best they could. As to planting any new trees to conserve the old ones, the farmers would have thought it a madman's dream.[3]

Such attitudes and economic imperatives drove colonization. Roads, then railroads, penetrated the eastern and central Canadian woods, providing access for immigrants seeking land. The timber industry expanded towards the north and west, migrating from the depleted forests of New Brunswick, southern Quebec, and the Great Lakes region. This industry exported its products widely, tying Canada tightly to first the British imperial economy, and subsequently to the American. On the Prairies, railways, guns, and fences reordered the landscape from one dominated by bison into a domesticated frontier of ranches and wheat farms.[4]

Even as settlers transformed the wilderness, governments set about the large-scale task of imposing order and value. Surveyors covered the landscape, imposing upon the chaotic patterns of hills, streams, and valleys the straight lines and orderly rectangles of road allowances and private ownership.[5] The drive to catalogue the landscape and its wealth also helped generate interest in organized scientific activity, in the form of geological and botanical surveys. Through the Geological Survey (established in 1842), as well as other agencies, the Canadian government promoted an "inventory" of Canada and its resources. The immediate motivation was economic: surveys of soils, plants, and trees could help define its agricultural potential, while geological surveys found deposits of coal and other minerals essential to industry. But such activities also had political benefits. What more effective way was there to exhibit the possibilities of a transcontinental nation and the valued role it could play within the British Empire than by cataloguing its natural wealth? After Confederation, scientists like John Macoun travelled throughout the Dominion, bringing back reports of fertile land and promoting settlement of the Canadian Northwest. Together the inventory sciences, especially geology and botany, by demonstrating the productivity and wealth of the young nation, buttressed the assumption underpinning John A. Macdonald's National Policy, of unlimited natural resources upon which Canada could build its future.[6]

Not only governments, but individuals became increasingly interested in the environment during the nineteenth century. By mid-century growing prosperity (for some) had created the circumstances in which amateur naturalists could gather during their leisure hours to share their interest in scientific matters. In the cities of the eastern colonies – Quebec City, Halifax, Montreal, Ottawa – nature and science provided a social occasion, as amateurs formed natural history societies, assembled catalogues, and built museums in which to display the diversity of life within their region. Their motivations also were diverse: to supplement one's education with an interesting hobby; to demonstrate through nature the wisdom and creativity of God; even to contribute in a small way to scientific discussions in Britain or America. Canada itself being a distinctive botanical and climatic region, even an amateur mapping the geographic distribution of species near his or her home could hope to make some contribution to science.[7] Other writers drew from their encounters with nature to make distinctive contributions to Canadian literature, as did Catherine Parr Traill, who arrived from England in 1832 to settle near what is now Peterborough.[8]

Interest in collections and inventories was rarely matched by concerns about protection of species or their habitats. In a country as vast as Canada, wildlife was widely regarded as virtually inexhaustible, and concerns about impacts on species – a closed season on partridge in Upper Canada (now, Ontario), declared in 1762 by Thomas Gage, Military Governor of Canada; an Act for the Preservation of Salmon, passed in 1806; an 1839 law establishing closed seasons for several game bird species, extended in 1856 to include fur-bearing animals – were limited and largely ineffective.[9]

An Orderly and Economic Landscape

Canada at the close of the nineteenth century was changing rapidly. The nation that had begun in 1867 on the shores of the Great Lakes, the St. Lawrence, and the Atlantic, now stretched across the continent, linked by the Canadian Pacific Railway. Rapidly growing cities in the East: Montreal, Toronto, Hamilton; and in the West: Winnipeg, Calgary, Vancouver; testified to a Canada becoming ever more urbanized and industrialized. With cities, factories, and offices becoming the reality for many, and as holidays in the countryside became more widely affordable, many came to value nature not just as a place to be subdued and turned to useful purpose, but as a source of solace, recreation, and regeneration. A "back to nature" movement emerged, as

hiking, camping, birdwatching and other out-
ren pursued "nature study" in school, and animal
hompson Seton and other writers appeared on
de tables.[10] For many Canadians, the "wilderness" –
gion somewhere north of settled areas; a place for
d for testing oneself against the rigours of nature –
eir ideas of their own and their nation's identity.
ient and business were anxious to encourage inclina-
ed Canadians and visitors alike to scenic areas. Their
most lasting efforts were the first national parks. In 1887 Banff National
Park (known initially as Rocky Mountain Park) was created, followed
over the next decade by other parks in or near the Rocky Mountains:
Yoho, Kootenay, Glacier, Mount Revelstoke, and Waterton Lakes. In
each case the motivation was not preservation, but development. The
landscape was raw material, a resource, to be transformed into an economic commodity able to attract visitors ready to spend on train tick-
ets and hotel rooms. With roads, lodges, even mines and logging
camps, wilderness would become a "park" amenable to orderly
exploitation. To restrict development to safeguard habitat for wildlife
would have been considered ludicrous. Similarly, dramatic features of
the landscape, such as Niagara Falls, were packaged and sold as attractions – the foundation of local tourist industries.[11]

The push for orderly exploitation of resources was expressed not
only in new parks, but in an emerging movement to manage resources
in an efficient, business-like way using scientific expertise. By the 1880s
the consequences of rapacious exploitation of forest resources were
coming more sharply into focus. They included wasteful cutting,
destructive wildfires, droughts and floods in denuded watersheds (as
described in 1864 by George Perkins Marsh in his classic, *Man and Nature*),
and a persistent boom and bust cycle, in which towns would prosper
for a while before going extinct once local forests were exhausted.
Many of these concerns were expressed at an American Forestry
Association Congress in 1882 in Montreal. Afterwards, the federal government and some provinces began cautious interventions, protecting
forests from fire, and collecting information on their status. Such
activities reflected some of the first inklings that it was an appropriate
function for governments in Canada to manage (and not simply survey) natural resources; in doing so, governments would co-operate

actively with private industry, pursuing a shared goal of efficient, profitable resource extraction.[12] This close, supportive relationship between government and industry, becoming evident by 1900, would dominate resource management for the next century.

Both Ontario and Quebec also began to establish parks. Such initiatives reflected an emerging view of forests as other than land simply waiting for the plow. Instead, as the timber industry became more concerned about supplies of raw materials (and as governments responded to these concerns) forests became themselves worth protecting, not from cutting, but from conversion to other uses. When, for example, Algonquin Park was created in 1893, the chief concern was to maintain timber and water supplies. Settlement would be restricted, to ensure that forests would not be converted to farmland, and because forested watersheds would ensure steady streamflows necessary for floating logs to mills. Similar motivations were at work in Quebec, in the creation of Laurentide and Mont Tremblant parks in 1895. Overall, parks were seen as economic propositions, expected to pay their way in timber as well as through a growing recreational industry.[14]

In 1898 Ontario also passed a Forest Reserves Act, and over the next decade created a series of reserves intended for sustained-yield forest harvesting as well as recreation. Quebec soon followed with its own network of reserves. It is questionable whether these reserves actually affected forestry practices. At least, however, by bringing together logging and recreation in the same areas the possibilities and limitations of this "sharing" of the landscape became more evident. Recreational interests, such as canoe-oriented youth clubs on Lake Temagami, may have even sometimes moderated harvesting activity. Several reserves ultimately became provincial parks, including Quetico and a fragment of the Temagami Reserve, now known as Lady Evelyn-Smoothwater Wilderness Park. Whatever their effectiveness, these reserves signaled an increasing interest in scientific approaches to resource management that drew from the American Progressive Conservation movement and was reflected in the development of schools of forestry at the University of Toronto in 1907 and elsewhere.[15] Managing the impact of industrial society on the Canadian wilderness became defined, in effect, as a technical problem.

In 1909 the Commission of Conservation was established as an independent agency within the federal government. Inspired in part by American ideas about efficiency in resource management and by the notion of bringing expertise to bear on resource problems, the Commission, under the leadership of Clifford Sifton, devoted itself to studies of natural resources and their prospects for development. Until its abolition in 1921, it surveyed resource stocks, catalogued the waste and environmental destruction accompanying their development, and even examined the implications of the urban environment for public health and well-being. The commission also considered the status of fish and wildlife, and the state of game laws. Its perspective on species, nevertheless, focused, as did resource management generally, on those species of most direct economic interest.[16] The Commission of Conservation was one way in which the Canadian government began to express some commitment to aspects of the environment, while enhancing possibilities for outdoor recreation. This commitment was not widely felt – most Canadian initiatives at the time were the product of a few well-connected Ottawa civil servants who shared an interest in wildlife and conservation, including James White, James Harkin, Duncan Campbell Scott, and, especially, Gordon Hewitt.[17]

Professional resource management would rarely favour species beyond those considered valuable by the forest industry. Neither did the advent of conservation impede the depletion of forests across much of the country. In well-settled regions such as New Brunswick, the halcyon days of the timber trade had already passed by, leaving depleted forests and impoverished communities. Across the continent on the British Columbia frontier, in contrast, industry was only now gearing up for a century-long liquidation of a forest that had taken half a millennium to grow.[18]

Concerns about certain wildlife species, and the possibility even of their extinction, did become more apparent in the last years of the nineteenth century. Atlantic salmon had once been enormously abundant in the streams flowing into Lake Ontario. An observer in 1869 observed that they "were so plentiful forty years ago that men killed them with clubs and pitchforks, women seined them with flannel petticoats, and settlers bought and paid for farms and built houses from the sale of salmon."[19] By the 1850s they were rare, the victim of impassable dams erected on almost every spawning stream, of silting up and reduced flow of streams as a result of deforestation, and of overfishing.[20] There was no lack of evidence of the continental impact of humans on other species. The bison was nearly gone by 1885, and other large species were predicted to follow, while the sun was setting on passenger pigeons, the Eskimo curlew, and the great auk, among other bird species. In the 1890s two Royal Commissions lamented the "fantastical desecration of wildlife" and called for stronger laws on hunting and fishing. Naturalists agitated for bird sanctuaries, following Jack Miner's example, who in 1904 established his first sanctuary, in Kingsville, Ontario. Such initiatives reflected to some a moral extension of the conservation movement – an expression of concern not only about resources useful to humans, but about the well-being of other species, inspired at least in part by the spiritual, sentimental visions of wilderness provided by John Muir and other American preservationists.[21] Hewitt, the Dominion entomologist, sought to inspire such a vision among his fellow citizens:

> It lies within our power to preserve for ourselves, but more particularly for posterity for whom we hold it in trust, the wild life of this country. It rests with us to prove that the advance of civilization into the more remote sections of Canada does not imply the total destruction of the wild life, but that civilization in its true sense signifies the elimination of the spirit of barbarism and the introduction of an enlightened attitude.[22]

But this concern was selective, limited to those species that humans found valuable, or attractive, or that did not compete with us. Other species remained "vermin." In 1886 W.F. Witcher, sent by the Ministry of the Interior to assess the new Banff Park, listed those animals that were unwelcome there: "Wolves, coyotes, foxes, lynxes, skunks, weasels, wild cats, porcupines, and badgers should be destroyed.... The same may be said of eagles, falcons, owls, hawks and other inferior rapaces, if too numerous; including also piscivorous specimens, such as loons, mergansers, kingfishers and cormorants."[23] And decades later Hewitt, after extolling the need to protect wildlife, drew a firm line between the deserving and the undeserving: "Any rational system of wild-life protection must take into account the control of the predatory species of mammals and birds. And while the complete extermination of such predatory species is not possible, desirable, or necessary, a degree of control must be exercised to prevent such an increase in numbers as would affect the abundance of the non-predatory species."[24]

However, another signpost of changing attitudes came in 1911, with the Forest Reserves and National Parks Act. It shifted the purpose of parks from being "primarily places of business," to places where "there will be no business except such as is absolutely necessary for the recreation of the people."[25] A separate Dominion Parks Branch was also established, under Harkin's leadership; over the next twenty-five years nine new national parks appeared. However, the implications of the 1911 Act were mixed, reflecting the complex politics of conservation of its time. While it expanded the Rocky Mountain Forest Reserve, and created or expanded reserves elsewhere (but without controlling cutting in those reserves), it drastically reduced the size of some parks, including Banff and Jasper (only in 1914 would their boundaries be restored).[26]

Other initiatives also followed. In 1914 and 1915 three national sanctuaries were established on the prairies for the endangered pronghorn. In 1919 Point Pelee National Park was created, protecting a crucial site on the north shore of Lake Erie for thousands of migratory birds. Unlike other parks, Point Pelee came into existence primarily as a wildlife habitat, rather than for its commercial benefits.

Conservation concerns also began to appear in Canada's external relations. In 1911 Canada was party to the North Pacific Fur Seal Convention, which imposed controls on a rapacious international sealing industry. In 1916 the Migratory Birds Convention Treaty was concluded with the United States, establishing a basis for international cooperation in wildfowl protection.[27]

The early decades of the twentieth century also witnessed the emergence of ecological research in Canada. For several subsequent decades many ecologists focused primarily on the aquatic environment, particularly studies of fish: their population and distribution, food sources, and physical and chemical environment. Their motivation was primarily economic: while the Biological Board of Canada (in operation between 1912 and 1937, when it was replaced by the Fisheries Research Board of Canada) functioned independently, its political support, and therefore funding, depended on the economic significance of the fisheries.[28] Such was also the case with the Ontario Fisheries Research Laboratory, established with provincial support in 1922. Studies of birds, including their distribution and ecology, also became significant.[29]

But even as the Canadian wilderness was becoming valued for its economic promise, recreational potential, scientific possibilities, or as refuge for certain species, another presence was being erased. Native people had long inhabited and used the landscape; their customary activities now were often prohibited, displaced by those more valued by the dominant society. The Act creating Algonquin Park outlawed the traditional activities of the Algonquins: hunting and trapping were forbidden, and all fishing was placed under the control of a permit system. A similar regime was imposed when Quetico Park was created in 1913.[30] The 1917 Migratory Birds Convention Act continued a Canadian tradition of contravening traditional and treaty-based Native hunting rights. This was deliberate: Hewitt and other officials, expressing both a paternalistic regard for Native welfare and an assumption that Natives would eventually be assimilated into white society, sought to protect Aboriginals from their supposed tendency to exhaust their food supply.[31] In these and other ways, such as in portrayals of the landscape by artists, the Aboriginal presence was removed, transforming Canada from a place long inhabited to an unoccupied frontier awaiting colonization and the imposition of a new economic and moral order.[32]

A Wider View

As Canadians entered the twentieth century, encountering a world war, prosperity (for some) in the 1920s, then depression and a second war, their relationship with their living environment became more complex, as nature remained essential to their economy, society, and national identity.

The National Parks Act of 1930 expressed one sentiment: the need to preserve at least a few areas of the landscape from development. The Act prohibited mineral exploitation, allowed only limited use of green timber, and reinforced the concept of parks as game sanctuaries. But

parks were al⸺   ⸺mic resources. With
Canadians exp⸺   ⸺on, and with a steady
flow northward⸺   ⸺e a great contribution
to the tourism in   ⸺his colleagues within
the evolving pro⸺   ⸺f the National Parks
Branch were alway⸺   ⸺ot alone in doing so:
in 1923 the Nationa⸺   ⸺was formed, the first
private organizatio⸺

The 1930 Act exe⸺   ⸺ement of Canadians'
attitude towards t⸺   ⸺ that different areas
should be devoted t⸺   the Act asserted federal control over na⸺⸺⸺ ⸺⸺⸺⸺ ⸺⸺⸺ from most development, at the same time the western provinces gained control over
resources everywhere else in the region, effectively establishing the
regime that would foster their rapid development for the rest of the
century.

A chief motive for assigning specific uses to specific places is to
reduce conflict: between, for example, Canadians' interest in outdoor
recreation and preservation of scenery, and the western provinces'
desire to encourage resource development. This motive was also much
in evidence in evolving approaches to managing parks, especially in
Ontario. By the 1930s interest in preserving natural areas was growing.
In 1934 the Federation of Ontario Naturalists, then only three years old,
published "Sanctuaries and the Preservation of Wildlife in Ontario," in
which it argued that the purpose of provincial parks should be not
only economic activity, but the "preservation of representative samples of natural conditions." Four years later, their campaign against
logging in Algonquin Park led Frank MacDougall, an innovative professional forester and the superintendent of Algonquin Park, to introduce a "multiple use" policy for the park. The idea was to restrict logging in certain special areas, such as beside lakes and portage trails, and
within certain small nature reserves, so that it and recreational activities could continue to coexist. Once MacDougall became deputy minister of the Ontario Department of Lands and Forests (a post he held
from 1941 to 1966), he extended this policy across several of the largest
parks in Ontario, forestalling, if only for a while, potential conflicts
between recreational users and resource industries.[14]

The potential for conflicts also indicated how Canadians' attitudes towards natural areas and wildlife were evolving. Many Canadians had for long adhered to a straightforward moral calculation: those species that served human interests – by providing food or other commodities, or by gratifying aesthetic sensibilities (the majestic elk, the gentle deer) – were "good"; those that ate crops or competed with us for game animals were "bad." Persistent cultural perspectives reinforced these calculations: certain species, like the wolf, had long been viewed as "evil," "bloodthirsty," or "cruel," particularly in relation to those species, such as deer, that more easily aroused our sympathy. Such perspectives drove efforts to control, even exterminate, certain species. During each year of the 1920s a bounty was paid on up to 100,000 coyotes across Canada, while within national parks, hunting and trapping predators remained part of every warden's job description.[35]

By the 1930s, however, such ideas were being revised and even rejected. In part, this was the result of insights from the science of ecology. In particular, an American incident became a symbol of the dangers of meddling with complex ecological systems. By the 1920s, predators in the Kaibab National Forest in Arizona had been systematically exterminated. As a result, deer populations exploded, ate every scrap of food, and then starved to death by the tens of thousands. Ecologists and other scientists, including the American conservationist Aldo Leopold, drew from this and other experiences the lesson that predators, and indeed all species, may have some role in nature, even if they are of no apparent direct value to humans.[36]

However, attitudes towards certain species were often slow to change. This was evident in the time it took for wolves to be accepted, even valued as an essential feature of wilderness. As late as 1958 it was considered part of a park ranger's job to shoot wolves in Algonquin Park. In contrast, two decades later park visitors would be drawn on summer evenings to listen to wolves responding to naturalists' imitations of their howls. In Ontario wolf bounties were repealed only in 1972, and in the Northwest Territories only in 1975.

If many were beginning to take a wider view of nature, an important element of Canadians' relationship with their environment – resource extraction – was focusing ever more tightly on a few species. This was particularly evident in forestry. In British Columbia, industrial forestry made its way to centre stage, as a new regulatory regime provided secure access to forests. By the late 1930s concerns were being expressed about impending timber shortages in the province. The solution, as advocated by the Sloan Commission of 1944-45, was "sustained yield," through which there would be ensured "a perpetual yield of wood of commercially usable quality ... of equal or increasing volume."[37]

In the name of sustained yield much of the provincial forest became classified as Tree Farm Licenses or Public Sustained Yield Units, and generous allowable annual cuts encouraged companies to invest in new mills, roads, and heavy equipment. With surprisingly little public debate, conversion of much of the province from diverse forests to plantations of single-species, even-aged tree farms, or simply to degraded clear-cuts because of inadequate reforestation, accelerated.[38] Professional forest management reinforced this perspective, presenting a view of forests not as complex, diverse assemblages of many species, but as predominantly one or a few species, valued only in terms of production of fiber and timber.

By the 1950s, these factors – interest in outdoor recreation; evolving ideas about ecology and wildlife; and the industrialization of resource exploitation – were all becoming ever more important elements of Canadians' relationship with nature. These elements were not, however, always compatible, and in this fact lay the inevitability of eventual conflict over the future of the living environment.

An Environmental Revolution

In the 1960s the environment emerged as a major political issue. A Lake Erie that might be "dying," smog over cities, traces of pesticides everywhere all suggested that Canadians had become a dominant, even malignant factor on their landscape. Television programs and books like Rachel Carson's *Silent Spring* explained what these phenomena meant, even as greater economic security and more leisure time encouraged Canadians to concern themselves with not only the necessities of life, but the amenities – clean air, clean water, pristine wilderness – that could only be provided by a healthy environment.[39] Environmental issues assumed a permanent place on the political landscape, with the creation of Environment Canada, provincial environment ministries or agencies, and an array of environmental laws and regulations.[40]

Ideas about ecology and diversity were part of this environmental revolution. Influential voices advocated an environmental ethic based on ecological diversity: Aldo Leopold wrote about the role of diversity in maintaining the integrity of ecological systems; Carson portrayed the impacts of pesticides on all species, not just those of economic significance; and many ecologists argued that the stability of ecosystems was related to their diversity: a simple ecosystem was a more vulnerable one. A common message emerged: protecting the diversity of life on earth must be an environmental priority.[41]

These concerns about the diversity of species had numerous impacts on how Canadians related to their environment. Provincial wildlife departments expanded their attention beyond those few bird or game species that had been their traditional focus. Scientists began to identify endangered species, and these departments assembled lists of them, and began to consider how to protect both the species and their habitats. These changes were especially apparent in the work of the Canadian Wildlife Service (the most important wildlife research agency in Canada). For decades it had focused on a few species of economic significance, such as caribou. In the 1960s its activities began to encompass a wider range of species and their habitats, including aspects of the effects of pollutants, such as petroleum and pesticides. The discovery of toxic chemicals, such as DDT, in the tissues of polar bears and other northern species brought to everyone's attention the ubiquitousness of these invisible threats.

A broader view of wildlife was also evident in the supplanting or supplementing of provincial Game Acts, designed primarily to regulate hunting and trapping of game species, with Wildlife Acts. Beginning in 1971 with British Columbia and Ontario, several provinces began to provide legal recognition for endangered species. For example, by 1974 the Ontario Endangered Species Act was protecting four species: the peregrine falcon, bald eagle, timber rattlesnake, and blue racer. The Canada Wildlife Act of 1973 expanded federal activities in wildlife beyond migratory birds, to include all wild animals and their habitats, in cooperation with the provinces.[42] In 1976 a symposium on

Canada's threatened species and habitats brought together knowledge of the issue, and identified priorities for action. It led the following year to the formation of COSEWIC, a committee of experts charged with maintaining a single, credible list of endangered species, that could focus attention on those species requiring urgent attention.[43]

These initiatives were shaped by the realities of federal-provincial relations. As Ted Mosquin observed in the mid-1970s: "the federal government here, through the Canadian Wildlife Service, has been working on a list of endangered species, but it is all very hush-hush because of fear of treading on the toes of the provinces."[44] Because the provinces, under the constitution, have jurisdiction over wildlife, the Migratory Birds Convention Act was, until the 1973 Canada Wildlife Act, the only federal legislation relating to wildlife. The absence of a strong federal role was especially evident when compared with the United States, where the federal government enacted a strong Endangered Species Act in 1973. Instead, the Canadian Wildlife Service has focused on research, and on work in national parks and the territories, ceding the primary role in protection and management of endangered species to the provinces. This has been, as Kathryn Harrison has noted, a persistent theme of Canadian environmental politics: the tendency of the provinces to protect their authority over economically valuable resources and federal reluctance to assert itself in environmental issues whenever its jurisdictional right to do so may be contested, unless overwhelming public pressure compels them to do so.[45]

For many Canadians, the most important initiative relating to species and their habitats was the rapid expansion of national and provincial parks systems. Between 1968 and 1978 ten new national parks appeared. Provincial parks also surged in number; in Ontario, for example, the number of provincial parks grew from eight in 1954 to 108 in 1970.

Parks proliferated partly in response to the demand for space for outdoor recreation. More Canadians now had the opportunity to enjoy their parks: visits to national parks alone rose from five million in 1960 to 18 million in 1970. But when they arrived, they often found the parks inadequate as recreational areas. In many cases they were becoming too crowded, as people overwhelmed the natural and scenic features they had come to enjoy. For many years the numbers of parks had remained nearly static, even as pressure built to create new ones. In Quebec, for example, no additional parks had been created since 1938 (and no new parks would appear until 1977; instead, already existing parks were consolidated, and some hunting and fishing reserves were created).[46]

However, parks also began to be created not just to meet recreational demands, but because of interest in preserving ecological features of the landscape. Parks had tended to be located where scenic attractions promised to draw tourists, such as the Rocky Mountains, or in response to other local demands or conditions. There was no overall plan to protect ecologically significant features across Canada, or to ensure that the natural diversity of the nation would be protected. By the late 1960s, however, parks began to appear in response to ecological priorities. For example, Polar Bear Provincial Park in northern Ontario, Gros Morne National Park in Newfoundland, and Kluane National Park in the Yukon were chosen because they included threatened habitats and endangered species.

Much of the initial advocacy for choosing parks on ecological principles came from naturalists and ecologists. In 1958 the Federation of Ontario Naturalists (FON) published an "Outline of a Basis for a Parks Policy for Ontario" that suggested such an approach, as well as the establishment of nature reserves.[47] Over the following decade the activists and scientists of the FON and related organizations would develop a sustained critique of Ontario parks policies. Other groups also formed to make the case for protecting ecologically significant areas of the landscape. In 1963 the National and Provincial Parks Association of Canada (now the Canadian Parks and Wilderness Society) was created to advocate for new parks across the nation. Regional organizations also formed, such as the Alberta Wilderness Association and the Western Canada Wilderness Committee.

Accompanying advocacy for more parks was the argument that parks management should focus not simply on maximizing recreational opportunities, but on preserving ecological values. This shift began to be expressed in the 1960s. It, too, reflected how innovations in park practices often emerged in response to pressure from outside government. A leading figure in efforts to change parks management strategies was Douglas Pimlott (1920-78), professor of zoology at the University of Toronto and a prominent wolf researcher. In his own work he had helped change attitudes towards the wolf, by demonstrating both their ecological role and their complex social behaviour.[48] In his activism, he and his colleagues convinced many that a primary goal in managing parks should be to maintain them in a natural state.

During the 1960s, then, both the creation and the management of parks became open to a wider range of influences. This was part of a larger trend in environmental politics, as citizens of many nations became more reluctant to defer to political or expert authority. Through the influence of environmental groups and the general public – including millions of park visitors each year – the selecting and managing of parks evolved from being activities conducted within an administrative system closed to most outside influences, to being open to participation by a wide variety of interests.

By the same token, the creation of new parks sometimes created controversy. In New Brunswick, Kouchibouguac National Park (created in 1969), and Gros Morne in Newfoundland (1970), displaced some small communities and long-standing land uses. This led, especially in New Brunswick, to protests and court action.

Controversies over parks often demonstrated how ideas concerning the balance between resource exploitation, recreation, and protection of natural areas had shifted over the years. In Ontario, multiple-use management of large provincial parks such as Algonquin and Lake Superior, seen in the 1940s as an acceptable compromise between timber-cutting and recreation, had by the late 1960s been rejected by environmentalists and by much of the public, who saw shoreline reserves and other modest controls on forest harvesting as ineffectual. In part a reflection of greater ecological awareness, including knowledge of how some species depend on an extensive habitat for survival, such attitudes were also a product of the changing nature of industrial forestry. The intensity of its practices, including year-round cutting and the use of large trucks and other heavy equipment, made conflict between resource extraction and environmentalists inevitable.

In 1968 Pimlott and other concerned individuals formed the Algonquin Wildlands League (AWL). Over the next several years it played a central role in making logging within parks, and the protection of wilderness generally, a major provincial issue. By 1974, after several years of public hearings and debate, environmentalists had achieved some partial victories: Quetico had been reclassified as a "primitive" park, prohibiting logging. But in Algonquin, while certain areas had been zoned for recreational uses only, 77 per cent of the park remained open for logging.[49]

In the aftermath of these battles over individual parks, environmentalists in Ontario shifted their focus to making the case for an overall plan for the parks system.[50] In 1978 the provincial government committed itself to completing a park system that would represent the entire natural heritage of the province. Setting this goal effectively changed the politics of parks: instead of being focused mostly on local controversies, parks became a province-wide issue, with environmental groups throughout Ontario sharing a common agenda.

Conflicts within Canadian parks did not occur only between visitors and resource industries. As visitor numbers continued to increase, their impact on the nature they had come to enjoy became ever more evident. In response, managers in several provinces and within the national parks system began to develop strategies for classification and zoning, whereby recreational activities and facilities would be concentrated within certain parks, or in particular areas within parks, leaving other, more ecologically sensitive parks or areas less exposed to these activities. It became recognized that, particularly within provincial park systems, certain parks were for primarily recreational use, while others were intended to protect significant natural areas.

Systems of classification and zoning also represented another increasingly significant element of parks: reliance on professional, science-based methods of choosing and managing parks. By developing a scientific basis for decisions about parks, it was hoped that ecological values would be more effectively protected. It was also hoped that conflicts would be reduced, as park decisions could be justified not on political or economic grounds – which could always lead to disagreement – but on scientific grounds, which might be more readily acceptable to opposing interests.

By 1970 Parks Canada had identified the need for such an approach to establishing new parks, guided not by local political or economic priorities, but by science. During the next decade planners used scientific information about ecological and climatic communities to formulate a list of 39 terrestrial and nine marine natural regions that together represented the natural diversity of the nation. The national parks system, it was then proposed, would be complete once a representative area within each region had been protected.[51] Similarly, in the late 1970s new provincial parks in Ontario were identified by a process within which a landscape analysis underpinned the setting of priorities within each region, thereby throwing scientific weight behind the arguments for establishing each park. Such a process bore fruit in 1983 when, after several years of planning, the Ontario government announced that it would establish 155 new parks, adding about two million hectares to the park system.[52]

Increasing public concerns, conflicts, and a large but contested role for expertise in managing these conflicts also became evident in other aspects of Canadian environmental issues. Some of the most heated debates related to exploitation of resources: hydroelectric dam development in Labrador, Quebec, Manitoba, and British Columbia; mining in western and eastern Canada; even the possibility of exporting water to the United States. Of special relevance to species and habitats were debates concerning forests. In British Columbia, the province most dependent on forestry, concerns focused on failed reforestation, the inadequacy of sustained yield management, and the prospect of a "falldown" in timber supply as old-growth forests were liquidated. These concerns, and an awakening demand that wilderness and wildlife values be considered in forest planning, forced a wider debate about the future of the provincial forests.[53]

Debates over resource development and alternative visions of the environment were significant in northern Canada. In the late 1960s the Arctic faced the prospect of massive oil and gas developments. In response, ecologists and others mobilized in groups, like the Canadian Arctic Resources Committee, to advocate extreme caution in these developments, because of the fragile nature of northern ecosystems. This fragility stemmed in part from the relatively few species found in the North. As Max Dunbar, a prominent Canadian marine biologist noted, the "upsetting of this already rather shaky equilibrium by man's activity is probably very easy to do, and hence one must suppose that the north is more, rather than less, sensitive to pollutants and other environmental dislocations."[54] Such ideas complemented long-standing views, as expressed in explorers' journals, in art, and in literature, of the Arctic as a sublime, uninhabited wilderness.[55]

But in the 1970s portrayals of the north as a fragile wilderness conflicted with intense interest within both industry and government in developing oil and gas resources. Vast sums were spent on resource exploration on the northern "frontier," in the hopes that this region could be fully integrated, through pipelines and other developments, with southern markets.

However, another northern "vision," that had long existed, now also became prominent in the 1970s: that of the North as a homeland, the value of which could be measured not by resources shipped south, but in terms of the identity and ways of life of Native peoples who had lived there for thousands of years. Thomas Berger recognized this vision, and its contrast with how the dominant Canadian society viewed the North, in his 1977 report of the Mackenzie Valley Pipeline Inquiry, *Northern Frontier – Northern Homeland*.[56]

The conflict between these visions of the north as a frontier or as a homeland was immediately evident. Less obvious, at least to many environmentalists, was that their view of a northern wilderness might not correspond to that held by Natives, who regarded hunting of wildlife as integral to the economic, social, and cultural integrity of northern communities. Overall, these views exemplify different ideas about northern species: as requiring protection from humans, as superfluous to the economic viability of the North, or as important sources of "country food" and an important factor in the northern traditional economy. These views continue to shape northern environmental controversies, over issues as diverse as the creation of national parks, the rules governing resource exploitation, and the hunting and trapping of northern wildlife.[57]

The importance today of the North as a homeland – evident most recently in the creation in 1999 of the new territory of Nunavut – reflects the increasing significance of Aboriginal perspectives on the environment. Once ignored, these perspectives now carry weight in areas ranging from the design of new national parks, particularly in northern Canada, to the development of new regimes for managing hunting and fishing, to the increasing attention being paid to traditional ecological knowledge: the understanding of nature built up by people through generations of living on the land and using its resources.[58]

Biodiversity Becomes International

In the last two decades biodiversity has emerged as a major international environmental issue. To be sure, the issue has long had an international component, as reflected in action on certain endangered species, from the whooping crane to whales. In 1975 Canada became a signatory to the Convention on International Trade in Endangered Species (CITES), negotiated two years before. CITES took its place alongside a few other international initiatives focusing on habitats, such as the 1971 (Ramsar) Convention on Wetlands of International Importance Especially as Waterfowl Habitat, and UNESCO's Man and the Biosphere Program.

However, only in the 1980s did the notion of "biological diversity" emerge as a unifying theme in international environmental affairs, combining elements of both science and policy: an appreciation of the vast diversity of life and of the combination of initiatives necessary to safeguard it. The term "biodiversity" itself achieved prominence at a 1986 conference in Washington, D.C.[59] The following year, the World Commission on Environment and Development (also known as the Brundtland Commission) recommended that all nations commit to the simple but ambitious goal of protecting 12 per cent of their land area.[60] A Convention on Biological Diversity was a major product of the 1992 United Nations Conference on Environment and Development (the "Earth Summit"). In force since December 1993, the Convention exemplifies the central importance of biodiversity in international environmental affairs.

Biodiversity – signifying concern for the status of the broad range of biological diversity, and not just certain favoured species – has also become an increasingly important element of environmental policy in Canada. The low point was reached in 1985, when Suzanne Blais-Grenier, the first Minister of the Environment in the government of Prime Minister Brian Mulroney, cut substantially the budget of Environment Canada, particularly that of the Canadian Wildlife

Service.[61] However, within a few years a federal commitment to biodiversity had begun to be expressed. In 1988 a national strategy for the recovery of endangered species was established; two years later a new national wildlife policy expressed a federal commitment to protect all species and their habitats.[62] Protection of natural areas also regained a place in the national agenda, not least through the complex political manoeuvres surrounding the creation of new national parks, such as South Moresby in British Columbia's Queen Charlotte Islands.

Environmental organizations played a major part in the creation of South Moresby Park.[63] This reflected their increasingly important role in setting the biodiversity agenda, and in encouraging commitments from federal and provincial governments. In September 1989 World Wildlife Fund Canada and the Canadian Parks and Wilderness Society launched the "Endangered Spaces" campaign. Central to this campaign is the goal (inspired by the Brundtland Commission), of protecting at least 12 per cent of Canada's land area by the year 2000. By the following year Lucien Bouchard, the then federal Environment Minister, had committed his government to completing the national park system, including five new national parks on land by 1996, and agreements on 13 more by 2000. But progress since then has been slow, while efforts to pass a Canadian Endangered Species Protection Act testify to the continuing significance (if not dominance) of biodiversity in national politics.

Conclusion

Canadians' changing attitudes and actions regarding biodiversity exemplify our evolving relationship with the living environment. We can summarize briefly what this history tells us by returning to Worster's ideas about the levels of this relationship. Immediately evident is the first level: how the environment itself has shaped our relationship with it. The vastness of forests, fertile land, and other resources convinced many Canadians that their future lay in exploiting these resources. More recently, interest in recreation has been stimulated by the abundance of lakes, mountains, and other places where humans can enjoy nature. The diversity of life and landscapes has stimulated scientific curiosity about the environment.

The successive exploitation and depletion of resources, as people have spread westwards across the country, and the emergence of new economic resources, such as the scenery within parks that attracts tourists, exemplify the second level of this relationship: that of our work in nature – drawing from it the commodities that remain a basis of our economy.

Finally, we encounter changing ideas. One aspect of this is the distance we have travelled from the notion that all of nature exists for our benefit, to the more widely accepted view that, as wilderness or homeland, the environment is not solely ours to consume. Parks have been transformed from economic opportunities – scenic playgrounds, and sanctuary for a few favoured species – to places in which human impacts are being minimized. Wilderness has been transformed from something to be subdued and remade, to a place to be preserved, and observed with care. Scientific perspectives have broadened: from considering only those species of immediate economic importance, to examining entire ecosystems, while clarifying the roles of certain species, such as wolves and other predators. Ideas about the land and national identity and about the balance between using and preserving the landscape have also been encountered in this history. As the following chapters attest, Canadians' relationship with other species and with their living environment is a complex one; and so, too, have been the pathways we have travelled in defining this relationship.

Notes

1. Donald Worster, "Doing Environmental History," in Worster, ed., *The Ends of the Earth: Perspectives on Modern Environmental History* (Cambridge: Cambridge University Press, 1985), 289-307.
2. An introduction to this earlier history is Ramsay Cook, "1492 and All That: Making a Garden Out of Wilderness," in Chad Gaffield and Pam Gaffield, *Consuming Canada: Readings in Environmental History* (Toronto: Copp Clark, 1995), 62-80.
3. Stephen Leacock, "The Boy I Left Behind Me," in *The Penguin Stephen Leacock*, selected and introduced by Robertson Davies (Markham, Ont.: Penguin Books Canada, 1981), 378.
4. A.R.M. Lower, *The North American Assault on the Canadian Forest* (Toronto:

Ryerson Press, 1938); Barry Potyondi, *In Palliser's Triangle: Living in the Grasslands 1850-1930* (Saskatoon: Purich Publishing, 1995).

5. John Ladell, *They Left Their Mark: Surveyors and Their Role in the Settlement of Ontario* (Toronto: Dundurn Press, 1993).

6. Suzanne Zeller, *Inventing Canada: Early Victorian Science and the Idea of a Transcontinental Nation* (Toronto: University of Toronto Press, 1987); W.A. Waiser, *The Field Naturalist: John Macoun, the Geological Survey, and Natural Science* (Toronto: University of Toronto Press, 1989).

7. Zeller, *Inventing Canada*; Carl Berger, *Science, God, and Nature in Victorian Canada* (Toronto: University of Toronto Press, 1983).

8. Catharine Parr Traill, *The Backwoods of Canada*, ed. Michael Peterman (Ottawa: Carleton University Press, 1997).

9. Janet Foster, *Working for Wildlife: The Beginning of Preservation in Canada*, 2nd ed. (Toronto: University of Toronto Press, 1998), 9-10.

10. George Altmeyer, "Three Ideas of Nature in Canada, 1893-1914," *Journal of Canadian Studies* 11 (1976): 21-36.

11. Robert Craig Brown, "The Doctrine of Usefulness: Natural Resource and National Park Policy in Canada, 1886-1914," in J.G. Nelson, ed., *Canadian Parks in Perspective* (Montreal: Harvest House, 1969), 46-62; Kevin McNamee, "From Wild Places to Endangered Spaces: A History of Canada's National Parks," in Philip Dearden and Rick Rollins, eds., *Parks and Protected Areas in Canada: Planning and Management* (Toronto: Oxford University Press, 1993), 17-44; Leslie Bella, *Parks for Profit* (Montreal: Harvest House, 1987); Patricia Jasen, *Wild Things: Nature, Culture and Tourism in Ontario, 1790-1914* (Toronto: University of Toronto Press, 1995).

12. H.V. Nelles, *The Politics of Development: Forests, Mines and Hydro-electric Power in Ontario, 1849-1941* (Toronto: Macmillan of Canada, 1974).

13. Yves Hébert, "Conservation, culture et identité: La création du Parc des Laurentides et du Parc de la Montagne Tremblante, 1894-1938," in John Marsh and Bruce Hodgins, eds., *Changing Parks: The History, Future and Cultural Context of Parks and Heritage Landscapes* (Toronto: Natural Heritage/Natural History, 1998), 140-59.

14. Gerald Killan, *Protected Places: A History of Ontario's Provincial Parks System* (Toronto: Dundurn Press, 1993).

15. Altmeyer, "Three Ideas." On forest reserves, see Bruce Hodgins, "Contexts of the Temagami Predicament," in Matt Bray and Ashley Thompson, eds., *Temagami: A Debate on Wilderness* (Toronto: Dundurn Press,

1990), 123-39; Bruce Hodgins, R. Peter Gillis, and Jamie Benidickson, "The Ontario Experiments in Forest Reserves," in Marsh and Hodgins, eds., *Changing Parks*, 77-93.

16. Michel Girard, *L'Ecologisme retrouvé: Essor et Declin de la commission de la conservation du Canada* (Ottawa: Presses de L'Université d'Ottawa, 1994).

17. Foster, *Working for Wildlife*; Dan Gottesman, "Native Hunting and the Migratory Birds Convention Act: Historical, Political and Ideological Perspectives," *Journal of Canadian Studies* 18, 3 (1983): 67-89.

18. Gilbert Allardyce, "The Vexed Question of Sawdust: River Pollution in Nineteenth-Century New Brunswick," *Dalhousie Review* 52 (1972): 177-90; Richard Rajala, *Clearcutting the Pacific Rain Forest: Production, Science, and Regulation* (Vancouver: University of British Columbia Press, 1998); R. Peter Gillis and Thomas Roach, *Lost Initiatives: Canada's Forest Industries, Forest Policy and Forest Conservation* (New York: Greenwood Press, 1986).

19. Excerpt from *Annual Report, Canadian Dept. of Marine and Fisheries for Year ending June 30, 1869*, quoted in Marshall McDonald, "Additional Fish-Cultural Stations," in *Report, 1889/91*, U.S. Commission of Fish and Fisheries (Washington: Government Printing Office, 1893), 58.

20. Richard Nettle, *The Salmon Fisheries of the St. Lawrence and its Tributaries* (Montreal: John Lovell, 1857).

21. Roderick Frazier Nash, *The Rights of Nature: A History of Environmental Ethics* (Madison: University of Wisconsin Press, 1989); Max Oelschlaeger, *The Idea of Wilderness* (New Haven: Yale University Press, 1991).

22. C. Gordon Hewitt, *The Conservation of the Wild Life of Canada* (New York: Charles Scribner's Sons, 1921), 1-2.

23. As quoted in Alan MacEachern, "Rationality and Rationalization in Canadian National Parks Predator Policy," in Gaffield and Gaffield, *Consuming Canada*, 198.

24. Hewitt, *Conservation of the Wild Life*, 193. As Hewitt made clear, the definition of wolves, coyotes, and other predators as "enemies" had a great deal to do with their appetite for livestock. Immediate human needs remained the measure of what aspects of nature should be preserved.

25. McNamee, "From Wild Places," 22.

26. R. Peter Gillis and Thomas R. Roach, "The American Influence on Conservation in Canada: 1899-1911," *Journal of Forest History* (1986): 160-74.

27. Alvin C. Glueck, "Canada's Splendid Bargain: The North Pacific Fur Seal Convention of 1911," *Canadian Historical Review* 63, 2 (1982): 179-201; Briton

Cooper Busch, *The War against the Seals: A History of the North American Seal Fishery* (Montreal and Kingston: McGill-Queen's University Press, 1985).

28. Kenneth Johnstone, *The Aquatic Explorers: A History of the Fisheries Research Board of Canada* (Toronto: University of Toronto Press, 1977).

29. Marianne Ainley, *Restless Energy: A Biography of William Rowan, 1891-1957* (Montreal: Vehicule Press, 1993); John Cranmer-Byng, "A Life with Birds: Percy A. Taverner, Canadian Ornithologist, 1875-1947," *Canadian Field Naturalist* 110, 1, spec. issue (1996).

30. Bruce Hodgins and Kerry Cannon, "The Aboriginal Presence in Ontario Parks and Other Protected Places," in Marsh and Hodgins, *Changing Parks*, 50-76.

31. Gottesman, "Native Hunting."

32. Jonathan Bordo, "Jack Pine – Wilderness sublime or the erasure of the aboriginal presence from the landscape," *Journal of Canadian Studies* 27, 4: (1992-93): 98-128.

33. McNamee, "From Wild Places."

34. Killan, *Protected Places.*

35. MacEachern, "Rationality and Rationalization."

36. Aldo Leopold, *A Sand County Almanac* (Oxford: Oxford University Press, 1949); Thomas Dunlap, *Saving America's Wildlife* (Princeton, N.J.: Princeton University Press, 1988).

37. Hon. Gordon McG. Sloan, *Report of the Commissioner on the Forest Resource of British Columbia, 1945* (Victoria: Charles F. Banfield, 1945), Q127, quoted in Jeremy Wilson, "Forest Conservation in British Columbia, 1935-85: Reflections on a Barren Political Debate," *BC Studies* 76, 4 (1987/88).

38. Wilson, "Forest Conservation in British Columbia."

39. Rachel Carson, *Silent Spring* (Boston: Houghton Mifflin, 1962); Samuel Hays, *Beauty, Health and Permanence: Environmental Politics in the United States, 1955-1985* (Cambridge: Cambridge University Press, 1987).

40. G. Bruce Doern and Thomas Conway, *The Greening of Canada: Federal Institutions and Decisions* (Toronto: University of Toronto Press, 1994); Kathryn Harrison, *Passing the Buck: Federalism and Canadian Environmental Policy* (Vancouver: University of British Columbia Press, 1996).

41. Leopold, *Sand County Almanac*; Carson, *Silent Spring*. That the stability of an ecosystem is related to its diversity would eventually be questioned by ecologists; while not entirely rejected, the notion is now seen as only useful in certain limited situations.

42. Darryl Stewart, *Canadian Endangered Species* (Toronto: Gage, 1974); Michael Singleton, "Endangered Species Legislation in Canada," in Theodore Mosquin and Cecile Suchal, *Canada's Threatened Species and Habitats: Proceedings of the Symposium on Canada's Threatened Species and Habitats, May 20-24, 1976* (Ottawa: Canadian Nature Federation, 1977), 19-21.

43. Francis R. Cook and Dalton Muir, "The Committee on the Status of Endangered Wildlife in Canada (COSEWIC): History and Progress," *Canadian Field-Naturalist* 98, 1 (1984): 63-70.

44. Charles H. Callison, "Endangered Species and Habitats: The Role of Non-Governmental Organizations," in Mosquin and Suchal, 182.

45. Harrison, *Passing the Buck*.

46. Hébert, "Conservation, culture et identité."

47. Killan, *Protected Places*.

48. J. Bruce Falls, "Douglas H. Pimlott: Lessons for Action," *Nature Canada* 8, 2 (1979): 18-23.

49. Gerald Killan and George Warecki, "The Algonquin Wildlands League and the Emergence of Environmental Politics in Ontario, 1965-1974," *Environmental History Review* 16, 4 (1992): 1-27.

50. See, for example, the publications *Wilderness Now* and *Wilderness in Ontario*.

51. Dennis Carter-Edwards, "The History of National Parks in Ontario," in Marsh and Hodgins, *Changing Parks*, 94-106.

52. Killan, *Protected Places*.

53. Wilson, "Forest Conservation in British Columbia"; Ken Drushka, Bob Nixon, and Ray Travers, eds., *Touch Wood: BC Forests at the Crossroads* (Madeira Park, B.C.: Harbour Publishing, 1993).

54. Max Dunbar, *Environment and Good Sense: An Introduction to Environmental Damage and Control in Canada* (Montreal and Kingston: McGill-Queen's University Press, 1971).

55. Shelagh Grant, "Arctic Wilderness — And Other Mythologies," *Journal of Canadian Studies* 32, 2 (1998): 27-39.

56. Thomas Berger, *Northern Frontier, Northern Homeland: The Report of the Mackenzie Valley Pipeline Inquiry*, 2 vols. (Toronto: James Lorimer, 1977).

57. See, for example, Robert Page, *Northern Development: The Canadian Dilemma* (Toronto: McClelland & Stewart, 1986); P. Sabin, "Voices from the Hydrocarbon Frontier: Canada's Mackenzie Valley Pipeline Inquiry (1974-1977)," *Environmental History Review* 19, 1 (1995): 17-48; George Wenzel, *Animal Rights, Human Rights: Ecology, Economy, and Ideology in the Canadian Arctic*

(Toronto: University of Toronto Press, 1991).

58. Lawrence Berg, Terry Fenge, and Philip Dearden, "The Role of Aboriginal Peoples in National Park Designation, Planning, and Management in Canada," in Dearden and Rollins, eds., *Parks and Protected Areas*, 225-55; Dene Cultural Institute, "Traditional Ecological Knowledge and Environmental Assessment," reproduced in Gaffield and Gaffield, eds., *Consuming Canada*, 340-65.

59. E.O. Wilson, *Biodiversity* (Washington: National Academy Press, 1988).

60. World Commission on Environment and Development, *Our Common Future* (Oxford: Oxford University Press, 1987).

61. Doern and Conway, *Greening of Canada*.

62. Wildlife Ministers' Council of Canada, *A Wildlife Policy for Canada* (Ottawa: Canadian Wildlife Service, 1990).

63. Elizabeth May, *Paradise Won: The Struggle for South Moresby* (Toronto: McClelland & Stewart, 1990).

Further Reading

Bocking, Stephen. *Ecologists and Environmental Politics: A History of Contemporary Ecology*. New Haven: Yale University Press, 1997.

Foster, Janet. *Working for Wildlife: The Beginning of Preservation in Canada*, 2nd ed. Toronto: University of Toronto Press, 1998.

Gaffield, Chad, and Pam Gaffield. *Consuming Canada: Readings in Environmental History*. Toronto: Copp Clark, 1995.

Gillis, R. Peter, and Thomas Roach. *Lost Initiatives: Canada's Forest Industries, Forest Policy and Forest Conservation*. New York: Greenwood Press, 1986.

Killan, Gerald. *Protected Places: A History of Ontario's Provincial Parks System*. Toronto: Dundurn Press, 1993.

Marsh, John, and Bruce Hodgins, eds. *Changing Parks: The History, Future and Cultural Context of Parks and Heritage Landscapes*. Toronto: Natural Heritage/Natural History, 1998.

Zeller, Suzanne. *Inventing Canada: Early Victorian Science and the Idea of a Transcontinental Nation*. Toronto: University of Toronto Press, 1987.

Bob Page

Banff National Park:
The Historic Legacy for
Biodiversity

B IODIVERSITY PROTECTION REMAINS AN ESSENTIAL component of the environmental agenda, but public discussion of the required policy tools has been limited. Almost everywhere expanding development presses in on remaining secure habitat. The species toll is documented in scientific reports and television specials. While the evidence is clear, the ability of governments to craft an effective policy response remains elusive. Endangered species legislation dies on the order paper in Ottawa and the scientific process for identifying threatened and endangered species is facing political challenge.[1] The weakness of the policy tools is compounded by the lack of political will in enforcing them. Habitat protection seems to strike at one of the most fundamental and sensitive of political issues: the ownership and use of public and private lands. Where new programs are attempted they seem mired in controversy. In Alberta, for example, conflicting interests and opinions have led the Special Places 2000 Program to an impasse. In this situation the viability of existing protected habitat like Banff National Park becomes all the more critical.[2] This chapter will explore the policy controversies relating to Banff and explain how the historic legacy has contributed to the present scene.

Importing Tourists to Banff

The central dilemma for Banff National Park today is the contradiction between the contemporary ecological expectations in the National

Parks Act (1988) and Banff's historic role as a world-class tourism destination. Today many see an inconsistency between the legislated mandate for "ecological integrity" and the scale and nature of approved development. Yet an explanation can be found in the century-old heritage of commercial events and forces in the region. Banff is both a reflection of its history and a prisoner of its past. While future development can be excluded, lawful businesses operating for decades are difficult for any government to remove. To what extent do threats to biodiversity justify decommissioning? Environmentalists and the local business community have very different answers to that question. The former wish to stress the principles of protection inherent in the 1988 Act while the latter wish to protect their historic way of doing business. Thus far the power of the historic forces seems to have prevailed.

The context of the debate goes back over a century to 1885, when the government of John A. Macdonald designated the first areas of the Park around the hot springs. The railway was already present and the CPR was the "godfather" of the Park's establishment. In its early days the Park was intended to enhance railway traffic and revenues through the development of high quality tourism for the rich of North America and Europe. Cornelius Van Horne of the CPR captured the commercial strategy neatly: " If we cannot export the scenery, we'll import the tourists." [3] To ensure the quality of the commercial establishments, the federal government would regulate the area as a national park, keeping out low-class establishments and limiting competition to protect their investment in the railway. Only after the 1880s did conservation begin to appear as part of the mandate. In the following decades mining, lumbering, and other resource developments were phased out to enhance the Park and the visitor experience.

The Canadian Pacific architecture and marketing strategy emphasized the exhilarating nature of the mountain experience and the exquisite beauty of the mountain landscapes. The appeal was to the viewing of rugged grandeur and the experience of mountain hiking in clean, bracing air. Right from the beginning Banff played a critical role in launching and sustaining the Canadian tourism industry. It set a standard for the whole country. The CPR's colourful posters of Banff circled the globe and created an image for Canada.[4] (They are still prized collector's items as fine examples of a period genre.) Tourism dollars sustained the government's commitment to the mountain parks through two world wars and the Depression.

In this period aesthetics were more important than ecology. Forest fires and, later, flooding were suppressed to enhance conditions for visitors. Loss of these natural processes affected the integrity of ecosystems as well as individual species, such as elk. Construction of roads, railways, and dams disrupted streams, lakes, wetlands, and the complex ecosystems on which they were based.[5] Such projects were never subjected to the type of environmental impact assessment process, we expect under the existing Act and regulations. During the Park's first two decades legal and illegal hunting and fishing decimated the indigenous wildlife and fish populations. To compensate for this loss of natural biodiversity, park officials imported exotic species which were on show in fenced areas as a visitor attraction. Only in 1997 was the last remnant of this approach removed, with the closing of the Buffalo paddock across the highway from the town.[6] Banff National Park also portrayed biodiversity through an extensive collection of stuffed animals from around the world in the Banff Park Museum. Today this finely preserved log structure is a truly remarkable example of the attitudes and practices relating to wildlife during the early decades of the century. Clearly, aesthetics were more important than ecology. The museum took great care to preserve the colour of fur or feathers. Dead specimens were considered a legitimate alternative to living ecosystems and exotic species a substitute for indigenous wildlife. Above all, it was a way to provide nature, in a way that was acceptable at the time, to visitors whose interest had been fostered by the many nature and natural history societies flourishing in Canada.[7]

Developing Banff for Recreation

In the first decade of the twentieth century, Banff National Park began a more proactive protectionist policy with the founding of what later became the Wardens Service. Established to stop illegal hunting of wild life in the Park, the service came to espouse a broad protectionist philosophy decades before it became enshrined in policy documents from Ottawa. This remarkable cadre of committed professionals have been the most vigorous force for conservation biology and protection of biodiversity. Within the Park they have been a continuous voice for resisting compromises to the basic mission of the Park in the best traditions of public service. However, those who possess a vision of parks with a higher emphasis on tourism have often criticized their "anti-business" philosophy. In the current downsizing the crucial role that they have played in building and sustaining the traditions of the Park should be remembered.

After 1914 the nature of tourism and tourism impacts began to change. The relaxed affluence of the railway gave way to the different styles of auto tourism. New types of development emerged to serve middle-class patrons. Winding, narrow roads were cut through forest habitat. Banff was linked first to Calgary and then to Jasper and the B.C. interior. Costs of these public works were kept down by exploiting wartime detainees or work gangs of the unemployed during the Depression. Along the new roads, motor hotels and camp grounds sprang up to serve more visitors with moderately priced accommodation. The Park changed to reflect the social patterns of leisure activities in Canada. But Banff remained very largely a summer-only resort with the main disturbance of wildlife confined to those months.

While Banff's involvement in the national economy was mainly confined to the tourism and transportation sectors, there were exceptions in times of crisis. In 1941 under the War Measures Act and over the opposition of at least some park officials, the hydroelectric power dam and generating facilities at Lake Minnewanka were greatly expanded to provide electricity for new munitions plants in Calgary. The higher dam flooded areas of prime montane habitat while the annual fluctuations in lake levels affected shoreline and benthic (lake-bottom) communities. As a result of this and other projects, 42 per cent of the flowing waters within the Park have been impounded, disrupted, or diverted, severely impacting aquatic ecosystems.[8] Today it is difficult to remove facilities such as the Minnewanka Dam given the recreation they provide and their contribution to the Alberta economy as low-cost, peak-load generating capacity. There would also be offsetting environmental costs. Cutting hydro capacity would force greater use of coal-fired generation and with it CO_2 emissions, which contribute to global climate change. However, the Park and the utility are exploring ways of increasing stream flows to restore some of the original characteristics of the aquatic ecosystems.

Although hunting was banned during the early years of the Park, fishing was allowed as a concession to tourism. Over the years it has proved to be a very popular recreational pastime for residents and visitors alike with motorized craft on Lake Minnewanka or fly fishing from the shores of high alpine lakes. However, in order to increase the take and to provide fighting species for sport, various water bodies were stocked with alien species, which displaced indigenous species, such as bull trout – another example of recreational needs being given precedence over preservation. Parks Canada are now trying to address some of these issues with such partners as Trout Unlimited.

In the last half-century Banff National Park has changed dramatically with visitation rising from 500,000 to five million per year. The isolation and the solitude of the Park have been affected. The winding two-lane road from Calgary has been replaced by the four-lane divided Trans-Canada Highway with 18-wheelers running 24 hours a day on the "milk run" from Toronto to Vancouver. The Vermillion Lakes wetlands are cut on one side by the railway and on the other by the highway. The plug in the wildlife corridors around the town of Banff is virtually complete. The design of the transportation corridor has created some unforeseen ecological problems. When the four-lane highway was constructed the wildlife toll became alarming. To solve this problem, high wire mesh fencing was constructed. While this curbed the road kill, it now created a barrier to wildlife migration between the habitat on both sides of the highway, as well as increased predation of vulnerable species trapped along the fence. In the latest section of the Trans-Canada Highway to be twinned with the addition of two more lanes, two 50-metre-wide wildlife overpasses were installed. It is hoped that these new design features will be more successful than earlier underpasses and overcome the fragmentation of habitat caused by the highway.

For some time scientists have documented the rail kill, especially in winter, from the frequent CPR freight trains hauling grain and other commodities to the coast. While the CPR has expressed concern, effective measures have not been devised or implemented. With the mix of single- and two-lane sections, traffic control and speed are critical to the flow of export-bound grain. Derailments and grain spills have created further problems. The plowing of the line in winter attracts migrating wildlife only to trap them between snow banks when trains approach. But the basic problem is historic. The route of the transportation corridor was decided long ago and there is little chance of changing it, given the level of investment and the few passes through the Rockies. New design techniques and mitigation measures could ease some of the threats to biodiversity. The critical question, for which there is no answer in sight, is who will pay for these changes?

Contrasting Visions

During the 1960s and 1970s Banff responded as downhill skiing became a widely popular sport. Three commercial ski slopes were developed at Norquay, Sunshine, and Lake Louise. These developments represented a new commercial recreation industry for the Park, attracting both Canadian and foreign visitors. With many new winter visitors, Banff was converted in the late 1970s and early 1980s from a summer to an all-season resort. New hotels and other facilities received European and Asian visitors arriving by wide-body jets at the nearby Calgary International Airport, only 10 hours from Germany and 12 from Japan. The barrier of distance, which had for so long limited numbers of visitors, was now breaking down.

This enormously successful new tourism coincided with the rise of the new environmentalism in Canada. The simultaneous emergence of both phenomena changed the dynamics at Banff. In the 1960s a proposal was developed to expand the Lake Louise ski facilities as part of a bid for the Winter Olympics. The release of the proposal triggered a storm of protest and controversy about the extent of development within mountain national parks. Banff helped originate Canadian environmental groups and in turn became a continuing focus for their attention as the non-adversarial National and Provincial Parks Association was converted into the activist Canadian Parks and Wilderness Society (CPAWS).

The sponsors of the Lake Louise project appeared to have the backing of Parks Canada, and a fierce national debate erupted about the purpose of national parks and the nature of "appropriate" development within them. Eventually Jean Chrétien, the minister responsible for parks, rejected the proposal as too big and too socially exclusive, but in the process the debate about Banff changed. Dave Day, a former

Superintendent of Banff National Park, told the Banff-Bow Valley Task Force: "we have never gotten beyond that, never managed to recover from that."[9] This early battle among environmental and tourism groups over Banff wounded Parks Canada's integrity because it challenged the terms of their stewardship of national parks. At the root of the debate were two profoundly different visions of national parks: the protectionist vs. the recreational. In this battle Parks Canada sought to find a middle ground between the historic and the emerging protectionist visions. In doing so, they antagonized important elements in both camps.

In 1979 the government unveiled a new policy statement stressing that "Ecological and historical integrity are Parks Canada's first considerations" and that national parks must "be given the highest degree of protection." During the 1980s Parks Canada continued to experience strong pressure from environmental groups and the public seeking to entrench a more protectionist philosophy. The United Nations Brundtland Commission called in 1987 for the protection of 12 per cent of the land mass. In 1988 the first amendments to the National Parks Act since 1930 were passed by Parliament. The wording was clear. The first priority in parks zoning and visitor use management became the protection of "ecological integrity." This was defined as "the minimization of human impact on natural processes of ecological change" including "protecting intact ecosystems."[10] But even as these legislated changes occurred, development continued at Banff. There appeared to be a widening rift between events on the ground and policy in Ottawa. Environmental groups focused on the policy debate, while the business community addressed the development approvals process. Nowhere was the gap between the two sides as great as in Banff.

In 1994 Parks Canada attempted to convert the new Act of 1988 into a broad policy document entitled: "Guiding Principles and Operational Policies." In many ways this was an admirable document, especially for new parks and existing parks isolated from serious development pressures. Ecosystems were to be accorded "the highest degree of protection to ensure perpetuation of natural environments essentially unaltered by human activity." Parks decision-making was to be based on "internationally accepted principles and concepts of conservation biology." Actions that threaten parks ecosystems were not to be permitted. In every application of policy ecological integrity was to be "paramount." The goal was to protect the diversity of genetic stock, species, and ecosystems. Commercial ski slopes, golf courses, hydro-electric generation, and major tourism facilities were to be located outside the boundaries of national parks. While the policy statement did recognize the importance of tourism, it had to contribute to the overall goals of "maintaining and enhancing ecological and commemorative integrity."

However, the historic legacy and development pattern in Banff meant that it had now clearly become a non-conforming area of the national parks system. Certain anomalies were recognized in the document.[11] Further growth at Banff was already guaranteed by provisions for expansion in many commercial leases. Unless the federal government was prepared to embark upon a massive program of decommissioning, expropriation, and compensation the nature of Banff could not be turned around. Given the climate of opinion in the House of Commons and the budgetary deficit, there was no chance of that happening. The conflicting visions of Banff had to be reconciled in the context of declining staff and budgets for national parks in the 1990s.

The International Dimension

National Parks have an international as well as a national biodiversity policy dimension. In signing the International Biodiversity Convention in 1992, Canada assumed global responsibilities for stewardship on its territory. Article VIII of the Convention stresses some of the key biological considerations including protecting ecosystems, natural habitat, and viable populations of species. Other mandated objectives include: rehabilitation of degraded ecosystems, fostering the recovery of threatened species, and legislative measures to protect threatened species. This latter goal could best be achieved through protection of larger naturally evolving ecosystems via national parks and protected spaces.[12] While the scientific rationale for these goals was never well explained (beyond some limited efforts by Environment Canada), in 1995 Canada followed up on federal/provincial consultations by establishing a National Strategy on Biodiversity.

Other international obligations relating to Banff stem from

UNESCO's World Heritage Convention. Canada was a leader in establishing the Convention. In 1983 Canada applied to have Banff, Jasper, and surrounding provincial parks declared a World Heritage Site under the Convention. This designation involves responsibilities to the global community which are monitored by the International Union for the Conservation of Nature (IUCN). While it has no power to force compliance, the IUCN reports carry great weight in the international community, and therefore the potential for embarrassing governments. During the Banff-Bow Valley Study, the IUCN communicated its concerns about the levels of development and their impact on Bow Valley ecosystems.[1] The task force was also invited to report to the October 1996 IUCN World Congress in Montreal. Today the World Heritage Site status remains a matter of controversy: it is a sacred trust for the NGOs (non-government organizations) but a public annoyance to the local business community and many residents.

Banff in an Age of Limits

In the early and mid-1990s Parks Canada suffered fundamental cuts in operating and capital grants. While funding declined by over 25 per cent, its responsibilities increased with new parks and historic sites. In response parks have explored privatization and partnerships with those outside government. Privatization schemes have raised fears for job security, while partnerships with the private sector to download costs are raising fears about official relationships. Those who regulate parks are now asking for contributions from those they regulate. This puts officials in potentially difficult situations involving conflicting roles.

In areas like visitor information and interpretation the cuts in staff have been tragically deep. They constitute the interface with the public and fulfil the role of interpretation in educating visitors about ecological integrity. This is no criticism of the local staff, who attempt to cope under very trying circumstances; it is a criticism of management who put a low priority on the educational components in the Park's mandate. Research budgets have also suffered, but not as severely. However, people, especially trained experienced staff, are the most important resource. Morale has suffered; many experienced staff chose early retirement.[14] Their knowledge and experience, so valuable for the current challenges facing Banff and the other national parks, is hard to replace.

A number of biodiversity issues emerged in the 1996 Banff-Bow Valley Study Report (see Appendix to this chapter). The contemporary pressures on ecological integrity will not be dealt with in this article as the report speaks for itself. Several conclusions with a historic dimension are relevant to the themes of this chapter. The report concluded that while the Park operates under a clear legislative and policy mandate, it has suffered over the years from inconsistent application of the act and policy. This reflects a variety of factors, including the historic evolution of Banff, ad hoc decision-making, and weak political will in the face of vigorous interest-based lobbying.[15]

The interconnection between the bureaucracy and politics has also been important. In the past Parks officials were often put into difficult positions. Rejecting a development proposal meant an immediate appeal over their heads to Ottawa. In some cases the appeal would be successful and the project would be approved. This would result in a weakened policy framework and diminished will of local officials to enforce the rules. A tradition of compromise and a tendency to avoid clear rules emerged in Banff, in order to avoid complicating relations with the Ottawa political establishment. While some ministers attempted to resist this process, they were still subject to influence from the Prime Minister's Office and their own party. This political pragmatism promoted further expectations and political pressure from the business community, as well as cynicism on the part of environmental groups and others aware of the nature of the process. The intensity of the current battles reflects this flexibility and pragmatism in enforcing the Act and policy.

Another historic factor complicating biodiversity protection is the traditional rivalry between Ottawa and the provinces over public lands policy surrounding national parks. As the Banff-Bow Valley Study documented, the long term preservation of species requires unprecedented co-operation, considering the migratory nature of species and the size of habitat required. However, fragmentation of this habitat is under way as development approaches Park boundaries in both British Columbia and Alberta. The core habitat within the national parks must be complemented by provincial protected areas and secure corridors between them. Development that is not permitted within the Park is also moving beyond: Canmore, with an annual growth rate approaching 10 per cent, resents being the location for the overflow from Banff. Such problems can be addressed only by regional, federal, provincial, and municipal cooperation. But there is little evidence of an end to the traditional rivalry between Ottawa and Edmonton; without co-operation the viability of ecosystems within the Park will be eroded by events beyond.

Conclusion

It is critically important to understand how history has undermined the effectiveness of the current Parks Act and policy as they relate to Banff National Park. At the core of the current problems are a series of historical anomalies, such as the Canadian Pacific Railway, the Trans-Canada Highway, extensive hotel and commercial complexes, ski slopes, the town site, the golf course, and the hydroelectric facilities. All were in place before current legislation and policy were formulated. They are not likely to be eliminated. But the current problems in Banff involve much more than just physical facilities. They involve the vision of the Park, attitudes to appropriate use, and management philosophy and practices. In this era of transition from the age of recreation to the age of ecology, controversies and tension were inevitable. Interests are never abandoned without a fight, and practices lag behind legislated intentions. In the words of the Banff-Bow Valley Study Report, addressed to the minister in 1996:

> The magnitude of the required change speaks to the past degree of drift towards unsustainability. The Banff Bow Valley is truly at the crossroads.... The effort to bring the Park back on track will require dedication and a long lasting commitment to the task, to the concept of national parks and future generations. It will require a courageous approach involving personal, political, and collective will.[16]

Banff is at a critical point where political will must be exerted if the goals of the Act are to be achieved. Only time will tell if that collective will is present to defend the biodiversity of Banff National Park.

Appendix

The Banff-Bow Valley: At the Crossroads

Between July 1994 and October 1996 the Banff-Bow Valley Task Force reviewed the evolution of Banff National Park, the policies and forces that affect it, and its present ecological status, with a mandate to develop a vision for the future of the park and to recommend actions to preserve or enhance the ecological integrity while balancing the other social and economic considerations of the National Parks Act. The following material has been condensed from the *Technical Report* and the *Summary Report*. The general conclusion of the task force was succinct and blunt:

> "It is our belief ... that current trends, if allowed to continue, will lead to the destruction of the conditions in the Banff-Bow Valley that are required for a national park."

Key Task Force Conclusions[17]

1 While Parks Canada has clear and comprehensive legislation and policies, Banff has suffered from inconsistent application of them. Some of the explanation lies in the historic evolution of the Park; some in ad hoc decision-making; and some from weak political will in the face of interest-based lobbying.

2 While ecological integrity is the focus of the Act and policy, it has been and continues to be increasingly compromised because of the level of human-use development, including the railway and the highway.

3 While the scientific evidence supports the above conclusion, a significant portion of the population seeing the natural beauty do not understand the ecological impacts that have occurred.

4 The current growth rates in visitor numbers and development, if allowed to continue, will cause serious and irreversible harm to the ecological integrity of Banff National Park. Stricter limits to growth must be imposed. The built heritage is also disappearing.

5 More effective methods of managing and limiting human use are required in Banff.

6 To maintain natural landscapes and processes, natural disturbances such as fire and flooding must be restored.

7 Existing anomalies such as the Trans-Canada Highway, the Canadian Pacific Railway, and the Minnewanka Dam, while continuing to exist, must update their designs to reflect the most advanced science and ecological and engineering practices.

8 Tourism must to a greater extent reflect the values of the Park and contribute to the achievement of ecological integrity and the quality of the visitor experience.

9 While mountain tourism will continue to expand in Alberta, the new facilities will have to be located outside the Park boundaries. Regional co-ordination and co-operative management initiatives are essential to the ecological integrity within the Park and in terms of the wider ecosystems beyond.

10 Current growth in the number of residents and infrastructures at Banff and Lake Louise is inconsistent with the principles of a national park. In some areas, facilities must be downsized, relocated, or removed.

11 Public scepticism and lack of trust in the development decision-making process requires that it be overhauled with new forms of broader-

based public involvement and shared decision-making to enhance accountability.

12 Visitors must be better informed about the Park's natural and cultural heritage, the role of protected areas, and the ecological challenges facing the Park. Improvements in education, awareness, and interpretation programs are required to promote greater feelings of personal responsibility and stewardship.

13 Parks management is central to Banff's future and it must begin with a comprehensive revision to the Banff National Park Management Plan.

14 Current funding is inadequate to implement the Report's recommendations and new sources of revenue are proposed.

Issues and Recommended Actions[18]

Development and activities inside and outside the Park continue to have a detrimental effect on terrestrial and aquatic ecosystems in the Banff-Bow Valley and the surrounding region. Important environmental concerns include:

- fragmentation of the landscape and habitat;

- the difficulty wildlife face in moving between major areas of protected habitat;

- loss of aquatic habitat;

- the effect of dams on the movement, diversity, and viability of fish and aquatic organisms;

- human-caused mortality of fish and wildlife;

- the effect of fire suppression and water regulation on vegetation;

- loss of the montane habitat;

- altered predator-prey relationships;

- wildlife-human conflicts;

- the effect of sewage on water quality;

- the introduction of non-native plants and fish.

To maintain and restore the ecological integrity of the Valley's terrestrial and aquatic ecosystems, the task force made a number of recommendations for specific places within the Park. In addition, numerous actions for aquatic and terrestrial ecosystems were presented to be considered on a Park-wide basis.

Aquatic Ecosystems

The recommendations for aquatic ecosystems relate mainly to reducing nutrients and restoring flows and native species:

- encourage sport fishing to eliminate non-native fish;

- end sport fishing in lakes and streams that have only native fish, and in the long term, eliminate fishing in the Park;

- reintroduce bull trout and cutthroat trout in selected lakes and streams;

- designate benchmark aquatic systems;

- prepare an emergency response plan for spills;

- participate in programs to reduce the long range transport of air pollutants.

Planning

To achieve maximum efficiency, a number of the site-specific recommendations require a holistic approach. The task force therefore recommends a comprehensive approach to planning in the following areas: aircraft use, water regulation, stream channelization, the Trans-Canada Highway, the railway, native vegetation, new facilities, and management of human use. There is a particular need to re-examine the long-range plans for the ski hills and to define the appropriate size of each area in terms of capacity and the type and number of runs, lifts, and other on-hill facilities, especially in relation to the on-site, off-site, and cumulative effects on ecological integrity.

Regional Management

- Parks Canada, Alberta, and British Columbia should work together on initiatives to:

- manage garbage;

- prepare a wildlife response plan;

- manage hunting;

- reduce landscape fragmentation;

- co-ordinate fire management.

Communication

Many of the recommended actions to restore and maintain ecological integrity will require visitors and residents to change their use, their behaviour, and their expectations. To encourage public support and co-operation, Parks Canada, the Park's communities, and commercial operators must foster a better understanding of the Park's ecosystems, the impact of humans on these ecosystems, the urgency for change, and the way recommended actions will affect individual use of the park. To do this will require public information programs on a wide range of subjects.

Research and Monitoring

Although we have a substantial amount of information on the Park's ecosystems, a number of important data gaps remain. These include baseline information on species, the response of ecosystems to human use, cumulative effects, and the effectiveness of environmental protection measures. There is also an urgent need to update and improve information about visitor activities, the quality of the visitor experience, visitor satisfaction, and the effectiveness of human-use management techniques.

A National and International Tourism Destination Model

Protecting ecological integrity is a foundation for the Park's success as a tourist destination. Studies clearly show that wildlife and majestic scenery are the main reasons people visit Banff National Park. Naturally this appeal would be more difficult to maintain in a national park where ecological integrity has been impaired.

The task force believes that Parks Canada, in collaboration with the local and regional tourism sector, should adopt a new model of tourism in the Banff-Bow Valley. We have called this new model "Touchstone for the Canadian Rockies." This theme seeks to convey to Canadians, and to all citizens of the world, that we intend Banff National Park to set a clear standard for the way tourism can support and enhance ecological integrity within an environmentally sensitive tourism destination. It is a theme that will pervade the whole Park, binding together the efforts of everyone who seeks to realize the tourism potential of the Banff-Bow Valley.

The goal of the Tourism Destination Model is to provide unique and memorable experiences for all visitors. It seeks to do this in a manner that respects the ecological integrity of the region, while laying the foundations for a lasting, sustainable tourist destination in the Valley.

In brief, our objective is to create a very special kind of tourism destination. More specifically, we see Banff National Park as a place that:

- fully respects the ecological integrity of its unique setting;

- reflects the values of Canadians;

- is accessible to all Canadians on a fair and equitable basis, regardless of income, age, physical ability, or place of residence;

- seeks to inspire and enable visitors to learn about, understand, and better appreciate nature and the mountain culture in the Canadian Rockies;

- within the constraints of ecological integrity, allows and encourages visitors to enjoy recreational experiences that are judged appropriate;

- recognizes its importance to the economic vitality of the local region and to the economy of Canada;

- recognizes its very special role in Canada as a vehicle for inspiring and fostering national pride and national unity;

- recognizes that nature is not free, and that pricing must reflect Banff's obligations as a national park;

- acknowledges the diverse interests of Canadians;

- provides authentic rather than artificial experiences.

In our efforts to realize the Touchstone Tourism Destination Model, we must seek to provide visitors with a range of experiences, each of which contributes in some way to learning, understanding, and appreciating nature and the Rocky Mountain culture in the Banff-Bow Valley. Once again, this is the core of the Tourism Destination Model. Promotional efforts should target those visitors who seek these experiences.

As a tourist destination, Banff National Park will contain three distinct components based on the five major zones in the Park:

Zones I to III – Wilderness, Special Preservation, and Natural Environment – will remain wilderness areas where human use is highly controlled (e.g., quotas, permits). The highest quality nature experience is provided here.

Zones IV – Outdoor Recreation – will provide a range of heritage-related and recreational experiences involving readily accessible trails and other specialized facilities.

Zones V – the hamlet of Lake Louise and the town of Banff – will provide basic and essential services for the large number of people who visit the Park.

Key Actions

Achieving the Tourism Destination Model will require Parks Canada and the tourism sector to work together on:

- a comprehensive tourism destination management information system, supported by a strong visitor research program;

- research to determine which visitor experiences are consistent with ecological integrity;

- developing a broad range of high-quality experiences that will foster an improved understanding of nature and the Rocky Mountain Culture;

- a comprehensive educational program, including the construction of a major interpretation centre in the town of Banff;

- opportunities for visitors to learn about the Park in as many tourism operations as possible;

- enhancing the visual appeal of the town of Banff, the hamlet of Lake Louise, and other facilities in the Park;

- ensuring that all Canadians have an equal opportunity to experience Banff National Park;

- marketing programs that enhance the appeal of Banff National Park, while ensuring that visitors have realistic expectations about what the Park can offer;

- making sure that all visitors feel welcome;

- fostering national unity and pride through recognition of the importance of Banff National Park to Canadians;

- programs that ensure a strong and fair contribution of financial and human resources to support the protection and operation of the Park.

Human Use

Currently, there is little direct management of human use in the Park, a situation people generally prefer. It is, however, a situation that cannot continue. If nothing is done to manage human use, the damage to the Park's environment could become irreversible. While human use may require some restrictions, it should not be looked at as a limitation on people's freedom. It should be seen, instead, as a means to protect the Park for future generations, while allowing as many people as possible to enjoy the experiences and activities it has to offer.

Principles for Human-Use Management

To complement the general principles that guided the Banff-Bow Valley Study, the task force developed some specific principles for its work on human-use management.

1 Maintaining ecological integrity in the entire Park is paramount. Levels of use in the wilderness and more developed zones must not harm the ecological integrity in other areas.

2 All management decisions about human use must be based on the

principles of precaution. When there are no data to guide managers in making decisions, the principles of precaution and the maintenance of ecological integrity take precedence over social, economic, or political choices. Uncertainty about the impact of a decision necessitates a conservative approach.

3   It is important to maintain visitor satisfaction in all designated zones, while respecting the need to protect the Park's natural and cultural resources.

4   It is important to maintain sustainable tourism.

5   To the greatest extent possible, the effect of human use in the communities should remain within their boundaries. It should not affect the ecological integrity of the rest of the Park.

6   Any system to manage human use in the Park must consider equity of access by Canadians. Allocation of use must be fair and equitable and accommodate the largest number of people possible, without infringing on ecological integrity or visitor satisfaction. Residents or other special interest groups must not have preferential access.

7   Any group that proposes to increase use beyond current levels must demonstrate that it will not have a negative impact on ecological integrity or visitor enjoyment. The responsibility for demonstrating the acceptability of the proposed change rests with those proposing the change.

8   Public involvement is crucial in the allocation of human use and in the implementation and successful operation of human-use management systems.

9   The opportunity to see, enjoy, and learn about wildlife is achieved through education and interpretation and by reducing the risk of human/wildlife conflicts.

Past Travels: Future Directions[19]

Let's look forward to the year 2025. Let's imagine walking with our grandchildren through Banff National Park. Let us look through their eyes at the legacy we hold in trust for them.

What Could Have Been

In the early 1990s, Parks Canada, the Canadian people, and the residents and businesses in the Banff-Bow Valley found themselves at a crossroads. They faced a perplexing choice. More than five million people visited Banff National Park every year, a number that was growing by more than 5 per cent annually; the town of Banff would soon be a city with more than 10,000 residents; the region outside the Park was one of the fastest-growing areas in Alberta; the scenic value of the Canadian Rockies was drawing increasing numbers of international visitors; pressure continued to twin the Trans-Canada Highway; public funding was in a dramatic decline; the future viability of populations of native fish and wild animals was in question; evidence pointed to seriously impaired aquatic and terrestrial ecosystems; a lack of trust, inconsistent decision-making, and an uncertain future fuelled tensions among the key interests in the Valley. This was a road that would very likely lead to the destruction of the values for which Banff National Park was created, and for which it qualified as a World Heritage site.

Faced with this bleak future, Canadians made a choice that meant some sacrifice by everyone. The choice was to preserve what had become a symbol of Canada's commitment to protected areas and an icon on the world tourism stage. In so doing, Canadians decided that the Park's ecosystems would be the envy of the world, would support a strong and vital national and international tourism industry, and would contribute to the essential life-support systems of all people.

The Decisions Made

In a true spirit of co-operation and understanding, all interests in the Valley came together to craft a common vision of the future. This vision was founded on such fundamental values as respect for others; for nature in and of itself; for safe, healthy, and hospitable communities; for open, shared decision-making; and for wilderness preservation as a cornerstone of Canada's image around the world.

The tourism industry, in co-operation with Parks Canada, implemented a new Tourism Destination Model. Visitors adjusted their expectations and behaviour to help reduce the impact of human use on critical wildlife habitat. In the process, they gained a new appreciation of the environment. They no longer saw it as a limitless resource to be exploited, but as a "fountain of life" supporting biodiversity and in need of protection.

The Park's communities focused on their role as visitor centres, providing basic and essential services. The town of Banff, together with other regional communities, devised an aggressive growth management strategy to preserve and, in some cases, restore the character of the town, preserve the quality of life for residents, and enhance the experience of visitors. Parks Canada implemented a comprehensive ecosystem management program, with the support of residents, visitors, and industry. This program complemented similar ecosystem-based management programs in neighbouring jurisdictions.

Over time, uses and services that were either not appropriate for a national park, or not needed to meet the basic needs of visitors, were phased out. Services that directly contributed to the benefit, education, and enjoyment of visitors were offered in their place. Finally, decision-making in the Valley, whether by government or by the private sector, sought to consider all points of view. Consistency and fairness were watchwords.

The New Order

Banff National Park has been described as unique by many people — some for its natural splendour; some for the combination of wilderness and comfort it offers; some for the excesses in development and use. The new order offers other ways to describe the Park. Even with millions of visitors coming each year, grizzly bears now roam traditional ranges. The number of wolves has increased and animals move freely through the valley. Elk populations are more in balance. Bull trout flourish in waters from which they had disappeared. More rivers flow freely. Vegetation patterns better resemble the natural variability seen in the early years of the Park. The Park's national transportation corridor is a demonstration area for leading-edge technologies designed to perpetuate natural systems.

Interests in the community and beyond, once torn apart by debate about which road to take, now have strong partnerships. They took seriously their responsibilities and achieved their vision. People from the world over enjoy hiking, camping, observing wildlife, and learning about the Park's natural and cultural heritage. They leave knowing that Banff National Park continues to be the icon it once was, and understanding the value of protected areas for all humankind. Administrators of protected areas around the world look to Banff National Park for solutions to the challenges that human use poses for them.

Events Since Delivery of the Report

With the release of the report in October 1996 Parks Canada began the process of implementing the nearly 500 recommendations from the study. A task force chaired by the assistant deputy minister of Parks Canada worked in the months following. Further public consultation took place in Banff. In April 1997 the minister brought down the new Banff National Park Management Plan, which incorporated many of the study recommendations. In her introduction to the Plan, Heritage Minister Sheila Copps paid tribute to the Study for its "unique contribution to helping us better understand the role that science plays in making our decisions" and said it "will continue to be a source of inspiration for decades to come." While Parks Canada continues the process of implementing the report, many of the controversies concerning development and the impacts of visitors continue in Banff.

Notes

1. As this article was being finalized there were media reports that the deliberations of the Committee on the Status of Endangered Wildlife in Canada, the listing body of scientists and wildlife experts, would now be

subject to yearly political review of its work before public announcement. Only time will show if these fears are realized. See *Calgary Herald*, April 12, 1998.

2. The author chaired the Banff-Bow Study Task Force of the federal government, a $2.5 million, 27-month inquiry into Banff issues. In October 1996 it filed its 432-page report complete with nearly 500 recommendations: *Banff-Bow Valley: At the Crossroads, Technical Report*, hereafter referred to as *Technical Report*. I wish to acknowledge a huge debt to my colleagues on the task force and all those who contributed to the Banff-Bow Valley Study.

3. Walter Hildebrandt, *Historical Analysis of Parks Canada and Banff National Park 1968-1995*, Background Report, Banff-Bow Valley Study (Banff, 1995), 44.

4. Ted Hart, *The Selling of Canada: The CPR and the Beginning of Canadian Tourism* (Banff: Altitude Publishing, 1983).

5. See *Technical Report*, 158-211, for discussion of natural processes and the aquatic ecosystems.

6. *Technical Report*, 142. Tourist and bus operators kept the buffalo paddock open for years after Parks Canada wished to see it closed.

7. Ibid., 280; B. Sandford, *The Book of Banff* (Banff: Friends of Banff National Park, 1994), 111.

8. *Technical Report*, 158-74, 8-9.

9. Hildebrandt, *Historical Analysis*, 62-66.

10. *Technical Report*, 8-9.

11. *Guiding Principles and Operational Policies* (Ottawa: Heritage Canada, 1994).

12. *Technical Report*, 11.

13. Ibid., 8-9, as well as personal communications between various IUCN officials and the Chair, Banff-Bow Valley Task Force 1995-96.

14. Personal communications and discussions with various Parks personnel, 1995-97.

15. *Technical Report*, 11.

16. Ibid., 360.

17. Abridged from ibid., 11-12.

18. Adapted from Banff-Bow Valley Task Force, *Summary Report*, October 1996, 33-50.

19. Adapted from ibid., 67-68.

Further Reading

Bella, Leslie. *Parks for Profit*. Montreal: Harvest House, 1987.

Dearden, Philip, and Rick Rollins, eds. *Parks and Protected Areas in Canada: Planning and Management*. Toronto: Oxford University Press, 1993.

Hildebrandt, Walter. *Historical Analysis of Parks Canada and Banff National Park, 1968-1995*. Background Report, Banff-Bow Valley Study, Banff, 1995.

Lowery, W.L. *The Capacity for Wonder: Preserving National Parks*. Washington: Brookings Institution, 1994.

Lothian, W.F. *A History of Canada's National Parks*, 4 vols. Ottawa, 1976-81.

Page, R., et al. *Banff-Bow Valley: At the Crossroads, Technical Report*. Report of the Banff-Bow Valley Task Force to Hon. Sheila Copps, October 1996.

Parks Canada. *Banff National Park: Management Plan*. Ottawa, 1997.

Sandford, Robert. *The Book of Banff*. Banff: Friends of Banff National Park, 1994.

Part Two: The Ecology of Biodiversity

Ted Mosquin	**Status of and Trends in**
	Canadian Biodiversity

C

ANADIAN BIODIVERSITY CAN BE MEASURED IN TWO WAYS.
First, we can record and describe what is happening to biodiversity
itself – both today and in the past – say, over the last 25 or 250 years.
Such a description would establish the *relative condition* of this country's
genes, species, ecosystems, ecological functions/processes, and
water/land/air matrix (in which biodiversity is embedded) in comparison to some norm or standard. Another way to examine the state of
biodiversity is to document how the actions of people, especially environmental organizations, government departments, or large corporations are causing positive and negative trends in the quality and quantity of biodiversity in terrestrial, freshwater, and marine regions of
Canada.

A wide range of evidence indicates that, with some noteworthy
exceptions, trends in biodiversity in Canada are decidedly negative – in
terms of both biodiversity and the actions of people. This chapter provides a brief summary of my observations on both of these aspects of
the Canadian scene over the past two decades, supplemented with
some representative examples.

How Can the State of Biodiversity Be Determined?

To assess the status of a country's biodiversity a baseline norm or standard is essential. The most scientifically objective standard can only be
the relatively "wild" and "uncontaminated" condition of ecosystems

and their organisms that evolved naturally and was present in a region before major human influences (agriculture, forestry, industrialization, toxification, urbanization, overpopulation) altered the evolving norm. "Normal" in this sense means that over hundreds of millions of years the planetary ecosphere has generated the kinds of ecosystems on land and sea that now define the natural order or baseline for biodiversity in any land or sea region of the planetary ecosphere. On this basis, for Canada, the mid-eighteenth century would be an acceptable standard against which deviations can be usefully judged or measured.[1] In the mid-eighteenth century the land- and seascapes of Canada were relatively unmodified by industrial technology. Using this standard as the norm, the state of biodiversity for any part of any country would be that which describes the differences between the present condition and what would otherwise have been the natural condition for the area or region. Norms thus defined recognize that for our planet the ecologically sustainable state is that of evolving natural or near-natural ecosystems.

It follows that the essential elements of normal ecosystems of this planet's ecosphere are: natural prairie, old-growth forests, untrawled ocean floors, clean water in lakes and rivers, clean air, soils with their natural microflora and fauna, organisms uncontaminated with toxic, man-made chemicals or with heavy metals or human-produced radionuclides and – above all – population levels of each species under natural regulation. The notion of ecosystem/ecosphere norms for our planet recognizes that some perturbations (fires in grassland or boreal forest, hurricanes, abundance cycles of many herbivores and carnivores, diseases or starvation of overabundant species) are part of the natural order. The dilemma for humanity is that (at our peril, in my view) biological, ecological, and medical science have enabled our species to escape from laws governing the stability of planetary norms. Considering that the earth and its resources are finite, this escape, logically, is temporary.

Trends in the state of the different parts of biodiversity – genes, species, ecosystems, ecological functions/processes and the water/land/air matrix – can be determined or inferred from historic records, scientific monitoring information, and by direct observations. One's approach to assessing trends is necessarily different depending on which part of biodiversity one is considering.

Trends in Genetic Diversity

Each individual species is unique and has its own standard or norm for genetic diversity within its community. Assuming that the standard could be known, then deviations (losses or gains of unique genes) presumably could be discovered and measured. Important deviations would include human-caused mutations, loss of genes due to habitat fragmentation, or extirpations of entire genetically unique populations. While many techniques exist for measuring or monitoring changes in genetic diversity, experimental work is prohibitively expensive and tracking changes is not practicable. All that reasonably can be done is to infer deviations from historic norms, or to determine which wild populations likely contain unique genes of adaptive value and, hence, would be worthy of conservation. This approach is regularly used in Canada.

By far the greatest deviations from normal genetic diversity have taken place in agricultural regions of the country. Agriculture causes the complete annihilation of native species and natural ecosystems from large regions, sometimes leaving small fragments in spots that are inaccessible to machines or livestock. Use of pesticides is pervasive and legal. We may infer that in heavily farmed areas millions of unique genes have been lost forever. Similarly, industrial forestry activities – where old-growth forests are eliminated over large landscapes – extensively alter normal genetic variation.[2] In marine environments federal overfishing policies have led to drastically reduced ecological integrity through the destruction of food chains and the elimination of benthic habitat (see Chapter 5).

A specific concern in Canada is the loss of uniquely hardy genes that enable dozens of species to survive in marginal populations at the extreme geographical limits of their ranges.[3] There are literally thousands of Canadian species in dozens of genera that contain populations at the northern fringes of the range for the species. This is particularly true of species having their principal ranges in the United States. Parts of southern Canada where many such populations occur in the northern extremities of their ranges include: southern Vancouver Island and the Gulf Islands (clarkia; Enos Lake sticklebacks), the valleys of southern B.C. (pallid rat; short-horned lizard, canyon wren, many plants); the southern Canadian prairies (yucca, cushion cactus, sand lily, some lupins, dozens of other plants), southern Ontario (Kentucky coffee tree, blue ash, bluehearts, many other plants), and southern Nova Scotia (Atlantic whitefish, eastern mountain avens, golden crest, pink coreopsis). Likewise, many arctic tundra species reach their southern limits in boreal parts of Canada (subarctic disjuncts along the north shore of Lake Superior such as Franklin's lady's-slipper, encrusted saxifrage, several woodsia ferns, willows, low sandwort, and others). These populations should be candidates for genetic uniqueness.

In Canada, governments and NGOs already make use of the inference approach in developing programs to attempt to protect and restore genetically unique populations. The Canadian Wildlife Service (CWS) publishes *Recovery: An Endangered Species Newsletter* and an annual *RENEW Report* describing some of this work, indicating funding sources and people involved with several dozen recovery projects for geographically marginal populations, such as the Nova Scotia population of the Blanding's turtle, Blanchard's cricket frog, black-footed ferret, blue racer, burrowing owl, Peary caribou, swift fox, and some others. These efforts are aimed not at entire species, but at marginal populations that are known or suspected of having genetically unique adaptive traits.

Trends in Taxonomic Diversity

The standard for judging deviations from normal taxonomic (i.e., identifiable) diversity is based on a different criterion from that of genetic diversity. The only practical standard possible is the *numbers of native taxa* (species, genera, families, etc.) present in an area or region at the mid-eighteenth century baseline. Percentages of native species lost can be plotted against the number of species in the estimated "original" indigenous fauna and flora, while realizing that the causes of loss of indigenous organisms is either direct human activity (such as farming) or the competitive impact of introduced alien species (such as loosestrife or zebra mussels). However, hundreds of alien plant and animal species are now firmly established, and while they were not part of the norm of 1750, they are here to stay and their presence cannot be ignored in any assessment of trends in taxonomic composition. The more invasive and aggressive of these alien species reduce natural biodiversity because they displace native species and ecosystems.

A great deal is known about trends in taxonomic biodiversity in Canada but only about our larger organisms, and with some exceptions the news is not good. In the early 1990s, I carried out a complete census of Canada's taxonomic biodiversity, including groups in marine regions.[4] The survey revealed that Canada has an estimated 140,000 species (excluding viruses) of which only 70,000 are known to science. According to literature and specialist taxonomists, 70,000 species (almost all small invertebrates and micro-organisms) still remain to be discovered, named, and classified.

The effect of habitat fragmentation, particularly in forested, agricultural, and urbanizing areas has an enormous impact upon resident taxonomic biodiversity.[5] Habitat fragmentation across much of southern Canada not only extirpates species and local races but is inevitably accompanied by increases in predatory species such as crows, grackles, jays, and raccoons, and also by increased nest parasitism by cowbirds. Increases in these species is a net negative factor for taxonomic biodiversity because they prey on woodland nesting birds in such regions. Another factor believed to be causing declines in woodland birds is extensive and accelerating clear-cut logging, resulting in the destruction of forest canopies required for protection, food, and nesting.

Woodland bird species in continuing decline include:

- brown creeper (cause: unknown);

- rose-breasted grosbeak (cause: possibly loss of winter habitat);

- ovenbird (cause: possibly high mortality from smashing into windows);

- some woodland thrushes, most vireos, pewees, small flycatchers, tanagers (cause: possibly loss of winter habitat in the tropics);

- murrelet; spotted owl (cause: loss of old-growth forests due to clear-cut logging);

- pileated woodpecker in Ontario (cause: not known)

- golden-crowned kinglet in Ontario (cause: not known);

- half-dozen warbler species (cause: loss of habitat in Canada due to extensive clear-cutting in the boreal forest, that is, loss of habitat).

Some non-woodland species — gray catbird, northern water thrush, brown thrasher, rufous-sided towhee, sage grouse, burrowing owl, some shore birds, puffins, some duck species, and others — are also in decline.[6]

Yet other taxonomic groups in decline include many insect groups. For example, parasitic wasps (of which we have hundreds of species) have undergone catastrophic collapses since 1970.[7] Many sea birds and sea mammals (such as the Pribilof fur seal) are decreasing; the cause is believed to be starvation caused by extensive overfishing. Currently, federal government policy allows for the overfishing of critical food chain species: herring of the west coast and the capelin of the Atlantic coast. In forested regions where acid rain is prevalent, I believe that soil fungi essential for symbiosis with tree roots probably also are in decline as is the case in the increasingly acidified soils of Europe. Lichens over large regions are in serious decline, due mainly to continuing acid precipitation.[8] As well, crustaceans, molluscs, frogs, salamanders, and fish in our increasingly acidified, over-fertilized, and pesticide-laden ditches, creeks, lakes, and rivers are disappearing (and sometimes developing gross deformities) over large sections of southern Canada. The federal government approves farm pesticides that cause debilitating deformities in frogs.

While many species are decreasing, a few are increasing, sometimes due to active management programs. Among increasing species and groups are: wild geese of several species, red-eyed vireo, yellow-bellied sapsucker, ruby-throated hummingbird, white pelican, great-crested flycatcher, whooping crane, red-breasted nuthatch, veery, yellow warbler, northern cardinal, muskox, gray whale, and a few others. Causes for the increases are sometimes due to deliberate human activities (whooping crane, white pelican, gray whale) but more often the causes are unknown or speculative.

Management programs aimed at increasing the numbers of individuals of those species that are at risk are described in the most recent

Recovery Newsletter (1998) published by the Canadian Wildlife Service and in the current *RENEW Report* No. 8 (1998). The latter provides an overview of research and recovery activities undertaken over the past decade across Canada. Since 1988 the CWS RENEW (Recovery of Nationally Endangered Wildlife) program has brought 50 species under its mandate and approved recovery plans for 19 species at risk. It also describes recovery activities for 13 mammals, 22 birds, one amphibian, five reptiles, and one ecosystem that provides essential habitat for three birds and one reptile. Among the over 300 species officially designated to be at risk, RENEW's efforts have helped with down-listing the ferruginous hawk (from threatened in 1980 to vulnerable in 1995) and the tundra peregrine falcon (from threatened in 1978 to vulnerable in 1992), as well as the de-listing of some others like the Baird's sparrow and the prairie long-tailed weasel (even though no effort was made to assist the latter two). Success stories have included the multiplication of the wood bison (establishment of additional self-sustaining colonies), restoration of the anatum peregrine falcon, and the swift fox. The *RENEW Report* also lists a number of ongoing recent programs designed to help with the recovery of species with extremely low population numbers. While these programs deserve public support, progress so far only scratches the surface, considering that thousands of species are now estimated to be at risk.[9]

It is no mystery that the great losses of native species and the increasing numbers of species at risk are caused by destructive human activities driven by the push for higher human populations and ever more economic development at the expense of ecosystem quality and integrity. These impacts can be expressed not only in terms of the extinction of species. For example, in the "Carolinian Forest" of southern Ontario, while some 97 per cent of the forest has been annihilated, nearly all plant species originally present are still found locally in isolated fragments of their former range,[10] although some are now very rare, being reduced to one or two small colonies. Similarly, in the area of the former Regina Prairie some of the genetic variants of most species adapted to these clay soils have almost certainly vanished, while the many native species (i.e., taxonomic diversity) formerly colonizing the prairie are still present in the province although in small numbers and greatly fragmented ecosystems. To cite yet another example, logging practices across Canada are such as to drastically alter the "native" flora and fauna over extensive regions of the country. Yet, taxonomic diversity on the larger scale remains, although often drastically altered in terms of the relative abundance and evenness of distribution of native species in areas of severe impact, such as clearcuts. However, because of the incompleteness of taxonomic studies and biological inventories in Canada, one cannot use direct evidence to determine total losses of native species as compared to the 1750 norm.

Species lost from all groups since approximately 1750 can also be crudely estimated by making extrapolations based on the few better-known groups of rare, vulnerable, threatened, and endangered species and populations whose status has already been determined by the Committee on the Status of Endangered Species in Canada (COSEWIC) and by some other studies.[11] Applying the percentage from COSEWIC's well studied groups it was estimated that in Canada today there are at least 8,000 species that are vulnerable, threatened, endangered, extirpated, or extinct even though the status of just over 300 has been formally determined.

Changes in Ecosystem Diversity

Deviations from ecosystem norms are easy to observe directly, particularly in terrestrial ecosystems. An airline flight over the Canadian landscape displays the enormity of ecosystem changes in many parts of southern Canada and across the boreal forest. Despite the scale of past destruction, the seemingly inexorable trend today is towards ever greater destruction, transformation, and loss, aided and abetted by official provincial and federal government policies and programs.

Where are ecosystems being seriously damaged or restored in recent years? The biggest impacts to terrestrial ecosystems are coming from a steady increase in the amounts of forest clear-cutting promoted by provincial governments. Between 1970 and 1989 the annual allowable cut increased from a total of 121.4 million cubic metres to 191.4 million cubic metres.[12] Some provincial governments (Manitoba, Ontario, Quebec) continue with support for clear-cutting, often in provincial parks. The phrase "Brazil of the North" is not unjustified.

In the Canadian prairies, 1 per cent of tall-grass prairie remains and a small effort is being made privately at restoration; 19 per cent of mixed-grass prairie (but modified by ranching) remains, and only 16 per cent of aspen parkland.[13] In 1998 the Saskatchewan Plains Research Centre published a "Saskatchewan Prairie Conservation Action Plan" outlining a vision for the conservation and restoration of native prairie in the province and outlining five goals with associated objectives. However, many of the privately held remaining prairies are being seeded with exotic grasses and forbs so as to increase their carrying capacity for livestock. The Action Plan is intended to inspire and guide owners of such properties, encouraging them to place greater value on conserving native biodiversity.

In agricultural and urbanizing regions drainage and pollution of wetlands and waterways continues and farmers are being allowed by governments to continue the use of fertilizers and new kinds of pesticides that affect biodiversity in soils, rivers, and lakes. Large regions of northern Alberta are being "opened up" for agriculture with ongoing annihilation of entire ecosystems. On the plus side for biodiversity, some parts of southern Ontario, Quebec, and the Maritimes continue to be abandoned by farmers (for economic reasons) and here normal biodiversity is slowly returning – a flickering hope that ever more areas of formerly devastated farmland will be abandoned so that natural ecosystems can regenerate.

Trends in Functional Diversity

Research literature and social dialogue on the importance of ecological functions of organisms and natural ecosystems is just emerging.[14] Functions describe what organisms and ecosystems actually do (and what their ancestors have done) to have caused the world to be the way it is.[15] Functions determine integrity and health of lands, waters, and organisms themselves. It is suggested that the reader turn to Chapter 6 of this book and contemplate each of the first 15 functions (primary production to food chains) and try to visualize how drastically different (and less valuable and impoverished) the world would be if even one or two of these functions were absent. Yet, humans are demolishing them in ever wider regions of the planet.

Loss of the orderly functioning, or balance, of nature has already had drastic consequences, including huge increases in species misery and human poverty in many parts of the world. When natural forests, prairies, coral reefs, estuaries, or the benthic ecosystems on oceanic continental shelves are grossly degraded and impoverished by human exploitation or conversion, there are pervasive and drastic consequences, namely the de-stabilizing of the ancient, orderly, and stable functioning both of the affected regions and of more distant lands and seas.

While we can draw conclusions about trends in the vitality of functions from looking at what is happening to species and ecosystems that carry out these functions, I know of no study in which resource managers, politicians, or corporations requested or carried out assessments of the consequences of destabilizing ecological/ecospheric functions in any area of the planet.

Trends in the "Abiotic" Part of Biodiversity

As noted in Chapter 6 the "abiotic" matrix within which biota are embedded has profoundly determined the form, structure, and functions of biodiversity, while the evolving organisms themselves profoundly affected the nature and quality of the ecosphere. For millions of years the "abiotic" matrix of the ecosphere has been self-cleansing, becoming less radioactive, less toxic, and more conducive and benign to organisms. Heavy metals were slowly sequestered away in sediments. Living things themselves participated in this purification process (for example, through oxygen formation, and mineralization by bacteria). These "normative" ecospheric processes have now been reversed by industrial societies, with catastrophic effects on biodiversity.

Statistics on trends in some of the "abiotic" aspects of biodiversity have been assembled by Statistics Canada, Environment Canada, and others.[16] For example, excellent monitoring records are available on factors such as: global production of CFCs; global carbon dioxide (CO_2) emissions; ocean dumping permits issued; soil toxification; compaction and erosion on agricultural lands; effluents from pulp and paper mills; heavy metal emissions: cadmium, mercury, copper, chromium, manganese, nickel, and antimony; reported oil spills;

emissions of nitrogen oxides and sulphur dioxide; production of toxics; synthetic organic compounds; commercial agricultural fertilizer application by sub-basin; agricultural pesticide expenditures and densities by sub-basin; and dozens of others.

While the changes taking place in the abiotic part of the ecosphere are of paramount importance to the future of biodiversity, these changes cannot be described adequately within this chapter and indeed form a subject beyond the scope of this volume. But generally, we are witnessing the accelerating toxification of all parts of the ecosphere and near-unprecedented extinctions and extirpations of species. This ominous trend is being driven by government policies and cultural attitudes respecting human population, by corporate activities such as mining, and by the continuing legal manufacture and dispersal of thousands of toxic substances that the ecosphere cannot assimilate. A particularly ominous trend is the toxification of the Arctic food chain. This is affecting large animals such as polar bears, seals, walrus, whales, and others that feed at the tops of food chains. This trend, like so many others, is taking place with the knowledge of governments and of corporations that are responsible for the manufacture of the toxic substances.

Some Destructive Trends in Human Actions Affecting Biodiversity

This chapter on biodiversity trends would not be complete without a brief mention of some of the actions of people in powerful positions that are impeding efforts to understand and conserve biodiversity. These destructive activities fall roughly into four categories: (1) the rise of government and corporate greenwash; (2) decreases or elimination of support for biodiversity research; (3) losses of unique agricultural plant and animal varieties; (4) efforts by large corporations and their friends in government to weaken or eliminate biodiversity protection and conservation legislation.

The Rise of Government/Corporate Greenwash

The purpose of propaganda is to deceive. In Canada, it is common for provincial governments and some federal agencies to spend substantial public dollars and allocate staff time to generate information aimed at confusing and misleading the concerned public about government and corporate policies and programs affecting biodiversity. Particularly since the early 1980s there has been a marked increase in the use of spin doctors and/or dishonest consultants hired to write documents and to develop media packages that present biodiversity-destroying governmental policies and activities in a friendly green light when in fact both policies and activities are designed to increase development and production of market goods and not to protect or restore biodiversity and already damaged environments.

Anti-environmental literature – designed to make bad government policy and action look good in the eyes of the public – has come to be known as "greenwash" or "ecospeak."[17] A lexicon of terminology has emerged, which, in the hands of capable spin doctors, can make a biodiversity-destroying department appear like a shepherd tending a flock of sheep or a mother caring for her child. Be wary of phrases like: sustainable development, natural heritage value, environmental and resource stewardship, environmental commitment, environmental benefits, balancing development and environment, eco-efficiency, enhancing biodiversity, management on an ecosystem basis, and many other similar phrases that have become part of the foot-dragging, anti-environmental lexicon. Greenwash phrases permeate deceitful propaganda literature. The claims made have little relevance to what is actually happening to nature and its organisms on the ground and in freshwater and marine regions. One of the more extreme kinds of greenwash comes in the form of oxymoronic expressions that portray a falsehood as the truth. Two such phrases are: "Agriculture in Harmony with Nature"[18] and "Lands for Life."

Let's examine some recent literature produced by Agriculture and Agri-Food Canada. This department has been actively involved in drafting the Articles of the Convention on Biological Diversity, and thereafter in developing the Canadian Biodiversity Conservation Strategy.[19] In late 1997 AAFC produced five publications on biodiversity; these have since been circulated across Canada.[20]

"Agriculture in Harmony..."?

These publications, and especially *Agriculture in Harmony with Nature* and *Profile of Production Trends and Environmental Issues in Canada's Agriculture and*

Agri-Food Sector, provide some of the best examples I have found of anti-environmental greenwash. The *Harmony* booklet claims to be AAFC's "first sustainable development strategy." The message written for the Minister of Agriculture makes the following preposterous claim:

> Sustainability in agriculture and agri-food sector means a thriving industry, a safe and high-quality supply of agricultural products, new market opportunities both at home and throughout the world, and a fair sharing of the benefits among all peoples. Essential to all of this is a healthy environment – unspoiled lakes and rivers, healthy and productive soils and good clean air.

Where is there mention of the need for major roll-backs of agricultural pesticides that are affecting the fertility and life cycles of numerous native species of birds, animals, fish, and others? And there's hardly a mention of the need for alternatives to those artificial fertilizers that are degrading ecosystems and destroying so much biodiversity in streams, lakes, and rivers. The publications ostensibly claim a deep concern for the environment and for biodiversity, while the record shows that for many decades AAFC has worked assiduously to undercut the efforts of conservation-minded government departments and environmental organizations. There is little mention of organic agriculture, which is the only kind of agriculture that seeks at least partial harmony with nature. Indeed, AAFC has no budget for research and extension services in organic agriculture, thus revealing a focus on support for the agri-business sector. The AAFC conducts no research and produces no literature that would be useful to organic farmers. Indeed, it is difficult to distinguish AAFC's policies and interests from those of large agri-business seed and chemical corporations. There is scant evidence that AAFC represents the interest of the Canadian public in moving towards sustainable agriculture and a healthful environment.

Yet another example of AAFC deception can be found in their *Action Plan* for implementing the Canadian Biodiversity Strategy.[21] Comparison of these two documents reveals that the *Action Plan* adheres to an entirely different set of goals and objectives than does the Strategy, thus avoiding commitments made by AAFC while participating in and drafting the Strategy. The Strategy has five goals, while the

AAFC plan has only four, entirely different goals. The stated objectives are also entirely different.

Finally, the illustrations on the cover of all five of the above AAFC publications depict family bliss and serene country scenes rich in wildlife, lovely vegetables, cows grazing in pastoral settings. There is no hint of the fertilizers and pesticides that are wiping out native bio-diversity in nearby rivers and streams or contaminating wildlife in Canada and beyond.

"Lands for Life"

Here is another example of a self-contradictory title, given by the Ontario government to an enormous planning exercise, the purpose of which was to determine the best future uses of some 46 million hectares of Crown lands of Ontario. The title itself gives the impression that this is a positive process. In fact, the reported favourite option of the government is to turn most of this vast region over to the private sector to manage under the rules of the global marketplace. Just how this would generate more life on these lands is never explained, and indeed turning these lands over to the private sector to manage would certainly result in far less life and more death for many species and ecosystems than ever in the past. But the phrase does reveal the influential power of greenwash.

Special Places 2000 Program

Another high-profile example of the use of greenwash is the Alberta government's efforts to avoid the passage of strong, protective legisla-tion for the province's "Special Places 2000 Program." This program, which aimed to allocate 46 sites (1.3 million acres) for the protection of nature, was subverted by the government's spin doctors, who wrote letters to newspapers containing misinformation designed to confuse the concerned public about the protection issue. The government changed the program to one where a simple stroke of the pen of the minister responsible could allow oil and gas exploration, mining, dams, clear-cuts, power lines, and strip mines in and near these places.

Regretfully, space does not permit a review of many other green-wash publications and related programs. Some of the best crafted and most misleading I have seen are published by large forestry companies in B.C. and by "wise use" organizations.

Eliminating Research in Biodiversity

A major ongoing trend over the past several decades has been the downgrading and/or elimination of biodiversity research by both federal and provincial governments. The paradox behind this trend is that major federal resource departments (Environment, Forestry, Agriculture, Fisheries, Canadian Museum of Nature) as well as all provinces participated in the establishment of the 1992 Convention on Biological Diversity (CBD), and Article 12 of the CBD calls upon signatory countries to carry out research in order to fill extensive gaps in our knowledge about biodiversity.[22] The most important gaps exist at the interface between biodiversity, conservation, sustainable use, and development.[23] Notwithstanding the CBD commitment, there is an abundance of evidence that Canada and the provinces are in serious violation of Article 12. Here are some examples of Canada's sorry record in biodiversity research:

Agriculture and Agri-Food Canada

Agriculture and Agri-Food Canada has cut professional biodiversity staff in all fields: botany from 12 to three or four; mycology from 10 to four; and entomology from about 35 to a dozen. Remaining staff have been left with few or no assistants. All fieldwork has been abandoned, with many of the remaining scientists spending their time in chemistry labs (conducting research of little relevance to biodiversity) and/or at computer terminals. It is ironic that AAFC is emasculating biodiversity research while spending tax dollars to produce a plethora of greenwash publications extolling their caring attitude towards biodiversity conservation.

Fisheries and Oceans Canada

This department terminated the Fisheries Research Board of Canada and the Arctic Biological Research Station. Professional staff have been reduced by 40 to 50 per cent. Many scientists had been researching the ecology of the fresh and marine waters, including dynamics of ocean processes, food chains, and the like. Remaining fisheries scientists and researchers are narrowly focused on "stock" management rather than on ecosystem-based management. Noteworthy research into the taxonomy of marine and freshwater biota has largely been terminated.

Natural Resources Canada (formerly Forestry Canada)

Petawawa Forest Experimental Station at Chalk River, Ontario has been closed. The number of biodiversity-related research positions at the Petawawa station was reduced from about a dozen to zero. Other locations across the country have suffered similar fates. Responsibility for forest-related research has been largely left to the provinces, where politicians are more subject to lobby pressures from international forestry companies with little interest in basic biodiversity research.

The Canadian Museum of Nature

The professional biodiversity research staff has been reduced in many fields: botany, invertebrate zoology, mammalogy, ornithology, malacology, bryology, and others. In the early 1970s staff totalled 24 to 26; this has been reduced to about 14 today. Research into birds, mammals, amphibians, and reptiles – so important to the Canadian public – has been terminated. Assistance to remaining scientists is also greatly reduced and fieldwork essentially eliminated. Reduced financial support from the federal government is one reason for this attrition. Admittedly, the museum has a new building, but almost no space was provided for growth of collections, library, or staff. Remaining scientists are crammed into tiny open pens that would be suitable for hens in egg factories. Further, in the biodiversity publications field, one by one over the past two decades the CMN has terminated all six of its serialized and/or occasional scientific publications on biodiversity. The remaining scientists have no "in house" place to publish their research. To top it off, a new, ambitious publication entitled *Global Biodiversity* started in 1991 was terminated in March 1999.

Environment Canada

The many changes at Environment Canada are due largely to budget cuts and shifts in research priorities. Major cuts to research took place in 1985. Research into northern wildlife has decreased, although work is continuing on some species at risk, such as polar bears and Peary caribou. The Experimental Lakes Project (run by world-famous scientist, David Schindler) was abruptly terminated before the project was completed. There has been an increased emphasis on toxicology and a decreased emphasis on waterfowl and other game species. Environment Canada's world-renowned State of the Environment Reporting system[24] has been virtually closed down. This means that trends in the "abiotic" matrix in which biodiversity is embedded will cease to be monitored as thoroughly as they were in the past decade.

Motives for Downsizing

What can be said about the motives behind downsizing basic taxonomic and ecological biodiversity field research? One motive must surely be that such research does not immediately produce commodities for selling in the global marketplace. Another, more likely, motive is that: "it's safer not to know." Basic knowledge about how nature functions and what is happening to species and normal ecosystems can interfere with bureaucratic and political decisions. It takes no research to cut down a forest, plow up a piece of prairie, or scavenge the continental shelf with huge draggers and trawlers. In the absence of ecological research there can be no public discourse on the reasons for the degradation of ecosystems or valued biological resources, such as salmon or cod. Management decisions also cannot take the health of the resource into account. The result will be over-exploitation. The few scientists who know the reasons for over-exploitation are sometimes muzzled by the bureaucracy – as has happened in AAFC, Health Canada, Environment Canada, and Fisheries and Oceans Canada. Scientific data on what is happening to biodiversity are a threat to the corporate bottom line, to aspiring bureaucrats, and to politicians whom they advise and support. Too many of Canada's political, corporate, and political élites seem to believe that without solid scientific research and knowledge an informed public discourse and criticism of government and corporate policies and programs are impossible.

Restrictions on biodiversity research represent a profound contempt for the public interest, the public's need to be informed, and the public's right to know. Biodiversity research at the federal level is being allowed to die — a trend contrary to Canada's formal commitment under the Convention on Biological Diversity. Downgrading research on species and natural ecosystems leads to an increasing societal ignorance of how the planet and its ecosphere function. The consequence is that the public is unable to act in defence of its own long-term interests.

Losing Unique Plant Cultivars and Animal Breeds

Another significant step backwards in protecting Canadian biodiversity was passage of the Canada Seeds Act. This law, supported by the agri-business industry, is designed to makes it illegal for farmers to sell any unregistered variety of cultivated plant or animal.[25] Its passage suggests that the Canadian government is no longer trying to prevent extinction of unique old cultivars and breeds. This topic is covered in detail by Bob Wildfong in Chapter 7.

Weakening Biodiversity Conservation Legislation

Over the past 15 years, there has been a determined effort by developers, free-marketeers, and their friends in government to water down international agreements and federal, provincial, and municipal legislation and by-laws intended to conserve biodiversity and protect the environment. This topic is discussed by Ian Attridge in Chapter 14. International trade agreements, such as NAFTA and the World Trade Organization, also contain clauses that enable nations and corporations to take legal action against any government *that tries to restrict trade for the purpose of preventing the import of toxic substances* (that impact on biodiversity) or that prevents imports of species at risk in other parts of the world.

It is not to the credit of corporate and governmental élites of Canada that biodiversity in this country should continue to be incrementally toxified, eliminated, or otherwise degraded to the extent that the ecosphere cannot function in its natural, normal, and secure manner. Genes, species, ecosystems, ecological functions, and the "abiotic" matrix continue to be over-exploited and lost under the impact of increasing human numbers and irresponsible government policies and legislation. Efforts by environmental organizations and some government departments (such as Environment Canada) constitute small steps to reduce a few of these trends. However, with the popular liberal belief in never-ending economic growth and never-ending development, a turnaround in the attrition of biodiversity is surely not yet at hand. In the meantime, we are losing more of the healthfully functioning, life-sustaining, and intrinsically beautiful ecosphere.

Notes

1. T. Mosquin, P.G. Whiting, and D.E. McAllister, *Canada's Biodiversity: The Variety of Life, its Status, Economic Benefits, Conservation Costs and Unmet Needs* (Ottawa: Canadian Centre for Biodiversity, Canadian Museum of Nature, 1995), ch. 3.

2. Bill Freedman, Stephen Woodley, and Judy Loo, "Forestry Practices and biodiversity, with particular reference to the Maritime Provinces of eastern Canada," *Environmental Review* 2 (1994): 33-78.

3. J.A. Burnett, C.T. Dauphine, S.H. McCrindle, and T. Mosquin, *On the Brink: Endangered Species in Canada* (Saskatoon: Western Producer Books, 1989); G.G.E. Scudder, "The Adaptive Significance of Marginal Populations," Proceedings of the National Workshop on Effects of Habitat Alteration on Salmonid Stocks, *Can. Special Pub. on Fisheries and Aquatic Resources* 105 (1989): 180-85; G.G.E. Scudder, "Marginal Populations and Environmental Change" (draft, 1993).

4. Mosquin et al., *Canada's Biodiversity*.

5. Roger Lewin, "Sources and Sinks Complicate Ecology," *Science* 243 (1989): 477-78.

6. John Terborgh, "Why American Songbirds are Vanishing," *Scientific American* (May 1992): 8-10; *RENEW Report* No. 8 (1998).

7. Lubomyr Masner, "The Nearctic species of *Duta* Nixon (Hymenoptera: Scelionidae), Egg Parasitoids of Common Crickets (Orthoptera: Grillidae)," *Canadian Entomologist* 123 (1991): 777-93.

8. E. Brodo, personal communication.

9. Mosquin et al., *Canada's Biodiversity*.

10. Michael J. Oldham, *Environmentally Significant Areas of the Essex Region* (Essex, Ont.: Essex Region Conservation Authority, 1983).

11. Mosquin et al., *Canada's Biodiversity*.

12. Environment Canada, *The State of Canada's Environment* (Ottawa: Government of Canada, 1991).

13. World Wildlife Fund, *Prairie Conservation Action Plan, 1989-1994* (Toronto, 1989).

14. E. Schultze and H.A. Mooney, *Biodiversity and Ecosystem Function* (Berlin: Springer-Verlag, 1993); Mosquin et al., *Canada's Biodiversity*; Edward Goldsmith, *The Way: An Ecological World View* (Devon, U.K.: Themis Books, 1996); Gretchen C. Daily, ed., *Nature's Services; Societal Dependence on Natural Ecosystems* (Washington: Island Press, 1997); Holmes Rolston III, "Global Environmental Ethics: A Valuable Earth," in Richard L. Knight and Sarah F. Bates, eds., *A New Century of Natural Resource Management* (Washington: Island Press, 1995), 349-66.

15. Holmes Rolston III, "Can and Ought We Follow Nature?" *Environmental Ethics* 1, 1 (1979): 7-31, Holmes Rolston III, "Environmental Ethics: Values in and Duties to the Natural World," in F. Herbert Bormann and Stephen R. Kellert, eds., *The Broken Circle: Ecology, Economics, Ethics* (New Haven: Yale University Press, 1991), 73-96; Rolston, "Global Environmental Ethics."

16. Statistics Canada, *Human Activity and the Environment 1991*. Cat. no. 11-509E (1991); Environment Canada, *The State of Canada's Environment* (1991, 1996).

17. C. David Fowle, "Will Ecospeak Make a Difference?" Maple, Ont.: Ontario Ministry of Natural Resources, Research, Science and Technology Branch, Research Technical Paper No. 3, 1994; Stan Rowe, "Ecosystems and Intellectual Puzzles." Maple, Ont.: Ontario Ministry of Natural Resources, Research, Science and Technology Branch, Research Technical Paper No. 2, 1994.

18. Agriculture and Agri-Food Canada (AAFC), *Agriculture in Harmony with Nature: Strategy for Environmentally Sustainable Agriculture and Agri-food Development in Canada* (Ottawa, 1997).

19. Environment Canada, *Canadian Biodiversity Strategy: Canada's Response to the Convention on Biological Diversity* (Ottawa: Minister of Supply and Services, 1995).

20. AAFC, *Agriculture in Harmony*; AAFC, *Biodiversity in Agriculture; Agriculture and Agri-Food Canada's Action Plan; Implementing the Canadian Biodiversity Strategy*

(1997); AAFC, *Biodiversity Initiatives; Canadian Agricultural Producers; Implementing the Canadian Biodiversity Strategy* (1997); AAFC, *Profile of Production Trends and Environmental Issues in Canada's Agriculture and Agri-Food Sector* (1997).

21. Environment Canada, *Canadian Biodiversity Strategy*.

22. International Union for the Conservation of Nature, "Guide to the Convention on Biological Diversity," IUCN Environmental Law Centre, Environmental Policy and Law Paper No. 30, 1994.

23. WRI, IUCN, and UNEP, *Global Biodiversity Strategy: Guidelines for Action to Save, Study and Use Earth's Biotic Wealth Sustainably and Equitably* (Washington: World Resources Institute; Gland, Switzerland: IUCN; Nairobi: United Nations Environment Program, 1992).

24. Environment Canada, *The State of Canada's Environment* (Ottawa, 1986, 1991, 1996).

25. Sue Strickland, *Heirloom Vegetables: A Home Gardener's Guide to Finding and Growing Vegetables from the Past* (London: Gaia Books, 1988); Susan Rempel, "The Power of Seeds," *Global Biodiversity* 8, 2 (1998): 21-22.

Further Reading

Agriculture and Agri-Food Canada. *Agriculture in Harmony with Nature: Strategy for Environmentally Sustainable Agriculture and Agri-food Development in Canada*. Ottawa, 1997. [Recommended only as an excellent example of Canadian green-wash literature.]

Environment Canada. *The State of Canada's Environment*. Ottawa, 1996.

Environment Canada. *Conserving Wildlife Diversity: Implementing the Canadian Biodiversity Strategy*. Ottawa, 1998.

Environment Canada, Biodiversity Convention Office. *Learning About Biodiversity: A First Look at the Theory and Practice of Biodiversity Education, Awareness and Training in Canada*. Ottawa, 1998.

Environment Canada, Biodiversity Convention Office. *Caring for Canada's Biodiversity*. Ottawa: Public Works and Government Services Canada, 1998.

Fowle, David C. "Will Ecospeak Make a Difference?" Maple, Ont.: Ontario Ministry of Natural Resources, Research, Science and Technology Branch, Research Technical Paper No. 3, 1994.

Don E. McAllister

Biodiversity in Canadian
Fresh and Marine Waters

F RESHWATER AND MARINE ECOSYSTEMS IN CANADA CONTAIN a diversity of elements: kelp forests with sea urchins and sea otters; deep-sea hydrothermal vents with bacteria tolerant of boiling temperatures and one-metre long worms fuelled by hot sulphur-laden springs; billions of tiny diatoms gathering sun rays on the underside of sea ice, the base of a food chain that includes crustaceans, Arctic cod, seals, and polar bears; springtails on snow; wetlands, covering 14 per cent of the country, invaded by exotic purple loosestrife.

Canada has large areas of aquatic ecosystems (Figure 1); and given its vertical dimension, the marine environment is likely the largest in vol-

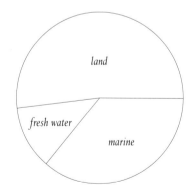

Figure 1: Relative Area of Land, Freshwater, and Marine Environments in Canada

(as portion of 17.8 million sq. km)

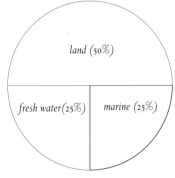

Figure 2: Percentage of Species in Each Environment

(percentage of 71,000 described species)

ume of any element of the Canadian environment.[1] These ecosystems — and particularly freshwater ecosystems, given their small size — are also richly endowed with species (Figure 2).

However, human activities pose a range of threats to these ecosystems. Some of these threats affect these ecosystems directly, such as the use of destructive fishing gear, and inappropriate logging practices. But equally important are the root causes of these threats, including the failure of governments to regulate harvesting activities effectively, the pressures of a global economy, and continuing growth in the world's human population. Our limited scientific knowledge impedes our ability to protect aquatic life.

Characteristics of the Aquatic Environment

Aquatic environments are more stable in terms of temperature than are terrestrial environments. The greater density, hence buoyant, effect of water means that skeletons of aquatic organisms need not be strong enough to oppose gravitational forces. Some aquatic animals, like jellyfish and comb jellies, lack even skeletons. On the other hand, aquatic organisms not dwelling at the surface or the bottom need to develop buoyancy control to conserve energy or to avoid "falling" upwards or downwards.

At the species level, aquatic environments are less diverse than terrestrial environments. About 23 per cent of Canada's species are freshwater, 25 per cent are marine, while 51 per cent are terrestrial.[2] These percentages refer to the number of known species, some 71,000: those that have been discovered, named, and classified by science. But it is estimated that there remain at least 68,000 additional species awaiting discovery by science, excluding viruses. Adding viruses might double the number. Much of terrestrial and a considerable portion of freshwater species diversity is composed of insects.

The diversity picture reverses when we examine the phyletic level. Of the 63 major phyla in Canada, two-thirds are dominantly or exclusively marine, while one-third are dominantly terrestrial or freshwater. We can expect that genetic diversity, tied to phyletic diversity, will be highest in the oceans where the thicker branches of the tree of life are found.

Canada has been a vigorous participant and leader in the drafting, signature, and ratification of the Biodiversity Convention. It has developed its own national strategy with participation by federal and provincial governments, environmental organizations, industry, and other sectors.[3] Implementation has not been as vigorous. Cutbacks in federal and provincial departments have hampered implementation. New federal fisheries and oceans acts have been passed, but the draft act on endangered species and ecosystems failed to. Some of the 2,000 environmental organizations in Canada deal with freshwater and marine environmental issues. They play a key role in public awareness, education, research, and on-the-ground activities.[4]

Establishment of aquatic protected areas has lagged behind protection for terrestrial areas. Freshwater ecosystems and species often have been protected only incidentally within terrestrial protected areas. Marine protected areas are beginning to receive more consideration by Parks Canada, and under Department of Fisheries and Oceans legislation.[5]

Freshwater Biodiversity

Fresh waters in Canada occur in solid and liquid form. One hundred thousand glaciers, permafrost, and permanent snow-cover in the Arctic and alpine zones lock up considerable volumes of water. In winter, surface waters in rivers and lakes may be frozen to a metre or more in thickness. Two million lakes, countless rivers, and wetlands contain most surface fresh waters. But soil moisture and ground water volumes exceed surface fresh waters. Water also comprises a vital part of living organisms. Evaporation and evapotranspiration form a vital link in the hydrological cycle.

Canada's land area (excluding rivers and lakes), essentially its drainage basin, occupies 9,215,430 km². Wetlands, including fresh and saltwater marshes, wooded swamps, bogs, seasonably flooded forests, and sloughs, cover about 14 per cent of Canada's land surface, while lakes and rivers cover about 755,180 km² or about 8 per cent of the land area.[6] Those values are higher than for most countries. The rivers drain about 9 per cent of the world's renewable water supply with about 60 per cent flowing into the Arctic Ocean, most of the rest into the Pacific and Atlantic oceans, and a tiny fraction into the Gulf of Mexico. Lake Superior's area (in Canada and the U.S.) is 84,124 km^2 while Great Bear Lake occupies 31,790 km^2. Canada's longest river system, the Mackenzie, extends 4,240 km and drains an area of 1,804,000 km^2.

Ecosystems

Canada possesses a variety of freshwater ecosystems, including lakes, ponds, temporary pools, streams, rivers, springs, marshes, swamps, fens, bogs, groundwater, and estuaries. Ice and snow, tree cavities, hot-springs, and cave waters are smaller but biotically interesting aquatic ecosystems. A few algae and springtails live on or in snow. Micro-organisms have been discovered hundreds of metres underground in Saskatchewan.

Lower reaches of rivers may be dominated by euryhaline (tolerant of salt water) and anadromous species; but sometimes the latter may migrate several thousand kilometres inland, as in, for example, the Yukon River basin. These migrations can transport significant amounts of energy and nutrients into upstream aquatic and riparian environments; nutrients that may foster the growth of stream-side trees.

One can approach ecosystems also from the standpoint of drainage basins. The World Wildlife Fund U.S. has recently mapped the biotical-ly distinctive basins of North America. At large-scale levels, such as between the Pacific drainage basin and those lying east of the Rockies, there can be major differences in biota. For example, minnow family members, such as the redside shiner, *Richardsonius balteatus*, and the squawfish, *Ptychocheilus oregonense* are found almost entirely in Pacific drainages. Terrestrial ecosystems and human activities within a basin have a profound affect on the rivers, lakes, and wetlands in that basin. It is, therefore, often most useful to consider management issues in terms of drainage basins.

Species

Twenty-three per cent of the known species of animals, plants, and micro-organisms in Canada occur in freshwater, while 72 per cent of major phyla occur in that environment. These species include 177 freshwater, 26 anadromous, and one catadromous fish, 179 freshwater molluscs, and 11 freshwater crayfish. Of Canada's 15,200 fungi, 1,095 or 7 per cent occur in fresh water; of 2,980 native flowering plants, 15 per cent or about 447 species occur in fresh water. About 32 per cent of bacteria are freshwater, and between 80 per cent and 98 per cent of 2,460 algal species live in freshwater. Of 745 species of mayflies, dragonflies, and stoneflies, 50 per cent may be said to be freshwater in that their eggs and larvae are freshwater while the adult stages are terrestrial (or aerial).[7]

Canada was almost completely ice-covered during the last glaciation, the Wisconsin, which lasted until about 10,000 years ago. Many species now in Canada re-invaded from glacial refugia, for the most part outside of Canada. This has meant that few are endemic to Canada, that is, originated within it. However, taxonomic investigations are increasing the number of known endemic species. Between 1 and 5 per cent of terrestrial and aquatic Canadian species in most taxa are estimated to be endemic.[8] Canadian freshwater endemics include a blind subterranean amphipod, *Stygobromus canadensis*, from Castelguard Cave, Banff National Park, Alberta; the copper redhorse, *Moxostoma hubbsi*, from the St. Lawrence basin near Montreal, and an oligochaete worm, *Henlea yukonensis*, from an unglaciated area in Yukon.

Freshwater species tend to be fewer towards the north. For example, only three of Canada's 50 freshwater mussels are found north of 60° N. Lat., none of Canada's 11 species of crayfish are known north of 60°, and only 41 of Canada's 181 freshwater fish species occur in the Northwest Territories.[9] Figure 3, using an equal-area grid, shows how the number of species of freshwater molluscs around Hudson Bay decline northward, but are richer in western basins, perhaps due to postglacial Lake Agassiz connections. Equal-area grids are useful in analysing and portraying geographic patterns in biodiversity, since most geographic units, like countries, provinces, and islands, are unequal in area, making the effects of area and species density more difficult to decipher.[10]

Superimposed on this north-south trend are regional hotspots: areas with high numbers of species. Two prominent ones are in southern Ontario and southern British Columbia, with southern Ontario

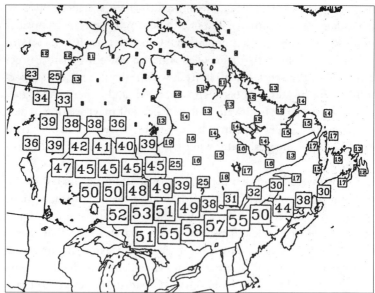

having the most species of fish, molluscs, and crayfish, including nine
of the 11 species of crayfish found in Ontario.

Status of and Threats to Biodiversity

By 1997 the Committee on the Status of Endangered Wildlife in Canada
(COSEWIC) had classified 62 species, subspecies, or distinct populations
of freshwater fishes as being extinct, endangered, threatened, or vulnerable. That means that almost one-third of Canada's freshwater
species are at risk. From the point of view of fisheries, 10 of 30 basin
stocks (Pacific, Arctic, and Atlantic) of important fisheries species are in
poor or very poor condition. Four of 41 species of Canadian amphibians
were at risk as of 1997.[11]

In many parts of southern Canada more than two-thirds of all wetlands have been lost.[12] Nationally this represents 14 per cent of all wetlands, a total of 200,000 km^2. The principle factor leading to loss of wetlands are their drainage or filling for farmland, municipal development, transportation, or because they are deprived of seasonal water
supplies by dams. Loss of wetlands has contributed to the decline this
century of duck populations from 200 million to about 30 million. This

loss has slowed in recent years because of legislation, while programs like the North American Waterfowl Management Plan have even restored some wetlands, although the gains are small compared to the losses.[13]

Immediate Threats

Dams

About 20,000 km² of land, the size of Lake Ontario, are now covered by hydroelectric dam reservoirs. There are more than 650 large dams, over 80 per cent of which are for generating hydroelectric power. Dams have a variety of environmental impacts. They change upstream environments from running waters to lake-like still waters. They block fish migrations unless functional fish ladders are included. Downstream, they affect the seasonality of flow, temperature, and turbidity. A number of ecosystems rely on a seasonal natural rise in water levels, be it from spring runoff or summer increases in flow from glacial melt. That flooding should not be confused with flooding due to rapid runoff resulting from inappropriate forestry or agricultural practices.

If we assume that the downstream effects of large dams extend 200 km, then Canada's large dams affect 130,000 km of rivers. The W.A.C. Bennett Dam in British Columbia disrupted annual flooding in the Athabasca-Peace Delta, 1,200 km downstream, causing conversion of 25 per cent of its wet grasslands to forest habitats. Inter-drainage diversions may result in the transfer of fish, plants, bacteria, and viruses from one basin to another.[14]

Agriculture

In Canada 680,000 km² are devoted to agriculture on improved farmland (cropland, improved pasture, summer fallow) and unimproved farmland. This represents 7 per cent of the land surface of Canada, but it could also be understood as almost 14 per cent of the land area of the southern half of Canada, where most agriculture and freshwater biodiversity is located.

Agriculture can have a range of impacts on aquatic biodiversity, including: drainage of wetlands; turbidity and sedimentation resulting from runoff of bare, tilled soil; eutrophication from fertilizer or manure runoff; runoff bearing toxic farm chemicals including pesticides; drawing of surface or ground waters for irrigation; and removal of riparian vegetation by stock or for cropland.

However, appropriate agricultural practices can benefit aquatic biodiversity. For example, a considerable amount of land in the Caribou region of British Columbia is kept in fairly natural condition for cattle grazing, thereby protecting aquatic ecosystems from cropland impacts. Many prairie farmers, on their own or through programs like that of Ducks Unlimited, conserve potholes and marshes, providing habitat for a rich variety of species. The 11 per cent of farms in Quebec that are organic disperse no pesticides into the aquatic environment.

The impacts of agriculture on one taxonomic group, frogs, are of particular note. Concern has grown around the globe about disappearing frog populations and the increasing proportion of frogs with deformities. For the last seven years Dr. Martin Ouellet of the Redpath Museum, McGill University, has been researching frog deformities in Quebec. He and his co-workers have collected thousands of specimens from hundreds of localities. Grotesque frogs are not unusual on a 250-km stretch along both sides of the St. Lawrence River from Montreal northeastward to Montmagny, Quebec. This includes 25 deformities in 16 species of amphibians, including both frogs and salamanders. These deformities include a frog with an eye in the back, one with legs growing from its belly, ones with one or both hind legs missing, ones with clogged and diseased livers, and ones that look like males but are female inside. On land that has not been sprayed with pesticides for many decades, an average of 1 per cent of the frogs are deformed, while on working farms that apply insecticides, fungicides, herbicides, and chemical fertilizers, 12 per cent of the frogs are deformed. Such deformities can be expected to contribute to lowered survival rates.[15]

According to Dr. David Green, professor of biology at McGill and former national co-ordinator of the Canadian Declining Amphibian Populations Task Force, of Canada's 66 frog, toad, and salamander species, 17 are in decline. Several of these 17 are designated as vulnerable or threatened species by COSEWIC, and most of these are western species, because of encroachment by farming and logging. For years Canadian farmers have been receiving public subsidies for draining wetlands. Clearly, Canadian farming practices are contributing to loss of frogs and other amphibians through agrichemicals. Unfortunately only modest funding has been available to study this decline in Canada.

The use of pesticides is reinforced by the planting of genetically uniform crops over large areas. Such low diversity varieties are a ready feast for pests. One then goes through a familiar cycle: a new crop and a new pesticide are developed, pests develop resistance to the pesticide, and either a new crop or a new pesticide is again developed. Crop varieties that are bioengineered to tolerate pesticides lock farmers into pesticide use. Pesticide-producing genes inserted into crops also go through the same pesticide effectiveness-resistance cycle as externally sprayed pesticides.

Aquatic species feel the impact of pesticides transported by runoff or by atmospheric fallout into their ecosystems. Toxaphene applied to cotton crops thousands of kilometres away is found in fish in Lac Laberge, Yukon Territory. This demonstrates the distances that atmospheric transport, and then distillation in cold climates, can transport pesticides.

Forestry

Forests provide a number of ecological services for aquatic ecosystems. Forests are a key element in hydrological cycles. Foliage, leaf litter, woody debris, and soil humus absorb much of the moisture from rainfall, and pass some along to soil moisture and ground water, whence it flows slowly to wetlands and streams or lakes. Intact forests slow runoff into streams, evening out the flow and thereby diminishing freshets and periods of drought. Trees, aided by mycorrhizal fungi, absorb moisture and transpire it into the air where it forms clouds, whereupon the cycle repeats itself. Clear-cutting short-circuits this cycle: more of the water flows rapidly to streams and thence to the sea; freshets are higher and droughts are longer and deeper. Periods of low water reduce living space and are more vulnerable to temperature fluctuations.

Leafs, twigs, branches and tree trunks that fall into streams are a primary source of food for invertebrates, which in turn serve as food for species higher on the food chain. Despite regulations to the contrary, some forest product companies still cut bank-side trees. Fallen branches and trunks are vital elements in forming stream, lake, and even marine habitats. They provide flow diversions, pools, and shelter under or beside which invertebrates and fishes shelter and feed.[16] Clear-cutting results in more erosion, especially when bank areas are cut. That in turn means stream habitat changes from sand, gravel, and rocks to mud, and the water becomes more turbid; these are all changes likely to reduce biodiversity of invertebrates and fish. Those impacts may be magnified when the clear-cuts are large, on sloping land or on unstable soils.

Exotic Species and Populations

The number of alien species in Canada's fresh waters is growing. Some introductions were intentional, like the carp, *Cyprinus carpio*, while others, like the zebra mussel, *Dreissena polymorpha*, were introduced accidentally. Yet others were introduced into the United States and spread northwards into our waters. Some species are indigenous to Canada but have been transferred into areas where they were not native. For example, rainbow trout, *Oncorhynchus mykiss*, have been introduced from western to eastern Canada. Some alien species like the zebra mussel and the purple loosestrife, *Lythrum salicaria*, have spread widely and are displacing native species and transforming ecosystems. Precautions with ballast water emptying (the zebra mussel, for example, entered the Great Lakes by way of the ballast water of a freighter) may reduce the incidence of alien species introductions. Twenty-three per cent of Canada's terrestrial and aquatic flowering plants are alien species, as are 18 per cent of its crayfish, 6 per cent of its freshwater fishes, and 2 per cent of its amphibian species.[17]

The introduction of exotic populations, stocks, subspecies, or species may result in hybridizations between the local and the introduced stocks — a kind of genetic pollution that can extirpate the local species. Widespread planting of fish from hatcheries, whether from wild or domesticated stock, disrupts the genetics and adaptation of local populations.[18] Aquaculture is one of the most rapidly growing industries in Canada. The escape of individuals from aquaculture ponds or pens have similar implications as the escape of other exotic species, with genetic threats actually increased when the stocks are specially bred, or possess transgenic genes. Introduction of aquaculture stocks also pose the risk of introducing diseases, pests, and parasites.

While each of these impacts on aquatic species is significant, it is also important to consider the root causes of these impacts in contemporary society. These root causes include the continued growth in the human population in Canada; market forces, and the frequent reluctance of governments to regulate effectively the activities of the private sector, particularly when these activities have environmental impacts; and the pressures of globalization, including those imposed by NAFTA and other trade agreements, which can tend to reduce the ability of governments to act in accordance with the democratically expressed wishes of their citizens.[19]

A new globalization threat has recently reared its head. In December 1998 Sun Belt Water Inc. of California began seeking millions in compensation under NAFTA rules for lost trade caused when the B.C. government banned exports of bulk water. Should it win, the precedent would establish that water is to be treated as a commercial commodity like oil or gas, greatly restricting the ability of Canadian governments to regulate its export. Such a precedent would ignore the fact that water is also a vital environment for biodiversity and biological resources. It would also eliminate Canadian sovereignty and capacity to make decisions based on environmental, societal, and future-generational needs, as well as trade considerations. The NAFTA tribunal that would rule on this dispute will likely consist of trade specialists, not known for their environmental qualifications. Canada is considering submitting the issue to the International Joint Commission, a joint U.S.-Canada body that deals with transboundary water and atmosphere issues.

Marine Biodiversity

Canadian marine waters cover some 6.5 million km^2 within the 200-nautical mile exclusive economic zone (EEZ) on Canada's Pacific and Atlantic coasts, and within Canada's Arctic sector. Canada's coastline is the second-longest in the world, with 29,489 km or 11 per cent on the Pacific coast including islands, 165,000 km or 68 per cent on the Arctic coast (excluding southeastern Baffin Island, Hudson Strait, and Ungava Bay), and 52,000 km or 21 per cent on the Atlantic coast.

Marine Ecosystems

Most marine species occur on the bottom. In the estuary and Gulf of St. Lawrence, for example, 83.7 per cent of the species are benthic, 9.0 per cent are parasitic, 6.0 per cent are zooplanktonic (in the water column), and 0.3 per cent are nektonic (living on or just under the water surface).[20] This high proportion of benthic species is probably comparable to that found in other marine areas. However, many benthic species have pelagic eggs or larvae, many of which occur in the upper photic zone.

While land plants are largely macroscopic, the majority of marine plants, aside from a few like seaweeds, seagrasses, and mangroves, are microscopic. The pastures of the sea are mostly invisible to the naked eye. Nevertheless, it is on these invisible pastures of diatoms, cyanobacteria, and others that almost all animal life in the sea depends.

Marine ecosystems can be classified in terms of large-scale zones. For example, all of Canada is covered by two biogeographic zones established by J.C. Briggs: Cold-temperate waters (on the Atlantic coast, the Western Atlantic Boreal Region; and on the Pacific coast, the Oregon Province) and Cold (Arctic) waters.[21] These zones can be very useful in distinguishing areas with common biota and moderate to high levels of endemism.

The small-scale ecosystems of Canadian marine waters are too many and varied to catalogue in this chapter. However, a few examples will give an idea of their variety: wrack (the seaweed cast up on the shore, consumed by sand hoppers and dipterans, themselves fed upon by land and shore birds); the space between sand grains inhabited by meiofauna; kelp forests (habitat for hundreds of species from sea urchins to sea otters); numerous sediment types (containing the infauna, species that live in the mud); eelgrass beds (used by limpets, snails, sticklebacks, and pipefish); the surface film (used by neuston, small species on or just under the surface); inclined or vertical rock faces (used by gorgonian sea fans, sea anemones, sponges, etc.); and the bathypelagic zone (home to luminous fish that migrate upward at night and downward at dawn).[22] An unusual type of ecosystem forms around hydrothermal vents, some found off the west coast, that discharge hot, mineral-laden water. Bacteria extract energy from sulphur compounds; molluscs, crabs, shrimps, and 60-cm long tubeworms are among the species inhabiting these ecosystems.[23]

Consider the significance of one obscure ecosystem. Certain tidal mudflats in the upper Bay of Fundy are home to a tube-building amphipod, *Corophium volutator* (see Figure 4). It feeds on detritus supplied to the marine ecosystem from the neighbouring saltmarshes by the ebb and flow of Fundy's great tides. Feeding on the amphipod are semi-palmated sandpipers (*Ereunetes pusillus*), 1.4 million of which funnel through the area in July and August. This food fuels the sandpiper for a 4,300 km non-stop transoceanic flight to South American wintering grounds. There are many other obscure ecosystems. Polychaete worms provide food to fish on Canada's well-known Atlantic fishing banks. Floating logs are used by seabirds as resting places, places of attachment for goose barnacles, burrows for teredos, and when they sink they serve as food and habitat for wood and debris munchers.[24]

The effective conservation of biodiversity and ecosystem-based management of biological resources will depend on developing hierarchical marine ecosystem classifications that encompass this diversity. The author is working on a model of such a classification for the west coast. Such a classification presents significant challenges. While terrestrial vegetation systems, being visible, are relatively easy to identify and map, marine ecosystems differ in that much of the "vegetation" is planktonic, and much of the three-dimensional structural biological diversity is zoological, such as coral reefs. Nevertheless, hierarchical marine ecosystem classifications, including physical and biological elements from large- to small-scales are possible.[25]

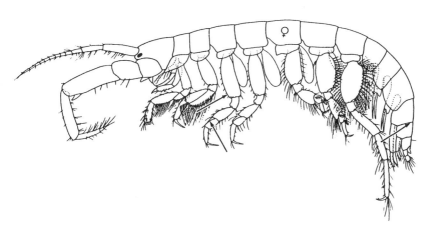

Figure 4: Corophium volutator, a tube-building amphipod from Bay of Fundy tidal mudflats.

Marine Species

Twenty-five per cent of all known species of microbiota, plants, and animals in Canada — some 17,750 species — are marine. This is slightly more than are found in fresh water.[26] About 5,000 marine species have been described from British Columbia, but this estimate did not include bacteria; 2,214 metazoan invertebrates have been listed as present in the Gulf of St. Lawrence.[27] But many taxonomic groups lack recent treatments for Canadian waters or lack them entirely. This lack hampers ecological and genetic research, conservation, resource management, and the development of new bio-industries.

Table 1 gives the number of species in most of the larger (more species-rich) groups of biota.[28] Of the 20,445 listed, only 48.3 per cent are scientifically named and classified. There is room for venturesome students of taxonomy. Of the named species, ecological and life history information is sparse, and information on geographic distribution is spotty. Grid-based biological surveys would provide the basis for sound distribution maps.

The oceans are richer in phyla than are land and fresh water. In Canada two-thirds of the 63 major phyla are predominantly marine.[29] About 84 per cent of phyla occur in marine environments, compared with 72 per cent in freshwater and only 66 per cent on land. As in the case of fresh water, most groups contain higher numbers of species in southern marine waters than in the north. For example, only 137 or 13 per cent of Canada's marine fish are found in the Arctic seas between Alaska and Labrador.

The Pacific coast is generally richer in species than the Atlantic coast, though the former spans only 48° to 55° North latitude compared to the latter's span of 42° to 60°. This is shown in Table 2, suggesting there are almost twice as many species in the Pacific than in the Atlantic.[30]

There are also hotspots of marine species richness in Canada. The west coast of Canada has one of the richest marine algae or seaweed floras in the world.[31] Most of the 639 seaweed species and subspecies in 281 genera occurring in the Pacific Northwest (Oregon to southeast Alaska) are found in British Columbia. The southern Atlantic coast of Canada has more species of stickleback, *Gasterosteidae*, than any other region of the world: fourspine stickleback, *Apeltes quadracu;* threespine stickleback, *Gasterosteus aculeatus*; blackspotted stickleback, *Gasterosteus wheatland;* white stickleback, *Gasterosteus* sp.; and the ninespine stickleback, *Pungitius pungitius* (not to mention the brook stickleback, *Culaea inconstans,* found in inland waters).

Endemism seems to be less common in northern marine waters than in fresh waters. In part this reflects the interconnectedness of the oceans compared to the isolation of drainage basins. But it may also reflect the fact that there has been less study of marine species. Nevertheless, there are some marine endemics in Canada, including the Y-prickleback, *Allolumpenus hypochromis* (though there is a doubtful California record), and the pixie poatcher, *Occella impi,* from northern B.C. V. Tunnicliffe has estimated that there are 293 marine invertebrate endemics in B.C. (excluding microbiota), or 7.8 per cent of the 3,771 species known. She suspected that with further study the ranges of some of these local endemics would be expanded beyond B.C.; those species would no longer then be considered endemic to B.C.[32]

Dr. Edward L. Bousfield (*in litt.*) informs me that there are 43 species of amphipods known only from the Pacific coast of Canada, mostly intertidal and shallow marine littoral species, e.g., *Rhepoxynius boreovariatus* Jarrett and Bousfield. On the Atlantic coast there are only two endemics, including *Haploops fundiensis* Wildish and Dickinson, 1982. However, that would be swelled to 32 species, if those (mostly deepwater benthic and epi-benthic species) recently discovered by Pierre Brunel are described. Doubtless the ranges of some of these will be extended with further research and some of those will no longer be classified as Canadian endemics.

Indigenous cultures also have important knowledge systems. The Haida people in Gwaia (Queen Charlotte Islands) possess knowledge about over 40 species of marine invertebrates, including razor clams, shrimp, octopus, giant red sea urchins, and Alaska king crabs.[33] The people of the Hudson Bay bioregion also possess extensive knowledge of their marine environment.[34]

Status of and Threats to Marine Biodiversity

A few marine species are extinct in Canada. These include the eelgrass limpet, *Lotea alveus*; the sea mink, *Musetelus macrodon*; the great auk, *Pinguinis impenni;* and the Labrador duck, *Camptorhynchus labradoricus,* which

Figure 5:
Gorgonian seacorn
coral, Primnoa
residaeformis
specimen, from seafan
groves being clearcut by
trawlers off Nova
Scotia. Specimens have
been aged at
500 years old.

Photo courtesy of Derek Jones, Canadian Ocean Habitat Protection Society.

occurred on the Atlantic coast. The sea otter, *Enhydra lutris*, was extirpated from the Pacific coast, but has been reintroduced from elsewhere and is now successfully breeding. Endangered species include the Acadian whitefish, *Coregonus huntsmani*, the St. Lawrence population of the beluga, *Delphinapterus leucas*, and the leatherback turtle, *Dermochelys coriacea*.[35]

The stocks of a number of important fisheries species are severely depressed. These include the Atlantic cod, *Gadus morhua*, the coho salmon, *Oncorhynchus kisutch*, and the American lobster, *Homarus americanus*. Even populations of fish species caught incidentally, but not sought by fishers, such as the barndoor skate, *Raja laevis*, are at very low levels in some areas.

Marine ecosystems under pressure from human activities include eelgrass beds, affected by near-shore development; woody debris, the marine supply of which is diminishing due to logging and dams; and the clear-cutting of gorgonian groves due to trawling activities (Figure 5).[36] Shoreline development (construction, marinas, wharves, and log booming) has caused the loss of about 40 per cent of shore habitats in Howe Sound, near Vancouver.[37] Large-scale habitat losses have occurred in 12 estuaries in the Canadian portion of the Gulf of Maine. These losses continue, despite some local reversals. Only if this decline was halted could a return to the days of thriving coastal communities, abundant marine species, and healthy marine ecosystems be expected.[38] Southern B.C., most of Nova Scotia, and parts of Prince Edward Island, Quebec, and Newfoundland have been mapped as being at high risk due to development.[39] Marine ecosystems at the global level are particularly disturbed at three interfaces: the land-sea interface, the atmosphere-sea surface interface, and the water column-sea bed interface.[40]

Four factors that pose particular threats to marine biodiversity include the use of mobile fishing gear, the overall level of fishing activity, pollution, and climate change.[41]

The seabed is significantly affected by mobile fishing gear. It has been calculated that 29,970 km² of seabed have been dragged over by trawl nets, and trawl doors cut grooves that totalled over 4.3 million km on the Canadian Atlantic continental shelf.[42] The continued disturbance of fine and coarse sediments, gravel and stones, and even rock surfaces by fishing gear threatens sessile biota and infauna and all the species that depend on them for habitat and food. The loss of seafan or gorgonian groves has already been mentioned; these can attain ages of at least 500 years; their recovery, therefore, will take centuries.[43]

Mobile gear such as demersal fish and shrimp trawls catch large quantities of unwanted species and sizes of fish and invertebrates. This bycatch may include forage fish or young of target species, thereby disturbing the trophic web or directly affecting future catches. It is desirable to replace or redesign gear that has significant impacts on habitat, or that results in a large bycatch. A step in the right direction is the design by Fisheries and Oceans Canada of a fish grating which greatly reduces the bycatch of fishes in shrimp trawling. Demersal fish trawls should be the next target for replacement or major redesign.

The use of destructive fishing gear also reflects the operation of basic aspects of our economic system. This is seen, for example, when individual transferable quotas (ITQ harvest shares) are transferred from individual fishers with non-mobile gear, such as longlines and fish traps, to corporate fishers with powerful ships and large mobile gear, causing more habitat damage and bycatch.

It is also generally admitted that fishing levels have been too high for anadromous, pelagic, and demersal stocks, such as salmon, herring, cod, and lobster. In part this is due to overcapacity. Rockfishes (*Sebastes*), which live for decades, and giant geoduc clams, which have an average age of 70 years, if fished down, take a long time to recover their population.

The depletion of such species as herring can affect the populations of other species, such as sea birds and harbour porpoises. Unfortunately, we have not yet finished identifying and mapping the occurrence of stocks of Canadian commercial species, diminishing our capacity to manage and conserve them. However, about one-third of Strait of Georgia Pacific salmon stocks, excluding those of the Fraser River, have been lost.[44]

These issues indicate the need for ecosystem-based fisheries management, directed as much towards monitoring and maintenance of habitat and trophic webs as to regulation of the stocks of target species. This would require taxonomic and ecological research to provide marine ecosystem classifications and to map their geographic occurrence. Populations of commercial species are the product of healthy ecosystems, and fisheries managers are, in effect, caretakers of marine biodiversity who should use such tools as marine protected areas and the periodic fallowing of fishing grounds. The shift from single-species towards ecosystem-based management will require expanded resources; but fisheries departments in Canada have instead had their resources reduced.

The upper photic zone, the sea surface and especially the neuston: places where exchanges of energy, gases, droplets, and particles take place with the atmosphere, are suffering considerable stress.[45] Widespread floating debris and oil slicks, and increased ultraviolet radiation are among the impacts on this zone. Oil is especially harmful to sea birds, the eggs and larvae of marine fish, and invertebrates. One hundred thousand sea birds are oiled off Newfoundland each year. Eggs and larvae of many species are concentrated near the sea surface, and are especially sensitive to toxins in petroleum compounds. A tin-based ingredient in antifouling paint (TBT) has been shown to cause the development of male genitals in female snails. This is only one of the man-made compounds that can adversely affect reproduction, development, or normal hormone function.[46] Pollution from pulp mills and other sources has led to the closure of shellfish beds and other fisheries.

Sea ice is one of Canada's largest marine ecosystems. Its continued shrinkage as a result of climate change (Arctic sea ice has already shrunk by 14 per cent between 1978 and 1994) risks more rapid warming of the Arctic as less solar energy is reflected into space by this snow-covered solar "mirror," and as less carbon dioxide is carried down into the deep Arctic sea by cold saline water.[47] Ian Stirling, a Canadian Wildlife Service biologist, has tentatively linked weight loss and a decline in polar bear birth rates with longer ice-free summers, when bears have trouble finding seals for food.[48]

In the past, warming effects from El Niños have reduced southern California kelp forests.[49] Will climate warming currently under way along the B.C. coast affect kelp forests there? Sea surface temperatures in B.C. have shown a significant one degree Celsius warming trend during the last century.[50] Climate change — in this case, lower temperatures — has been blamed for reduced catches of Atlantic cod. It is worth recalling that global warming does not mean ocean temperatures will uniformly rise, only that the average temperature will increase.

Conclusions

Governments and other sectors of Canadian society can take several steps in response to the threats to aquatic biodiversity described in this chapter. These include:

1   Move biological resource management in agriculture, forestry, and fisheries to an ecosystem-based approach. Label products produced by genetic engineering. Verify and eco-label products produced in an environmentally benign manner, to provide consumer choice.

2   Replace fishing gear that has impacts on habitat, or that results in large bycatches, with environmentally congenial gear.

3 Carry out freshwater and marine biological surveys to enable mapping of aquatic ecosystems, to contribute specimens and information for ecosystem classification and taxonomic research.

4 Fill in the gaps in taxonomic research, discovering, naming, and classifying as yet undiscovered species and producing distribution maps for each species (using data from surveys). Provide identification guides for micro-organisms, fauna, and flora at levels for biologists and, as appropriate, for naturalists and eco-tourists. Establish or strengthen provincial natural history museums. Unite federal taxonomic researchers, collections, their libraries, and other resources, now located in three departments, within one organization. Establish a national natural history database, accessible on the Internet, of the occurrence in space and time of Canadian micro-organisms, fauna, and flora.

5 Establish a national hierarchical ecosystem classification for fresh and marine waters, and help develop global systems to assist research, conservation of biodiversity, and ecosystem-based management of resources.

6 Re-establish and strengthen Canadian capacity to monitor environmental health, and share the resulting reports by paper and by Internet.[51]

7 Include the status of biodiversity capital, and annual deficit or gain, as part of Canada's gross domestic product reporting system.

8 Revise international agreements, where needed, and ensure that any new agreements conserve biological diversity and resources and do not diminish government capacity to ensure healthy ecosystems and species populations. Include in appropriate agreements the requirement that neighbouring nations should be consulted before exotic species are introduced into common bodies of water.

9 Establish networks of permanent (not "floating") protected areas so as to represent all Canadian freshwater and marine ecosystems and protect viable populations of species, including those in deep waters. Work

in international fora, such as the International Convention on Biological Diversity, to establish marine protected areas in areas beyond national boundaries. Propose the establishment of marine protected areas as a tool to solve contested marine boundaries between nations. Never use the threat of fishing down populations to resolve questions of sharing fisheries based on species that cross international boundaries.

10 Strengthen civil society and democratic processes so that citizens and their elected governments have the powers needed to assure healthy ecosystems for wild species and humanity, and that neither domestic nor transnational corporations shall unduly influence the course of democratic government process.

Notes

I wish to acknowledge the assistance of the following: Dr. Edward L. Bousfield provided information on amphipods. Dr. C.-T. Shih reviewed the manuscript. Elisabeth Janssen kindly proofread one of the final drafts of the manuscript. Derek Jones of the Canadian Ocean Habitat Protection Society provided the photograph of the seacorn coral.

1. E. Norse, "Capsizing the cradle of life," *Global Biodiversity* 4, 1 (1994): 4-7.
2. T. Mosquin et al., *Canada's Biodiversity* (Ottawa: Canadian Museum of Nature, 1995).
3. Environment Canada, *Canadian Environmental Strategy: Canada's Response to the Convention on Biological Diversity* (Ottawa, 1995).
4. L. Beckman, "Marine Conservation in Canada: Perspective on What Public Policy Should Look Like," in *Ocean Yearbook 13* (Chicago: International Ocean Institute, 1998), 211-44.
5. Parks Canada, *Implementing the Canadian Biodiversity Strategy: Protected Areas* (Ottawa, 1997).
6. J. Linton, *Beneath the Surface: The State of Water in Canada* (Ottawa: Canadian Wildlife Federation, 1997); Canada, *The State of Canada's Environment* (Ottawa, 1996).
7. Mosquin et al., *Canada's Biodiversity*; for fish, see D.E. McAllister, "A list of the fishes of Canada," *Syllogeus* (National Museum of Natural Sciences,

Ottawa) 64 (1990): 1-310; for molluscs, see A.H. Clarke, *The Freshwater Molluscs of Canada* (Ottawa: National Museum of Natural Sciences, 1981); for crayfish, see P. Hamr, *Conservation Status of Canadian Freshwater Crayfishes* (Toronto: World Wildlife Fund Canada and the Canadian Nature Federation, 1998); for algae, see M. Poulin, P.B. Hamilton, and M. Proulx, "Catalogue des algues d'eau douce du Québec, Canada," *Canadian Field-Naturalist* 109, 1 (1995): 27-110.

8. Mosquin et al., *Canada's Biodiversity*.

9. Clarke, *Freshwater Molluscs*; Hamr, *Crayfishes*; W.B. Scott and E.J. Crossman, "Freshwater fishes of Canada," *Fisheries Research Board of Canada Bulletin* 184 (1973): 1-966.

10. D.E. McAllister, F.W. Schueler, C.M. Roberts, and J.P. Hawkins, "Mapping and GIS analysis of the global distribution of coral reef fishes on an equal-area grid," in R.I. Miller, ed., *Mapping the Diversity of Nature*, (London: Chapman and Hall, 1994), 155-73.

11. F.R. Cook, *Introduction to Canadian Amphibians and Reptiles* (Ottawa: National Museum of Natural Sciences, 1984); Linton, *Beneath the Surface*.

12. Canada, *State of Canada's Environment*.

13. Linton, *Beneath the Surface*.

14. Canada, *State of Canada's Environment*.

15. T. Colburn, D. Dumanoski, and J.P. Myers, *Our Stolen Future* (New York: Dutton, 1996).

16. C. Maser and J.R. Sedell, *From the Forest to the Sea: The Ecology of Wood in Streams, Rivers, Estuaries and Oceans* (Delray Beach, Fla.: St. Lucie Press, 1994).

17. Mosquin et al., *Canada's Biodiversity*; Hamr, *Crayfishes*; McAllister, "Fishes of Canada"; Cook, *Amphibians and Reptiles*.

18. M.M. Ferguson, "The genetic impact of introduced fishes on native species," *Canadian Journal of Zoology* 68 (1990): 2053-57.

19. For a fuller discussion of the root causes of loss of freshwater biodiversity, see: D.E. McAllister, A.L. Hamilton, and B. Harvey, "Global freshwater biodiversity: Striving for the integrity of freshwater ecosystems," *Sea Wind* 11, 3 (1997): 1140.

20. P. Brunel, L. Bossé, and G. Lamarche, "Catalogue of the marine invertebrates of the estuary and Gulf of St. Lawrence," *Canadian Special Publication of Fisheries and Aquatic Sciences* 126 (1998): 1-405.

21. J.C. Briggs, *Marine Zoogeography* (New York: McGraw-Hill, 1974); see also B.P. Hayden, G.C. Ray, and R. Dolan, "Classification of coastal and marine

environments," *Environmental Conservation* 11 (1984): 199-207; Alan Longhurst, *Ecological Geography of the Sea*, (San Diego: Academic Press, 1998).

22. E.F. Ricketts, J. Calvin, and J.W. Hedgepeth, *Between Pacific Tides*, revised by D.W. Phillips (Stanford, Calif.: Stanford University Press, 1985).

23. V. Tunnicliffe, "Lessons from deep, hot places," *Global Biodiversity* 6, 1 (1996): 19-22.

24. Maser and Sedell, *From the Forest to the Sea*.

25. See, for example, F.P. Holthus and J.E. Maragos, "Marine ecosystem classification for the tropical island Pacific," in Maragos, M.N.A. Peterson, L.G. Eldridge, J.E. Bardach, and H.F. Takeuchi, eds., *Marine and Coastal Biodiversity in the Tropical Island Pacific Region.* (Honolulu: East-West Center, Ocean Policy Institute and Pacific Island Association, 1995), 239-78.

26. Mosquin et al., *Canada's Biodiversity*.

27. V. Tunnicliffe, "Biodiversity: The marine biota of British Columbia," in M.A. Fenger, E.H. Miller, J.A. Johnson, and E.J.R. Williams, eds., *Our Living Legacy: Proceedings of a Symposium on Biological Diversity* (Victoria: Royal British Columbia Museum, 1993), 191-200; Brunel et al., *Catalogue of the Marine Invertebrates*.

28. These are derived from Mosquin et al., *Canada's Biodiversity*.

29. Ibid.

30. P. Lambert, "Biodiversity of marine invertebrates in British Columbia," in L.E. Harding and E. McCullum, eds., *Biodiversity in British Columbia* (Ottawa: Canadian Wildlife Service, Environment Canada, 1994), 57-69.

31. M.W. Hawkes, "Seaweeds of British Columbia: Biodiversity, ecology, and conservation status," *Canadian Biodiversity* 1, 3 (1991): 4-11.

32. Tunnicliffe, "Biodiversity."

33. D. Ellis, *The Knowledge and Usage of Marine Invertebrates by the Skidegate Haida People of the Queen Charlotte Islands* (Skidegate, B.C.: Queen Charlotte Islands Museum Society, 1981).

34. M. McDonald, L. Arragutainaq, and Z. Novalinga, *Voices from the Bay: Traditional Ecological Knowledge of Inuit and Cree in the Hudson Bay Bioregion* (Ottawa: Canadian Arctic Resources Committee and Environmental Committee of Municipality of Sanikiluaq, 1997).

35. For a full list of endangered, threatened, or vulnerable species, see the reports of the Committee on the Status of Endangered Wildlife in Canada (COSEWIC).

36. Maser and Sedell, *From the Forest to the Sea*; L. Behnken, "Southeast Alaska

trawl closure: A case study in risk-averse management," *Sea Wind* 7, 1
(1993): 8-14.; H. Breeze, with D.S. Davis, M. Butler and mapping by V.
Kostylev, "Distribution and status of deep sea corals off Nova Scotia,"
Ecology Action Centre, Marine Issues Committee Special Publication No.
1 (1997): 1-58; M.J. Risk, D.E. McAllister, and L. Behnken, "Conservation of
cold- and warm-water seafans: Threatened ancient gorgonian corals," *Sea
Wind* 12, 1 (1998): 2-21.

37. L.E. Harding, "Threats to biodiversity in the Strait of Georgia," in
Harding and McCullum, eds., *Biodiversity in British Columbia*, 293-305.

38. J. Harvey, D. Coon, and J. Abouchar, *Habitat Lost: Taking the Pulse of Estuaries
in the Canadian Gulf of Maine* (Fredericton: Conservation Council of New
Brunswick, 1998).

39. D. Bryant, E. Rodenburg, T. Cox, and D. Nielsen, "Coastlines at risk: An
index of potential development-related threats to coastal ecosystems,"
World Resources Institute Indicator Brief, 1996.

40. D.E. McAllister, "The crises in marine biodiversity and key knowledge,"
*Proceedings of Pacem In Maribus, Panel 1. The nature of the crisis: Philosophical and his-
torical, cultural and ethical dimensions of knowledge* (Halifax, 1998).

41. For more ample discussions, see E. Norse, *Global Marine Biological diversity: A
Strategy for Building Conservation into Decision Making* (Washington: Island Press,
1993); D.E. McAllister, "Status of the World Ocean and its Biodiversity,"
Sea Wind 9, 4 (1995): 1-72; C. de Fontaubert et al., *Biodiversity in the Seas*
(Cambridge: IUCN, 1996).

42. S.N. Messieh, T.W. Powell, D.L. Peer, and P.J. Crawford, "The effects of
trawling, dredging and ocean dumping on the eastern Canadian continental shelf sea bed," *Continental Shelf Research* 11, 8 (1991): 1237-63.

43. Risk et al., "Conservation of cold- and warm-water seafans."

44. Harding, "Threats to biodiversity"; D. Ellis, "The Strait of Georgia Pacific
herring controversy," *Sea Wind* 12, 3 (1998): 16-19.

45. D.E. McAllister, "Oil slicks: A threat to eggs, embryos and larvae of
marine fishes and to fisheries?" *Sea Wind* 12, 2 (1998): 27-31; McAllister,
"Crises in marine biodiversity."

46. Lambert, "Biodiversity of marine invertebrates"; Colborn et al., *Our Stolen
Future.*

47. D.E. McAllister, "Measuring Arctic Ocean icepack shrinkage and warming: The planetary solar mirror and global thermostat," *Sea Wind* 5, 4
(1991): 19-24; *Ottawa Citizen*, November 23, 1998.

48. *Maclean's*, October 5, 1998, 54.
49. M.J. Tegner and P.K. Dayton, "El Niño effects on southern California kelp forest communities," *Advances in Ecological Research* 17 (1987): 243-79.
50. H. Freeland, "Sea surface temperatures off Vancouver Island," in R. Forbes, ed., *Pacific Coast Research on Toxic Marine Algae*, Canadian Technical Report on Hydrographic and Ocean Science, No. 135, 1991.
51. Beckman, "Marine Conservation."

Further Reading

Canada. *The State of Canada's Environment*. Ottawa, 1996.

de Fontaubert, C., D.R. Downes, and T.S. Agardy. *Biodiversity in the Seas: Implementing the Convention on Biological Diversity in Marine and Coastal Habitats*. Gland, Switzerland, and Cambridge: IUCN, 1996.

Harding, L.E., and E. McCullum, eds. *Biodiversity in British Columbia*. Ottawa: Canadian Wildlife Service, Environment Canada.

Linton, J. *Beneath the Surface: The State of Water in Canada*. Ottawa: Canadian Wildlife Federation, 1997.

McAllister, D.E. "Status of the World Ocean and its Biodiversity," *Sea Wind* 9, 4 (1995): 1-72.

Mosquin, T., P.G. Whiting, and D.E. McAllister. *Canada's Biodiversity: The Variety of Life, Its Status, Economic Benefits, Conservation Costs and Unmet Needs*. Ottawa: Canadian Museum of Nature, 1995.

Norse, E. *Global Marine Biological Diversity: A Strategy for Building Conservation into Decision Making*. Washington: Island Press, 1993.

Shih, C.-T., D. Laubitz, and I. Sutherland, eds. *Bibliographia Invertebratorum Aquaticorum Canadensum*, 8 vols. Ottawa: National Museum of Natural Sciences (now the Canadian Museum of Nature), 1983-1986.

Wells, P.G., and S.J. Rolston. *Health of Our Oceans. A Status Report on Canadian Marine Environmental Quality*. Dartmouth and Ottawa: Environment Canada, Conservation and Protection, 1991.

Canadian Museum of Nature home page: http://www.nature.ca

Fisheries and Oceans Canada home page: http://www.ncr.dfo.ca/

Parks Canada National Marine Conservation Areas home page: http://parkscanada.pch.gc.ca/mmca/mmca/index.htm

Ted Mosquin

The Roles of Biodiversity in Creating and Maintaining the Ecosphere

T HIS CHAPTER[1] CONSIDERS SEVERAL INTRIGUING QUESTIONS. First, what specific functions of ecosystems and their organisms have enabled the unfolding and evolution of such a complex and astounding biodiversity in marine, freshwater, and terrestrial regions of the earth? Second, which of these functions have been most instrumental in creating the ecosphere that humans encountered when they first arrived on the scene? By ecosphere I mean the whole living earth – a deep magma/solid rock/soil/sediment layer, a water layer at the surface, an atmospheric layer, together with their contained assemblage of organisms – the biotic communities that have evolved and within which organisms are intricately linked. This chapter identifies and describes 18 functions of biodiversity. Together, they illuminate the seemingly mysterious and miraculous workings not only of ecosystems and their individual species but of the ecosphere as a whole.

Imagine yourself walking in a natural forest or native grassland or perhaps snorkelling through a rich marine kelp bed or coral reef, and reflecting on the following sorts of questions: What ecological processes are going on here? Which organisms are carrying them out? Which organisms are relatively independent and which are symbiotically linked to others? How does energy flow among these species? Who is doing the recycling? What systems of communication mediate processes such as reproduction and dispersal? Who is producing the oxygen? How did it come to be that such harmonious and co-operative communities exist? Then imagine yourself in a corn or potato field or in a salmon holding tank at the edge of the sea. Again ask yourself the same questions, but also ask which functions are completely absent or are present only due to human management.

By describing functions of ecosystems and organisms, readers will be better able to assess the true value of different parts of biodiversity and of the ecosphere. This chapter should also help to develop an eco-centric perspective on nature that emphasizes the value of nature as something more than a source of economic commodities. It will help to expose the narrow, selfish, and earth-destroying argument that "capricious nature" offers no guidelines for our conduct, and that therefore ecosystem management must respond exclusively to what people want.[2]

For 3.5 billion years organisms and ecosystems have been integral elements of the evolution and gradual emergence of the ecosphere. Organisms and ecosystems together created the ecosphere (with essential energy from the sun) as humans found it. We are ourselves one consequence of the workings of the highly stable and complex functioning of the emerging ecosphere. But what exactly are these functions? What are the linkages between them and to what extent are they mutually exclusive?

This chapter considers the value of ecospheric functions to the ecosphere as a whole. This is in sharp contrast to the purely anthro-pocentric approach to valuing "nature's services," described by other authors (see Table 1).[3] The anthropocentric values identified by these authors are a subset of the 18 "intrinsic" functions outlined here. Defining ecospheric functions as "ecoservices" assumes that only humans have high value and that wild species and natural ecosystems are valuable only if they have commodity or instrumental value (i.e., are "of service") to humans.

The notion of intrinsic value recognizes that objects, whether species, individuals, or things, have an innate worth, regardless of immediately apparent human benefits.[4] When human wants are over-valued, the earth is devalued, taken for granted, and abused as a mere commodity – to the long-range detriment of other forms of life. Thus, this chapter does not ask the question: What do organisms and ecosys-

A

Table 1:
Two Anthropocentric
Approaches to Valuing
"Nature's Services"

1. Gas regulation (regulation of atmospheric chemical composition)
2. Climate regulation (global and local levels)
3. Disturbance regulation (storm protection, flood control, etc.)
4. Water regulation (provisioning of water for agriculture, industry, transport)
5. Water supply (provisioning of water by watersheds, reservoirs, aquifers)
6. Erosion control and sediment retention
7. Soil formation (weathering of rock and accumulation of organic material)
8. Nutrient cycling
9. Waste treatment (recovery and breakdown of toxics, nutrients, etc.)
10. Pollination (provisioning of pollinators for reproduction of plants)
11. Biological control
12. Refugia (habitat for harvested species)
13. Food production (production of fish, game, crops, nuts, including subsistence farming and fishing)
14. Raw materials (production of timber, fuel, or fodder)
15. Genetic resources (sources of unique biological materials for agriculture, medicine, and the like)
16. Recreation (providing opportunities for recreational activities)
17. Cultural (providing opportunities for non-commercial uses)

B

1. Purification of air and water
2. Mitigation of floods and droughts
3. Detoxification and decomposition of wastes
4. Generation and renewal of soil fertility
5. Pollination of crops and natural vegetation
6. Control of the vast majority of agricultural pests
7. Dispersal of seeds and transportation of nutrients
8. Maintenance of biodiversity, from which humanity has derived key elements of its agricultural, medicinal, and industrial enterprise
9. Protection from the sun's harmful ultraviolet rays
10. Partial stabilization of climate
11. Moderation of temperature extremes and the force of winds and waves
12. Support of diverse human cultures
13. Providing of aesthetic beauty and intellectual stimulation that lift the human spirit

Sources: Robert Costanza *et al.,* "The value of the world's ecosystem services and natural capital," *Nature,* May 15, 1997; Gretchen C. Daily, ed. *Nature's Services: Societal Dependence on Natural Ecosystems* (Washington: Island Press, 1997).

tems do for people? Rather, what have wild organisms and ecosystems done (and what are their modern-day descendants continuing to do) to create the world as humans found it? Ecospheric functions are those processes that organisms and ecosystems perform or participate in, and that provide products and/or consequences for themselves, for other species and ecosystems in the community or region, or even in more distant lands. As natural processes that have evolved in organisms and ecosystems, they have enabled major new life forms to thrive, new functions to evolve, and more complex ecosystems to flourish.

Paleontology has revealed that wilderness ecosystems and wild species have lasted for eons. Such systems represent the normal environments, or norms, of the ecosphere. All organisms within wilderness systems represent the end-products of evolution within these norms. The survival of natural or wild ecosystems with their "normal" species therefore provide the only known standards against which the success or failure of biological resource management (in forestry, agriculture, fisheries) and economic development can be judged. Agriculture, for example, is a major and drastic deviation from planetary norms, and economic "development" is laying waste to all parts of the earth. On the other hand, hunting and gathering cultures are entirely within the norms of the ecosphere. (While some species have been exterminated by hunting or gathering, nearly all animals engage in these activities, and have done so, and the ecosphere has nevertheless persisted for billions of years.) These norms can provide guidance for human conduct, by indicating what is stable, time-tested, and normal, rather than what is gratifying people's wishes at the expense of the earth. The only alternative norm is that which encompasses our own technologies, and these have not been tested for their long-term stability. Enormous damage is being done in the blind belief that technology is intrinsically beneficial and natural systems and species limitless commodities, to be cared for and nurtured only if they appear immediately to be of instrumental value to humans. The modern ideology that says to nature,"Adapt to humanity; serve humanity or die," is drastically altering all of the normal ecospheric functions of our planet.

Many of the functions of organisms and ecosystems described in this chapter have been widely explored.[5] It deals with those functions that can be described as ecocentric – what ecosystems and their species do and have done to cause the world to become the way it is.

The Meaning of Biodiversity

In this chapter the broadest possible meaning of biodiversity is adopted. Biodiversity has been described as "the variety of life and its processes in an area."[6] To this we can add the popular way of recognizing the ecological concept, "that everything is connected to everything else."[7] The four key words in these definitions are *variety, processes, connections,* and *area.* The inclusion of "area" is essential because it is only in a physical context that variety, processes, and connections have meaning. "Area" also is essential when we are talking about conservation, preservation, or restoration of biodiversity. After all, the only real proof of loss or gain of biodiversity is *what is actually happening* to the forms of life *on the ground* and *in fresh and marine waters.*

While this description provides for general insight into why biodiversity demands our concern, it is not adequate for scientific analysis of the basic parts of biodiversity. We need a more rigorous definition.

Table 2 outlines the scientifically definable and inseparable parts of

1. *Genetic variation*: Genetic material in all individuals of all living things.
2. *Taxonomic variation*: Taken together, all taxonomic groups in nature — sub-species, species, genera, families, orders, classes, phyla, and the five kingdoms.
3. *Ecosystem variation*: Ecosystems, i.e., three-dimensional (volumetric) spaces on the surface of our planet where organisms dwell — including all abiotic matter therein, from the deepest rocks and oceans to high up in the atmosphere with inputs and outputs of energy from and to adjoining ecosystems.
4. *Functions, or "ecoservices"*: The specific processes that organisms and ecosystems carry out that affect themselves, their immediate neighbours and surrounds, communities in which they live, and the ecosphere as a whole. Functions describe what organisms and ecosystems actually do (and have done) to enable the emergence and evolution of the ecosphere.
5. *The abiotic matrix*: The enveloping rock, soil, sediment, water, and air that organisms and ecosystems have participated in creating and within which all are embedded.

Table 2:
The Five Parts of
Biodiversity

A. Functions Performed Primarily by Individual Organisms

1. Primary production — creation of many kinds and forms of biomass though photosynthesis and (around deep sea vents) chemosynthesis

2. Oxygen production — by oxygen-producing bacteria, algae, and plants

3. Sequestering of carbon dioxide

4. Herbivory — the eating of primary producers by bacteria, protozoa, fungi, and animals

5. Carnivory — the eating of protozoa, fungi, and animals by protozoa and animals

6. Control of soil erosion

B. Functions Involving Interactions among Low Numbers of Different Kinds of Organisms (These functions are carried out by usually very unrelated species in an area, often in immediate proximity, or from time to time.)

7. Population moderation — a powerful and essential aspect of herbivory and carnivory — includes diseases, parasitism on overabundant species

8. Seed and spore dispersal (plants); migration and larval dispersal (animals)

9. Symbiosis (mutually beneficial, intimate, co-evolved associations — extremely widespread and variable in nature)
   a. nitrogen fixation (esp. bacteria and algae in higher organisms; lichen partnerships)
   b. pollination involving insects, birds, etc.
   c. mycorrhiza (fungi and plant roots)
   d. enable food digestion (bacteria and fungi in animals)
   e. "fish cleaners" on coral reefs
   f. dozens/hundreds of others

C. Complex Functions Involving Interactions among Large Numbers of Different Organisms (These functions represent an increased level of complexity.)

10. Soil and sediment creation/bioturbation

11. Moderation of macro and microclimate

12. Decomposition (primary and secondary detritivory, including digestion, mineralization of organic compounds, fermentation, etc.)

13. Maintenance of 3-dimensional structures (consequences of multicellularity — trees, shrubs, herbs, kelp, larger animals, forests, soils; creation of "habitat")

14. Communication (both intra- and inter-specific) — i.e., sight, sound, taste, smell, touch via colour, shapes, pheromones, mimicry, camouflage, bioluminescence, radar, etc.

Table 3 continued.

> **D. Ecosystem Functions and Processes** (These are dependent on most or all of the above contributory functions of organisms.)
>
> 15. Food webs and chains (trophic structure)
>
> 16. Biogeochemical nutrient cycling and transport via individuals, local and sectoral ecosystems, and the ecosphere as a whole
>
> 17. Stability (consequences of complexity, connectedness, keystone species, deceptive 'redundancy,' generalist behaviour, trophic structure, succession, and some others)
>
> 18. Harmony (combinations of form, movement, structure, and functions resulting in a proportionate, orderly, co-operative condition — pervasive in individuals, natural ecosystems, and ultimately in the ordered and harmonious functioning of the ecosphere as a whole.)
>
> *Sources*: Adapted from T. Mosquin, "A conceptual framework for the ecological functions of biodiversity," *Global Diversity* 4,3 (1994): 2-16; T. Mosquin *et al.*, *Canada's Biodiversity* (Ottawa: Canadian Museum of Nature, 1995).

biodiversity: genes, taxonomic groups, ecosystems, functions, and the abiotic. Three of these parts (genes, taxonomic groups, and ecosystems) are widely recognized and discussed in the literature.[8] The meaning of these three components is widely understood and they will not be further reviewed here. But failing to consider functions and the abiotic component produces a simplistic and highly misleading notion of the meaning and importance of biodiversity. In particular, the abiotic (inorganic, inanimate, physical) part is as essential as the life-giving water/air/soil/ sediment/mineral environment within which organisms and ecosystems evolved, in which they are inextricably embedded, and without which they cannot live.[9] Fish could not have evolved without water, birds without air, or trees without soil.

Framework for the Functions

Table 3 identifies 18 ecospheric functions of organisms and ecosystems. They are organized into four groups of increasing complexity: starting with those carried out mainly by individual organisms; those performed by small numbers of very different species; and those that are the result of hundreds or thousands of different species working together at community, region, or landscape scale.

The least complex of the functions is primary production (Function 1). It mainly involves organisms operating independently – although, of course, within the abiotic ecosphere and with the energy of the sun. The most complex functions are those of stability and harmony (Functions 17 and 18). These depend on most if not all of the other functions. The functions contributing to ecosystem-level biodiversity may include very different combinations of functions depending on the particular ecosystem. Generally, the table illustrates that the more complex a function, the more it relates to, even depends upon, other functions.

Functions are best appreciated in terms of long-term evolutionary processes. When a unique process (here called a function) originated, it made possible the evolution of other novel things or functions. Thus, as the framework illustrates, the complexity of nature has increased as new functions have been made possible by the evolution of other functions. One could think of this increasing complexity through time as a kind of "law of ecospheric functions." If one were to suggest a general rule it might be that "all ecospheric functions except primary production are derived from and dependent upon pre-existing functions." It appears highly probable that these functions enabled the ecosphere to evolve, persist and become increasingly complex and stable over several billion years.[10] Obviously, for areas heavily altered by human activities, the number of functions are greatly reduced or impaired while one or two may be vastly expanded. For example, primary production in a cornfield is achieved at the expense of the many functions that were carried out in the natural prairie or forest which the cornfield replaced. As well, the variety and total number of functions would vary greatly in different areas and climatic zones. Additional reconsideration of numbers of species involved in these functions as well as a further review of the biological and ecological literature could result in an improved classification, particularly as the activities of taxonomically little known groups of organisms are studied in soils and in freshwater and marine ecosystems.

Ecospheric functions are sometimes referred to as "ecoservices."[11] This term should not be misunderstood. All organisms "service" themselves in addition to carrying out functions that benefit other species or the community. Herbivores did not evolve only to provide a service to carnivores, yet herbivory is a necessary service to carnivory, since only after herbivory originated (independently in a great many different animal taxonomic groups) were carnivores able to evolve.

Ecospheric functions are "polyphyletic," meaning that similar functions (e.g., nitrogen fixation, decomposition, carnivory, symbiosis, similar food webs, communication) arose repeatedly in different phylogenetic groups. Thus, in all ecosystems there was a consistent increase in complexity and harmony. We do not yet understand why evolution causes the emergence of similar functions in dozens of entirely different groups.[12] One can only observe that within entirely different taxa, innate processes are at work that make possible the emergence of parallel functions in different groups.

Ecological/Ecospheric Functions Described

Primary Production – Function 1

Primary production is the capture of energy from sunlight through photosynthesis and associated production of carbohydrates, fats, proteins, and other organic compounds needed by all herbivores. A second group of primary producers that live near deep sea vents relies on chemosynthesis to capture energy from sulphur compounds. But it is not primary production as such that is responsible for the megadiversity of herbivores, carnivores, and detritivores. Rather, it is the sheer variety of organisms engaged in primary production, the stupendous variety of carbohydrates, proteins, and fats produced, and the great diversity of forms in which biomass is produced. Some primary producers are photosynthetic bacteria, which feed protozoans, which feed microinvertebrates which feed larger invertebrates, and vertebrates – as in aquatic ecosystems. Other primary producers are so large and diverse (trees, shrubs, herbs) as to create habitat (both within themselves and as 3-D ecosystems [Function 16]) for all manner of terrestrial life.

Taxonomic groups that perform this function include cyanobacteria, chloroxobacteria, archaebacteria, all algal phyla, lichens, mosses, and all (except saprophytic) vascular plants. Primary production can sometimes be greatly increased through symbiotic associations among organisms.[13]

Oxygen Production – Function 2

All free oxygen in the air, water, and soils has been generated over billions of years, first by photosynthetic bacteria, then by algae, and eventually also by higher plants. This has had two entirely different beneficial results. First, all the free oxygen available today is necessary for the life of aerobic biota and for decomposition (Function 13). Second, this oxygen is the source of earth's protective ozone shield.[14] Free oxygen is produced by the same taxonomic groups as are engaged in photosynthetic primary production.

Sequestering of Carbon Dioxide – Function 3

Many different life forms contribute to the removal of carbon dioxide (CO_2) from the atmosphere, soils, and waters through mechanisms such as the precipitation of calcium salts, the amassing of organic deposits or of living biomass. While stress here is placed on CO_2, the role of living things in removing other compounds, particularly toxic substances, from ecosystems and adding them to accumulating muds or sediments is not insignificant. Taxonomic groups that sequester large amounts of CO_2 include marine cyanobacteria; algal protoctists, such as charophytes; chrysophytes (which make limestone plates and ooze); protozoan protoctists, such as *Globigerina* (which deposit massive layers of CO_2 in the form of marine chalk and limestone); hydroids (which create coral reefs); mosses, forbs, and woody plants (which deposit peat in fens, bogs, and marshes); and trees, shrubs, and herbs (which tie up biomass in living plants).

Herbivory – Function 4

Herbivory is the function of animals eating primary producers. The repeated emergence of this function early in the history of life on earth and among different groups of animals has made possible the diverse world of herbivores. Taxonomic groups where herbivory is the sole or dominant function are the filter feeders: protozoans, rotifers, many molluscs, and many crustaceans. Among non-filter-feeding herbivores are nematodes, millipedes, most insects, symphylids, springtails, waterbears, kinorhynchs, many echinoderms, many fish, amphibians (tadpoles), some reptiles, many birds, and many mammals.

Carnivory – Function 5

Carnivory is the eating of herbivores and other carnivores. Without it, trophic structures (Function 15) would be far simpler. Harmony in nature (Function 18) would also be much diminished. Taxonomic groups where carnivory is dominant are filter feeders: protozoans, sponges, hydroides, combjellies, various worm groups, molluscs, and many crustaceans. Among non-filter feeders, carnivores include spiders, many insects, all centipedes, all lampreys, sharks, most bony fishes, amphibians (adults, with one exception), most reptiles, many birds, and many mammals.

Both herbivory and carnivory constitute a kind of "superfunction" in which organisms eat other organisms. Predation is not considered to be a function but only part of the mechanism through which the carnivory function is performed. Herbivory and carnivory (including filter feeding) are inextricably linked to the detritivory (decomposition) function, since food needs to be digested to provide energy for living.

Control of Erosion – Function 6

The control of soil erosion, especially in terrestrial ecosystems, is a particularly powerful enabling function of vascular plants, since it can transform associated plant, animal, and micro-organism biodiversity. Aquatic vascular plants and some algal phyla also play an important role in estuaries and in riverine and lacustrine sites in reducing erosion. In shoreline marine areas, kelp beds and seagrass beds reduce loss of enriched sediment. In terrestrial regions, we may see extensive root growth, accumulation of an organic soil layer, litter accumulation, and recycling and retention of nutrients. In such circumstances, soil builds up faster than wind and/or water can carry it away. The consequence for biodiversity is the evolution of more complex and diverse ecosystems.

Population Moderation – Function 7

Population moderation refers to the limiting of runaway population increases or "blooms" of individual species. This function has commonly been described as maintaining the "balance of nature." The cyclical dynamics of predator/prey relationships and plant/herbivore relations, and diseases of humans provide examples of this function. Parasites often are major factors in controlling population. Humans are unique in that we have controlled numerous diseases, parasites, and predators on our own species to the extent that some feedback mechanisms formerly limiting our population have in some places ceased to operate. At least in the short term, humans have stretched the norms of the ecosphere. This has grave consequences for the health of the ecosphere. Taxonomic groups important in this population-moderation function include viruses, many phyla of bacteria, fungi, protozoa, many invertebrates, many herbivores, and many carnivores.

Seed, Spore, and Larval Dispersal; Migration – Function 8

This function is the spreading of propagules or reproductive animals to new areas where they might complete their life cycles or otherwise reproduce. This function enables individuals to reach the optimum range within which a species can survive and adapt. Dispersal is a characteristic function of all organisms and facilitates the emergence of new adaptive variants. This function is also critical to re-colonization and restoration of natural ecosystems where they have been destroyed or highly modified. Successful long-distance dispersal or migration of organisms also has been essential to the evolution of the world's unique endemics on remote oceanic islands or in similar terrestrial ecosystems in different parts of the world.

Symbiosis – Function 9

Symbiosis is the mutually beneficial, co-evolved association of a species with other (usually very unrelated) species. The degree of interdependency varies greatly. It may involve co-operation among three or more species. Symbiosis is one of the most powerful functions of the ecosphere because as unrelated organisms began to depend on each other, wholly new kinds of life forms originated. There are tens of thousands of co-evolved symbiotic systems in all ecosystems in virtually all phyla.[15] In the dawn of life symbiosis brought many submicroscopic organisms together permanently and, over eons, shaped the world of life as we know it today. In fact, all individual cells of "eucaryotes" (algae, protozoans, fungi, animals, and plants) are permanent symbiotic systems, indicating that ecological functions operate even at the cellular level. The loss of any species, however small, may decrease the possibilities of new forms of symbiosis and new life forms tomorrow.

Mycorrhizal associations are widespread between fungal hyphae and vascular plant roots, in which fungi enable more efficient mineral absorption by the root hairs. In temperate forests some 80 to 90 per cent of higher plants have roots associated with fungi.[16]

Lichens combine a green algae and/or a nitrogen-fixing cyanobacteria with a fungal partner. The algae or cyanobacteria provide nutrients to the fungal host, and in return receive living space. Some lichens contain both algal and cyanobacterial partners.[17] Symbiotic associations are found between coelenterates and algae growing in their cells; between bacteria and echinoderms;[18] between bacteria, protozoans, and/or fungi living in the gut of animals (essential for food digestion); between ants and aphids, and ants and fungi.

Bioluminescence is the emission of cool chemical light by some groups of organisms, such as plankton, many deep-water fish, some shallow-water fish, squids, and fireflies. It is a unique kind of symbiosis. While in some cases the organism produces the light itself, in many species the light is emitted by phosphorescing bacteria that the host shelters and nourishes. In oceanic waters bioluminescence caused by bacteria occurs in fish species that live in the darkness down to 500 metres. For fish the light enables them to recognize species and mates (a form of communication), attract prey, camouflage their silhouettes from prey species through "countershading," and startle and distract predators.[19]

Symbiosis is evident also in pollination, in which an enormous variety of insects, birds, and bats are adapted to pollinate tens of thousands of different species of flowering plants, and where plants have responded by evolving floral fragrances, reflectance spectra, flower forms, markings, and flowering-time sequences.

The biological complexity of pollination is underlined by the many forms mediated by abiotic matrices of biodiversity, wind and water, both of which are active agents of pollen transport between many plant species. In Canada, most trees, many shrubs, grasses, sedges, cattails, and many forbs are wind pollinated. Water carries pollen in marsh plants, such as the water shield, *Brassenia schreberi*, American eel grass, *Vallisneria americana*, the many species of *Potamogeton*, and others.

Impairment worldwide of many elements of symbiosis, through habitat fragmentation, pollution, pesticides, and other human activities, has already caused extinction of thousands of races and species.

Soil and Sediment Creation/Bioturbation – Function 10

The growth of roots and fungal hyphae, and tunneling by worms and other soil invertebrates builds, aerates, and maintains soils.[20] Soils are ecosystems created and maintained by a great variety of living organisms, present by the tens of thousands in each cubic centimetre of soil and sediment. Countless biochemical processes take place here, including decomposition, and recycling of carbon and nutrients. Many animals live in freshwater and marine sediments and help bring about a constant mixing of sediment and nutrients from deeper layers. Taxonomic groups that have major roles in carrying out this function include bacteria, cyanobacteria, algae, fungi, numerous invertebrate phyla including arachnids and insects, as well as plants (roots, leaves, dead trunks).

Moderation of Macro and Microclimate – Function 11

Macroclimate – the prevailing weather in a region, as well as meteorological conditions over a period of years – is an "abiotic" factor that powerfully determines biodiversity in a region. The distribution of major ecosystems such as tundra, boreal forest, prairie, or west coast rain forest is determined by macroclimate. However, once vegetation is firmly established, it then can affect the macroclimate, both locally and in distant areas. Ground cover (vegetation, snow, water, soil) greatly influences albedo (the percentage of sunlight reflected from an area) and this influences air temperature. In addition, transpiration from forest canopies and ground vegetation can significantly increase atmospheric humidity, affecting rainfall and determining the kind of biodiversity present. Air temperature and rainfall in more distant regions can also be affected.

In terrestrial ecosystems, plants have a profound effect upon groundlevel climate, as do macroalgae and eel grass in intertidal ecosystems. Trees, shrubs, forbs, grasses, and mosses, through effects on shade and humidity, moderate the microflora and fauna of an area. In areas devoid of plant cover (such as deserts or cultivated fields), extremes of light intensity, humidity, temperature, and wind can greatly affect the local flora and fauna. In deserts, uniquely adapted florae and faunae evolve in response to both macroclimate and micro-climate.

Decomposition (Primary and Secondary Detritivory) – Function 12

Decomposition (detritivory) is the natural recycling of residues of life. Most decomposers require oxygen (Function 2). Next to primary pro-duction, decomposition is the most important ecological function of organisms. A very wide range of life forms participate in decomposi-tion: from bacteria to protozoa, filter feeders, humans, and scavenging biota in all ecosystems, and also within many larger organisms (i.e., digestion). Fermentation is a specialized method of decomposition.

Primary detritivory is the absorption of free organic molecules as food. Bacteria obtain all their food this way, as do two phyla of marine worms. They metabolize these molecules to create nutritive blocks (called plaques) that are eaten by multitudes of protozoa and other plankton (Functions 2 and 3). These, together with photosynthesizing algae and cyanobacteria (Function 1) are the primary "pastures" for all freshwater and marine food chains.

Secondary detritivory is the "digesting" of animal and plant tissue and its degradation into simpler organic compounds. All filter feeders are secondary detritivores because they cannot discriminate between living planktonic organisms and floating dead tissue biomass. Life on earth could not survive without primary and secondary detritivores because there would be no way of cleansing the ecosphere of the "products" of life. Indeed, oil and coal may have been deposited only because the detritivory function had not yet by that time been perfected by the evolving ecosphere.

Many bacteria have developed a very powerful ecological function; that of ingesting organic molecules (toxics, oils, etc.) and reducing a portion of them to less harmful substances and minerals.[21] Mineralizing bacteria, since they metabolize toxic organic compounds (and return part of the molecule to harmless mineral matter) are hugely abundant in many ecosystems, and play an influential role in detoxifying soils and waters in local and regional ecosystems and the ecosphere as a whole.

Creation and Maintenance of 3-D Ecosystem Structures – Function 13

The capability of different phyla to evolve *multicellular* structures is the basis for this function. During the history of life on earth, the emergence of multicellular organisms has profoundly affected associated organisms and made possible the three-dimensional structure of ecosystems such as forests, tundra, prairie, kelp beds, submergent freshwater plant beds, coral reefs, and others. As well, most larger organisms provide homes for various biota, such as wood-boring insects, cavity-nesting birds and animals, and fish seeking the protection of coral reef structures. As a consequence of multicellularity, entire assemblages of life forms in all major groups have been able to evolve in and depend on these structures.

Marine taxonomic groups that dominate in this function include tall sponges, macro algae (green, red, and brown), and large sea animals; in terrestrial areas they include herbs, shrubs, trees, and large land animals; in freshwater areas all submergent vegetation and larger animals play roles. The three-dimensional structures can be submicroscopic: even single-celled organisms often have parasites, or have parasitic symbionts living within them.

Communication – Function 14

Communication is an ecological function because it has a profound effect upon the substance, nature, and quality of species and ecosystems. This is a widespread and essential function of all complex life forms. A diverse array of methods of contact between individuals of the same species and between different species have evolved and are now intrinsic to ecosystem processes.

Simple chemical sensory abilities enable more primitive organisms to communicate for purposes of reproduction or finding food. Among higher forms of life, communication includes the use of taste, sight, touch, sound, radar, sonar, the sending and detection of electric currents, and other specialized methods. Sight (between organisms and between organisms and their surroundings) influences all manner of activity: courtship, parenting, food gathering, migration, herding, flocking, and escape from carnivores and other threats. The capacity of some to perceive colour has had stupendous impact on the evolution of colour in birds, fish, mammals, and colour-perceiving insects, such as pollinating bees. Flower colours have evolved in response to the capacity of pollinating insects to see colour. Intricacies of mimicry, widespread among insects, is the result of the ability of insect-eating birds to perceive differences not only in the shape of their food but in its colour, taste, and behaviour. Pheromones released by female insects ready to mate attract males from more than a kilometre away. Substances released from injured skins of minnows alert other minnows to the possible presence of a predator.

The evolution of the ability to use sound in communication has also produced what can only be described as a wondrous diversity of bird, animal, and insect sound and song, enriching the harmonies of natural ecosystems beyond the bounds of human understanding. Much of the communication taking place in nature cannot even be sensed by humans, except through scientific instruments. For example, ultraviolet light reflected by many specialized flowers can be seen by some pollinating insects. In the sense that communication is the product of the evolution of biodiversity, there can be little doubt that much that is beautiful and meaningful vanishes as biodiversity is reduced.

Food Webs and Chains (Trophic Structure) – Function 15

The movement of energy through organisms in a community defines its trophic structure. It is considered as a separate ecological function because species utilize many trophic pathways and shift from one to another depending on what has been closed off by factors such as extirpations or habitat destruction. All food webs begin with primary production (Function 1). Most bacteria and all fungi, protozoans, and animals cannot manufacture their own food and hence are always at higher (dependent) trophic levels.[22]

Food webs usually are not discrete. Among plants and mammals, for example, a variety of primary producers are usually eaten by herbivores, which are then eaten by a number of omnivores and vertebrate carnivores. Humans regularly shift from eating algae to wheat to fungi to meat, consuming snails here and grasshoppers there, corn in one area and bowhead whales in another. Some species, however, are more limited when it comes to finding alternate sources of energy.

Trophic structure among micro-organisms and invertebrates can be amazingly interlinked and complex: many invertebrates are filter feeders, and most will ingest any bit of organic material whether it be phytoplankton, bacteria, other zooplankton, or detritus. In these circumstances there are many interlocking levels and "feedback" webs, because consumers are neither 100 per cent herbivorous grazers nor 100 per cent carnivorous predators. Movement through complex food webs is analogous to the way information can travel through the Internet.

Biogeochemical Nutrient Transport and Cycling – Function 16

This function describes the physical transport of nutrients (phosphorus, potassium, nitrogen, and trace elements) via living tissue and the abiotic part of the ecosphere. This is classed as an ecological function because of its effects upon the distribution and occurrence of ecosystems and the abundance of many species. Organisms that carry out this function include fungi (through hyphae in soils), plants (through root systems and leaf dispersal), and mobile animals (through animal droppings and upon death).

Nutrient pathways are pervasive and the processes complex. All major elements required by plants and animals move in cycles within the organic part of communities (the biosphere) and in the abiotic matrix of the ecosphere. All essential nutrients including trace elements are involved, and are recycled and reused again and again. The term "biogeochemical cycles" has been coined to emphasize that both organisms and the abiotic part of biodiversity play essential parts in this process. An indication of the scale and evolutionary consequences of these cycles can be provided by the example of calcium: all calcium carbonate of the great limestone deposits of the earth was precipitated from dissolved CO_2 by living organisms in marine systems. The importance of carbon-fixing organisms becomes more obvious when one considers that it comprises nearly the exclusive source of calcium in the bones of vertebrates and the exoskeletons and shells of invertebrates.

Human activities (through agriculture and industry and from our homes) add millions of tons of nutrients into waters, soils, and the atmosphere, causing major changes to ecosystems and species composition.

Stability – Function 17

Evidence of stability as an important ecospheric function has been provided by palaeontological and evolutionary research, that has revealed the remarkable persistence of natural communities and many of their component species. Over billions of years a stupendous variety of communities and species have evolved in marine, freshwater, and terrestrial ecosystems. While most organisms live their entire lives within only one of these three ecosystem types, numerous species have survived and evolved in two, such as amphibians, some reptiles (turtles), anadromous fish, sea birds that nest on land, and so on. Because of the great stability of ecosystems, so many phylogenetically distinct taxonomic groups and communities originated, became ever more diverse, acquired new and parallel functions, and extended themselves into all habitable parts of the earth. At the same time these organisms helped fashion an increasingly healthy and productive ecosphere, making it ever more possible for a great variety of organisms to thrive harmoniously.

Understanding why the ecosphere has been so unerringly and increasingly stable has been the subject of scientific inquiry. In recent years the Gaia Thesis has been proposed: that the earth's ecosphere is a system with certain self-regulating features, controlled by the combined activities of the biota and the abiotic environment.[3]

That even today's natural systems change only very slowly (major human impacts excepted) is encapsulated by the phrase "balance of nature," widely held to be self-evident to those of long life experience living relatively close to nature. To analyse and describe the elements of this emerged stability is a formidable task. Here follow some elements contributing to stability in nature to stimulate discussion and thought.

Complexity. We accept that increased complexity in naturally evolved ecosystems leads to greater stability.[24] Thus, ecosystems in a climax condition are considered to be optimally stable. Climax communities left on their own with no human management and no introductions of aggressive alien species have been extremely stable over eons. Without humans introducing alien species such ecosystems strongly resist invasion, although some naturally evolved ecosystems are vulnerable to randomly introduced alien species. However, the linkage between complexity and stability is rejected by the proponents of some ecological models who assume that an ecosystem's complexity should be measured only by the number of its parts.[25] Such models do not include the time component: how long the climax ecosystem evolved; nor do they consider the organization of the climax. Two recent authors noted that "stability may decrease or increase with reductions in species number in a given system, and the effect may be different in temperate, tropical, and Arctic habitats."[26] These authors did not make the vital distinction between those species naturally co-evolved within a system and aggressive, destructive aliens (such as loosestrife, zebra mussels, carp, chestnut blight, Dutch elm disease, and others).[27] In other words, these modelling exercises are hardly relevant to what actually goes on in nature.

Connectedness. The notion that "everything is connected to everything else" is essential to stability since species need to meet their requirements in consort with others and through cycles, trophic levels, dispersal, and other functions that involve most or all of them either recurrently or from time to time.

Redundancy. It has been argued that many genes, individuals, or even species in an ecosystem may be surplus to the requirements of the system.[28] A surplus species would be one whose functions are seemingly identical to those of a companion species. Thus, its elimination apparently would not significantly change the characteristics of the ecosystem. Examples would be: the loss of two species among 20 of single-celled, free-floating green algae in a pond; extinction of one of five species of bumblebees in a meadow (all opportunistic pollinators); or the death by disease of one of ten species of deciduous trees in a forest (all of which provide the principal canopy), as happened with the American chestnut. However, it is highly unlikely that such species are actually surplus to the ecosystem (in terms of functions and *potential* functions) since genetic and chemical differences may well indicate opportunities to interact uniquely with other species and to secure a more diverse evolutionary future. It has been suggested that redundancy provides long-term resilience to ecosystems.[29] If so, this could mean that it is a positive mechanism for increasing diversity and buffering ecosystems against abrupt change, thereby enhancing both short- and long-term stability.

Generalist Behaviour. Ecosystem stability would be enhanced when an important species such as a pollinating bee would care little as to which flowers were available for nectar and pollen, and so would pollinate numerous plants. Alternatively, when a particular carnivore could exploit many different kinds of prey, its survival would not be jeopardized by extirpation of one of its food species. These are examples of how fluctuations in species numbers are dampened by spreading risk more widely.[30]

Keystone species. A keystone species is one that has a disproportionate effect on the persistence of other species.[31] Obviously, the strength of the effect depends on how many other species are affected. Keystone species include: carnivores (mountain lions, killer whales, sea otters), herbivores (snowshoe hares, caribou), competitors (aggressive exotics, dominant forest trees), symbionts (major pollinators, mycorrhizal fungi of dominant trees), earth-movers (earthworms, pocket gophers); plants that alter the fire regime (producing major fire loads), and system processors (nitrogen-fixers, like lichens). The presence or absence of these keystone species will significantly affect the presence and abundance of certain species, and will help determine the stability or instability of the ecosystem.

Food webs/chains (trophic structure). The varying intricacies and lengths of food webs – from only a few, simple pathways to extremely complex cycles at many levels, such as occur when filter feeders are involved – may affect stability in a community. Humans have the most complex of all food chains, since they eat thousands of different species in most phyla either directly or by assimilating domesticated animals and plants. Complex webs enable dependent species to survive by shifting to alternate trophic pathways when one or several fail. However, according to some models, webs with more trophic levels undergo such severe fluctuations as to lead to the extirpation of top carnivores.[32] Again, however, we are dealing with models rather than real nature. The matter of species richness of herbivores and carnivores generated by complex trophic systems over large landscapes is insufficiently understood. However, since communities and organisms can move while ecosystems are geographically circumscribed, more complex trophic systems appear to foster more stability rather than less.

Community succession. Succession is defined as a continuous directional change in an ecosystem at a particular site lasting dozens or hundreds of years and involving both colonization and extirpation of species in response to innumerable factors. Succession occurs, for example, when old fields are recolonized by forest ecosystems. It is the unique genetic traits of each species that determine whether and at what rate it can participate in succession, and return to communities disturbed by human activities, fire, storms, insect herbivory, and other events.

The positive effect of natural fires and other local disturbances upon ecosystem stability are also evident within large landscape regions. Repeated fires or wind-throw in ecosystems prone to fire (boreal forest, lodgepole pine forest, prairie) greatly increase their overall complexity by creating numerous successional stages that can support a wider variety of biota. This phenomenon has been described for Banff National Park, where Parks Canada has instituted a fire management policy to encourage biodiversity through maintaining a permanent patchy fire-disturbance regime.[33]

Many ecological functions affect community succession, and act to determine the species present. One example is the mutualistic symbiosis between plants and various soil microbes in forest communities.[14] The presence or absence of mycorrhizal fungi can strongly determine the kind of succession that follows clearcutting and deep soil fire (where the fungal mat has been burned off), or that takes place in an area where one is attempting to restore a prairie after farming has been carried out for decades. Plant species that do not require linkages with mycorrhizal fungi are less constrained successionally since they can invade without the presence of the soil microbes which may take decades or longer to enter a degraded or destroyed ecosystem. Following disturbance, when the community at a site is considered to have reached a near "steady state" (i.e., no apparent net gain or loss of species over a period of time), succession would be so slow as not to be perceivable by humans.

Harmony – Function 18

Harmony is the overriding function of biodiversity: the consequence of the 17 functions already described. Harmony in nature is diverse, pervasive, and persistent, existing at all levels necessary to the maintenance of the whole. Harmony emerged slowly in both aquatic and terrestrial ecosystems. We can observe harmony in many aspects of the ecosphere: animal and plant form (trees, flowers, birds, fish, insects), the efficient grace of animal movement (swimming, flight, running); colours of birds, fish, insects, trees, leaves, flowers; radial or bilateral symmetries of individual animals and flowers. Even the world of micro-organisms is full of harmonies of many types. Another aspect of harmony is the innate capacity for hundreds and thousands of life forms to live together within a community or larger ecosystem, and to form linkages, co-adaptations, and symbioses. The developmental and physiological harmonies that have evolved within individual organisms constitute another level of harmony. Wholeness, completeness, health, and integrity are the broader aspects of the innate harmony function in the ecosphere.[15]

Harmony cannot be separated from the abiotic part of biodiversity:

the matrix of rivers, lakes, waterfalls, wind, oceanic surf, landforms, clouds, and all other abiotic conditions within which organisms and ecosystems evolved and apart from which they cannot survive. Indeed, since the beginning of life, organisms have dramatically changed and shaped the characteristics of the ecosphere.[36] Certain harmonies appear to be a consequence of the workings of the laws of nature. The deeper origins of the pervasive and persistent harmonies in nature may be due to an innate drive of organisms to achieve maximum "self-realization" or "self-organization" during their lifetime, a concept explored by a number of authors, including Arne Naess, Stuart Kaufmann, Edward Goldsmith, and Holmes Rolston.[37]

Harmony is hardly distinct from beauty, but "beauty" has a philosophical and ethical dimension and is a subject of discussion among philosophers. Therefore, some scientists[38] feel that to include beauty as another function of biodiversity is crossing a fine and dangerous line – unlike other functions, it is too subjective to measure by the methods of science. But the importance – or beauty – of harmony can be appreciated if we consider its obverse side. Disharmony is created when organisms or ecosystems are reduced to fragments or parts. A cut-off tree, a headless body are not harmonious entities.

At the level of ecosystems, harmony is reduced and violated when a road is cut through a previously natural forest, when a fully developed old forest is clear-cut, when a river is toxified by a sewer or pulp mill, when an oil spill bathes a rich intertidal shoreline, or when a coral reef disintegrates due to global warming or runoff of fertilizers from nearby human activities.

Conclusion

The ecospheric functions of biodiversity are far more pervasive, diverse, and complex than generally realized. When ecosystems are left undisturbed by humans, they exhibit an inherent organizing capability. Over billions of years life forms and ecosystems became ever more complex, leading to the emergence of a stable and harmonious ecosphere.

By identifying and classifying these ecological/ecospheric functions, one can better comprehend the creative, secure, and resilient path that the ecosphere has sustained and amplified since the beginnings of life. Certainly, the ecosphere has been super-stable and resilient, gaining in diversity, complexity, and internal harmonies over several billion years, interrupted by abrupt extinctions caused by several big comets – events from which the ecosphere was able to recover. That, given sufficient time, complexity begets increased stability is a remarkable phenomenon of our ecosphere.

By identifying ecocentric/ecospheric functions we can also provide a tool for ecologists, naturalists, environmentalists, ecophilosophers, foresters, and others who, like myself, have been troubled for years by the imprecise definitions of some widely used ecological terms – such as ecological processes, ecological functions, land health, ecological integrity, environmental quality, and ecological complexes.

Today, some writers view functions of the ecosphere through anthropocentric eyes, asking only, "What good is nature for commerce?" Instead, they should ask: "What do natural systems do and what have they done to create and secure the permanence, health, balanced productivity, and beauty of the world into which humanity came?" We live in an age when the time-tested functions of the ecosphere are being thoughtlessly and brutally modified by those who consider nature to be nothing but a source of commodities to satisfy humanity's selfish and short-term desires.

An extensive literature now exists on the toxification and destruction of ecosystems and the continuing overexploitation of species and ecosystems that carry out irreplaceable ecospheric functions. The commodification of nature remains official government policy, while an extensive greenwash literature provides cover for a great deal of destructive federal and provincial legislation and policies in agriculture, fisheries, forestry, and industry – particularly the chemical industry, which manufactures millions of tons of toxics every year for inevitable dispersal into the ecosphere.

Securing better insights into the long term consequences of impairment of each of the 18 functions will require an army of researchers. I am not aware of any government or institution in Canada where policy-makers or managers of forests, fisheries, agriculture, or the pesticide industry have carried out such analyses, or even care to. It would be to the long-term benefit of humankind to determine the scope of changes to ecospheric functions in almost any area of land or sea. But our circumstances are challenging. Where to start? How to measure? Thomas Berry provides an inspiration to thought and action when he notes that "the integral functioning of the natural world [can be] taken as the supreme model of managerial success."[39]

Notes

I wish to thank Drs. J. Stan Rowe, New Denver, B.C., Don E. McAllister, Perth, Ontario, and Stephen Bocking for their thoughtful reviews, all of which materially improved the article.

1. This is a revised version of material that first appeared in Ted Mosquin, "A conceptual framework for the ecological functions of biodiversity," *Global Biodiversity* 4, 3 (1994): 2-16; and Mosquin et al., *Canada's Biodiversity* (Ottawa: Canadian Museum of Nature, 1995).
2. For this argument, see Daniel B. Botkin, *Discordant Harmonies: A New Ecology for the 20th Century* (New York: Oxford University Press, 1990).
3. C. Perrings, "The Economic Value of Biodiversity," in V.H. Heywood and R.T. Watson, eds., *Global Biodiversity Assessment* (Cambridge: UNEP and Cambridge University Press, 1995); Robert Costanza et al., "The value of the world's ecosystem services and natural capital," *Nature*, May 15, 1997; Gretchen C. Daily, ed., *Nature's Services* (Washington: Island Press, 1997); Alan Drengson, *An Ecophilosopher's Exploration* (Victoria, B.C.: Lightstar Press, 1994).
4. T.A. More, J.R. Averill and T.H. Stevens, "Values and economics in environmental management: a perspective and critique," *Journal of Environmental Management* 48, 4 (1996): 397-409.
5. Aldo Leopold, *A Sand County Almanac* (Oxford: Oxford University Press, 1949); James Lovelock, *The Ages of Gaia* (New York: W.W. Norton, 1988); Peter Bunyard and Edward Goldsmith, *Gaia and Evolution: Proceedings of the Second Annual Camelford Conference on the Implications of the Gaia Thesis* (Bodmin, Cornwall: Abbey Press, 1989); M. Begon, J.L. Harper and C.R. Townsend, *Ecology: Individuals, Populations and Communities* (Oxford: Blackwell Scientific Publications, 1990); Richard C. Brusca and Gary J. Brusca, *Invertebrates* (Sunderland, Mass.: Sinaur Associates, 1990); Elliott A. Norse, *Global Marine Biodiversity Strategy; Building Conservation into Decision Making* (Redmond, Wash.:

Center for Marine Conservation, 1993); J.F. Grassle, P. Lasserre, A.D. McIntyre and G.C. Ray, *Marine Biodiversity and Ecosystem Function* (IUBS, SCOPE, UNESCO, Biology International No. 23, 1992), 1-19; E. Schultze and H.A. Mooney, *Biodiversity and Ecosystem Function* (Berlin: Springer-Verlag, 1993); Heywood and Watson, *Global Biodiversity Assessment.* See also books listed under "Further Reading."

6. H. Salwasser, "Conserving biological diversity," *For. Ecol. Management* 35 (1991): 79-90.

7. U. S. Council on Environmental Quality, *Incorporating Biodiversity Considerations into Environmental Impact Analysis and the National Environmental Policy Act* (1993).

8. World Resources Institute, "Global Biodiversity Strategy" (Draft) (WRI, IUCN and UNEP, 1991); World Conservation Monitoring Centre, *Global Biodiversity: Status of the Earth's Living Resources* (London: Chapman and Hill, 1992); Environment Canada, *The State of Canada's Environment* (Ottawa, 1991); Environment Canada, *The State of Canada's Environment* (Ottawa, 1996).

9. J. Stan Rowe, "What on Earth is environment?" *Trumpeter* 6, 4 (1990): 123-26; Rowe, *Home Place: Essays in Ecology* (Edmonton: NeWest; Toronto: Canadian Parks and Wilderness Society, 1990); Rowe, "Biodiversity at the landscape level," Workshop on Biodiversity, Vancouver, March 1994. All five parts of biodiversity are examined in Mosquin et al., *Canada's Biodiversity,* which presents a detailed rationale for this classification together with rationales for the standards or norms against which the state of the five parts of biodiversity can be assessed.

10. Lovelock, *Ages of Gaia;* Lovelock, *Gaia: The Practical Science of Planetary Medicine* (London: Gaia Books, 1991); Bunyard and Goldsmith, *Gaia and Evolution;* S.H. Schneider and P.J. Boston, eds., *Scientists on Gaia* (Cambridge, Mass.: MIT Press, 1991).

11. Paul R. Ehrlich and H.A. Mooney, "Extinction, Substitution, and Ecosystem Services," *BioScience* 33 (1983): 248-54; Mosquin, "A conceptual framework"; Mosquin et al., *Canada's Biodiversity;* Daily, *Nature's Services;* Costanza et al., "The value of the world's ecosystem."

12. Mosquin et al., *Canada's Biodiversity,* Appendix 1.

13. David L. Hawksworth, "The fungal dimension of biodiversity, magnitude, significance and conservation," *Mycological Review* 95 (1991): 641-55; Hawksworth, "Fungi: The Neglected Biodiversity Crucial to Ecosystem Function and Maintenance," *Canadian Biodiversity* 1, 4 (1992).

14. Schneider and Boston, *Scientists on Gaia*.

15. Sibil P. Parker, *Synopsis and Classification of Living Organisms*, 2 vols.(New York: McGraw Hill, 1982); Lynn Margulis and Karlene V. Schwartz, *Five Kingdoms: An Illustrated Guide to the Phyla of Life on Earth* (San Francisco: Freeman & Co., 1988); Brusca and Brusca, *Invertebrates*; Begon et al., *Ecology*.

16. Francois Le Tacon, Jean Gargage, and Geoff Carr, "The Use of Mycorrhizas in Temperate and Tropical Forests," *Symbiosis* 3 (1987): 179-206; Jeremy Cherfas, "Disappearing Mushrooms: Another Mass Extinction?" *Science* 254 (1991): 1458; J.M. Trappe, "Phylogenetic and ecological aspects of mycotrophy in angiosperms from an evolutionary standpoint," in G.G. Safir, ed., *Ecophysiology of Mycorrhizal Plants* (Boca Raton, Fla.: CRC, 1987), 2-25; Hawksworth, "Fungal Dimension"; Hawksworth, "Fungi."

17. Ernie Brodo, Canadian Museum of Nature, personal communication.

18. I. Bosch, "Symbiosis between bacteria and oceanic clonal sea star larvae in the western North Atlantic ocean," *Marine Biology* 114 (1992): 445-502.

19. Don E. McAllister, "The significance of ventral bioluminescence in fishes," *Journal of the Fisheries Research Board of Canada* 24, 3 (1967): 537-54; Frank H. Johnson and I. Haneda, *Bioluminescence in Progress: Proceedings of a Luminescence Conference* (Princeton, N.J.: Japan Society for the Promotion of Science and National Science Foundation and Princeton University Press, 1966).

20. Nyle Brady, *The Nature and Properties of Soils* (New York: Macmillan, 1984).

21. These bacteria are listed in Margulis and Schwartz, *Five Kingdoms*.

22. A detailed discussion of trophic structures is presented in Begon et al., *Ecology*, 798-815.

23. As discussed in Bunyard and Goldsmith, *Gaia in Evolution*; Schneider and Boston, *Scientists on Gaia*; E. Goldsmith, in *The Way: An Ecological World Vire* (Devon, U.K.: Themis Books, 1996).

24. Goldsmith, *The Way*, 324-29.

25. Robert M. May, *Stability and Complexity in Model Ecosystems* (Princeton, N.J.: Princeton University Press, 1973).

26. Schultze and Mooney, *Biodiversity and Ecosystem Function*, 507.

27. See list in Mosquin et al., *Canada's Biodiversity*, 64-66.

28. This is discussed in J.H. Lawson and V.K. Brown, "Redundancy in ecosystems," in Schultze and Mooney, *Biodiversity and Ecosystem Function*, 255-70; Goldsmith, *The Way*, ch. 53.

29. Perrings, "Economic Value."

30. Lawson and Brown, "Redundancy in ecosystems."

31. W.J. Bond, "Keystone species," in Schultze and Mooney, *Biodiversity and Ecosystem Function.*

32. Begon et al., *Ecology.*

33. C.A. White and I.R. Pengelly, "Fire as a natural process and a management tool: the Banff National Park Experience," paper presented at the Cypress Hills Forest Management Workshop, October 2-4, 1992, Medicine Hat, Alta. Society of Grassland Naturalists; C.A. White, P. Paquet, and H. Purves, "Nursing Humpty's Syndrome: Bow Valley Ecological Restoration," paper presented at the Fourth Annual Conference on Ecological Restoration, sponsored by the Canadian Council on Ecological Areas, August, 1992, Waterloo, Ont.

34. Hawksworth, "Fungi"; D.J. Read, D.H. Lewis, A.H. Fitter, and I.J. Alexander, *Mycorrhizas in Ecosystems Symposium* (Wallingford, U.K.: CAB International, 1993).

35. A brief description of the harmony function is provided by R. Augros and G. Stancieu, *The New Biology: Discovering the Wisdom in Nature* (Boston: New Science Library, 1988), 130-55.

36. James E. Lovelock, *Gaia: A New Look at Life on Earth* (Oxford: Oxford University Press, 1979); Lovelock, *Ages of Gaia*; Lovelock, *Gaia: The Practical Science*; Schneider and Boston, *Scientists on Gaia*; Goldsmith, *The Way.*

37. Arne Naess, *Ecology, Community and Life Style: An Outline of an Ecosophy* (New York: Cambridge University Press, 1989); Stuart Kaufmann, *At Home in the Universe* (Oxford: Oxford University Press, 1995); Goldsmith, *The Way*; Holmes Rolston III, "On Behalf of Bioexuberance," *The Trumpeter* 5, 1 (Winter 1988): 26-29.

38. Philip P. Hanson, *Environmental Ethics: Philosophical and Policy Perspectives* (Burnaby, B.C.: Institute for the Humanities, Simon Fraser University, 1986); J. Stan Rowe, "In praise of beauty," in Hanson, *Environmental Ethics: Philosophical and Policy Perspectives*, 45-47.

39. Susan Meeker-Lowry, *Economics as if the Earth Really Mattered: A Catalyst Guide to Socially Conscious Investing* (Santa Cruz, Calif.: Catalyst, New Society Publishers, 1988).

Further Reading

Daily, Gretchen C., ed. *Nature's Services: Societal Dependence on Natural Ecosystems.* Washington: Island Press, 1997.

Goldsmith, Edward. *The Way: An Ecological World View.* Devon, U.K: Themis Books, 1996.

Kaufman, Stuart. *At Home in the Universe: The Search for the Laws of Self-Organization and Complexity.* Oxford: Oxford University Press, 1995.

Lovelock, James. *Gaia: The Practical Science of Planetary Medicine.* London: Gaia Books, 1991.

Mosquin, Ted, Peter G. Whiting, and Don E. McAllister. *Canada's Biodiversity: The Variety of Life, Its Status, Economic Benefits, Conservation Costs and Unmet Needs.* Ottawa: Canadian Museum of Nature, 1995.

Orr, David W. *Earth in Mind: On Education, Environment and the Human Prospect.* Washington: Island Press, 1994.

Rowe, J. Stan. "From Shallow to Deep Ecological Philosophy," *The Trumpeter* 13, 1 (1996): 123-26.

Schneider, Stephen H,. and Penelope J. Boston, eds. *Scientists on Gaia.* Cambridge, Mass.: MIT Press, 1991.

Wilson, Edward O. *The Diversity of Life.* Cambridge, Mass.: Belknap Press of Harvard University, 1992.

Bob Wildfong   **The Chain of Seeds:**

Biodiversity and Agriculture

E VER SINCE THE FIRST FARMERS TURNED THE SOIL, THE ABILITY to acquire viable, well-adapted seeds has allowed human beings to form civilizations, set up permanent settlements, and build cities, supported by a reliable and bountiful source of food. Many times, they have had to change their kinds of food crops. As people moved to different areas of the world and developed different farming technologies, from simple ploughs to giant combines, their seeds changed with them.

It is this ability to change that has made plants so important. Without the possibility of adaptation, controlled breeding, and selection, it would be impossible to grow acres of corn as far north as Canada, wheat would be no more than a wild grass, and all apples would be tiny crabapples. Throughout history, hundreds of species of plants have diverged from their wild roots and become the basis of our food, our clothing, and our urban landscapes. Hardly any of these domesticated plants could live without human care. We inherit thousands of varieties of useful plants that exist only because farmers and gardeners have grown them, produced seeds, and grown them again. Our plants are a chain, a chain of seed-saving, and that chain is breaking.

A Quick History of Seeds

To understand the issues affecting crop diversity in modern times, we must understand the natural and human history of our food system.

In the 1920s and 1930s, the Russian biologist and explorer N.I. Vavilov studied the genetic distribution of cultivated plants throughout the world and discovered that their greatest natural diversity occurred in several tropical and subtropical regions. He concluded that crop plants had originated in these regions, which he called "gene centres," later to be known as "centres of diversity."[1]

Independently, in those areas of the world where edible grains grew in the wild agriculture apparently began.Wheat, barley, and millet were domesticated in North Africa; beans and corn in Central and South America; rice in east Asia. Early hunter-gatherers discovered that these grains could be planted intentionally, putting an end to the nomadic need to travel to find enough food.[2] When the earliest farmers began cultivating food-grain crops, seeds were part of their harvest: some of the kernels of wheat and millet were set aside to be sown at planting time. In contrast to our modern concept of buying seeds as an' input, farmers used seeds as part of a self-renewing cycle.

Until recently, farmers had an enormous selection of wild plants to include in their seed stocks. Wild relatives of crop plants that displayed drought tolerance, insect resistance, or other favourable qualities would be brought into cultivation to eventually give those strengths to the cultivated crop. Since each farmer could propagate a slightly different set of varieties, or a different ensemble of plant genes, a staggering number of useful plant varieties evolved on the farms of Africa, Latin America, and Asia.

The seeds grown by traditional farmers are often called "landraces" or "Farmers' Varieties." These are mixed, highly diverse populations. In a field of traditional African landrace wheat, the plants are genetically heterogeneous. Many slightly different plants grow side by side, creating a form of crop insurance. If dry weather suits certain plants, then those plants thrive. If the weather turns cold and wet, others grow better. Either way, there is usually an adequate harvest, and rarely a total crop failure.

Traditional farmers trade seeds with one another, always searching for those that grow best on their particular patch of land. The best grains are saved for planting and only the second-grade seeds are used for food. High-land farmers and low-land farmers often have different types of plants, fields on sand and fields on clay support different types, all developed through the ancient cycle of natural and human selection.

The United States and Canada, like most Western nations, are not in a genetic centre of diversity and are considered to be "gene-poor." So poor, in fact, that when prairie wheat breeders wish to introduce a new characteristic (such as resistance to a new disease), they almost always have to turn to plant varieties in North Africa, the centre of diversity for wheat.[3] Indeed, few foods are of North American origin. Except for a few items, such as Jerusalem artichokes and some berries, almost everything we grow and eat originated in other countries. Originally, settlers brought seeds from their homelands, which gradually adapted to the Canadian climate through natural selection, often becoming somewhat different from the original varieties.

Because Canadian seed companies were scarce until the mid-1800s, especially in newly settled areas, most farmers had to grow their own seeds. Neighbours often grew different varieties, and families passed unique strains of seeds from generation to generation, like precious heirlooms. Since most seeds were produced in the same area as they were planted, natural and human selection created various "regionally adapted" varieties.[4] So it was that in 1900, it is estimated that over 7,500 different varieties of apples existed in North America.[5] Estimates of the numbers of heirloom, non-commercialized varieties of grains, vegetables, legumes, tree fruits, and other food plants also number in the thousands. Indeed, many countries, whether in centres of diversity or not, had a wide range of distinct crop varieties before the turn of the century.

Declining Diversity

The United Nations Food and Agriculture Organization (FAO) estimates that since the beginning of this century, about 75 per cent of the worldwide genetic diversity of agricultural crops has been lost.[6] The erosion of this genetic treasure has occurred in rich and poor countries alike, but it has been especially rapid in the industrialized world. There are many reasons for this catastrophic loss of plant gene stocks, but most boil down to a common theme: there are far fewer seed-growers today than ever before. Farmers and gardeners, who have traditionally been seed producers, have all but given up the age-old practices of on-farm breeding and seed-saving and have become passive seed consumers. The 10,000-year legacy of millions of individual growers is now perpetuated by a scant few seed companies.

In the early part of the twentieth century, seed houses began to replace the seed-saving and breeding activities of individual farmers. Originally, small family-owned seed houses across the country together maintained and produced thousands of varieties of regionally adapted seeds. Each company sold only a few dozen kinds of seed, but the selections were different from region to region. Since long-distance transportation was limited and expensive, most seeds were locally produced, and the varieties of distant regions were rarely traded.

Once efficient rail transportation and especially a reliable rural parcel post service became common, the inventories of seed companies from coast to coast became available to nearly all Canadians. It was no longer necessary for farmers and gardeners to purchase their seeds locally. Soon the seed industry began to converge on a narrower course.

When large seed companies buy their smaller competitors, many of the varieties originally grown and sold by the smaller companies are discontinued. Generally, it is more profitable for a large seed company to sell a few mass-market varieties than many little-known seeds. The economies of scale which come from producing and selling fewer varieties, but more of each kind, allow the modern corporate seed giants to sell the same seeds coast-to-coast at a greater profit than by selling some varieties to the Maritimes and others to the Prairies, even though those areas have quite different growing conditions.

Since 1984, over 125 seed companies in Canada and the United States have gone out of business. Many more have been bought out by pharmaceutical and chemical companies.[7] There is a clear correlation between the concentration of seed company ownership and the number of varieties which fall out of production each year. For instance, in 1981 there were 50 varieties of non-hybrid broccoli on the market whereas in 1994 only 38 were available.[8]

Many seed companies are being bought out by pharmaceutical and chemical companies. Most of the leading agro-chemical manufacturers are introducing varieties of major crops (corn, soybeans, cotton, potatoes, canola) that are genetically engineered to be resistant to their leading herbicides, increasing the demand for both their chemical products and their seeds. Examples include "Roundup Ready" corn, cotton, soybeans, and canola, a line of crops genetically engineered by Monsanto Company to be resistant to its own Roundup herbicide. Roundup Ready corn, produced by Monsanto-owned DeKalb Genetics Corporation, is a collection of five varieties of hybrid corn that have been rapidly embraced by farmers. Only a few years after its introduction, over 13,000 farmers planted Roundup Ready corn in 1998 on over one million acres in the U.S. and Canada. DeKalb expects this acreage to increase to three or four million acres in 1999.[9]

Putting aside debate about the health and environmental effects of transgenic crops, it is worrisome that so many farmers – presumably because of compelling business reasons – choose to grow a very small number of patented crop varieties. These displace other important crop varieties, leading to the further decline in genetic diversity on Canadian farms.

To make matters worse for global genetic security, the very centres of crop diversity where our food crops originated are now being threatened. These areas are the vital reservoirs of plant varieties that the world uses in modern breeding. Unfortunately, they also tend to be in regions of civil and economic instability. Many farms and their precious seed collections are threatened by war and brutal governments. In developing countries where traditional fields were once rich in diverse, well-adapted plants, Western-style farms are moving in. For too long we have depended on the subsistence farmers of the world to conserve our crop diversity on their farms. Who will save the seeds now?

Gene Banks

Ever since distinct cultivated varieties of plants began to be bred under controlled conditions, people have amassed collections of seeds. Breeders have always recognized the importance of having a wide and deep gene pool. Creating a new type of tomato is not the same process as making a new kind of toaster. Technology tends to build on itself, but breeding often turns back to the old. The "right" gene might be found in an old or obsolete variety, or even in a wild relative. Breeders attempt to gather a wide assembly of strains of a certain plant in the hope that some of them will prove useful given future threats, such as a new disease, a new strain of fungus, or a thinning ozone layer.

In the 1960s, the United Nations Food and Agriculture Organization (FAO) recognized that plant genetic stocks needed to be conserved for the future, and it was generally felt that long-term institutional storage would be an adequate solution. The UN formed an international system of gene banks, which currently maintains over one million samples of seeds, fruit trees, fibre plants, potatoes, and other plants of economic importance.[10] Seed samples are exchanged free of charge throughout the world to scientists, breeders and seed companies, which in turn use the samples to develop commercial seeds for farmers and gardeners.

Agriculture Canada Plant Gene Resources, Canada's agency in the international system, currently maintains over 100,000 samples in its seed collection. In 1998, it moved its main seed bank to a new facility in Saskatoon, where seeds are stored in a giant underground freezer and are expected to remain viable for up to 100 years.

The U.S. National Plant Germplasm System's collection is up to about 450,000 samples[11] and the former Soviet Union had an excellent gene bank system of about the same size. Still, this represents a tiny fraction of the plants on which we depend for our food. Recall that the genes needed for wheat breeding are often found in North African fields, which contain far more wheat varieties than have been formally studied or documented.

In 1996, the FAO published the first State of the World report on global plant gene resources.[12] It paints a grim picture. Worldwide, 48 per cent of stored seeds need to be regenerated. Even with the best storage facilities, gene banks must plant their seeds from time to time, grow more, and replenish their stocks. It is an expensive and laborious operation. Some gene banks, especially those in poorer countries, could be storing more dead than living seeds.

The gene banks have a huge task, and inadequate funding to fulfil their mandate. The gradual erosion of genetic diversity is hardly a political priority, but even if it were, it is doubtful that the world could afford to conserve all of the currently unexplored and undocumented plants by such a costly, institutionalized method. Besides being expensive, the centralized system of gene banks is susceptible to natural disasters, war, and economic instability.[13]

Alternatives

The international gene bank system is operated by scientists for the benefit of seed companies and farmers. An alternative approach is to involve farmers more directly in seed conservation. This builds on the fact that even today, smallholders and subsistence farmers throughout the world who continue to select their own seeds from their own fields each year conserve more plant genes than all the gene banks and seed companies put together.[14] This approach is recognized in the UN Biodiversity Convention,[15] and in the FAO Leipzig Declaration,[16] which called for "a new and more productive partnership between scientists and farmers." It encourages the marriage of the technical ability of publicly funded gene banks with the labour force and traditional knowledge of ordinary farmers and gardeners.

The Seeds of Survival (SOS) program of the Unitarian Service Committee (USC) Canada has received international praise for its pioneering work involving this sort of collaboration. USC Canada is a 54-year-old international development organization which began the SOS project in Ethiopia after the famine of the early 1980s. Civil war and drought had disrupted the traditional cycles of seed-saving and many people had been forced to eat their treasured seeds. The bountiful indigenous varieties of barley, wheat, and sorghum were decimated in many parts of the country.[17]

USC Canada helped to link the farmers with scientists from the Ethiopian gene bank.[18] In 1988, USC-sponsored Ethiopian scientists released samples of indigenous seeds from the gene bank and worked closely with traditional farmers who multiplied the seeds and returned them to the SOS project to be shared with others. Gradually, on-farm seed stocks were restored and at the project's peak in 1995, almost 20,000 farmers were growing the rescued varieties.[19] The scientists reported great enthusiasm among participating farmers as the native crops outperformed imported seed varieties.[20]

There are many approaches to seed conservation throughout the world. One common strategy is to put a threatened plant into commercial use so that it is naturally multiplied as it is used. This strategy has certain benefits over the gene-bank approach. Seeds frozen for decades in gene banks are literally frozen in time. They remain viable, but they do not adapt. Farming conditions might have become very different when the seeds are taken out of storage. In contrast, seeds that are collected and replanted every year have a chance to adapt to changing conditions. The two approaches of on-farm and in-storage conservation complement each other by solving different problems.

The ability of individuals to enact change has long been underestimated in seed conservation circles. The Seed Savers Exchange, the U.S. grandfather of grassroots seed-saving groups, has grown from a few gardeners into an 8,000-member network that combines the best features of popular enthusiasm and institutional expertise. Closer to home, Seeds of Diversity Canada co-ordinates the grassroots seed-saving efforts of its 1,500 members. These organizations allow interested and capable gardeners and farmers to acquire endangered varieties of garden plants, learn correct seed-saving methods, and share their multiplied seeds with others. This enthusiastic workforce can also be partnered with the scientific expertise and technical facilities of the public gene banks, allowing significant specimens to be backed up in long-term storage.

Thousands of gardeners have enhanced their hobby by adopting a rare plant, perhaps an heirloom tomato, perhaps a rare kind of melon, or the purple-top strap-leaf turnips I grow at home, producing seeds and sharing them with other seed-savers. About 20,000 varieties are being conserved this way in North America.[21] There are hundreds of thousands of endangered varieties of garden plants, but there are at least that many gardeners who could adopt a variety.

Seeds of Diversity Canada has extended its principle of "conservation through use" to help develop commercial markets for threatened and "heritage" vegetables. Certain produce distributors in the U.S. have found lucrative niche markets selling unusual vegetables and fruit to gourmet restaurants.[22] Chefs are eager to work with produce of interesting colours, shapes, and textures. Many farmers are interested in growing these unusual varieties, but a suitable distribution system does not exist in Canada. Seeds of Diversity sees market forces as a key to ensuring the conservation of these varieties, and is working to develop this niche market.[23]

The chain of seeds has been forged by hundreds of generations of farmers, and now it is up to us to secure the next link by passing this ancient inheritance on to the next generation. For the sake of global food security, it is vital that the world conserve the genetic diversity contained in both seed banks and farmers' fields, and that the issue of genetic conservation be brought into the light of political awareness. Conservation strategies must be broadened to include the participation of farmers and grassroots seed-savers. The responsibility for future food security is shared by all: the scientist, the diplomat, and the backyard gardener.

Appendix   Farm Animals: Diversity is Declining (Jy Chiperzak)

Soil and plant diversity are not all that is being lost in our new agriculture. Farm animals are also disappearing as a result of the industrialization of agriculture. Of the 4,000 breeds of livestock thought to exist worldwide, 27 per cent of them are at risk of becoming extinct. We are losing 5 per cent of our breeds every year, almost one breed of cow, horse, or pig per week.

In Canada we are not immune from this genetic erosion. Of our 220 livestock breeds, about 60 are rare or endangered. In the early 1990s Rare Breeds Canada found only 45 pure Cotswold sheep left in Canada, where there were once tens of thousands. Kerry cattle, Berkshire pigs, White Jersey Giant chickens all teeter on the brink of disappearing from our farms. In just this last year, Canada has lost the English Saddleback pig, and the Large Black pig is critically threatened.

The most dramatic losses of farm animal biodiversity are occurring in the poultry (egg, broiler, and turkey) and swine industries. Mass market demand in Canada and throughout the world means that poultry and swine are raised in high-density, controlled environments. One poultry complex in California has close to one million laying birds. The eggs it produces could satisfy the entire Canadian market west of Ontario. The birds are all of highly selected strains with very narrow genetic variability. Even with its high levels of disease risk, this system is being looked upon as a model for the future of other livestock.

Only a handful of multinational companies own all of the "élite" breeding lines to produce the commercial laying and broiler birds for the world. The many breeds and genetic lines that were once the mainstay of the family farm are rapidly disappearing. Early commercial strains such as the Plymouth Barred Rock, Brown Leghorn, and Canada's Chantecler have only remnant populations left with many flocks consisting of fewer than 50 birds. Thus, the lowly chicken, the most universal and important animal food source, is probably in greater need of conservation than any other.

The turkey industry is even more tightly controlled, with only three multinationals owning all the "élite" genetic stocks globally. The turkey has been so tampered with genetically that, because of its size and huge breast (people eat more white meat than dark), the commercial turkey can no longer breed naturally. Today our traditional Christmas turkey is the product of genetic manipulation and artificial insemination. Dr. Roy Crawford of Rare Breeds International says that "the gene pool is so small that one catastrophe like a major disease could wipe them all out."

What we are doing is putting all our eggs in one basket for the sake of short-term economic gains. We no longer measure progress in the multigenerational time frame needed to fully realize the impacts of much of our decision-making. Crawford underlines the need for the conservation of biodiversity: "Maintenance of biological diversity, in all its many aspects, is essentially an insurance policy for future needs. Canada cannot afford to be complacent with regards [to] its animal genetic resources.... There is an urgent need for Canadians to undertake conservation action as both long- and short-term insurance against our changing needs."

Notes

1. N.W. Simmons, ed., *Evolution of Crop Plants* (New York: Longman, 1976).
2. Vavilov's centres of diversity are described in detail in A.C. Zevan and J.M.J. de Wet, *Dictionary of Cultivated Plants and their Regions of Diversity* (Wageningen, Netherlands: Centre for Agricultural Publishing and Documentation, 1982).
3. Personal conversation with Dr. Melaku Worede, Director of Plant Genetic Resources Center/Ethiopia, Chair of United Nations Food and Agriculture Organization's Commission on Plant Genetic Resources, 1993.
4. My studies of early Canadian seed catalogues (pre-1900) indicate that home-grown or regionally developed varieties were commonly grown and sold. Many of these cultivars can be linked to particular families or places in the areas where they were first commercialized.
5. Estimate reported by members of the North American Fruit Explorers (NAFEX), 1997.
6. United Nations Food and Agriculture Organization, *State of the World's Plant Gene Resources for Food and Agriculture* (Rome: FAO, 1996).
7. Kent Whealy, *Seed Savers Exchange Garden Seed Inventory*, 4th ed. (Decorah, Iowa: Seed Saver Publications, 1995), lists all non-hybrid commercial seed offerings in North America. See also Hope Shand, *Human Nature: Agricultural Biodiversity and Farm-based Security* (New York: Rural Advancement Foundation International and FAO, 1997). For several years the decline in competition was steep, but since about 1990 several new seed companies have appeared, specializing in rare and "heritage" garden vegetables and flowers. There are encouraging signs that the swelling interest in heritage flowers, fruit, and vegetables is helping to keep them in cultivation, but industry-wide seed inventories show that many varieties still fall out of production every year.
8. Whealy, *Inventory*. Hybrid varieties are not considered since they cannot be re-propagated from seed – they must be made by crossing two non-hybrid varieties.
9. DeKalb Genetics Corporation, DeKalb, Illinois, October 1998.
10. FAO, *State of the World's Plant Gene Resources*.
11. USDA-Agricultural Research Service, "Seeds for Our Future," U.S. Department of Agriculture, Office of Communications, 1996.
12. FAO, *State of the World's Plant Gene Resources*.

13. Hurricane Andrew partly destroyed a field collection of tropical fruit trees in Florida in August 1992. The gene bank station in the former Soviet state of Georgia was "all but destroyed" in the civil war. Staff took seeds with them as they fled, but much of the collection was lost. See: *Diversity* 9, 4 (1993) and 10, 1 (1994). Since the breakup of the Soviet Union, the once-secure Vavilov Institute gene bank system is now critically underfunded and understaffed.

14. Shand, *Human Nature*.

15. Biodiversity Convention, Agenda 21 (New York: UNCED, 1992), ch. 14.57: Objectives of program area for conservation and sustainable utilization of plant genetic resources for food and sustainable agriculture: "(c) Not later than the year 2000, to adopt policies and strengthen or establish programmes for in-situ on-farm and ex-situ conservation and sustainable use of plant genetic resources for food and agriculture, integrated into strategies and programmes for sustainable agriculture."

16. FAO, Fourth International Technical Conference on Plant Genetic Resources, Leipzig, Germany, June 1996.

17. Personal communications with Dr. Melaku Worede and Hailu Getu, two of the scientists involved in the project, 1994-97.

18. Ethiopian "On-farm Landrace Conservation and Enhancement Project," detailed in Melaku Worede and Hailu Mekbib, "Linking genetic resources conservation to farmers in Ethiopia," in Walter de Boef, Kojo Amanor, Kate Wellard, and Anthony Bebbington, eds., *Cultivating Knowledge* (London: Intermediate Technology Publications, 1993), 78-84.

19. From Unitarian Service Committee (USC) Canada promotional literature, 1995.

20. Personal communications with Dr. Melaku Worede and Hailu Getu, 1994-97.

21. According to Kent Whealy, director of Seed Savers Exchange, closing address at "Preserving Crop Biodiversity and Saving Seeds in the Northeast," Pennsylvania State University College of Agricultural Sciences, November 15, 1997, SSE has over 18,000 unique varieties in its collection at Heritage Farm. According to Seeds of Diversity Canada staff, the 1998 SODC seed listing contains over 1,500 unique varieties. There is probably substantial overlap between the two organizations, but there are undoubtedly many varieties grown by members that are not listed.

22. Indian Rock Produce Inc. of Bucks County, Pennsylvania, a specialty pro-

duce distributor, is seeking farmers to help it meet the demand for heritage vegetables in the restaurant trade.

23. Jim Dyer, *Business Plan for Niche Market Development of Minor or Heritage Crops* (Toronto: Seeds of Diversity Canada, 1998).

Further Reading

Ashworth, Suzanne. *Seed to Seed*. Decorah, Iowa: Seed Saver Publications, 1991.

Fowler, Cary, and Pat Mooney. *Shattering: Food, Politics and the Loss of Genetic Diversity*. Tucson: University of Arizona Press, 1990.

Shand, Hope. *Human Nature: Agricultural Biodiversity and Farm-based Food Security*. New York: Rural Advancement Foundation International, United Nations Food and Agriculture Organization, 1997.

Stickland, Sue, and Kent Whealy. *Heirloom Vegetables: A Home Gardener's Guide to Finding and Growing Vegetables from the Past*. New York: Fireside Publishing, 1998.

Weaver, William Woys, and Peter Hatch. *Heirloom Vegetable Gardening : A Master Gardener's Guide to Planting, Growing, Seed Saving, and Cultural History*. New York: Henry Holt & Company, 1997.

Whealy, Kent. *Seed Savers Exchange Garden Seed Inventory*, 4th ed. Decorah, Iowa: Seed Saver Publications, 1995.

Woodhead, Eileen. *Early Canadian Gardening: An 1827 Nursery Catalogue*. Montreal and Kingston: McGill-Queen's University Press, 1998.

Contacts

USC Canada, 56 Sparks Street, Ottawa Ont. K1P 5B1 (613) 234-6827

Seeds of Diversity Canada, Box 36, Stn. Q, Toronto, Ont. M4T 2L7 (905) 623-0353 *mail@seeds.ca* http://www.seeds.ca

Seed Savers Exchange, 3076 North Winn Rd., Decorah, Iowa 52101 (319) 382-5990

Rural Advancement Foundation International (RAFI), 110 Osborne St., Suite 202, Winnipeg, Manitoba R3L 1Y5 (204) 453-5259 rafi@rafi.org http://www.rafi.ca

Part Three: Ideas, Knowledge, and Values

Russel Lawrence Barsh   **Taking Indigenous Science**

Seriously

I N THE EARLY 1990S CONTROVERSY ERUPTED OVER A PROPOSED diamond mine on land claimed by Dene people in the Northwest Territories. Broken Hill Pty. (BHP), an Australian mining conglomerate, had announced the discovery of a large pipe of diamond-bearing kimberlite in 1994. Dene hunters in the area were quick to express concerns about the effects of mining on the health and migration routes of caribou.[1]

The Environmental Assessment Panel struck by the federal government to review BHP's mining application decided to give equal weight to science and to traditional Dene knowledge. Some critics charged that this violated the principle of the separation of church and state set out in the Canadian Charter of Rights and Freedoms.[2] They advanced two arguments to support this claim: (1) to the extent that traditional knowledge consists of nothing more than "spiritual" teachings and values, it is *not science* because it cannot be challenged or verified by non-Aboriginal people; (2) to the extent that traditional knowledge includes first-hand observations of ecosystems, it is merely a body of *raw data* and must be subjected to verification and systematization by scientists.

Critics further charged that Aboriginal leaders concoct claims of traditional knowledge simply to ransom development projects and extort funds from Ottawa. As the principal consumers of wildlife and fish in the North, it was argued, Aboriginal peoples have a selfish interest in resisting new conservation measures, and deploy claims of traditional knowledge to deflect legitimate ecological concerns.

This chapter outlines some of the reasons why indigenous peoples, ecologists, and conservationists often fail to collaborate effectively. These reasons include ethnocentrism, mistrust, and cultural differences in the way ecological data are collected, systematized, and described. Particular attention is given to the comparative strengths of indigenous science, the ways indigenous peoples formulate questions and design models to account for their observations, the extent to which indigenous ecology is valid and reliable, and the role of ethics in indigenous knowledge systems. Examples of the potential applications of indigenous models and field methods are drawn from the author's current work in Blackfoot territory in Alberta.

The biodiversity concept challenges governments to shift from the species-by-species conservation strategies of the past to an ecosystem approach. However, our knowledge of the adaptability of particular ecosystems and their possible alternative, stable states is limited by a lack of local historical data. To obtain such information we could launch long-term experiments in selected locations.[3] Or, we could learn from the indigenous people who have long inhabited, sustainably utilized, and extensively modified local ecosystems. Their knowledge is especially important in Canada. Most of Canada was occupied exclusively by indigenous people until the end of the last century, and nearly half of Canada still is indigenous territory today.

Indigenous knowledge nonetheless continues to be underutilized in Canada. For example, although one recent study confirmed the reliability of Inuit hunters' recollections of caribou numbers and seasonal movements, the authors did not try to determine whether their informants were using models of caribou ecology for forecasting.[4] If indigenous people are treated merely as passive recorders, and not as active researchers and model-builders, a great deal of the potential value of indigenous science will continue to be overlooked or lost.

Trust and Transparency

Trust is a central issue. Non-Aboriginal people have been taught historically to despise, resent, fear, or (at best) to pity Aboriginal people, who, it is presumed, will grasp any opportunity to "get even."[5] Aboriginal people, in turn, have ample historical reasons to mistrust most of their neighbours and nearly all government officials, and have encountered science chiefly as a rationale for seizing their lands and restricting their liberty.

Aboriginal leaders are no doubt sometimes guilty of mystifying indigenous knowledge for selfish, short-sighted ends, but non-Aboriginal politicians invoke "science" to justify their policies and programs as well. Aboriginal scholars are capable of making substantial errors, but then so are mainstream scientists — especially in fields such as forecasting the oscillations of wildlife populations, as illustrated by the recent collapses of Canada's "managed" salmon and cod stocks. All human knowledge is imperfect and susceptible to manipulation and abuse. Aboriginal peoples argue that their scientific errors have rarely affected the planet on a catastrophic scale, however.

The critics of indigenous knowledge are doubly suspicious because of their inability to discover its precise methods or contents. Similarly, Aboriginal people tend to mistrust Western science because of its preoccupation with seemingly obscure and impenetrable symbolic languages, such as nonparametric statistics and fractal geometry. When a Western-trained ecologist wants to talk about logistic functions, an Aboriginal elder may describe population dynamics in songs and dances. We speak about the same phenomena using different languages.

Miscommunication and mistrust have been perpetuated on both sides for different reasons. Western-trained scientists are taught to be materialists — that is, to believe in what they can feel, see, and weigh. As such, they tend to dismiss explanations couched in moral or spiritual terms. They also tend to regard the use of mathematics as a guarantee against contaminating their models with culture. Scientists, nonetheless, draw on their values and experience in designing models, whether or not they admit it. For example, while using "competition" to model ecosystems reflects Western ideals, indigenous peoples may describe the same processes as "co-operation." Expressing such ideas mathematically does not render them culture-free.

Aboriginal communities have concerns about sharing knowledge with people they do not yet trust to use it wisely. This reluctance may be expressed in terms of sacredness, but it also reflects practical concerns, such as opposing commercial exploitation of indigenous botanical or medical knowledge, and fears that their knowledge will be used against them.[6] There is, moreover, a widespread perception among

Aboriginal people today that indigenous knowledge systems have been fragmented and are in decay. This has led to anxiety over exposing them to critical scrutiny. The number of individuals who are *fully* trained in (say) physiology or pharmacology has arguably fallen dramatically since the early years of this century, as has their ability to practise their skills openly and with public respect. In many communities, efforts to reconstruct and renew indigenous knowledge systems began only in the 1970s, after the dismantling of residential schools, and the departure of Indian Agents and missionaries.

Even the most candid Aboriginal leaders are reluctant to discuss the damage already done to indigenous knowledge systems, fearing that honesty on this subject would merely strengthen the arguments of those who dismiss indigenous knowledge as mystification and romanticism. However, a tragic result of silence is inaction, and the further neglect and decay of indigenous sciences.

An alternative would be to create conditions in which indigenous science is taken seriously enough to motivate young people to learn it in all of its depth and complexity. This is not simply a matter of repeating a few generalizations about holism or the connectedness of nature. Rather, it takes years of study. Only with a full appreciation of the details can they ever feel sufficient confidence to begin reconstructing lost elements, or making critical comparisons with mainstream science.[7]

Potential Contributions

It is as important not to trivialize indigenous science as it is to avoid dismissing it as non-empirical. Even ardent defenders of the value of indigenous knowledge frequently underestimate its scientific content.

Wildlife managers were relatively quick to appreciate the role of hunters and fishers as observers, not only of the current distribution and numbers of species, but of historical conditions. People who spend their year travelling the land accumulate an irreplaceable long-term record, elements of which they may pass on to their descendants. For instance, my colleagues and I constructed an 85-year chronology of the impacts of seasonal floods on vegetation and wildlife along a two-kilometre segment of the Oldman River by overlaying the recollections of people who had grown up, hunted, gathered medicines, and raised cattle there.[8] Our eyewitness record was consistent with available physical evidence, such as surficial geology and dendrochronology, but was more precise as to the timing and location of changes and much richer in terms of the number of changes identified. Sequential variation in notable species – those with some local utility – could be mapped to a very fine grid.

Indigenous knowledge is not merely a database, however. As long-time observers of ecosystems, indigenous people discover *associations* in space and time, such as seasonal changes in the trophic dynamics of communities, and successional changes in the structure of communities. Knowledge of associations is obviously related to a practical problem: locating resources, and harvesting them when they are most accessible, or their qualities are most desirable. Some knowledge of associations is embedded in taxonomy. Among the Salish peoples of Puget Sound, for example, salmon taxonomy includes a model of competitive relationships – that is, which species prevails in competition for spawning habitat in the region's rivers. Associations may also be embedded in stories, in symbology such as Dene "maps" and the birchbark scrolls of the Ojibway *midewin* lodge,[9] or in ritual performances.

Figure 1

When indigenous people move through a familiar landscape, they augment their ability to monitor ecological processes by observing the behaviour and vocalizations of species that have more acute senses.

On Kodiak Island (Alaska), for example, I was able to reconstruct some of the historical impacts of earthquakes by asking local fishers for a chronology of changes in places where target species congregate in the Karluk River. The key was the preference of certain species for water of more or less depth, velocity, and turbidity. Using local knowledge of flatfish, we discovered (among other things) that part of the river bed had tipped appreciably during the 1964 earthquake.

The associations detected by indigenous people raise tantalizing questions on issues as diverse as plant physiology and human medicine. Why do Aboriginal peoples from Cape Breton to Lake Superior agree that a certain medicine found growing in marshes is most effective when its roots are dug after a particularly cold winter freeze? What explains the association, observed in Blackfoot territory, between early-summer cactus blooms and late-summer berry production? Indigenous people may sometimes appear indifferent to the *causes* of these relationships, but this does not mean that indigenous knowledge is not a rich, systematic repository of reliable models.[10] Once again, the purpose of indigenous science is likely to be forecasting, rather than modifying the system. What is sought is precise and highly reliable information about how things behave, and how their behaviour may change in response to a variety of existing forces. Theories and laws that transcend existing systems achieve practical importance only when we wish to find ways of redesigning system structures: turning a forest into a wheatfield or a desert into a cotton plantation.

Empiricism and Indigenous Science

What is indigenous science, then, and how good is it? Indigenous science is both *empirical* and *systematic*, like Western science. Indigenous science differs, however, in its focus, in the analogies used to build models, and in the choice of methods and tools of observation. I will use indigenous ecology to illustrate these points.

Indigenous peoples tend to view the biosphere as relatively chaotic.[11] Although there is an underlying cyclical pattern to events, unpredictable forces (often described as *tricksters*) continually intervene and divert the flow. Countervailing stability can be achieved to some extent through *relationships*. Relationships include kinship and alliances, which may extend to animals, plants, and landforms as well as humans. Each human family inherits from its ancestors a network of relationships with all the beings that share its territory. Each human generation must learn its relationships, renew them, and adapt them to stresses and change.

This viewpoint is entirely consistent with Western conceptions of biophysical processes. Long-term studies of climate change are revealing many superimposed cycles or oscillations in the physical environment, such as longer- and shorter-term trends in temperature and precipitation. Despite these patterns, there is considerable seasonal and annual unpredictability, which varies locally. Western scientists had to disburden themselves of mechanical, deterministic models of the biosphere before accepting the world as statistical *and* chaotic – which is the way indigenous peoples viewed the world all along.

What about the stabilizing role of relationships? It is a way of conceptualizing the adaptability of ecosystems. All of the species in an ecosystem (including humans) share trophic relationships. They may relate to each other as predator and prey, co-predators, comensuals, or

Figure 2

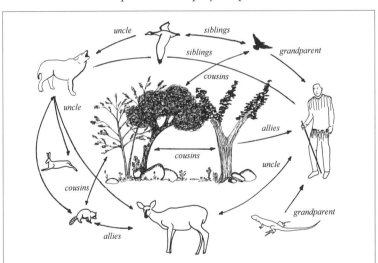

Indigenous peoples conceive of other species as conscious and strategic, and view the landscape as the product of a large number of historical conflicts, treaties, and marriages between species. The ecosystem is not merely a food chain, but a social network.

symbionts. Trophic relationships change in response to changes in the environment, and changes in the food-gathering and defensive behaviour of each species. For example, humans and wolves both are predators of moose. If moose grow scarce or "shy," humans and wolves must both readjust their hunting strategies relative to each other. Or, if wolves learn better ways of harassing and tiring moose, humans must find ways of regaining the balance of predation efficiency with wolves or switch to another prey. Continuity and gradual adaptive change in ecological relationships is indeed the means by which species survive change, and ecosystems remain relatively stable over time.

At one level, then, we can say that indigenous science describes the same processes as Western science using different metaphors. This difference in metaphors has important implications for the way we pose questions, however. Indigenous peoples describe ecosystems as *social* systems.[12] Consciousness, will, and strategic thinking are ascribed to all species. Species may feel responsibilities to each other, as well as resentments. They may try to outsmart each other – usually with bad consequences. Thinking this way tends to make *behaviour* the focus of inquiry, rather than the physical structures or populations of plants and animals.

Western biology and indigenous science accordingly approached the issue of adaptation from different directions. Western scholars began with the study of comparative anatomy. Indigenous peoples focussed on what we now call behavioural co-evolution. Each scientific system has relative strength in describing different aspects of the same process. Significantly, the anatomical perspective deals with changes in entire species (or higher taxa) over very long time periods. The behavioural perspective is highly localized in time and space: behavioural change can be seen in a single pond or grove of trees over a few seasons.[13]

To a considerable degree, moreover, indigenous peoples have been, and continue to be, direct participants in behavioural adaptation. The hunter must find ways of adjusting to the defensive strategies adopted by prey species, while avoiding conflicts with powerful co-predators such as wolves, lions, bears, and toothed whales. The horticulturalist must study and continually readapt to the foraging strategies of insects, birds, and other garden foragers. These experiences reinforce the idea that other species act strategically, and must be either outsmarted or brought into co-operative relationships. At the same time, participant observation of behavioural adaptation can produce extraordinarily rich empirical models of the behavioural flexibility of individual species.

If its foundation is participant-observation, indigenous ecology cannot be called "traditional" knowledge, since it involves an ongoing process of interaction with the ecosystem, observation of the results, and revision of models. Moreover, indigenous ecology often describes ecosystems that have been modified extensively by indigenous peoples themselves, such as prairies created and maintained by means of frequent burning.[14] Indeed, indigenous production systems could have originated with extrapolations from natural processes. Swidden horticulture, for example, could easily have been developed on the basis of observations of plant succession following natural wildfires.

Participant-observing involves some methods and tools that could raise doubts in the minds of Western scientists. The observer who interacts intensively over a long period of time with animals, for instance, is likely to learn subtle cues to animals' behaviour. These cues may be so subtle that the observer is unconscious of them and, if questioned, may attribute his/her insights to empathy, or to spirituality. For example, anyone who has lived with a dog will appreciate the head-and-eye movement cues identified in recent field studies of wolves as signals of mood, desire, and stress.

Whatever may be its source, the observer's unconscious knowledge can make an important contribution to modelling and forecasting. This is similar to the experience of a Western ethnographer, primatologist, or natural historian who observes whole communities for long periods. While most Western scholars downplay the possibility of some kind of direct link or communication of animals with non-humans,[15] indigenous peoples find this not only plausible, but entirely consistent with their conception that all species are conscious and strategic.

What About Verification?

Indigenous peoples needed to recognize patterns in ecosystems in order to survive. Critics acknowledge this but argue (inconsistently) that "[w]ithout writing, observations could not be recorded, measured, and analyzed systematically," resulting in the acceptance of imprecise and untested beliefs.[16] Human survival is a severe test of knowledge, however, compared to peer review and the possible loss of professional status. In the short term, at least, Western scientists are unlikely to starve or freeze to death, with their families and neighbours, if their models have errors.

Hunting peoples must forecast the abundance, seasonal migrations, daily movements, and defensive behaviour of wildlife. Horticultural peoples must be able to forecast climate patterns, crop growth, and the behaviour of insects and other competitors. Only supermarket cultures could believe that any real ecosystem is so abundant that people need not always be reducing risk through forecasting and improving their forecasting models.

What has been used has been tested by use. This is not to argue against further testing, nor against testing with Western criteria and tools. The strictest approach would involve two experimental hurdles. The first hurdle would be confirming that the indigenous model *is* used by the people concerned, and that they are satisfied with the results. This would involve data on prior forecasts and outcomes. We should be willing to presume that the model is a good predictor; otherwise people would not continue to use it in ways that affect their very lives.

The second hurdle would involve comparing the model's predictions with random chance. If, for example, wildlife in their seasonal migration had used a particular route 20 per cent of the time in the past, then indigenous models should be able to forecast the use of that route with better than 20 per cent accuracy. The people concerned are clearly on to something if their model passes such a hurdle.

Unfortunately, one may have some practical problems applying this second test. Indigenous models are multi-layered, and may include moral as well as empirical lessons. For example, star lore may provide tools for anticipating seasonal changes but also may include stories teaching social values, such as justice and generosity.[17] These layers may be confused when Westerners record indigenous knowledge hastily or incompletely, without scrupulous attention to all of the embedded details. It is crucial to identify and test the empirical layers of models.

Furthermore, it can prove extremely difficult to determine the actual probability of the kinds of events forecast by indigenous models, such as wildlife migration routes. If these routes vary greatly from year to year, indigenous forecasting models could be very useful, as well as important sources of insights regarding the factors determining annual variation. But to test indigenous models, we would need to have data on *all* of the routes actually taken by wildlife over a large number of years, so that we can calculate the probability that *any one route* will be taken in the future. Sufficient data to make such comparisons usually will be lacking. Until such data can be gathered, indigenous models may be the best forecasting tools available.

It must also be recognized that indigenous science is preoccupied with forecasting relatively *local* phenomena, rather than the discovery of "universal" patterns or "laws."[18] Like any knowledge system, indigenous science should be used and evaluated only in the context of its purpose. The people of a particular house-group or village may be very successful at predicting the annual movements of a nearby caribou herd, which they might attribute symbolically to a social relationship with that herd. This does *not* mean that they know – or claim to know – everything about caribou behaviour or ecology generally. It *does* mean that wildlife ecologists should treat this local model of caribou herd movements as established until proven otherwise, since it is likely to be based on a large, locally specific data set.

Unfortunately, indigenous models have rarely been tested rigorously within their local context. In a refreshing exception, zoologists tested the ability of San hunters in Namibia's Kaudom Game Reserve to reconstruct the composition and behaviour of wildlife populations from spoor.[19] A conventionally trained British zoologist observed wildlife activity in various parts of the Game Reserve, then challenged a team of four San hunters to visit each observation site and reconstruct the scene and the sequence of events. There was nearly perfect agreement on individual animals' size, age, sex, and activities, even after the lapse of several days. Significantly, the San team often engaged in a spirited discussion among themselves before venturing an opinion about a particular site, showing that the models upon which they relied were capable of being verbalized.

Ever since indigenous peoples began asserting claims to wildlife, and justifying their claims (at least in part) on the grounds of sound stewardship, however, some Western scholars have felt obliged to prove that *all* human cultures are equally rapacious: once possessed of the capacity to wreck ecosystems, they will do so. This is the premise of Hobbes's *Leviathan* and subsequent ideological justifications of states with a monopoly of power to regulate human behaviour: the mass *must* be controlled by a rational élite. But in their enthusiasm for proving Hobbes right, scientists have made some serious analytical errors.

One long-standing challenge to indigenous ecology has been the attribution of Pleistocene megafaunal extinctions to overharvesting by indigenous Americans. The original proponent of "overkill" did little more than note that most of the larger mammals native to the Americas, such as mammoths and giraffes, disappeared after the last glaciation – the time that humans were long believed to have arrived from Asia. He was aware of the growing evidence for a much older human presence, but argued that: "Whether or not prehistoric people were in the Americas earlier, 11,000 B.P. is the time of unmistakable appearance of Paleo-Indian hunters using distinctive projectile points."[20] This change in style was "presumably" accompanied by a "rapid and catastrophic change in human behavior, with the relaxation of any preexisting restraints on excessive hunting."[21] Inferring behaviour from stylistic change is highly speculative, and makes the entire argument fallacious because it is circular, thus: stylistic change *must* have been associated with excessive hunting, because it is synchronous with the disappearance of megafauna, which *must* have been caused by excessive hunting.

The overkill argument has another major flaw: many megafauna did *not* disappear 11,000 years ago, including important food species, such as moose and elk. In defence of the overkill hypothesis, it has been argued that these species originally migrated from Asia where they had already become "conditioned" to human hunting.[22] Why, then, were these Asian megafauna better able to adapt behaviourally to hunting pressure than American megafauna?

Critical studies of hunting among contemporary indigenous peoples are also flawed. A 1995 report on the Piro in Amazonian Peru argued that Amazonian wildlife has *not* become extinct only because humans lack the physical capacity to exterminate them.[23] To support this, the author showed that Piro hunting was opportunistic: hunters harvested whatever they encountered. When a prey population declines, hunters encounter fewer members of that species, and more members of other prey species. The result is a self-regulatory mechanism that obviates the need for conscious human planning.

The difficulty with this line of research has been its focus upon only one way in which hunters exercise *self-restraint*: selectivity in their choice of prey.[24] Selective harvesting of older individuals or of males should have less impact on the prey population's reproductive rate than harvesting younger individuals and females. The Piro do not appear to make this distinction, and their harvest of some species has been disproportionately female. There are many other ways of ensuring the survival of prey species, however, including limiting the size of the *human* population.[25] A better approach would have been to ask the Piro themselves how they ensure a sustainable supply of prey, and then see if their behaviour is consistent with their own model. Piro still hunt less selectively than nearby settlers, for example.[26] Is this as a result of thoughtlessness, or does it reflect Piro ethics?

It is important to recognize the extent to which the Piro and nearly all other contemporary hunting peoples have been affected by settlers. Not only do settlers introduce tools such as shotguns and flashlights, which increase indigenous peoples' killing power, but settlers reduce wildlife themselves by hunting, logging, and polluting ecosystems. It is frequently the case that contemporary hunting societies overharvest their ecosystems simply because they are competing with forces outside of their control for whatever food sources remain available to them.

Empiricism and Ethics

Where does "spirituality" come in? The easiest way for Western-trained scientists to understand indigenous peoples' references to the spiritual foundations of knowledge is to substitute the word "ethics." Few scientists would dispute the importance of professional ethics, or disagree with the proposition that ethics, albeit normative in nature, can be integrated into the conduct and application of sound research. Indeed, few scientists would argue that religious convictions are so incompatible with objective inquiry that only atheists can be good scientists.

Western scientific ethics are largely humanistic, based on the assignment of moral values to human life and human well-being.

Indigenous ethics tend to be more "ecumenical," assigning moral values to all living and non-living entities. Indigenous peoples also tend to believe that the physical universe is continuously in flux, and that the moral order of the universe is continually *renegotiated* between humans, animals, and other beings. Western ethics generally assume that humans make moral choices for the rest of the planet.

There is no reason why a person cannot be conscientiously ethical or religious *and* painstakingly empirical. Indigenous knowledge systems differ from contemporary Western science in the *centrality* of ethics, however. In indigenous pedagogies, ethical knowledge precedes technical knowledge; the medical student must learn to be human before she is taught how to locate, identify, and prepare herbals. Indeed, indigenous peoples tend to regard ethical conduct as a condition of discovery: nature reveals itself to those who behave respectfully. There is an intriguing logic to this belief. Believing that animals have spirits and volition, for example, is not only a normative basis for avoiding cruelty and waste, but an invitation to take the behaviour of animals seriously. Moreover, beliefs in non-human volition focus our attention on individual variations and on the unexpected. If we do not think of animals and plants as mere machines, but rather as individuals somewhat like ourselves, we tend to be far more suspicious of generalizations about them.

In this way, indigenous peoples' ethical framework inclines them to seek and discover a different side of nature — variance rather than sameness. Western and indigenous traditions are not incompatible, in this light, but complementary. The Western scientist asks, what makes all magpies similar? A Blackfoot scientist asks, why is *this* magpie *different* from the others?

As some view Western intellectual history, the two great triumphs of the modern era were the liberation of reason from religion (rationality) and the liberation of the individual from inherited relationships or responsibilities (individualism). Science has become the symbolic embodiment of these achievements. Science is associated in scientists' minds with reason and truth, family and religion with sentiment and faith. Anyone who admits to spiritual beliefs is liable to be accused of irrationality, and his or her position on any other subject may be dismissed as mere sentimentality.

Western scholars' anxiety over sentimentality and faith is the product of a particular historical experience: the domination of European society for a thousand years by a bureaucratic system of religion (the Church) and inherited social relationships (feudalism). Indigenous knowledge systems have developed within different social and political contexts. A Christian biologist must take care lest she be suspected of allowing her beliefs (for example, about Divine creation) to influence her evaluation of empirical data, but this is because churches in the past have wielded power and demanded unquestioning obedience. Such an assumption need not be made of contemporary believers. Again, the same suspicions may not be justified in the case, say, of a Dene biologist who says that – as a Dene woman – she respects all life.

Renewal and Synergy

Indigenous knowledge is not static data that can be extracted and recorded for future study. It is dynamic, experimental, and generally entrusted to specialists who maintain and develop distinct *disciplines* of knowledge within their own societies, each with its own system of theories, models, methods, and ethics.

The organization of the control of knowledge differs considerably among indigenous peoples. Teaching may be entrusted to individuals or to sacred societies, and protocols for seeking and borrowing knowledge differ greatly depending on the subject. Ordinarily, knowledge is only shared for a specific purpose, not to satisfy the learner's curiosity, or to enable the learner to gain status. The learner must establish a formal relationship with a teacher, and begin by providing services to the teacher and the community as humble as cutting firewood, or taking offerings into the forest. Services instil humility, self-discipline, and respect for life. Learning ethics in this way is not an alienated intellectual process, but social and emotional. Rituals reinforce the emotive element of learning.

What is required for Aboriginal people to regain meaningful control of their own land and future, and for all of us to build a better understanding of ecosystems, is a renaissance built on the renewal of people, rather than the rediscovery and translation of ancient books. Western scientists must help – through research collaborations with

Aboriginal scholars and elders, and educational programs that challenge students to learn and compare both knowledge systems.

In southern Alberta we are exploring several areas of potential collaboration between indigenous scientists and university scientists. One evolving field of shared interest, directly relevant to the goals of the Convention on Biological Diversity, is water conservation. The relatively arid prairies and foothills of southern Alberta fall within the ancestral domain of the Blackfoot Confederacy.[27] The Oldman River, so named for the Blackfoot trickster-transformer *Napi* ("the Old Man"), deeply dissects this terrain, forming a web of "Napi tracks" that long formed the critical axes of Blackfoot travel, subsistence, and memory. The Oldman has been tapped for irrigation canals since the early years of the century. A major barricade dam was recently constructed amid strong opposition from many Blackfoot people, as well as environmental groups. Feedlots, meat-packing plants, and the runoff of agricultural chemicals are jeopardizing water quality. Water quantity and quality are key limiting factors to the growth of population and agriculture – a concern shared by Blackfoot communities and their non-Aboriginal neighbours.

What makes Blackfoot territory particularly challenging, in terms of biodiversity and sustainable development, is the volatility of its climate. Daily, seasonal, and annual fluctuations in weather patterns can be severe. Hail and snow may fall in August. In winter, mornings of -20° can be followed by afternoons of +20°, driven by fierce winds that evaporate snow cover in an hour or two. Growing seasons can vary by months from year to year, superimposed on a longer cycle of warming and cooling so severe that early British explorers described a desert, while dryland farmers arriving a half-century later enjoyed many years of adequate rain and bumper crops before the land dried out again.

This natural volatility is mirrored in Blackfoot cosmology, which emphasizes the dynamic, chaotic character of the universe and the role of random or playful forces. Human security within this flux depends, above all, on understanding motivations and maintaining relationships. Among the Hopi and Zuni of Arizona, by comparison, the universe is seen to follow far more precise, fixed cycles – a reasonable way of modelling a relatively more stable and predictable ecosystem.

As a matter of physical survival, Blackfoot needed to be masters at forecasting the distribution and movements of elk, bison, and antelope, as well as the distribution and abundance of plants used for medicine and food, all of which varied as a function of pronounced fluctuations in rainfall. Intercepting migrating bison at one of the region's many stone pounds or natural jumps was no mean feat, nor was planning trips to foraging sites in an environment where many species of plants produce shoots or fruit only once every few years, depending on warmth and water. In more volatile ecosystems, forecasting is not only more challenging but more important – especially when food and water sources are so widely dispersed that errors in planning travel routes can be fatal. No wonder that the most powerful Blackfoot ceremonial tool is the Beaver Bundle: beavers control the flow of water. This is a symbolic association and a nexus for practical knowledge, since the behaviour of beavers is an indicator of changes in river flows.

As long-time systematic observers and modellers of hydrology and ecology in the Oldman River watershed, Blackfoot can contribute to our understanding of the ecology of water in this highly variable system. For example, we need very deep historical records of species' responses to fluctuations in moisture to estimate the *limits* of their adaptability. This knowledge could be particularly useful in forecasting the effects of impounding and redistributing water for irrigation or industry, and the effects of new patterns of climate change. Blackfoot knowledge of recent changes in *how* species respond to variations in moisture levels could tell us a great deal about the cumulative impacts of agriculture and industry on local ecosystems.

Conclusions

Indigenous science has much to contribute to contemporary efforts to conserve and benefit from biodiversity. Its contributions include models of ecosystem dynamics based on past observations, interactions, and modifications, as well as methods of observing and modelling that can complement Western tools and methods in future research. However, existing publications on indigenous knowledge frequently provide instead only a partial perspective. It is important to recognize that:

1 Indigenous knowledge systems can be highly specialized, and the commitment of time and effort required to get beyond elementary propositions can be considerable. This probably contributes to the impression, in published studies, that indigenous knowledge is relatively superficial or static.

2 Indigenous knowledge is not merely an accumulation of data, but includes models, theories, and methods that – in ecology – focus on behavioural processes rather than physical structures or the genetics and size of populations.

3 Indigenous knowledge is expressed in models that analogize to social relationships and interweave empirical findings as well as moral propositions. Outside observers often confuse the two levels of meaning or focus on the moral level.

4 Indigenous knowledge is verified through use, as evident in the survival of the community and in the reputations of specialized practitioners.

5 Preliminary confirmation of the reliability of indigenous models can be derived by reconstructing the history of their use.

Notes

1. Marc G. Stevenson, "Indigenous knowledge in environmental assessment," *Arctic* 49, 3 (1997): 278-91; Susan Wismer, "The nasty game: how environmental assessment is failing Aboriginal communities in Canada's North," *Alternatives* 22, 4 (1996): 10-17.

2. The following exchange is representative: Albert Howard and Frances Widdowson, "Traditional knowledge threatens environmental assessment," *Policy Options/Options Politiques* 17, 9 (1996): 34-36; Fikret Berkes and Thomas Henley, "Co-management and traditional knowledge: threat or opportunity?" ibid. 18, 2 (1997): 29-31; Marc G. Stevenson, "Ignorance and prejudice threaten environmental assessment," ibid. 18, 2 (1997): 25-28; Albert Howard and Frances Widdowson, "Traditional knowledge advocates weave a tangled web," ibid. 18, 3 (1997): 46-48.

3. Peter Arcese and A.R.E. Sinclair, "The role of protected areas as ecological baselines," *Journal of Wildlife Management* 61, 3 (1997): 587-602. Compare R.A. Lautenschlager, "Biodiversity is dead," *Wildlife Society Bulletin* 25, 3 (1997): 679-85.

4 . Michael A.D. Ferguson and François Messier, "Collection and analysis of traditional ecological knowledge about a population of Arctic Tundra caribou," *Arctic* 50, 1 (1997): 17-28. Observations made by different hunters were largely consistent with each other and with whatever historical records existed. Hunters *were* asked to speculate about the reasons for annual fluctuations in the size of caribou herds, but their answers – which might have revealed underlying ecological models – were not reported.

5. Niels W. Braroe, *Indian and White: Self-Image and Interaction in a Canadian Plains Community* (Stanford, Calif.: Stanford University Press, 1975).

6. On selective biological weapons, a key concern of indigenous peoples who have recently mobilized against the Human Genome Diversity Project, see Benno Muller-Hill, "The shadow of genetic injustice," *Nature* 362 (April 8, 1993): 491-92.

7. A further condition for the renewal of indigenous knowledge is some form of legal recognition of the rights of its traditional custodians. Indigenous and non-indigenous scholars agree that existing patent and copyright laws would be inadequate. See Stephen B. Brush and Doreen Stabinsky, *Valuing Local Knowledge: Indigenous People and Intellectual Property Rights* (Washington: Island Press, 1996); Darrell A. Posey and Graham Dutfield, *Beyond Intellectual Property: Toward Traditional Resource Rights for Indigenous Peoples and Local Communities* (Ottawa: International Development Research Centre, 1996); Rural Advancement Foundation International, *Conserving Indigenous Knowledge: Integrating Two Systems of Innovation* (New York: United Nations Development Program, 1994).

8. Fieldwork conducted in 1995 by Faye Morning Bull under an agreement with the Peigan Nation, which is sole proprietor of the data.

9. Selwyn Dewdney, *The Sacred Scrolls of the Southern Ojibway* (Toronto: University of Toronto Press, 1975); Hugh Brody, *Maps and Dreams: Indians and the British Columbia Frontie* (Vancouver: Douglas & McIntyre, 1988).

10. I make the distinction here between *models*, which describe how the world works, and *theories*, which attempt to explain models in terms of general laws.

11. There are wide differences in this regard between hunting peoples, particularly those who inhabit highly volatile ecosystems, and farming societies. The former tend to view the cosmos as more chaotic than the latter. The Blackfoot, described below, fall close to one end of this spectrum of cosmologies; the Pueblos of the American Southwest near the other. Alfonso Ortiz, *The Tewa World: Space, Time, Being, and Becoming in a Pueblo Society* (Chicago: University of Chicago Press, 1969).

12. See Philippe Descola, *In the Society of Nature: A Native Ecology in Amazonia*, trans. Nora Scott (Cambridge: Cambridge University Press, 1994), for an excellent study of the use of social relationships as a model of ecology among the Achuar of Ecuador.

13. The behavioural approach can be more efficient as well. For example, levels of physiological stress in caribou could be monitored through observation rather than by capturing and testing individual animals; Stevenson, "Indigenous knowledge."

14. Russel L. Barsh, "Fire on the land," *Alternatives Journal* 23, 4 (1997): 36-40.

15. There are certainly exceptions, such as Frans de Waal's *Chimpanzee Politics: Power and Sex Among Apes* (Baltimore: Johns Hopkins University Press, 1989).

16. Howard and Widdowson, "Tangled web," 47.

17. Compare G. Reichel-Dolmatoff, "Cosmology as ecological analysis: a view from the rain forest," *Man* 11, 3 (1976): 307-18, which shows how Tukano cosmology maps the flow of energy through the forest.

18. It is interesting that scientists still use the term "laws" to describe consistent patterns, since this implies the existence of a Creator by whose decree these patterns exist.

19. P.E. Stander, Ghau, D. Tsisaba, Oma, and Ui, "Tracking and the interpretation of spoor: a scientifically sound method in ecology," *Journal of Zoology* 242, 2 (1997): 329-41.

20. Paul S. Martin, "Prehistoric overkill: the global model," in Paul S. Martin and Richard G. Klein, eds., *Quaternary Extinctions: A Prehistoric Revolution* (Tucson: University of Arizona Press, 1984), 363.

21. Ibid., 370.

22. Ibid., 368. Charles E. Kay, "Aboriginal overkill: The role of Native Americans in structuring Western ecosystems," *Human Nature* 5, 4 (1994): 359-98, presents evidence that elk declined as a component of Native diets about 500 years ago, and argues that this was due to excessive hunting. If true, this undermines Martin's attempt to explain why elk *survived*.

23. Michael Alvard, "Intraspecific prey choice by Amazonian hunters," *Current Anthropology* 36, 5 (1995): 789-802.

24. The Piro did tend to target *larger* species (higher protein yields for the energy and materials invested in the hunt).

25. Russel Barsh, "Indigenous peoples' perspectives on population and development," *Boston College Environmental Affairs Law Review* 21, 2 (1994): 257-70. Alvard, "Intraspecific prey choice," 790, observes that a small group can sustain itself "in spite of the absence of any proactive conservation on their part," begging the question of why the group *remains* small.

26. Kent H. Redford and John G. Robinson, "The game of choice: Patterns of Indian and colonist hunting in the Neotropics," *American Anthropologist* 89, 4 (1987): 650-67.

27. My deep appreciation to Darryl Pard and Gerry Potts for sharing an overview of Blackfoot water philosophy with my colleagues and students as part of the development of our collaboration.

Further reading

Brush, Stephen B., and Doreen Stabinsky. *Valuing Local Knowledge: Indigenous People and Intellectual Property Rights*. Washington: Island Press, 1996.

Descola, Philippe. *In the Society of Nature: A Native Ecology in Amazonia*, trans. Nora Scott. Cambridge: Cambridge University Press, 1994.

Reed, Richard. *Forest Dwellers, Forest Protectors: Indigenous Models for International Development*. Boston: Allyn & Bacon, 1997.

Sillitoe, Paul. *Roots of the Earth: Crops in the Highlands of Papua New Guinea*. Manchester: Manchester University Press, 1983.

Stevens, Stan, ed. *Conservation through Cultural Survival: Indigenous Peoples and Protected Areas*. Washington: Island Press, 1997.

Williams, Nancy M., and Eugene S. Hunn, eds. *Resource Managers: North American and Australian Hunter-Gatherers*. Boulder, Colo.: Westview Press, 1982.

Richard K. Baydack   **Science and Biodiversity**

SCIENCE CAN BE THOUGHT OF AS KNOWLEDGE ACCUMULATED over time through systematic investigation. Essential to past developments, science will no doubt be a key to our future. People generally assume that science plays a critical role in biodiversity conservation, but how effectively does science fulfil this role? This chapter will consider this question in relation to one of the most significant conservation efforts ever attempted: the North American Waterfowl Management Plan.[1] The Plan, signed in 1986 by the governments of Canada and the United States, with Mexico becoming a full partner in 1994, is a co-operative international effort to reverse declines in waterfowl populations and their habitats.[2] As was acknowledged then in 1986, the major problem facing North American waterfowl was loss of their habitat:

> significant changes have occurred on the North American waterfowl scene. Large-scale alterations of the wetland and grassland habitat base by agriculture, urbanization, and industrial activities have affected the distribution and abundance of several species, resulting in new opportunities and problems. Although some goose populations have benefited from agricultural land use and protection afforded by expanding urban environments, most duck populations have not. Loss of nesting cover, wetland drainage, and degradation of migration and wintering habitat have contributed to long-term downward trends in some important duck populations.[3]

Prairie wetland:an essential habitat for migrating waterfowl

The goal of the NAWMP is to restore continental waterfowl populations to the levels of the mid-1970s. The 1986 Plan was updated in 1994, with a further revision planned for 1999. Approximately $1.5 billion U.S. were committed in 1986 to the Plan. The North American continent was subdivided into a number of joint ventures, which generally correspond to areas meeting certain seasonal requirements for waterfowl. Management occurs primarily at the joint venture level, with each federal government providing oversight and co-ordination. Unique partnerships have developed, involving various levels of government, the private sector, and local interests.[4]

Although the Plan originally focused on waterfowl, habitat management activities were implicitly seen as benefiting other species as well. In the 1994 Update, conservation of biodiversity and improved environmental quality were recognized as additional goals, and it was argued that the NAWMP "has made a substantial contribution to the conservation of biological diversity in addition to advancing waterfowl conservation," and was, therefore, one of the most clearly defined links in the chain of global programs that support biological diversity.[5]

The NAWMP raises significant issues concerning the relationship of science to biodiversity conservation. "Biodiversity" is a term that did not exist 20 years ago, but is now "one of the most commonly used expressions in the biological sciences."[6] Conservation of biodiversity is critical to the future of life on Earth, including humankind. But must biodiversity conservation be grounded in sound science — carefully controlled experiments described in enough detail to be replicable — in order for it to be legitimate? Is it possible to manage for biological diversity in the absence of scientific certainty?[7] Is it possible to have "good science" that is nevertheless uncertain? These questions are central to this chapter, which explores the relationship between science and biodiversity conservation, especially as seen in the North American Waterfowl Management Plan.

Definition and Focus

A first step in addressing the relationship of science to biodiversity conservation is the proper definition of terms. Some recent definitions of biodiversity include:

- the variety of life and its processes in a given area;

- the variety of and variability among living organisms and the ecological complexes of which they are part; this includes diversity within species, between species, and of ecosystems;

- the variability among living organisms from all sources including, inter alia, terrestrial, marine, and other aquatic ecosystems and the ecological complexes of which they are a part.[8]

There is no need for a single, "correct" definition of biodiversity; instead, those who use the term should select the definition most appropriate to their area of study.[9] However, terminology should also be carefully defined prior to initiating study and reporting findings. Strict application of appropriate definitions is essential to scientific credibility.

Within the North American Waterfowl Management Plan, however, definitions regarding biodiversity are often only implied, not specified. The 1986 Plan document suggested in several places that conservation of biodiversity would occur through various NAWMP activities, and by 1994, the Update had specified biodiversity conservation as a management goal. However, none of the major Plan documents actually define biodiversity, although references have been made to "other wetland-dependent wildlife."[10] More recently, the Plan has begun to feature the concept of biological diversity. All of the initial 1996 options, for example, assumed the Plan to be biodiversity-friendly, in the sense that habitat conservation projects are sensitive to the preservation of valuable ecological functions and endemic flora and fauna, as well as waterfowl. However, a closer reading of the options finds that they all relate primarily to avian species. Whether biodiversity conservation in the context of the NAWMP includes only avian species, wetland-dependent wildlife, or all wetland-dependent species has not been clarified. For the partners, the issue seemed to be not only the extent to which the Plan would actually address biodiversity conservation, but whether it would be publicly perceived to be doing so.[11]

Our Existing Knowledge

Our knowledge of biodiversity depends primarily on the work of three scientific disciplines: taxonomy, genetics, and ecology. The taxonomic classification of organisms into distinct biological classes (i.e., kingdom, phylum, class, order, family, genus, species) has allowed us to better understand and organize our thinking about life. Genetics has advanced our understanding of variety among populations, individuals, chromosomes, genes, and nucleotides. Ecology has provided us with an understanding of biomes, bioregions, landscapes, ecosystems, habitats, niches, and populations. Cultural diversity — human interactions with each of the above systems — must be considered in the conservation of biological diversity.[12] Future work in these disciplines will add to our understanding of biological diversity. But do we now have a sufficient database on which to build biodiversity concepts?

Humans have likely wondered about the diversity of life on earth for as long as we have inhabited the planet. Scientists began to classify life forms and develop the field of taxonomy as early as 400 BC. Since the eighteenth century, naturalists, such as Darwin, Humboldt, and Wallace, have discussed the relationship between organisms and their

photo: Jerry Valen DeMarco

environment, thus contributing to the early study of ecology. Mendel's experiments in the nineteenth century paved the way for the field of genetics.

While the science of biodiversity is, in a sense, centuries old, our current knowledge about the composition, distribution, abundance, and life histories of *most* plants and animals is incomplete, insufficient, unreliable, or non-existent.[13] Only for those groups most relevant to human concerns is our knowledge advancing. For the rest, we have thus far lived remarkably successfully with ignorance. But there is no shortcut: if we are to protect and conserve the complete array of bio-diversity found in our world, we must expand our knowledge beyond those species and ecosystems on which we depend directly.[14] What should our priorities be? On which organisms, and in which ecosystems? The study of biodiversity is revealing surprises and uniqueness, which suggests to some that predictive methods used heretofore, such as indicator species or the mapping of hotspots (areas especially rich in biodiversity), are of limited value. But if we claim that the study of bio-diversity is a "science," how do we deal with the incompleteness of our database?

Measurement of biological diversity must be carried out with careful attention to the uniqueness of particular habitats and species. Biodiversity is not a standardized, quantifiable entity, easily compared from location to location; and there is no universal "yardstick" by which success in its conservation can be measured.[15] One option is to engage a variety of indicator variables, applied at four levels of biological organization (regional landscape, community-ecosystem, population-species, and genetic), and including compositional, structural, and functional components. Specific indicators could encompass, for example: distribution, richness, and proportions of habitat types in a regional landscape; biomass and resource productivity in a community or ecosystem; population structure including sex and age ratios in a population; or allelic diversity in a genetic sample.[16] The variables to be measured must be appropriate to the objectives of a study. Hypothesis testing should be built into the work wherever possible, and careful attention to data collection and analysis is essential.

Within the North American Waterfowl Management Plan, measurement of biological diversity is somewhat problematic. This appears largely to be the result of an inconsistent database, which is reasonably strong for waterfowl, but terribly weak for other components of wetland ecosystems. For waterfowl populations, the Plan has clearly documented specific objectives for continental populations of ducks, geese, and swans, based upon levels of occurrence in the mid-70s.[17] Although these estimates may have considerable uncertainty,[18] their utility in establishing general goals for Plan partners is relatively clear. However, it is more difficult if not impossible to identify how large a population of each species each region (or "joint venture") will supply so as to achieve the continental goal. Similarly, the relationship between waterfowl-production goals and wintering areas has not been clearly established.[19] Nor has the specific amount of habitat needed in both production and wintering areas to achieve waterfowl population goals been precisely estimated.[20]

When the concept of biodiversity is expanded to include other species, the Plan encounters significantly greater difficulties. No objectives have been developed for non-waterfowl, wetland-dependent wildlife. This is partly due to the lack of definitive data. As a result, success for other species will have to depend on how accurately and comprehensively waterfowl serve as indicators of healthy wetland ecosystems.[21] In addition, the 1998 Update process has apparently restricted consideration of biodiversity to avian species.[22] To attempt to measure the Plan's success in conserving biological diversity in the myriad of wetland ecosystems across North America would be difficult indeed.

Science and Management

The application of science within a plan like the NAWMP raises difficult questions. Our knowledge base is incomplete, and yet management initiatives must continue. For example, Prairie Habitat Joint Venture programs were required to meet their objectives even before there was complete understanding of the systems to be managed.[23] How, then, should limited financial resources be allocated: how much should go to expanding our scientific knowledge base and how much to applying the knowledge that we already possess?

Such questions are essentially political: they are questions of assigning value. In selecting among competing alternatives, a decision-maker must compare and judge values. However, science does not consider values, but facts: organized, tested, and accepted knowledge.[24] While the *study* of biodiversity is a scientific matter, biodiversity *management* entails value judgements. Biodiversity management could be described, therefore, as the practice of using available scientific knowledge to achieve the goals of society with respect to biodiversity.

Many of these considerations hold true for the North American Waterfowl Management Plan. The word "management" within its title reflects a general direction and focus, although its construction and evaluation have by and large been directed by science. The Plan has been relatively well funded, although there is now more concern regarding support for future initiatives.[25] Decisions within the Plan often reflect non-scientific priorities. For example, while distribution of Plan funds to all areas of North America can be justified in terms of political priorities, biological realities considered alone would imply concentration of efforts in prairie breeding areas.[26] It would be appropriate, therefore, for Plan partners to specify which decisions are based on science and which are not. This would not only help to justify decisions, but would indicate to interested parties that various decisions are based on differing values.

Adaptive Resource Management

Recently, attempts have been made to better integrate science into the management process, through adaptive resource management (ARM).[27] The ARM concept was developed in the late 1970s by scientists at the University of British Columbia. The concept addresses the dual goals of achieving management objectives while at the same time gaining reliable knowledge.[28] It suggests that because knowledge of our natural world is imperfect, managers must "learn while doing" through "management by experiment."[29] Essentially, ARM seeks to address the sometimes conflicting objectives of researchers and managers:

> Researchers typically argue that management should not be undertaken until more is known, yet they seldom seem to agree about what is enough. Managers, on the other hand, typically respond based on their intuition and experience, and pressed to solve a problem before it worsens, contend that enough is known to proceed with management. To make matters worse, when the need for quick action is perceived, solutions may be implemented in ways that make it difficult to evaluate whether management is successful, and if not, why not. Adaptive management offers a potential solution to these dilemmas by encouraging research and management to be conducted simultaneously as one coordinated endeavor which should reduce uncertainty and improve management.[30]

The ARM concept, of managing while learning about the species or system being managed, has considerable appeal. Research results could be used to identify additional management alternatives and options. The ARM approach has been used, for example, in forest management, and its application within NAWMP has also been suggested.[31] Overall, ARM is leading to improved scientific undertakings in the study of biological diversity, by making it possible for research to be modified on the basis of practical experience.

However, adaptive management may have pitfalls. The great complexity of systems being managed is one confounding problem, as it is in any management approach.[32] Lack of controls over biological as well as social, economic, and political parameters can also restrict management options.[33] A further problem is that the "best available science" is seldom used in ARM; instead, conventional wisdom and anecdotal information seem to be more often used in designing alternative management scenarios.[34]

Use of the ARM approach in the North American Waterfowl Management Plan would require managers to adhere to a set of principles to assist them in evaluating whether their programs were achieving the desired outcomes. (1) The goals of management must be explicit and agreed to by those doing the assessment. (2) There must be a finite and succinct list of alternative management actions or policies. (3) The manager must be able to express biological uncertainties in terms of alternative hypotheses about how the managed system works.

Perhaps the greatest value of this type of analysis would be that it forces managers to think critically about what is involved in making decisions in the face of limited biological information. Even qualitative assessments can have value in structuring a problem and producing a shared perception of the issues. The challenge is that, in practice, as one author has noted, "managers must go where scientists fear to tread."[35]

Future Innovations and Research Needs

The study of biological diversity must be grounded in science. The application of science to biodiversity management should also adhere to scientific standards wherever possible. A pressing need in biodiversity study is enhanced communication and the sharing of research results. This is essential in such a fast-paced, evolving, and dynamic area of biological research. Communication should be encouraged by governments and the private sector; university departments might also be contracted to serve as disseminators of an advancing knowledge base. Internet-based or computerized databases could allow access to up-to-date information. An annual conference or workshop would encourage communication of research findings among diverse interests. Within the NAWMP, for example, habitat managers need immediately information collected from the Prairie Habitat Joint Venture Assessment Program, so as to improve their program implementation. The NAWMP could also serve as a model of information exchange through annual workshops or by integrating research seminars into a major conference. The Wildlife Society Annual Conference would provide an ideal opportunity for such an activity, thereby ensuring that each joint venture area could access information in a timely fashion.

Financial support of scientific investigation should be a priority. Long-term data collection, an essential ingredient of success, should be funded adequately. Partnerships may be needed to obtain sufficient financial support for research. One example of a partnership is the Prairie Habitat Joint Venture Assessment Program, a long-term research undertaking designed to add credible scientific knowledge to our waterfowl management database.[36] The need for combined efforts in research and management will continue. The North American Waterfowl Management Plan administrative structure could serve as an example of how evaluations can be done in tandem with regional and local management programs, enhancing the effectiveness of management in the absence of scientific certainty.[37]

The use of management activities to test hypotheses, and thereby to add to our knowledge of ecological systems (a basic element of adaptive resource management) has often been suggested as a means of improving the use of science in management. Much of the management philosophy of the NAWMP has adhered to ARM principles, and their continued application will provide valuable lessons to managers and scientists both within and outside the plan. Within the Prairie Habitat Joint Venture a number of investigations have been outlined that can demonstrate hypothesis testing, adaptive management, and a combination of the two, to better our understanding of waterfowl ecology and management.[38]

Finally, it must be recognized that action on biodiversity conservation cannot wait for complete scientific knowledge. Our knowledge base will not reach those lofty heights for some time.[39] Does this mean we must delay our management efforts? On the contrary. We should adhere to the principles of ARM, ensuring that management decisions are treated as experiments that will lead to an ever-expanding knowledge base. In this the North American Waterfowl Management Plan can continue to play a key role.

Notes

1. NAWMP, *North American Waterfowl Management Plan* (Washington: U.S. Department of the Interior, Fish and Wildlife Service; Ottawa: Environment Canada, Canadian Wildlife Service, 1986).

2. NAWMP, *Update to the North American Waterfowl Management Plan* (Washington: U.S. Department of the Interior; Ottawa: Environment Canada; Mexico City: Desarrollo Social Mexico, 1994).

3. NAWMP, *Waterfowl Management Plan*, 1986, 1.

4. T.G. Nerassen and J.W. Nelson, "Landscape planning and management in agro-ecosystems: the Canadian prairie experience," in: R.K. Baydack et al., eds., *Practical Approaches to the Conservation of Biological Diversity* (Washington: Island Press, 1999), 141-66.

5. NAWMP, *Update*.

6. E.O. Wilson, "Introduction to Biodiversity II," in M.J. Reaka-Kudla, D.E. Wilson, and Wilson, eds., *Biodiversity II: Understanding and Protecting Our Biological Resources* (Washington: Joseph Henry Press, 1997), 1-3.

7. D.A. Trauger, "Can we manage for biological diversity in the absence of scientific certainty?" in Baydack et al., eds., *Practical Approaches*, 195-202.

8. H. Salwasser, "Conserving biological diversity: a perspective on scope and approaches," *Forest Ecology and Management* 35 (1990): 75-90; United Nations Environment Program, "Fourth revised draft convention on biological diversity," 1991; Environment Canada, *The Canadian Biodiversity Strategy* (Ottawa: Environment Canada, 1996).

9. G. Skiba, "Are definitions really important?" *Biological Diversity Working Group Newsletter*, May 1994, 3. R.K. Baydack and H. Campa III, "Setting the context," in Baydack et al., eds., *Practical Approaches*, 3-16, provide a summary of 18 common definitions for biodiversity and trace their development during the recent past.

10. D. Sharp et al., *Evaluation Strategy for the North American Waterfowl Management Plan* (Washington: Continental Evaluation Team, 1992).

11. NAWMP, *Preparing for the 1998 Update: A Bridge to the Future* (Washington: North American Waterfowl Management Plan Update Working Group, 1996).

12. V.E. Heywood, ed., *Global Biodiversity Assessment* (New York: United Nations Environment Program, Cambridge University Press, 1995), estimates that at least 20 different fields of biological study have contributed to our understanding of biodiversity, as well as other fields in the sociocultural area.

13. N.L. Christensen et al., "The report of the Ecological Society of America committee on the scientific basis for ecosystem management," *Ecological Applications* 6 (1996): 665-91.

14. Heywood, *Global Biodiversity Assessment*.

15. Baydack and Campa, "Setting the context"; R.K. Baydack, "Why is measurement of biodiversity and ecosystem sustainability important?" Proceedings of The Wildlife Society Third Annual Conference, Cincinnati, October 1-5, 1997.

16. R.F. Noss, "Indicators for monitoring biodiversity: a hierarchical approach," *Conservation Biology* 4 (1990): 355-64.

17. NAWMP, *Update*.

18. F.A. Johnson et al., "Enhancing biological performance of the North American Waterfowl Management Plan," *Transactions of the North American Wildlife and Natural Resources Conference* 62 (1997): 377-85.

19. M.G. Anderson et al., "NAWMP evaluations: how can we generate the feedback that Plan partners need?" in J.T. Ratti, ed., *Proceedings of the 7th International Waterfowl Symposium* (Memphis: Ducks Unlimited, 1996), 250-57; M.G. Anderson et al., *Annual Report of the Continental Evaluation Team to the North American Waterfowl Management Plan Committee* (Washington: NAWMP Implementation Office, 1996).

20. Johnson et al., "Enhancing biological performance."

21. Sharp et al., *Evaluation Strategy*.

22. NAWMP, *Update*. This was apparently done for greater ease of understanding.

23. R.G. Clark and A.W. Diamond, "Restoring upland habitats in the Canadian prairies: lost opportunity or management by design?" *Transactions of the North American Wildlife and Natural Resources Conference* 58 (1993): 551-64.

24. J.A. Bailey, *Principles of Wildlife Management* (Toronto: Wiley, 1994).

25. NAWMP, *Update*.

26. Anderson et al., *Annual Report*.

27. T.E. Nudds, "Adaptive management and the conservation of biodiversity," in Baydack et al., eds., *Practical Approaches*, 179-93.

28. C.J. Walters, *Adaptive Management of Renewable Resources* (New York: Macmillan, 1986); R.A. Lancia et al., "ARM! For the future: adaptive resource management in the wildlife profession," *Wildlife Society Bulletin* 24 (1996): 436-42.

29. Nudds, "Adaptive management"; J. Macnab, "Wildlife management as scientific experimentation," *Wildlife Society Bulletin* 11 (1983): 397-401.
30. Lancia et al., "ARM! For the Future," 439.
31. Nudds, "Adaptive management," provides contrasting examples of how this approach has been used to determine effects of forest management activities in Alberta, Ontario, and Missouri. Clark and Diamond, "Restoring upland habitats," and Johnson et al., "Enhancing biological performance," have suggested how evaluation activities of the NAWMP can use the adaptive management approach in enhancing waterfowl habitat management decisions in prairie Canada.
32. J.W. Thomas, "Crossroads of science, policy, and conservation," Proceedings of The Wildlife Society First Annual Conference, Albuquerque, September 20-25, 1994.
33. D.M. Ehrenfeld, "The management of diversity: a conservation paradox," in F.H. Bormann and S.R. Kellert, eds., *Ecology, Economics, Ethics: The Broken Circle* (New Haven: Yale University Press, 1991), 26-39.
34. Trauger, "Scientific certainty?" in Baydack et al., eds., *Practical Approaches.*
35. R. Hilborn, "Can fisheries agencies learn from experience?" *Fisheries* 17 (1992): 6-14; With regard to the NAWMP, for example, Clark and Diamond, "Restoring upland habitats," suggest a variety of options that managers should consider in designing treatment options for waterfowl habitat development.
36. Anderson et al., "NAWMP evaluations."
37. Johnson et al., "Enhancing biological performance."
38. Clark and Diamond, "Restoring upland habitats."
39. Christensen et al., "The report."

Further reading

Baydack, R.K., H. Campa III, and J.B. Haufler, eds. *Practical Approaches to the Conservation of Biological Diversity.* Washington: Island Press, 1999.
Heywood, V.E., ed. *Global Biodiversity Assessment.* New York: United Nations Environment Program and Cambridge University Press, 1995.
Reaka-Kudla, M.J., D.E. Wilson, and E.O. Wilson, eds. *Biodiversity II: Understanding and Protecting Our Biological Resources.* Washington: Joseph Henry Press, 1997.
Walters, C.J. *Adaptive Management of Renewable Resources.* New York: Macmillan, 1986.

Nina-Marie E. Lister
and James J. Kay

Celebrating Diversity:
Adaptive Planning and
Biodiversity Conservation

W E ARE ONLY NOW BECOMING AWARE OF THE COMPLEXITY AND surprising dynamics of the living environment. The paradox of biodiversity science is that the more knowledge we acquire, the more uncertainty we encounter – which renders planning for conservation a sticky business indeed.

Biodiversity conservation in Canada is being undertaken by all levels of government, and by many non-government organizations, such as the Nature Conservancy of Canada, the Federation of Ontario Naturalists, and the Evergreen Foundation. The primary means of protecting biodiversity are *in situ* methods – that is, in their natural setting, in protected areas. Indeed, most conservation initiatives worldwide are based on protected areas, set aside because of natural heritage or economic resource values, or to protect species classified as endangered, threatened, vulnerable, or rare. In Canada, most protected areas are found within national and provincial parks systems. Local Environmentally Significant Areas, Ecological Reserves, Areas of Natural and Scientific Interest, Conservation Areas, and several World Biosphere Reserves also form part of the public protected areas network. However, the degree of biodiversity conservation depends largely on the definition of "protection" afforded by each type of area.

There are three key problems with this current approach. First, it does not generally reflect emerging scientific perspectives on ecosystems as complex and uncertain, and in which certain kinds of change are inevitable and normal. Second, values for biodiversity often are hidden within the decision-making process. Third, conservation planning remains largely dominated by expert-led, prescriptive, regulatory methods that rely almost entirely on publicly funded parks and protected areas. More creative approaches are needed if Canadians are to meet their national and international commitments to biodiversity protection.[1]

This chapter will consider an emerging approach, known as adaptive planning and management – an approach characterized by flexibility in learning through change, by the integration of science with values, and by resilience through the use of a diversity of innovative tools, methods, and perspectives. A case study of the Huron Natural Area in southwestern Ontario will demonstrate a practical application of this approach.

Becoming Flexible: Embracing Uncertainty and Complexity in Ecosystems

Until recently, most ecologists believed that ecosystems follow a linear path of development towards a particular, biologically diverse, and stable "climax" state. However, within the past 15 years, research has shown this view to be incomplete.[2] While ecosystems do generally develop from simple to more diverse, complex states, they may develop along any of many possible paths and states, or even flip suddenly into entirely new states. Ecosystems are cyclic and dynamic systems, marked by often sudden, unpredictable change.[3] Diversity, complexity, and uncertainty are normal, and we cannot predict exactly how or when ecosystems will change.

These insights are not yet reflected in biodiversity policy and planning, which continue to be based on the assumption that more knowledge leads to certainty, and therefore, predictability.[4] While this is generally true in certain deterministic science and engineering applications (such as mechanical physics and transportation engineering), it is not the case with complex living systems. Given what we are learning about ecosystem complexity and dynamics, it is clear that we cannot predict how ecosystems will evolve, change, and behave because they are such complex systems and, as such, inherently unpredictable. Of course, this does not mean we should entirely give up trying to plan and manage. Rather, we must accept and embrace change as a normal part of life.[5]

Insights from science should be fundamental to adaptive planning. This requires closer links between ecological science and conservation. Three strategies for doing this are to: (1) broaden the scientific basis of conservation to include all scales of biodiversity, not just species; (2) stop relying on the assumption that biodiversity makes ecosystems stable, and instead note the important ecological roles played by biodiversity; and (3) link conservation policies to experimentation, action research, and learning by doing.

Beyond Species

Biodiversity exists at all levels of the ecological hierarchy: from genes, to species, populations, communities, landscapes, and eventually biomes or whole ecosystems. Furthermore, biodiversity varies according to ecosystem perspective (or "type"), and the associated organizing process. For example, the organizing process for watersheds is water flow; for foodwebs it is nutrient and energy flows; and for species, it is reproduction. The notion of biodiversity as hierarchical is well established among ecologists and is integral to their newer work in ecosystem ecology. The implication of this view is that what happens on one level will not necessarily occur at another.[6] For example, loss or addition of a species may not affect the diversity of communities within a landscape, or the diversity of a foodweb, but clearly affects species diversity. Planning and management must, therefore, target the appropriate ecosystem scale and perspective, and must be supported by scientific investigation done at a relevant level. Thus, research on individual species may not be applicable to management of communities, foodwebs, or entire landscapes. By the same token research into ecological communities or landscapes may not provide much direct insight into species diversity issues. Yet all these forms of diversity are important.

Most conservation plans and policies have tended to focus on species,[7] likely because species are the most tangible, visible aspects of biodiversity. They are comparatively easy to measure, and much more research has been done on them than on other aspects of biodiversity. Many species also have a good deal of public appeal and can help "sell" conservation. This is particularly evident with large mammals such as bears, big cats, or caribou. The World Wildlife Fund, for example, has long known that people are more likely to open their hearts (and wallets) to conservation for the sake of cuddly bears or beautiful birds.

It also is widely believed that by protecting the habitat of the largest, longest-living, or most ecologically important ("keystone") species other species also will be protected.[8] However, this "umbrella" assumption often leads to habitat protection that does not always result in the target species being conserved.[9]

Ecologists do not all agree on the importance of particular species to ecosystems. Some argue that all species play significant roles, and that it would be a serious mistake to conserve only those species considered most critical. Others, however, suggest that most species are redundant, and only a fraction of them are critical to ecosystem structure and function.[10] These contrasting views leave planners with a conundrum: ecosystems may collapse before it is known which species are expendable.

This debate over the role of species in ecosystems is the product of a misguided search for simple rules to describe complex systems. To ask "which species play which role" is the wrong question. It assumes the system is static, and that the relationships between species is static. In an ecosystem that is constantly reorganising and evolving, so, too, are the relationships and roles of species. At one time a species may be crucial, but at other times appear unimportant. For example, after a disturbance in a forest such as a wind storm or fire, some species are crucial to the recovery process, but these same species may play apparently little role in a mature forest. Any species will appear to be essential or redundant, depending on the ecosystem, scale, perspective, and reorganizational state in which it is considered. It is not a matter of "either/or" but "when" species play particular functional roles.[11]

Species represent merely one aspect of biodiversity. A focus on them provides an insufficient basis for effective conservation policy. We don't even know the total number of species on earth, and this makes it difficult, if not impossible, to determine how much biodiversity loss has occurred, whether as a result of human activities, or of natural processes.[12] Instead of focusing narrowly on species, we would strengthen biodiversity policy by embracing a wider, more complex view– one that encompasses the many roles of biodiversity in ecosystems, at all scales and perspectives, and according to overall system function. In this way, biodiversity conservation may be more tightly linked with our new understanding of ecosystems.

The Problem of Stability

It has long been assumed that there is an inherent "balance" or stability in nature, which biodiversity helps to maintain. This, it has been suggested, is a strong argument for conserving biodiversity.[13] Many policies have been based, at least in part, on this assumption (for example, protected areas and parks management plans). However, this notion of stability is difficult to defend in scientific terms.[14] Even defining what is *meant* by "stability" is difficult – living systems experience many fluctuations, such as in the weather, populations, biomass, and so on.[15] The lack of a single, accepted definition for stability is also confusing and frustrating for policy-makers and planners.

More recent ecological ideas, based in part on complex "systems science," provide a revised perspective of living systems, in which the idea of a single "stable" state is replaced with that of a "shifting steady-state mosaic." In a forest, for example, there are different patches of forest, each of which is a different age. Each patch will grow to maturity and then fire, wind storm, pest outbreak, or some other disturbance will cause the trees in the patch to fall over and growth to start again. This process goes on in each patch on the landscape, so that at any given moment different parts of the landscape will be at every possible age. Which pieces are at a particular age changes with time. Hence, the mosaic of maturities is shifting constantly over the landscape, even though the landscape remains a forest.[16]

Ecosystems actually have multiple possible operating states, and may shift or diverge suddenly from any one of them. For example, in the Huron Natural Area case study, considered later in this chapter, part of the natural area is a closed, soft-maple swamp in a wetland community. However, changing flows of water can radically alter this state. Drying events, such as an extended drought, could change it to an upland forest community or grassland. If, in contrast, extended periods of flooding cause high water levels, it would become a marsh ecosystem. Red and silver maples will tolerate floods lasting as long as 30 per cent to 40 per cent of the growing season. Longer than this, and the trees will die, giving way to more water-tolerant herbaceous marsh vegetation. The feedback mechanism that maintains the swamp state is evapotranspiration (i.e., water pumping) by the trees. Too much water overwhelms the pumping capability of the trees and not enough shuts it down. The point is that the current state of the ecosystem is a function of its physical environment and the accidents of its history. Each of these three ecosystem states is, so far as we know, as ecologically healthy and appropriate as the others. There is no one "right" community for this landscape.

Ecosystems may even literally flip into a new state. These flips have been identified in the Great Lakes, where the dominant ecosystem moves from a benthic to a pelagic state quite suddenly. Change in an ecosystem as a result of natural catastrophe, such as fire, pest outbreak, or human-induced perturbation, is a normal and usually cyclic event.[17] We must infer that the ability of ecosystems to recover, reorganize, and adapt in the face of regular change, rather than stability, is critical to their survival.

Biodiversity is vital to ecosystems in this context: it is the basis of *resilience*, that is, the ability of an ecosystem to buffer itself from being pushed into another state, and also its ability to regenerate itself following a shift or other disturbance. Biodiversity could be considered as analogous to a library of information (some recorded long ago, and some only now being written), that provides not only a wide range of possible pathways for the future development of life, but learned repertoires for responding to environmental change and disturbance.[18]

Figure 1 depicts a modified version of Holling's dynamic cycle of ecosystem development. Living systems evolve discontinuously and intermittently. Following a sudden disturbance, an ecosystem reorganizes to "renew" itself or regenerate to a similar or perhaps different state. Immediately after a disturbance, biodiversity at many scales is critical: the abundance, distribution, and diversity of an ecosystem's

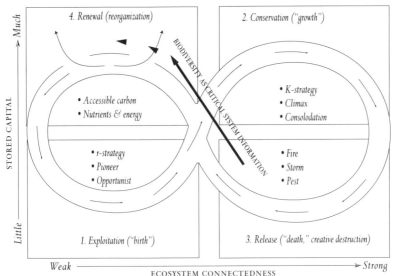

Figure 1:
Ecosystem Dynamics:
Holling's Modified
Figure Eight.

Source: C. S. Holling, "The Resilience of the Terestrial Ecosystem: Local Surprise and Global Change," in W. C. Clark and R. E. Munn, Eds., *Sustainable Development of the Biosphere* (Cambridge: Cambridge University Press, 1986)

structures (e.g., species) and functions (e.g., nutrient cycling) determine its ability to regenerate and reorganize itself, and establish its future pathway.

Biodiversity is vital to the normal, healthy functioning of ecosystems because the information it contains and the functions it serves constitute the key elements that determine how an ecosystem will self-organize. In effect, biodiversity forms the palette of future possibilities for an ecosystem.[19] The notion of biodiversity as an essential basis for ecosystem resilience provides a more powerful premise for conservation policy than does stability, and ultimately, a more robust basis for conservation plans.

Learning By Doing

This view of ecosystems as open, dynamic, complex, and uncertain (i.e., inherently unpredictable) has significant implications for conservation. We can never determine with precision the consequences of our actions. In effect, "environmental management" is an oxymoron, because we can never truly "manage" living systems.[20] What we can do is refocus our energies on those human activities that provide the context for the self-organizing processes in ecosystems.[21] This implies a profound change in environmental planning and management.

If uncertainty and regular change are inevitable, then we must learn to be flexible and adaptable.[22] But what does this mean in practice? Recalling the importance of multiple perspectives at various ecosystem scales, one of the first steps towards flexible adaptive planning is to use a diversity of approaches to conservation. This means emphasizing the small-scale, the experimental, and the action-oriented. Ecosystems may change in any number of possible ways, and so there may be an indefinite number of possibilities for conservation. Effective conservation planning, then, requires a diversity of tools, techniques, and methods.[23] Learning becomes a central goal, leading to continual improvement in planning and management – in short, to adaptation.

In conservation, we should consider demonstration projects that emphasise "learning-by-doing."[24] Such projects should be small enough that if they are not successful, they can fail "safely," without endangering an entire ecosystem, watershed, or habitat. Mistakes may provide experience that can be used in the future. Thus, the "surprising" nature of ecosystems can be turned into a learning opportunity rather than a liability. As Kai Lee observes, "experiments often bring surprises, but if resource management is recognized to be inherently uncertain, the surprises become opportunities to learn rather than failures to predict."[25]

Of course, conservation policies and plans must still be rooted in science, drawing on new knowledge in conservation biology, ecosystem, and landscape ecology.[26] But adaptive planning must also proceed on a broader scale, linked to experience as well as to research. Learning through experimentation and action also requires field-trained specialists, and more expertise and research in systematics and taxonomy – neither of which can be provided at present by Canadian universities. Conservationists and ecologists agree that conservation management and research needs more "boots not suits," and a stronger connection between knowledge and action.

There are significant barriers to learning through action. Planners and managers are not usually rewarded for perceived failure, no matter what lessons were learned. Being open, flexible, and adaptive to change often is discouraged.[27] We need, instead, to reward learning, so that decision-makers will be encouraged to experiment, to collaborate in sharing results, to learn from experience, and, overall, to be responsive to change.[28] Rewarding, rather than punishing, honest mistakes can help link knowledge and action. Trial and error is, after all, one way that humans learn.

"Learning by doing" means profound changes to our tradition of planning and management. It still is widely assumed that with enough research and knowledge, nature can be predicted and thereby controlled. But new insights from ecosystem ecology and complex-systems theory have shown that this is not how the "real world" actually works. If ecosystems are indeed dynamic, diverse, open to surprising and sudden change, then nature is not under our control. Adaptation and flexibility becomes essential. We must learn to live with nature. We must learn to look to multiple perspectives and values, at different scales and in different contexts if we wish to successfully manage our interactions within nature.

Integrating Science and Values: Beyond Prescriptive Planning

Sustainable development is about making choices, from the perspective of what we know about the limits to growth and the need for equity. As an integral component of sustainable development, biodiversity conservation incorporates aspects of both science and politics. Ecological realities can be determined to some extent through scientific inquiry and learned experience, but in a complex world, this knowledge illuminates not "solutions" but choices and trade-offs, the selection of which is driven by values.

Decision-making for biodiversity today relies largely on science to determine these choices, and rarely considers values explicitly. While it is widely acknowledged that biodiversity embraces a vibrant suite of social, economic, and spiritual, as well as non-human, biocentric values, we do not yet make real use of this rich texture of meanings in our conservation policies and plans.

The dominant reason for this is that much of institutionalized planning is rooted in a scientism known as the "rational-comprehensive approach." This approach is modelled on the scientific method and advocates objective decision-making. Planning is seen as a top-down, expert-driven, rational activity, relying on management through control.[29] But as we know through ecosystem research, biodiversity cannot be managed through prediction and control. In addition, in its social, cultural, economic, and political dimensions, biodiversity is very much about values, and this must be reflected in its management and conservation. The domains of science and values must, therefore, be integrated within conservation.

One way to begin integrating values into planning is through the use of visioning. Visioning is a planning tool, one of several now being used by many cities across Canada to generate consensus through shared perceptions of a desirable future.[30] It may also be a useful tool for integrating biodiversity values into conservation planning. Adaptive planning that integrates values and science (through visioning or another collaborative forum) is essentially a design process through which we collectively evaluate and decide which of many futures we wish to steer ourselves towards, through choices, trade-offs, trial and error, learning by doing, and flexible management.

The HNA Case Study

The Huron Natural Area (HNA), in Kitchener, Ontario, provides a useful case study of adaptive planning and management for conservation.[31] Like much of southwestern Ontario, the Kitchener area has undergone extensive urbanization. This has resulted in a fragmented, patchwork landscape. Much of the Kitchener area is comprised of upland, maple-beech (*Acer spp.* and *Fagus spp.*) forest remnants.

The Huron Natural Area is about 150 hectares, bounded by major roadways and a business park. Strasburg Creek, a stream supporting a population of brook trout (*Salvelinus fontinalis*), flows through the site. A provincially designated Class I wetland known as the Central Wetlands forms the eastern boundary of the area. The HNA is part of the Grand River Watershed, which, in turn, drains into Lake Erie. It was originally settled and much of it cleared and farmed in the late eighteenth and early nineteenth centuries. In the post-war years, much of the land was taken out of agricultural production and converted to industrial and residential uses. The site itself was largely abandoned during this period, although some restoration work, in the form of plantations and wetlands, was done during the 1940s. It had been considered for development of a suburban, commercial business park, but during the planning process its ecological diversity and potential as a park became evident.

The site contains a variety of ecological features, including pine plantations (*Pinus resinosa* and *Pinus strobus*), mature maple-beech forests (*Acer saccharum* and *Fagus grandifolia* dominating), old farm fields, ponds, a dry marsh, varied topography, and ground water recharge areas critical to Strasburg Creek. There are 14 different vegetation zones with 276 plant species, as well as a variety of glacial landforms. Overall, these features indicate an opportunity to retain an important example of the diverse landscape that once characterized much of southwestern Ontario. The city of Kitchener, in co-operation with local school boards, made a commitment in 1991 to preserve this area.

During the early 1990s, consultants identified the area's conservation and educational potential, university researchers examined its ecological processes, and the area was rezoned. The HNA was also incorporated with a Board of Directors and a formal partnership agreement was signed between the city and the two school boards. Adjacent land identified as essential to the integrity of the HNA is now being acquired. In 1995 a Master Planning Committee was struck and collaborative planning began. Figure 2 provides an example of a planning model being followed by the HNA Master Planning Committee. The team is essentially a partnership, with representatives from each relevant profession, science, and community interest. The Master Plan is being generated through collaboration between the team, the clients (Board of Directors), and the community of users.

The goal of the HNA Project was derived from the vision statements of participants at a Visioning Workshop held in 1995. The participants included representatives of the Steering, Citizens', Technical, and Master Planning Committees. A Citizens' Advisory Committee was established to assist with stewardship initiatives and implementing the plan.[12] The goal can be encapsulated in the stakeholders' statement: "Using our definition of ecological integrity,[13] we want to develop an

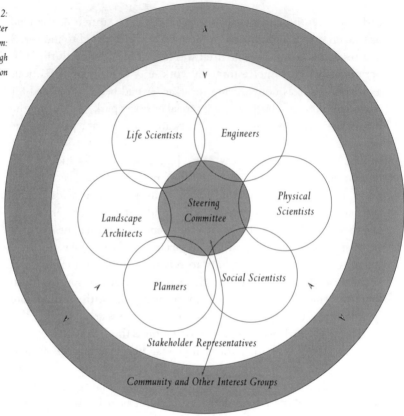

ecosystem-based management approach and complementary monitoring program which allow us to use the site sustainably while maintaining the valued ecosystem features."

Within the context of this goal, there are three key objectives: (1) to
promote an awareness of natural ecosystems as functioning, dynamic
entities; (2) to improve links between ecosystem science and municipal
land management decision-making within the Region of Kitchener-
Waterloo; and (3) to use the information gathered through the monitoring program to inform the planning and management process on a
continuing basis. These objectives will be promoted through a series of
demonstration projects within the HNA, as well as conservation and
educational activities at local schools and universities.

A variety of studies have been undertaken over the past seven years

photo: R. Shipley

on the ecosystem's abiotic, biotic, cultural, and energetic features.[34] The abiotic features include climate and hydrology; biotic features include wildlife communities as well as individual species and populations; cultural features include human use of the area and its cultural and heritage value; and ecosystem energetics include flows of energy and nutrients. These principles have been examined at a variety of scales, ranging from the Strasburg Creek sub-watershed to the Great Lakes Basin. Next steps will include ecological study, and results of preliminary monitoring data will be used to construct possible future ecosystem scenarios, which will be used to identify planning options, with the guidance of stakeholders and community participants.

At present, ecological study indicates two possible ecosystem states that now coexist, but are not likely to persist. The first supports a slow-moving, low-oxygen, warm-water stream interrupted by ponds and small wetlands, in which beaver (*Castor canadensis*) and muskrat (*Ondatra zibethicus*) shape and maintain the habitat and its communities. Several factors are shifting the ecosystem towards this state: the resident population of beaver, invading purple loosestrife (*Lythrum salicaria*), and nutrient-rich runoff from nearby agricultural areas, which depletes oxygen in the stream. The competing state is a fast-moving, highly oxygenated cold-water stream in which brook trout thrive. The latter state is perceived to be highly desirable, but likely would require intensive management to maintain.

In setting their goal and objectives for the area, the stakeholders have indicated a desire to protect a wide range of biodiversity, including both brook trout in the creek and the beaver ponds. But this may not be feasible, as the two populations belong to potentially mutually exclusive ecosystem states. A difficult choice may have to be made, in favour of one population over the other. In making this choice, the values of stakeholders and community members will play an essential role. This exemplifies the role of value judgements in making choices, for example, beaver versus trout.[35]

Clearly, developing a conservation management plan must be an iterative process, wherein information gained through ecological research and modeling feed into the planning process, and the results from this process feed back into model and scenario development, or perhaps into new goals based on changing values. This process continues until an acceptable ecosystem function and performance is observed. Ideally, the adaptive planning process will be used over the long-term, as the management of the HNA is continuously adapted to changing ecological, social, and economic conditions. Thus, the Huron Natural Area Project is a unique example of holistic, learning-based adaptive planning and management — truly, a process of "designing within nature."

Practising Resilience: Diversity in the Planner's Toolbox

Decisions today usually are based on particular sectors, such as agriculture, fisheries, or finance, rather than on the interdisciplinary issues affected by these sectors, such as changes in habitat, resource depletion, or poverty.[36] A tendency to reduce, simplify, and control natural systems often accompanies this approach. Our political institutions are not, as a rule, designed to be flexible, adaptive, resilient, or accommodating of change through learning: rather, they are designed to resist change through rigid, top-down structures based on a hierarchy of expertise.

This rigidity is perhaps best exemplified by the disjuncture between politics and ecology. Political boundaries (e.g., municipal/regional jurisdictions) are a major obstacle to dealing with ecological phenomena, including biodiversity, that cross these boundaries. Political decisions, which tend to fragment, manipulate, and control natural systems and which nearly always impose a single-ecosystem perspective, have also led to the homogenization of landscapes and, ultimately, the loss of biodiversity.[37] The consequences of this are that the ability to self-renew and regenerate complexity is diminished, and eventually lost. The result is a paradox: control-oriented management of biodiversity will reduce diversity.[38] This indicates an urgent need to create institutions and processes that engender diversity, and a plurality of perspectives, both in society and in nature.

In moving towards adaptive rather than control-oriented management, decision-makers must focus on ecosystem processes and resilience. There are three general criteria in planning for resilience: (1) in the absence of certainty and given the realities of ecological trade-offs, more voices, values, perspectives, and forms of knowledge must be drawn on to support responsible decision-making; (2) in the presence of complexity, collaborative processes are essential to better decisions (by including multiple perspectives, the lessons of history, and so on); and (3) changing conditions and a variety of possible solutions require more innovative and diverse planning tools and methods. Each of these criteria is being addressed in the Huron Natural Area, and is elaborated on in the following sections.

Redefining Expert Culture

Uncertainty is inevitable in ecosystems, and making predictions on the basis of mechanistic causal models is not possible. In addition, in any given circumstance there is more than one possible state for the ecosystem. These states represent different solutions to the problem of survival in a particular environment. Thus, there is no single ecologically "right" state for an ecosystem.[39] This realization, coupled with the inevitability of uncertainty, means that we can no longer rely on "experts" who know the "right answers." The alternative is to open decisions to a greater variety of players, disciplines, and voices, and their diversity of values, experiences, and perspectives.

Decision-making for conservation must become a co-operative endeavour that relies on shared learning through action. Many scientific disciplines, ecosystem perspectives, and related types of knowledge must contribute to the information used in decisions. Because neither social values nor conventional science alone can adequately describe ecosystems or biodiversity, a co-operative, interdisciplinary approach to research as well as practice is essential.[40] In the HNA, this approach, undertaken through a shared visioning exercise in which scientific experts, community leaders, ordinary citizens, and schoolchildren participated, continues today through various committees, input into the Master Plan, the education system, and local stewardship initiatives.

The challenge of implementing such an approach should not be underestimated. Our planning and decision-making structures are not designed for either co-operation or learning. Ours is a culture of experts, not usually questioned by those outside the discipline. In contrast, a more participatory and co-operative decision-making model demands much sharing, questioning and humility, as learning through action is not prescriptive, involves trial and error, and critical thinking.[41]

Such a model would benefit from the "democratization of science" in which the pursuit of *quality* decision-making (rather than a single solution or "truth") is the goal.[42] This is particularly applicable to dynamic, complex, uncertain, urgent conditions, as usually are encountered in efforts to protect biodiversity. Quality decision-making may be achieved by extending the conventional expert culture to include other voices and values as legitimate knowledge, such as the traditional ecological knowledge of indigenous cultures, landowners, lay naturalists, and cultural historians.[43] In doing so, a role for deeper participation and eventual collaboration in planning and decision-making is validated, and a more flexible approach to making decisions can emerge. This perspective can also be extended to research, in determining which disciplines and other forms of knowledge are ultimately used to support a value-driven planning process.

Figure 3 depicts how decision-making must change to deal adequately with complexity and uncertainty. On the left, a generalized sector-based and top-down structure is shown, in which a hierarchy of experts supplies information in relative isolation, i.e., separated by discipline. On the right, a more flexible and organic model is offered, in which many forms of knowledge and values – including conventional

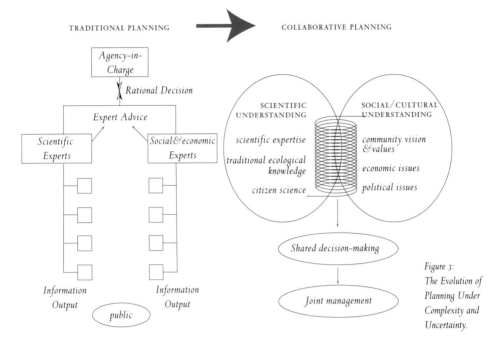

TRADITIONAL PLANNING → COLLABORATIVE PLANNING

Agency-in-Charge

Rational Decision

Expert Advice

Scientific Experts

Social & economic Experts

Information Output

Information Output

public

SCIENTIFIC UNDERSTANDING

scientific expertise

traditional ecological knowledge

citizen science

SOCIAL/CULTURAL UNDERSTANDING

community vision & values

economic issues

political issues

Shared decision-making

Joint management

Figure 3:
The Evolution of
Planning Under
Complexity and
Uncertainty.

science as well as citizen science, traditional ecological knowledge, and economic, political, and cultural values – are integrated into a collaborative, shared decision-making process. A collaborative model ideally incorporates both top-down (expert) and bottom-up (citizen or grassroots) approaches, as managers, planners, and field personnel must work iteratively to share knowledge.[44] Furthermore, citizen and community participants must possess a certain degree of scientific understanding and ecological literacy to contribute effectively.[45] This is also considered an important criterion of membership on the HNA Citizens' Advisory Committee, and can eventually lead to improved education and stewardship by the wider community.

Collaboration in Planning

Collaboration creates new possibilities, by breaking barriers and forging new paths. In this process, creative partnerships may be formed between stakeholders or various interest groups, thus promoting the integration of ecological, economic, and social values with science for biodiversity. Through sometimes unconventional alliances we can build new and exciting alternatives to the adversity and conflict that too often force us to choose convention over innovation. In the HNA, for example, co-operation between the public and separate (Roman Catholic) school boards and the municipal government set a precedent for breaking jurisdictional boundaries and creating a new business partnership.

Collaboration implies equity among participants in the planning process and, therefore, empowerment of different voices, opinions, values, and sources of information. The adaptive framework advocated here is based on interdisciplinary collaboration, feedback, and learning, by an integrated team of professionals from a wide range of disciplines, as well as community representatives and citizens working together towards a holistic conservation plan, with support by a Technical Advisory Committee and a Citizens' Advisory Committee. While it is true that collaborative planning can be time-consuming, there are clear benefits.

In a collaborative process such as the HNA Master Planning exercise, all issues and values are on the table from the start. This reduces miscommunication and enhances the potential for integrated, joint management. While collaboration usually takes longer, it is cost-effective in the long term, as it usually results in a single best planning solution that fulfils participants' goals and objectives without the need for several alternative plans. It should also not be overlooked that long-term community stewardship is a critical additional benefit – and this was a central goal of the HNA collaborative process.

Common sense and experience suggest that less fragmentation and more integration in decision-making results in a more holistic, relevant, and socially acceptable plan. However, there are several challenges involved in more open, flexible processes of decision-making. Planners and managers need to concern themselves with issues of empowerment, ethics, literacy, commitment, and timing.

Collaboration is critical in setting goals, through visioning, identifying values, and combining these with scientific information, as occurred in the HNA planning process, beginning with the Visioning Workshop. However, the conservation community will need to be vigilant to ensure that no single interest co-opts another, or that no special interest dominates. In conventional "citizen participation," in contrast, one powerful interest often permits only limited input from others (usually non-experts). A collaborative process differs in that decision-making power is distributed equally around the table, or at least is allocated by consensus when the process is being designed.[46]

It is also important that a full range of values for biodiversity be kept central to the planning process. This is critical to success because planning goals must reflect socially as well as ecologically desirable scenarios. Only by explicitly recognizing them can all values be validated and considered by participants and potential conflicts resolved.

It is also vital that participants in a collaborative process have a basic knowledge of the relevant science and policies, as well as an awareness of how collaboration works. Without a general willingness to learn, such a process may do more harm than good, particularly if one special interest or set of values dominates. Similarly, "experts" or technical information providers need to understand the collaborative process; they must understand that non-expert values are legitimate and must be considered before a plan can be implemented – even if these values are contradictory. This issue sometimes arose within the HNA process.

Participation in a collaborative planning process must also require a commitment to the process. There should be no "free entry" for latecomers who seek to shut down or stall a process which has been open and transparent. Conservation is more likely to succeed if members buy into the process they develop and feel a sense of ownership in it. Rules for participation and criteria for commitment can be determined by consensus at the outset.

Finally, there are strategic points for collaboration with the wider community in any planning process (see, e.g., Figure 4). In the early stages, an interactive ideas workshop might be held, through which a vision and project goals and objectives can be developed, as was done in the HNA project. From these and through feedback with the community, planning criteria can be established. The conservation plan and associated management strategy can be generated within a planning workshop in which community members participate with a master plan team. This should also be an interactive event, in which poster displays, building blocks, three-dimensional computer modelling, and other tactile and visual media can be used to help the community visualize and "feel" the expected results of various planning options. As the plan is further developed, the community may continue to provide feedback at key points and eventually may participate in monitoring and performance evaluation.

Ideally, all interested and capable parties should collaborate in shaping a conservation plan. However, this will only make a meaningful difference if the collaboration occurs from the outset. In our experience, collaboration in defining the vision, the goals, and the plan itself almost always results in a sense of stewardship by participants. This harnesses the dedicated energies of the wider community through formal involvement in conservation decision-making.[47] In the HNA project core members have remained committed and involved in the planning process for two years, and some for as long as six years.

Innovation in Strategies

While conservation advocates generally agree that biodiversity protection is in the public interest and should be a public responsibility, it would be problematic to continue to rely on the public-sector system of protected areas as the principal strategy of conservation, particularly in an era of government cut-backs and diminished political will. In moving towards more flexible and resilient planning for conservation we need to look to a more diverse range of methods and tools, including those offered through collaborative planning.

Our national parks system is admirable, but is in economic and ecological trouble. There has been a dramatic decrease in funding for creating, maintaining, and operating parks, and there is little political or economic motivation to set aside more large tracts of land.[48] At the same time, provincial parks systems and virtually all publicly funded protected areas, as well as related scientific research, have been affected by budget cuts. Several key biodiversity-related activities continue to decline: the federal government's interdisciplinary Tri-Council "Eco-Research" program was terminated in 1997; budgets of major museums for natural history collections are shrinking; there are few jobs for field-trained conservation biologists and ecologists; and university-level systematics and taxonomy courses have also declined, resulting in few new, trained field experts.

Our national parks and other protected areas protect only between 5.9 per cent and 7.1 per cent of Canada's land area. Clearly, other strategies need to be explored if Canada is to reach the target of 12 per cent protection. Fortunately, there has been considerable recent work in Canada on innovative planning strategies and associated tools for conservation. Promising conservation strategies include partnerships with the private sector; private protected areas; community-based land trusts; the use of creative zoning; and shared conservation through municipal and regional official plans, which make use of adjacent, established protected areas. The HNA is a prime example of a public-private partnership for conservation. Similarly, Georgian Bay Islands National Park has established a network of conservation supporters and advocates outside its official boundaries, but within its greater ecosystem. Through the use of a "vision map," park officials, in consultation with community groups, local planners, and landowners, have created a conceptual plan that identifies core ecological areas of interest and connecting corridors throughout the greater park ecosystem — many of which are on private or municipal lands, yet may nevertheless offer conservation potential through local land trusts, as stewardship areas, or protection by municipalities.[49]

Southwestern Ontario, known as the Carolinian bioregion, is an area rich with examples of alternative conservation planning strategies. A fragmented landscape and the unlikelihood of scattered natural areas ever being integrated together have forced conservation planners to rely on co-operation. For example, in 1984 the Natural Heritage League, in conjunction with the World Wildlife Fund, began a landowner contact program that led to creation of a private stewardship program.[50] Participation is voluntary and success in adding lands under conservation depends on co-operation by public and private landowners. While traditional planning tools are also used, including regulation and legislation, the distinctive feature of conservation is co-operation between regulated planning strategies and non-regulatory or voluntary strategies. Information on biodiversity is also collected and shared among various agencies and citizen action groups. Overall, such strategies serve to illustrate the potential of an integrative and collaborative framework for planning.

Towards Adaptive Planning In Practice

This chapter has established the need for an adaptive approach to conservation planning that integrates values, science, and policy into a decision-making framework in a rigorous and defensible way. Here, "rigour" means quality through an open, transparent, accountable, and collaborative process in which values for biodiversity are made explicit, and learned experience is fed back through regular plan reviews into ongoing management. While the adaptive management concept appeared in the ecological literature in the late 1970s, and has been evolving slowly ever since, only within the last few years has it begun to move from theory to practice.

Recently, scholars and practitioners have begun to synthesize the notions of complexity and uncertainty in ecosystems with ideas of how organizations can adapt to change. Biodiversity conservation is an ideal domain in which to play out this synthesis, because it highlights the mismatch between ecosystems and the decision-making structures through which we attempt to plan and manage them. The challenge is to reform decision making, from control-oriented, predictive, and interventionist *management of the environment*, to adaptive, flexible, and participatory *management of human activities*. In these ways, adaptive planning is a process that more closely models the living systems it is intended to shape, and that is responsive to change in these systems, responding to new ecological information before critical and irreversible thresholds are crossed. In this way, adaptive management is "to learn to manage *by change* rather than merely reacting to it."[51]

Figure 4 depicts an adaptive planning process, and reflects the general approach undertaken in the HNA project. Planning in an adaptive context is cyclic and continuous, and learning is a conscious activity, derived from information as it is acquired, which in turn is transformed into knowledge through adapted behaviour in the next planning cycle.[52] Although the planning process can begin anywhere, the "ideal" process begins with visioning (identifying "what is desirable"). The process proceeds with setting planning goals, objectives, and targets, planning criteria, and interactive workshops (in combination with ecological research, identifying "what is possible"). The process results in several forms of synthesized information, including conceptual models of how the local ecosystem works and how it relates to the broader social context; a master plan; and a management strategy. From this, the plan should be refined, implemented, and monitored, with lessons from experience being used to begin another planning cycle.

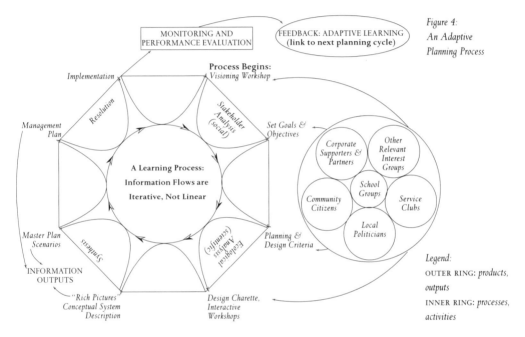

Figure 4:
An Adaptive
Planning Process

Conclusion

Conservation planning is in transition. At present, it is fraught with complexity and uncertainty – from the science it relies on, to the range of policy options and planning tools available, to the plurality of perspectives and diversity of voices needed. Conservation planning must become a more flexible, resilient, and adaptive process, based on proactive, collaborative learning and rooted in an interdisciplinary (and perhaps even transdisciplinary) art and science. In doing so, we engage in what is ultimately a process of *design*.

In moving towards more adaptive decision-making we may navigate the murky waters of uncertainty and complexity that are the hallmarks of our living environment. A new era is possible in which we value and celebrate the diversity of life, that while it confounds and frustrates, also inspires and motivates the human spirit. This is a paradox of life to be embraced by the challenge of *doing* adaptive planning, and therefore, designing *within* nature.

Notes

Research related to this paper was supported by an Eco-Research Doctoral Fellowship, through generous funding by the Canadian Tri-Council, 1994-97. Through parallel work, Dr. Ann Dale and Dr. Henry Regier have provided invaluable discussion and inspiration. Sincere thanks are also extended to the many planners, scientists, and community leaders in conservation who have participated in this research, and in particular, the hard-working group dedicated to the realization of the Huron Natural Area. Their shared experiences and thoughtful commentary on the changing face of conservation planning have contributed richly to the research on which this chapter is based.

1. The Canadian target is to complete an ecologically representative network of protected land areas by the year 2000 and marine areas by 2010. This target is advocated by the World Wildlife Fund Canada's Endangered Spaces Campaign, and was agreed to by the federal, territorial and provincial governments in 1992. See World Wildlife Fund, *Endangered Spaces Report: 1997-98, Number 8* (Ottawa: World Wildlife Fund Canada, 1998); A.M. Turner, C.D.A. Rubec, and E.B. Wiken, "Canadian Ecosystems: A Systems Approach to their Conservation," in J.H.M. Willison et al., *Science and the Management of Protected Areas* (Amsterdam: Elsevier, 1992), 117-27. Canada has also agreed to international targets ranging from 8 to 12 per cent of Canada's total land area to receive protected status.

2. See, for example, C.S. Holling et al., "Biodiversity in the functioning of ecosystems: An ecological primer and synthesis," in C. Perrings et al., eds., *Biodiversity Loss: Economic and Ecological Issues* (Cambridge: Cambridge University Press, 1995), 44-83; J.J. Kay, "A non-equilibrium thermodynamic framework for discussing ecosystem integrity," *Environmental Management* 15,

4 (1991): 483-95 [www.fes.uwaterloo.ca/u/jjkay/pubs/envmgmt/]; J.J. Kay and E. Schneider, "Embracing complexity: The challenge of the ecosystem approach," *Alternatives* 20, 3 (1994): 32-38; [www.fes.uwaterloo.ca/u/jjkay/pubs/alt/alt.html].

3. The evolution of this "new" or emerging paradigm in ecology is traced in N.-M. Lister, "A systems approach to biodiversity conservation planning," *Environmental Monitoring & Assessment* 49, 2-3 (1998): 123-55; see also Lister, "Celebrating Diversity: An Adaptive Planning Process for the Conservation of Biological Diversity in Urbanising Landscapes," Ph.D. dissertation, University of Waterloo, 1999.

4. Lister, "Celebrating Diversity."

5. Kay and Schneider, "Embracing complexity"; Lister, "A systems approach."

6. See T.F.H. Allen and T.W. Hoekstra, *Toward a Unified Ecology* (New York: Columbia University Press, 1992); B.G. Norton and R.E. Ulanowicz, "Scale and biodiversity policy: A hierarchical approach," *Ambio* 21, 3 (1992): 244-49; R.V. O'Neill et al., *A Hierarchical Concept of Ecosystems*, Monographs in Population Biology, No. 23 (Princeton, N.J.: Princeton University Press, 1986).

7. Many recent conservation policy documents and strategies still focus implicitly on species. See, for example, Environment Canada, *Canadian Biodiversity Strategy: Canada's Response to the Convention on Biodiversity* (Ottawa: Biodiversity Convention Office, Environment Canada, 1995).

8. For example, the World Wildlife Fund Canada's Endangered Spaces campaign is based on the principle that protected spaces means protected species.

9. D. Simberloff, "Flagships, umbrellas, and keystones: is single-species management passé in the landscape era?" *Biological Conservation* 83, 3 (1998): 247-57.

10. See P.R. Ehrlich and A.H. Ehrlich, *Extinction: The Causes and Consequences of the Disappearance of Species* (New York: Random House, 1981); Y. Baskin, *The Work of Nature: How the Diversity of Life Sustains Us* (Washington: Island Press, 1997); Holling et al., "Biodiversity in the functioning of ecosystems."

11. Lister, "A systems approach."

12. S.L. Pimm et al., "The future of biodiversity," *Science* 269 (July 21, 1995): 347-50.

13. Biodiversity Science Assessment Team, *Biodiversity in Canada: A Science Assessment for Environment Canada* (Ottawa: Environment Canada, 1994); S.L.

Pimm, *The Balance of Nature? Ecological Issues in the Conservation of Species and Communities* (Chicago: University of Chicago Press, 1991); O.T. Solbrig, "The origin and function of biodiversity," *Environment* 33, 5 (1991): 17-20, 34-38; P.J. Burton et al., "The value of managing for biodiversity," *Forestry Chronicle* 68, 2 (1992): 225-37; D. Tilman and J.A. Downing, "Biodiversity and stability in grasslands," *Nature* 367 (1994): 363-65.

14. On the range of varying interpretations of stability, arising from five distinct meanings: strict mathematical stability, resilience, variability, persistence, and resistance, see, for example, G.H. Orians, "Diversity, stability and maturity in natural ecosystems," in W.H. van Dobben and R.H. Lowe-McConnell, eds., *Unifying Concepts in Ecology* (The Hague: Junk B.V. Publishers, 1975), 139-50; G.H. Orians, R. Dirzo, and J.H. Cushman, "Impact of Biodiversity on Tropical Forest Ecosystem Processes," in H.A. Mooney et al., *Functional Roles of Biodiversity: A Global Perspective* Scientific Committee On Problems of the Environment, (Chichester: Wiley, 1996), 213-44; and Pimm, *The Balance of Nature?*

15. For a discussion of the diversity-stability hypothesis in ecology, see Biodiversity Science Assessment Team, *Biodiversity in Canada*; Kay and Schneider, "Embracing complexity."

16. F.H. Bormann and G.E. Likens, *Patterns and Process in a Forested Ecosystem* (Berlin: Springer-Verlag, 1979).

17. C.S. Holling, "The resilience of terrestrial ecosystems: Local surprise and global change," in W.C. Clark and R.E. Munn, eds., *Sustainable Development of the Biosphere* (Cambridge: Cambridge University Press, 1986), 292-320.

18. Holling et al., "Biodiversity in the functioning of ecosystems."

19. Lister, "A systems approach."

20. Kay and Schneider, "Embracing complexity"; N.-M. Lister, "Environmental management: Overcoming the oxymoron," *Ontario Planning Journal* 11, 4 (1996): 20.

21. T.F.H. Allen, B.L. Bandurski, and A.W. King, *The Ecosystem Approach: Theory and Ecosystem Integrity*, Report to the Great Lakes Science Advisory Board (Windsor, Ont.: International Joint Commission, 1993).

22. There is a small but growing literature on adaptive management. See Holling, "The resilience of terrestrial ecosystems"; K.N. Lee, *Compass and Gyroscope: Integrating Science and Politics for the Environment* (Washington: Island Press, 1993); Lister, "Celebrating Diversity"; C.J. Walters, *Adaptive Management of Renewable Resources* (New York: Macmillan, 1986); C.J. Walters

and C.S. Holling, "Large-scale management experiments and learning by doing," *Ecology* 71, 6 (1990): 2060-68.

23. R.E. Grumbine, "Reflections on 'what is ecosystem management?'" *Conservation Biology* 11, 1 (1997): 41-47.

24. R.D. Brunner and T.W. Clark, "A practice-based approach to ecosystem management," *Conservation Biology* 11, 1 (1997): 48-58; Lee, *Compass and Gyroscope*; Walters and Holling, "Large-scale management experiments"; M.P. Wells, "Biodiversity conservation and local development aspirations: new priorities for the 1990s," in C. Perrings et al., *Biodiversity Conservation: Problems and Policies* (Dordrecht: Kluwer Academic, 1994), 306-20.

25. Lee, *Compass and Gyroscope*, 56.

26. W. Suter, "Involving conservation biology in biodiversity strategy and action planning," *Biological Conservation* 83, 3 (1998): 235-37.

27. Grumbine, "Reflections."

28. See A. Dale, "Sustainable Development: A Framework of Governance," Ph.D. dissertation, McGill University, 1998; F. Westley, "Governing Design: The Management of Social Systems and Ecosystems Management," in L.H. Gunderson, C.S. Holling, and S.S. Light, eds., *Barriers and Bridges to the Renewal of Ecosystems and Institutions* (New York: Columbia University Press, 1995), 391-427; J. Woodhill and N.G. Riling, "The Second Wing of the Eagle: The Human Dimension in Learning Our Way to More Sustainable Futures," in Riling and M.A.E. Wagemakers, eds., *Facilitating Sustainable Agriculture: Participatory Learning and Adaptive Management in Times of Environmental Uncertainty* (Cambridge: Cambridge University Press, 1998), 47-71.

29. L.C. Dalton, "Why the rational model persists: The resistance of professional education and practice to alternative forms of planning," *Journal of Planning Education and Research* 5 (1986): 147-53.

30. Visioning is defined as the process of generating a "picture of the future in the eye of the mind," usually by a diverse group of stakeholders or citizen and expert participants at the outset of a planning exercise.

31. More detail about this case study can be found at: www.fes.uwaterloo.ca/u/jjkay/HNA/

32 Huron Natural Area Working Group, *The Huron Natural Area: An Application of the Ecosystem Approach* (Waterloo: Faculty of Environmental Studies, University of Waterloo, 1995).

33. Specifically, an ecosystem is in a state of integrity when three key characteristics are present: (1) ecosystem health — the system is in a state of

health, when it can maintain normal operations under normal environmental conditions; (2) resilience — the ability to cope with stress in a
changing environment; and (3) the ability to continue the process of self-
organization on an ongoing basis. The latter two characteristics
differentiate ecosystem integrity from ecosystem health. See J.J. Kay,
"The concept of ecological integrity, alternative theories of ecology, and
implications for decision-support indicators," in P.A. Victor, J.J. Kay, and
H.J. Ruitenbeek, eds., *Economic, Ecological and Decision Theories: Indicators of
Ecologically Sustainable Development* (Ottawa: Canadian Environmental
Advisory Council, 1991), 23-58; S. Woodley, J.J. Kay, and G.R. Francis, eds.,
Ecological Integrity and the Management of Ecosystems (Delray Beach, Fla.: St.
Lucie Press, 1993).

34. Huron Natural Area Working Group, *Huron Natural Area.*

35. B. Bass, R.E. Byers, and N.-M. Lister, "Integrating research on ecohydrol-
ogy and land use change with land use management," *Hydrological Processes*
12 (1998).

36. Dale, "Sustainable Development."

37. J.H. Kunstler, *The Geography of Nowhere: The Rise and Decline of America's Man-
Made Landscape* (New York: Simon & Schuster, 1993); V. Shiva,
"Monocultures of the Mind: Understanding the Threats to Biological and
Cultural Diversity," Inaugural Hopper Lecture, University of Guelph,
September 21, 1993.

38. D. Ehrenfeld, "The management of diversity: A conservation paradox,"
in F. H. Bormann and S. R. Kellert, eds., *Ecology, Economics, Ethics: The Broken
Circle* (New Haven: Yale University Press, 1991), 26-39.

39. Kay and Schneider, "Embracing complexity."

40. J. Ellsworth and L. Jones-Walters, "Ecosystem initiatives: Overcoming the
inherent risk in identifying environmental issues and decision makers,"
Public Policy Review (forthcoming).

41. Wells, "Biodiversity conservation"; Woodhill and Riling, "Second Wing of
the Eagle."

42. S.O. Funtowicz and J.R. Ravetz, "Science for the post-normal age," *Futures*
25, 7 (1993): 739-55; Funtowicz and Ravetz, "The worth of a songbird: ecological economics as a post-normal science," *Ecological Economics* 10 (1994):
197-207.

43. See, e.g., F. Berkes, C. Folke, and M. Gadgil, "Traditional ecological
knowledge, biodiversity, resilience and sustainability," in Perrings et al.,

eds., *Biodiversity Conservation*, 269-87; A. Irwin, *Citizen Science: A Study of People, Expertise and Sustainable Development* (London: Routledge, 1995).

44. D.W. Gilmore, "Ecosystem management: a needs driven, resource-use philosophy," *Forestry Chronicle* 73, 5 (1997): 560-64.

45. Irwin, *Citizen Science*; M. Zimmerman, *Science, Nonscience, and Nonsense: Approaching Environmental Literacy* (Baltimore: Johns Hopkins University Press, 1995).

46. Lister, "A systems approach."

47. K.A. Oxley, "Education in Support of the Ecosystem Approach at the Huron Natural Area," Master's thesis, University of Waterloo, 1998.

48. In 1993 Parks Canada was moved out of the Environment Canada ministry and into the Canadian Heritage ministry. Consequently, its funding, personnel, and access to scientific research and support previously provided by Environment Canada were significantly reduced.

49. N.-M. Lister, "Guidelines for Natural Heritage Conservation: Alternative Planning Methods for Ecological Protection in Ontario," M.Sc. research paper, Department of Geography, University of Toronto, 1992; see also Y.C. Wells, *Ontario's Natural Heritage: Options for Protection. A Manual for Conservation Organizations* (Toronto: Ontario Heritage Foundation, Ministry of Culture and Communications, 1989); Lister, "Celebrating Diversity."

50. Lister, "Guidelines."

51. Gunderson et al., eds., *Barriers and Bridges*, xi.

52. Lister, "Celebrating Diversity."

Further Reading

Baskin, Y. *The Work of Nature: How the Diversity of Life Sustains Us.* Washington: Island Press, 1997.

Capra, F. *The Web of Life: A New Scientific Understanding of Living Systems.* New York: Doubleday, 1996.

Golley, F.B. *A History of the Ecosystem Concept in Ecology: More than the Sum of the Parts.* New Haven: Yale University Press, 1993.

Gunderson, L.H., C.S. Holling, and S.S. Light, eds. *Barriers and Bridges to the Renewal of Ecosystems and Institutions.* New York: Columbia University Press, 1995.

Lee, K.N. *Compass and Gyroscope: Integrating Science and Politics for the Environment.* Washington: Island Press, 1993.

Perrings, C. C., K.-G. Mäler, C. Folke, C. S. Holling, and B.-O. Jansson, eds. *Biodiversity Loss: Economic and Ecological Issues.* Cambridge: Cambridge University Press, 1995.

Van der Ryn, S., and S. Cowan. *Ecological Design.* Washington: Island Press, 1996.

Weeks, W.W. *Beyond the Ark: Tools for An Ecosystem Approach to Conservation.* Washington: Island Press, 1997.

Peter Whiting

Economic Aspects of Canadian Biodiversity

ORN, OR MAIZE, WAS DEVELOPED FROM A GRASS BY INDIGEN-
ous peoples of the Americas approximately 7,000 years ago. Starting
with small cobs, less than a finger-length long, they bred cobs up to 20-
30 cm long, filled with richly nutritious yellow kernels. Worldwide,
corn production today is worth at least $50 billion annually and is a sta-
ple food for millions of people. The enormous contemporary
significance of corn and its origins in a species of grass provide a hint of
the economic value of biological diversity.

In 1992, prior to the United Nations Conference on Environment
and Development (UNCED) in Rio de Janeiro, Canada prepared a status
report on the country's biological diversity. This study was not merely
an inventory of Canadian biodiversity; in addition to detailed information on Canadian biological resources, it contained valuable assessments of the benefits and costs associated with Canada's biodiversity.[1]
This report has made an important contribution to our understanding
of biodiversity and its value in Canada. It was presented to the conference and has subsequently been used as an example for other countries
in the preparation of their biodiversity studies and conservation strategies. Further, it has helped draw attention to one of the achievements
of the 1992 conference – the International Convention on Biological
Diversity (CBD).

As this Convention recognized, economics has important roles to
play in ensuring the conservation and sustainable use of biodiversity.
Economics can suggest how to encourage activities that conserve it

and discourage those that eliminate biodiversity. It can also demonstrate why biodiversity is worth conserving, by evaluating and balancing both its positive and its negative implications for humans. Numerous economic uncertainties remain, particularly in estimating the value of biodiversity resources that are not used and cannot be bought or sold. Nevertheless, the value of Canada's biodiversity, both in total and in specific sectors and examples, can be estimated; such estimates demonstrate effectively the priority to be attached to biodiversity conservation.

Economics and the Biodiversity Convention

One of the many significant features of the International Convention on Biological Diversity was the recognition that economics plays an integral role both in understanding biodiversity and the reasons for its loss, and in creating solutions for its long-term conservation. The CBD explicitly incorporates economic principles in its articles. Even in the Preamble it states that the contracting parties are "conscious of the intrinsic value of biological diversity and of the ecological, genetic, social, economic, scientific, educational, cultural, recreational and, aesthetic values of biological diversity and its components."[2]

The objective of the Convention (Article 1) is even more precise in its relevance to the economic aspects of biodiversity conservation:

> The objectives of this convention, to be pursued in accordance with the relevant provisions, are the conservation of biological diversity, the sustainable use of its components and the fair and equitable sharing of the benefits arising out of the utilization of genetic resources....

In employing economics-oriented terms such as "intrinsic value," "sustainable use," and "equitable sharing of the benefits" the CBD clearly recognizes economics as having a significant role to play in ensuring the conservation, use, and the distribution of benefits arising from biological diversity.

A Role for Economics

Unfortunately, in some circles, "economics" is cast as the villain. This contrary view holds that "economics" is the reason (or one of the main causes) for loss of biological diversity and, therefore, should not be considered as part of the solution. While there may be some validity to this view, it must be remembered that economics is an evolving and expanding social science. If the view that "economics is the problem" has any credence, it is probably more correct to suggest that *commerce*, not economics, could be viewed as the actual culprit. Simply put, the prime objective of commerce is to maximize profits. Businesses must do this according to the rules which society sets, i.e., within the legislative and regulatory environment created by different levels of government. Within this environment and within the established rules, Canadian business is free to carry on activities that result in the earning of profits. "Commerce," as a science, is concerned with the most efficient way of achieving these profits within the constraints imposed by the regulatory environment. It is perhaps the pursuit of this commercial objective within an imperfectly framed regulatory environment that has been one of the many causes that have led to the loss of biodiversity. The challenge for governments is to create the right climate that allows businesses to prosper and grow while ensuring that the human and natural resources over which they have jurisdiction are used efficiently, equitably, and sustainably. These are issues central to economics.

The classical definition of "economics" describes a discipline concerned with the allocation of scarce resources among competing uses. Increasingly, economics is contributing to both commercial successes as much as it is contributing to public policy that helps create the climate for business and resources to be used efficiently and equitably. Economics, therefore, can indeed help with the conservation of biodiversity. It helps describe the means and conditions whereby public policies can have the desired effects of conserving biodiversity and it assists public policy-makers in understanding the likely economic consequences of their policies.

How can economics help conserve biodiversity? One way, as just noted above, is through analysis and development of public policy options and the selection of those that contribute to the sustainable use of biodiversity without threatening its extinction. Economics can be used to develop policy alternatives that responsible public agencies may wish to consider in their efforts to conserve or manage the use of biodiversity. For example, the development of policy instruments such as incentive measures to encourage activities that conserve biodiversity, or disincentives/penalties for those activities that produce a loss in biodiversity are possibilities. A broad range of such alternatives exist, each of which can take on many different forms; for example, tax incentives or subsidies for conservation efforts, and tax surcharges or restricted use designations as disincentives for activities leading to a loss in biodiversity.

Another way in which economics can assist with the equitable sharing of the benefits derived from biodiversity is through the valuation of biological diversity. Economics can illustrate how important biodiversity is. Economics can also help to answer other questions about biodiversity: What is its value? Who is benefiting from its use? How can we ensure that those who benefit absorb any associated costs and do not pass them on to others?

Public and private institutions are beginning to recognize that the valuation of biodiversity is a useful activity, but the importance of estimating the value of biodiversity still does not appear to be fully acknowledged in decisions today. Humanity is dependent on biodiversity and biological resources. When these resources are not properly valued or accorded sufficient importance, biodiversity conservation may be incorrectly viewed as a cost to society rather than as an investment in its future development. But when the benefits of biodiversity conservation are shown to exceed the costs of conserving these resources, a powerful and clear incentive for investing in biodiversity is established. Enlightened management should ensure the sustained flow of goods and services from biological diversity of direct benefit to humanity without reducing the productive capacity of the resource base. Taking stock and estimating the value of these resources is an essential first step.

A Balanced View of Biodiversity

When valuing biodiversity, a fundamental distinction to be made is between biological diversity and biological resources. The question is: what component is actually being valued – the "diversity" or the "biota"; or does the valuation of biodiversity just mean the valuation of a broad range of biota?

While no one would dispute that diverse biological resources are beneficial, indeed fundamental to our existence, there is nevertheless the need for a balanced view of biological resources that acknowledges both positive and negative aspects (or benefits and liabilities) associated with these resources. Current approaches of benefit measurement concentrate on those aspects of biodiversity that produce large benefits or are thought to produce large benefits (fishery or forestry resources, for example). However, consideration must be given equally to those biological resources that generate significant disbenefits (e.g., many bacteria and rodents).

A good example of both positive and negative characteristics within one species is the honeybee (*Apis mellifera*). The honeybee in North America, through pollination, annually contributes billions of dollars

Pollinating bees provide an economically important ecological service

photo: Jerry Valen DeMarco

to the fruit and vegetable industries, while producing a large and valuable honey crop. This same insect, however, also carries a nasty sting, which can result in medical costs, loss of performance (income, worker productivity), and, on occasion, death. The honeybee, therefore, has a positive/negative characteristic in terms of its relationship with humans. Furthermore, diversity within bees has itself caused substantial negative impacts on horticultural production: areas of the southern United States have been placed under quarantine to prevent the spread of the aggressive Africanized bee. While some biologists argue that this new strain of bee represents natural evolution and will ultimately triumph over its more docile relative, its presence today is nevertheless resulting in financial loss for agricultural producers in the affected areas as well as for apiarists who traditionally have supplied the area with itinerant bee colonies.

On a more general level, measuring the value of biodiversity as the combined value of resources ignores the nature of the individual. When the value of the insect world is measured this way, there is no accounting of the fact that some individual species (the crop-destroying locust or the disease-carrying mosquito or tsetse fly or the voracious spruce budworm) may *not* produce a net benefit and, in fact, actually result in costs, or disbenefits not only to humanity but to other species as well.

The following figure illustrates a balanced view of the different types of net benefits to be derived from biological resources. The chart assumes that the values are measured from a primarily human perspective (which does not preclude the inclusion of other value systems, e.g., ecosystem values) and that all direct and indirect values are or can be incorporated. Four quadrants are used to indicate the following:

Quadrant I: wholly positive values (no known disbenefits)
Quadrant II: positive and negative values, with the positive values outweighing the negative (i.e., >1)
Quadrant III: wholly negative values (no known benefits)
Quadrant IV: positive and negative values with the negative values outweighing the positive (i.e., <1)

If there is sufficient biological and economic information, a net (all-inclusive) value for *each* biological resource (especially at the species level) can be derived in such a way that each resource falls into one of the four quadrants. Clearly, from a human perspective, the net cumulative value for all biological resources is positive. At the same time this graph illustrates the dichotomous nature of many biological resources, in having both positive and negative values.

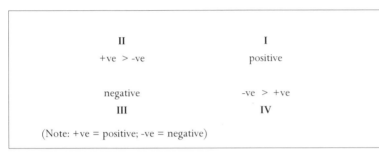

Figure 1:
Economic Values
Associated with
Biological
Resources

At this point, this scheme is a largely abstract one: it is not obvious where specific species would fit within it. A hypothetical distribution of how these values for all species might fit into the four quadrants, as represented by the percentage of biological resources, is:

Quadrant I: 5%
Quadrant II: 15%
Quadrant III: 5%
Quadrant IV: 10%
Unknown: 65%

This distribution, with its high proportion of "unknown," illustrates our current lack of knowledge of the existence of all biota (there are likely still many undiscovered species) and our ignorance of the benefits to be derived from most of those species that have been discovered. As more research is conducted on known species and as new species emerge, our understanding of biota and their relationship with humanity should grow. We will then be in a better position to know into which quadrant each fits. The important thing is to ensure that sufficient numbers and varieties of biota are conserved until we have a better understanding of the function, role, and importance of each species. Estimating the value of biota is an important aspect of these conservation efforts.

Recognizing that not all biota are entirely beneficial to humans is an important conclusion. Further, attempting to determine the relative merits of one species over another should contribute to the development of priorities for research, conservation, preservation, and use of individual species. Economic valuation can assist in that assessment.

What are some of the other conceptual and practical problems with trying to place a value on biodiversity?

Difficulties with Valuations

As I have noted, current efforts to value biodiversity tend to concentrate on the positive values only – the beneficial aspects. What types of values or sources of benefits should be included? And are other valuations more useful? For example, would it be better to measure the value of changes in biodiversity, rather than the total value? A recent United Nations Environment Program (UNEP) document indicates the great uncertainty that surrounds the issue:

> Countries will find that their efforts to measure the value of biological resources and diversity are hampered by tremendous uncertainty. There is uncertainty regarding biological measures of the qualities, quantities, diversity and interactions of biological resources. There is uncertainty of the various goods and services that flow to us from these resources or that may flow to us in the future. There is also uncertainty about the values members of our society place upon the flows of these goods and services and the values that future generations may place upon them. There is uncertainty about how human actions may impact biological resources and diversity and their associated goods and services but face the very real risk that the impacts of our actions may be irreversible. (UNEP, undated)

Economic value is measured anthropocentrically, i.e., from the perspective of humans. However, humans derive value from many different sources, including the satisfaction gained from other species and ecosystems that directly and indirectly contribute to some aspect of human welfare. This does not mean that humans realize the value of species and ecosystems that are fundamental to the species we value highly. In order to initiate a valuation, a framework for assessing value must be created and a perspective for valuation adopted. Ideally, values should not be double counted and, equally, values must not be overlooked. Various "taxonomies" of values have been used as guidelines for determining these values. Although it could be argued that there should be three frameworks, one for each level of biodiversity (genetic, species, ecosystems), an alternative, simple, but powerful framework is presented in Table 1. This framework allows data to be collected on the values associated with each of the major categories of biodiversity (with the exception of the last category: institutions). Inevitably, the categories used must represent a compromise between the ideal analytical framework and the form in which data are available.

Once a framework is devised, the kinds of values to be included in the valuation need to be specified. Because not all biodiversity values are determined in a market situation (where the forces of demand and supply dictate prices), many different types of values are used to derive estimates of value. Some are calculated (such as the value of substitutes, or replacement costs) and some are measured in various other ways (e.g., imputed values, contingent valuation methods).[3] It is important to recognize that it is not necessary that a good or service derived from biological resources be used or consumed directly for it to have an economic value. Biodiversity *use* values are only one type included in these valuations. Non-use values, which include option, existence, and bequest values, also are significant sources of benefit measures.

Use values are usually divided into two categories: direct use and indirect use. These can subdivided further (e.g., consumptive and non-consumptive, or type of use – subsistence, recreation, pharmaceutical, etc.), depending on how the results are to be used. Examples of direct use values of biodiversity include subsistence, timber, fishing, food production, fuelwood, recreation, industrial processes, and many others. Indirect use examples include nutrient cycling, watershed protection, climate regulation, nitrogen fixation, and others. Different uses impact on the genetic, species, and ecosystem levels of biological diversity.

Non-use, or "passive use" as some writers prefer, is usually considered to be comprised of three sources of value: option use benefits, existence value, and bequest value. These three sources of value are fre-

Table 1: Taxonomy of Biodiversity Economic Values

1. **Plants**
   1.1 Wild
      1.1.1 Forest trees
      1.1.2 Crops (fruits, wetland produce, etc.)
      1.1.3 Grazing
      1.1.4 Pharmaceuticals
      1.1.5 Other (aquatic, tundra, desert, other forest, non-forest, etc.)
   1.2 Cultivated
      1.2.1 Forest plantations
      1.2.2 Agricultural crops
      1.2.3 Horticultural (flowers, sod, shrubs, etc.)

2. **Animals**
   2.1 Wild
      2.1.1 Wildlife-related recreation
      2.1.2 Fishing (commercial, recreational)
      2.1.3 Trapping
      2.1.4 Other (insects, worms, etc.)
   2.2 Domesticated
      2.2.1 Agriculture (meat, dairy products, wool, etc.)
         2.2.1.1 agriculture (meat, dairy products, wool, etc.)
         2.2.1.2 fur farming
         2.2.1.3 game ranching
      2.2.2 Aquaculture
      2.2.3 Other (pets, scientific specimens, etc.)

3. **Micro-organisms**
   3.1 Wild
   3.2 Cultured
      3.2.1 Yeasts
      3.2.2 Bacteria for vaccines, medication
      3.2.3 Bacteria for agriculture, dairy products

4. **Ecosystems**
   4.1 National Parks/Reserves (all national parks, reserves, wildlife refuges)
   4.2 Provincial Parks
      4.2.1 Nature reserves
      4.2.2 Natural environment parks
   4.3 Ecological Reserves, Wildlife Refuges
   4.4 Public Protected Areas (natural environment areas, designated areas, Conservation Areas)
   4.5 Private/NGO Protected Areas (Ducks Unlimited, waterfowl parks, game reserves)
   4.6 Other (natural landscapes, eco-tourism, eco-art)

5. **Institutions**
   5.1 Museums
   5.2 Herbaria
   5.3 Botanical Gardens
   5.4 Aquaria/Aviaries
   5.5 Zoos
   5.6 Germplasm/Seed/Gene Banks
   5.7 Microbial Culture Collections
   5.8 Data Banks
   5.9 Other Research Institutions

quently termed "preservation values." Option value refers to the value placed on biodiversity that may be available for future possible use: by maintaining today's level of biodiversity we facilitate future options for its use. Existence value is simply the value that people place on the existence of biological diversity; i.e. it has some value to (some) people just because it exists. Bequest value is the value we place on making biodiversity available to future generations. While there is no standard ratio of the relative importance of non-use values to use values, some studies have found that when these preservation values are included in the estimation of overall benefits, the benefit estimate is more than five times the use value estimate alone.[4] Clearly, both use and non-use values contribute in important ways to the total value of biodiversity.

The measurement of non-use and non-market values (benefits and costs) can be contentious. There is no doubt that they exist, but their quantification into dollar values is a focus of considerable debate and research. Various approaches are being used to create dollar values for non-use benefits; many of these are termed "contingent valuation methods" (cvm). The term "contingent valuation" comes from the fact that the methodology depends on the assumption that a plausible market for the good or service can be created or simulated. This can be a contentious issue, and the methods used are frequently based on many assumptions, that raise concerns regarding reliability.

Canadian Biodiversity Values

Table 2 is a summary of several months' research into the value of Canada's biodiversity. It provides the best existing (but nevertheless incomplete) assessment of the importance of Canada's biological diversity, as measured by the benefits received by Canadians from biota in 1990.[5] The benefit values reported were calculated using a number of different methods, as briefly described above.

Plants	$28.2 billion
Animals	$25.7 billion
Micro-organisms	$3.1 billion
Ecosystems	$13.6 billion
Total	$70.6 billion

Table 2: First Estimated Value of Canada's Biodiversity, 1990

Dollar benefit values derived from plants were estimated to total $28.2 billion in 1990. Major contributions to this value were from agricultural and forestry biota. Farm cash receipts for grains, for example, were approximately $6.6 billion while other agricultural plant-related revenues were approximately $7 billion. Lumber and wood by-products generated revenues of approximately $7.5 billion. Not included in these figures are the many benefits derived from the use of plants for home consumption, including home grown produce, home grown and harvested fuelwood and timber for home use, and subsistence use of plant resources (such as berry picking). Also not included in these figures are the many, varied, and valuable ecosystem services provided by plants – primary production, oxygen production, nutrient transport, sequestering of carbon dioxide, control of soil erosion, moderation of macro- and microclimates, and many others. At the time this report was prepared, very little research on the valuation of benefits from these types of services had been completed.

Farm animals, wildlife, fish, pets, and other less familiar animal forms of biota also have considerable value. As in the case of plants these values are derived from a wide array of uses: food, fur, inputs to other processes, transportation, recreation, and many others. Livestock were estimated to have a value of approximately $11.3 billion in 1990. Canadians also place a high value on their wildlife; these are estimated at $6.1 billion annually, while recreational fisheries are estimated to have an annual value of approximately $4.1 billion. None of the values generated to date incorporates the more difficult to measure ecological functions or ecosystem services that animals contribute to our environment.

Micro-organisms are poorly understood and valued in economic terms, and yet life as we know it would not be possible without them. Yeasts, for example, are required in many processes, natural and man-made. Fungi, bacteria, and viruses are very important in the food, medical, forestry, and industrial sectors, contributing millions of dollars towards the value of final products and the processes leading to final products. Nevertheless, there are few published dollar values for these contributions.

Ecosystem values refer to the combined and synergistic benefits realized from plants, animals, and micro-organisms in a defined area. These values include ecosystem services as well as recreational, cultur-

Wildlife-watching and related recreational activivities make an impotant contribution to northern economies (watching musk-oxen on Victoria Island, Nunavut)

photo: Jerry Valen DeMarco

al, educational, and other benefits. The economic values derived from ecosystem services are difficult to estimate and only limited research has been carried out in this area.[6] Recreational benefits derived from the use of national parks, natural classes of provincial parks (as opposed to historic sites and picnic sites), and other defined areas have only recently been the subject of benefits research. Most economic research has concentrated on the economic impacts of these areas rather than on the benefits they produce. In the next section the results of a recent Ontario study examining the benefits produced by three provincial parks are provided as an example of this type of analysis.

Just as the benefits associated with biological diversity are difficult to measure, so are the costs associated with its conservation. Many different agencies and organizations in the public, private, and non-governmental sectors contribute to or participate in the conservation of biodiversity. Mostly their programs are directed at a broad array of objectives (not necessarily targeted strictly at biodiversity conservation), but these other objectives also support conservation of biodiversity. Allocating costs or attributing some portion of these organizations' costs to biodiversity conservation, therefore, becomes difficult.

The 1990 Canadian study estimated monetary costs that were *at least* $2.8 billion annually directed toward the conservation of biodiversity.

Specific Examples of Economic Values

Some specific examples of economic valuations of biodiversity and their significance are presented here.

Pollination

The pollen grain of the common mallow plant (*Malva*), possesses blunt-tipped spines that facilitate capture by insects. Pollen is the plant's method of exchanging hereditary genes with other members of its species, keeping in tune with its environment through evolution. The pollen of fruit trees, crops, and many wild plants depends on this partnership with insects. These linkages suggest humanity should care for insect diversity and avoid harm to the many beneficial or neutral species. The economic value of insect pollination in Canada is estimated at $1.2 billion annually.

Recreational and Ecological Benefits

A recent study of the benefits derived from three of Ontario's provincial parks – Quetico, Lake Superior, and Mattawa River – conservatively estimated the benefits to Ontario at $16 million annually. This study combined several economic valuation methods within an economic assessment framework that recognized three types of benefits: personal, business, and societal. Both quantitative and qualitative (descriptive) results were provided. The study showed that the parks are important both to the local communities and to the province, and produce a wide range of benefits. In addition, while results varied with each park, the study found that most of the personal use benefits accrued to areas other than Ontario. This was especially true for Quetico Provincial Park, which is located on the Canada-United States border and has the majority of its visitors coming from the U.S. It was found in Quetico's case that approximately 80 per cent of personal use benefits accrued to the United States and other countries. These benefits derived from the park by its non-Canadian visitors represent benefits to those other countries and an export from Canada. For managers of Quetico Park, while they were aware of the origins of their visitors, this study helped indicate the significance of the situation.

Medicinal Benefits

The western yew, *Taxus brevifolia*, is a small evergreen cone-bearing tree found on the west coast of North America, including Canada. A small tree (seldom exceeding 14 metres), it reaches maturity after 250-350 years. Its slow growth and often twisted trunk lead it to be of virtually no timber value, and it was not replanted when forests were cut. A few trees were taken for the sake of its springy wood – excellent for bows. A few years ago the bark of the western yew was found to contain taxol, a compound that selectively damages cancer cells. Clinical testing of taxol has shown its promise in combating breast, ovarian, and lung cancer. A successful drug of this nature could be worth millions of dollars. Guarding biodiversity preserves future options of developing similar products of value in medicine, industry, agriculture, and biotechnology.'

Conclusions

Biological diversity and biological resources, both important, are different. Consideration of the economic values associated with each should more often recognize the differences and similarities between them. Such research should help lead to the "operationalization" of biological diversity for further economic analysis. Biodiversity is not yet a sufficiently well-defined concept in economic terms and this has led to some confusion in economic analysis. For example, the specific values quoted above are mostly biological resource values; biological *diversity* has not been adequately addressed.

Determining the benefits associated with biological diversity is, in economic terms, a marginal analysis; that is, an analysis related to *changes*, not overall total values. The valuing of biological resources, however, is or can be a *total* values analysis. A true examination of the economics of biological diversity should perhaps be concerned with such tasks as: describing and analysing qualitatively and quantitatively the economic values associated with biodiversity; measuring changes in benefits and costs as genetic, species, and ecosystem diversity changes; examining the potential economic benefits and costs of genetic engineering (manufactured biodiversity); and examining the value of biological resources in one area of the world for breeding and diversity enhancement in other parts of the world. Inevitably, economic research on topics such as these will help direct biological research activities in Canada and elsewhere.

Economics clearly has a role to play in the conservation of biological diversity. While economics is not an exact social science, it is clear that economic values can nevertheless be useful for conservation purposes. Considerable conceptual and methodological development must occur in order for economics to make an even larger contribution to the sustainable use and equitable sharing of benefits arising from biological diversity.

Notes

1. The study was published in 1995. T. Mosquin, P.G. Whiting, and D.E. McAllister, *Canada's Biodiversity: The Variety of Life, Its Status, Economic Benefits, Conservation Costs and Unmet Needs*, (Ottawa: Canadian Museum of Nature, 1995).
2. United Nations Environment Program, Interim Secretariat for the Convention on Biological Diversity, *Convention on Biological Diversity*, Gland, Switzerland, November 1994.
3. Imputed values are derived through various means that result in a representative estimate of value. It could be based on input costs or other measures that contribute to a goods value. Contingent valuation methods are research methods used to estimate values for goods and/or services where no market exists.
4. L.D. Sanders, R.G. Walsh, and J.B. Loomis, "Toward Empirical Estimation of the Total Value of Protecting Rivers," *Water Resources Research* 26, 7 (July 1990): 1345-57.
5. The results reported in this section are drawn from Mosquin et al., *Canada's Biodiversity*.
6. See R. Costanza et al., "The Value of the World's Ecosystem Services and Natural Capital," *Nature* 387 (May 15, 1997): 253-60.
7. D.E. McAllister and E. Haber, "Western Yew — Precious Medicine," *Canadian Biodiversity* 1, 2 (Spring 1991): 2-4.

Further Reading

Costanza, R., et al. "The Value of the World's Ecosystem Services and
Natural Capital," *Nature* 387 (May 15, 1997): 253-60.

Mosquin, T., P.G. Whiting, and D.E. McAllister. *Canada's Biodiversity: The Variety
of Life, Its Status, Economic Benefits, Conservation Costs and Unmet Needs*. Ottawa:
Canadian Museum of Nature, 1995.

The Outspan Group. *Economic Benefits of Provincial Parks in Ontario: A Case Study
Approach*. Prepared for Ontario Parks (forthcoming).

Pearce, D., and D. Moran. *The Economic Value of Biodiversity*. London: Earthscan
Publications, 1994.

Small, E., and J. Cayouette. "Biodiversity Diamonds – the example of wild
corn," *Canadian Biodiversity* 2, 3 (Winter 1992): 24-28.

Swanson, T.M., and E.B. Barbier, eds. *Economics for the Wilds: Wildlife, Wildlands,
Diversity and Development*. London: Earthscan Publications, 1992.

United Nations Environment Program, *Guidelines for Country Studies on Biological
Diversity*. Nairobi, n.d.

United Nations Environment Program, Interim Secretariat for the
Convention on Biological Diversity. *Convention on Biological Diversity*. Gland,
Switzerland, November 1994.

Loren Vanderlinden
and John Eyles

Public Perspectives on
Biodiversity: Models and a
Case Study

SCIENTISTS, MANAGERS, POLICY-MAKERS, PUBLIC INTEREST
groups, and the general public all may recognize biodiversity as important and valuable; but each group has a unique perspective. Public support for biodiversity protection hinges on how well it strikes a chord in
the public psyche; and this, in turn, depends on how well it corre-
sponds to commonly held ideas about biodiversity. This chapter examines the Canadian public's perspective on biodiversity. It also presents
results from a study of public views of biodiversity, with reference to a
specific forest in southwestern Ontario.

Public views of biodiversity, like those of any complex environmental issue, are shaped by conceptual models and values that help people
make sense of their relationship to nature. These models and values
influence human attitudes and behaviour (including recreational
activities and purchasing and voting behaviour) that affect biodiversity. The public appears to identify most readily with an anthropocentric, utilitarian view of biodiversity, although they also acknowledge
moral and ethical values that transcend immediate utility. Our study
of human values and forest biodiversity showed how peoples' perspectives on biodiversity are most often conceptualized in terms of bio-

medical, economic, recreational, and aesthetic values. These perspectives also incorporate scientific explanations, and indeed, are often in tune with scientific models. However, members of the public also interpret science through the filters of their own values and culture. These filters determine the extent to which the public is willing to support environmental initiatives. The public is most likely to support campaigns to protect biodiversity if these campaigns highlight its links to human health and well-being, as well as our moral and ethical obligations to preserve diversity for future generations.

Scientific Views of Biodiversity

Biodiversity can be defined as simply an inventory of variety of life on earth,[1] but an adequate scientific definition is much more complex. Scientists measure diversity at the ecosystem, species, and genetic levels, and recognize it as a dynamic, evolving phenomenon.[2] Biodiversity may also be both symptom and sign: an indicator of the health of an ecosystem, and a portent of its ability to survive future stresses.

Providing habitat to two-thirds of the country's wildlife, Canadian forests, like those of other countries, are undeniably our most important reservoir of terrestrial biodiversity.[3] This rich heritage includes the west coast rain forests, the northern boreal forests, and the southeastern mixed deciduous forests.

However, here as much as anywhere, degradation of forests has led to diminished biodiversity. Over three-quarters of the nation's distinct terrestrial regions are at risk of biodiversity loss. Among these, forested areas, prairies, and wetlands are particularly vulnerable. British Columbia's old-growth Douglas fir forest and the Carolinian forests of southern Ontario are among those terrestrial regions classified as "seriously imperiled." The Carolinian forests in southern Ontario have been described as scarce, highly fragmented, vulnerable, and "an ecological disaster zone." These conditions reflect a long history of alteration, initiated by indigenous land uses and accelerated by European settlement and agriculture.[4]

Models of the factors affecting biodiversity indicate the complexity of the issue and the need for several perspectives. As Figure 1 indicates, Environmental Condition, which encompasses multiple indicators of biological diversity, is affected by both natural factors and human activity. As the figure also indicates, the state of biodiversity has socioeconomic and ecological effects. These effects in turn dictate societal responses, expressed in terms of human activities, which will then affect biological diversity both directly and indirectly. For example, in Canadian forests, logging coupled with natural forces, such as fire and insects, has steadily reduced habitat, with marked effects on biodiversity. Forest managers replanting logged or burnt areas with single species, even-aged "tree farms" further reduce the diversity of habitat. Logging roads can lead to additional human uses, such as hunting, urban development and other activities that increase opportunities for disturbances that will affect biodiversity. On the other hand, designating certain forests as protected areas is one societal response, as expressed through government policy, that helps to conserve forest biodiversity.

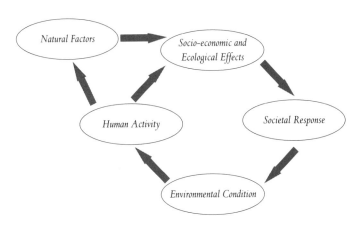

Figure 1:
The Interactions That
Influence Biodiversity

Source: Environment Canada, *State of the Environment Report*, 1997, Bulletin No. 97-1: 1.

Understanding biodiversity issues requires a broad perspective, encompassing both ecological and societal concerns. Societal concerns reflect what different stakeholders or interest groups deem important. If these values and related perceptions of environmental issues are not considered in efforts to protect biodiversity, then there is little hope of meaningful action.

Values for Biodiversity

In their efforts to influence the public's thinking about biodiversity, scientists have sought to answer the question "What is biodiversity good for?" by identifying a variety of values that may be derived from it. There are numerous classifications of the value of biodiversity; each provides a distinct view of its role in the natural world and in human society.[5] One common distinction is that drawn between utilitarian and non-utilitarian values. The former represents a wide range of values that contribute to human welfare in economic terms, both directly and indirectly, as well as several less quantifiable benefits. Direct economic values include the many goods that provide food, clothing, shelter, and raw materials for medical, industrial, or other commercial uses. Biodiversity's technological potential – the untapped resources and the genetic storehouse that it represents – is among these "use" values.

There is also a substantial indirect value to biodiversity in the form of the ecosystem services that it provides without cost to humans. These services, integral to the "global life-support system,"[6] include such fundamental processes as photosynthesis, maintenance of soil and water quality, regulation of climate and atmospheric gases, waste decomposition, nutrient cycling, biogeochemical cycles of carbon and nitrogen, natural pest control, and pollination.

Scientists are quick to point out that a precise dollar value cannot be estimated for ecosystem services. However, extrapolating from the costs of Biosphere 2, the sealed, self-contained ecological system that sustained eight people in the Arizona desert for two years at a cost of about $150 million U.S., some have estimated that provision of these same environmental services for the planet's current population would cost $3 x 10^{18}$, or three quintillion U.S. dollars![7]

Indirect value from biodiversity is recognized in the boost to local economies derived from recreation. Human well-being is enriched by the opportunity to spend time in natural settings and experience biodiversity. Communities have capitalized on people's willingness to pay for experiences in unique environments, hence, ecotourism has emerged as an important economic benefit of biodiversity. In Canada, the success of whale watching ventures on both the Atlantic and Pacific coasts demonstrates this value.

Biodiversity also implies a great variety of non-utilitarian, less tangible values. Whether or not they have obvious value to humans, all species have a right to exist, and we have an ethical responsibility to preserve that right. Ehrenfeld's "Noah principle" sums up this essential intrinsic value of biodiversity.[8]

The aesthetics of biodiversity are also part of its inherent value. Its beauty, richness, and interest engender emotional, spiritual, and transformative value. The aesthetics of nature move and restore people and are clearly part of why biodiversity has recreational and ecotourism worth. Edward O. Wilson and others suggest that this response to biodiversity, which they term "biophilia," is an evolutionary adaptation that reflects our orientation to areas of high resource value. As evidence of a deeply rooted biophilic response, they cite the allegedly universal appeal of scenic landscapes and activities such as gardening and visiting zoos and aquaria.[9]

Public perceptions and values for biodiversity

The public affects biodiversity both directly, as consumers and users of ecosystem goods and services, and indirectly, through the policies of elected governments.[10] Protection of biodiversity, therefore, depends on public understanding, support, and education. Public education is especially vital when, as is often the case, "individual and short-term economic incentives are inconsistent with the best interests of society over the long term."[11] Biodiversity conservation requires a global perspective, and a willingness to alter lifestyles and consumption patterns, and make sacrifices for the sake of future generations.

This also means that it is necessary to understand how the public perceives biodiversity, how it fits into their values and world view and how it varies from scientific perspectives. By doing so, we can explore why environmental initiatives may attract the public's support or its opposition, as well as the significance of differences between public and "expert" opinions.

The Public and Environmental issues

Data from opinion polls, surveys, voter and market behaviour suggest that the North American public has become increasingly aware and supportive of environmental initiatives.[12] As has been shown by the switch from aerosol to non-aerosol cans to reduce CFC emissions and by the appeal of "dolphin-friendly" tuna, public perceptions of environmental issues can have decisive impacts on consumer behaviour. These episodes, as well as changes in language and voting behaviour, indicate a fundamental change in public perceptions.[13]

The public appears to react most readily to simple, reductionist models and "iconic" issues such as the annual seal hunt in eastern Canada. This illustrates an influential source of information for the public: the media's dissemination of the messages of environmental and animal rights groups. But while this type of public response does elicit ethical concerns, it has drawbacks. It poses greater challenges for scientists working with complex, "grey" issues that have less tangible relevance to individual species. To be sure, protection of wildlife is a fundamental concern. However, it is only part of a broader ecological perspective on biodiversity.

In recent years public priorities have shifted. While the environment is still considered important, it has declined in significance compared to health, economic, and family issues. Biodiversity may therefore now be salient only if it is conveyed in terms that relate to the quality of human life.[14] This means that public support for biodiversity protection may depend on linking the priorities identified by science with those of society as a whole.

Canadians' perceptions of biodiversity

There has been relatively little study of Canadians' knowledge of biodiversity. One recent effort was a random telephone survey of more than 1,500 people.[15] This study suggested that the majority of Canadians are relatively uninformed about biological diversity: 36 per cent had no opinion and 28 per cent said that it meant nothing to them.[16] However, when given a brief definition and asked to consider what the most serious consequence of biodiversity loss would be, the most common response was that it would be "bad for the ecosystem and the balance of life on earth" (39 per cent). A clear majority (83 per cent) agreed that species extinction would likely threaten earth's ability to sustain life, while smaller numbers cited intergenerational equity (30 per cent), the ecosystem services of oxygen and water (25 per cent), moral considerations (12 per cent), and cures for human diseases (8 per cent) as reasons to justify biodiversity preservation.[17] At the same time, 20 per cent had no opinion regarding the effects of biodiversity loss.

The major perceived contributions to biodiversity loss were general pollution levels (33 per cent), destruction of habitat (18 per cent), over-consumption of resources by a growing human population (13 per cent) and commercial resource activities in agriculture, forestry, and fisheries (10 per cent). About 85 per cent agreed that individuals have a role in curtailing loss of biodiversity, citing actions such as recycling (22 per cent), reducing consumption (14 per cent) and purchasing "green" products (14 per cent).

Work by World Wildlife Fund Canada provides additional insight into public perceptions. Their goal was to become more effective in demonstrating the relevance of biodiversity to society, and to shift the public mind-set from an aesthetic view of nature, as exemplified by such sentiments as "Nature really should be preserved – it's so pretty and I love hiking," to the view that biodiversity preservation has direct implications for human welfare, as expressed by such sentiments as "My quality of life is in jeopardy. WWF is working to save the earth's biological diversity/web of life, of which I am part. By supporting WWF, I am helping to preserve myself." As part of this effort, they commissioned focus group research to help guide their plans for biodiversity advertising campaigns.[18] Respondents were not a random selection of the public, but rather were selected to have at least a "minimal degree" of philanthropism and sensitivity to environmental issues, as reflected in their donation habits and use of blue boxes for recycling. This study identified some knowledge of biodiversity among them, including the perception that it should be preserved for future generations, for moral reasons (citing the rights of wildlife), and to prevent effects on the food chain. About half the respondents also cited the discovery of new biopharmaceuticals as an important benefit for humans from biodiversity.

These results highlight some fundamental difficulties in surveying public opinion on environmental topics. One difficulty relates to language. While over half of the 1,500 telephone respondents had no opinion of or did not understand the significance of biodiversity, this may reflect unfamiliarity with scientific terminology as much as being genuinely uninformed. The language of science can hinder public understanding. Notably, when survey respondents were provided with a definition of biodiversity, there were fewer "no opinion" responses to the remaining questions, suggesting that biodiversity can indeed be understood when people are given non-technical explanations. In contrast, the WWF focus group participants were chosen specifically on the basis of evidence that they had an environmental sensitivity and therefore might have a broader understanding of biodiversity. In our discussion of our case study of public opinion of forest biodiversity, we will explore further these two types of sampling.

Canadians' perceptions of biodiversity to some extent mirror those identified in the American public, with, however, some differences. In 1993 Defenders of Wildlife commissioned a random telephone survey of more than 1,200 Americans. Almost three-quarters of the sample were uninformed about declining biological diversity, and very few correctly linked habitat destruction and species loss.[19] The survey, "Biodiversity in the Next Millennium," conducted in 1998 for the American Museum of Natural History, revealed that 61 per cent of the American public is still "not very" or "not at all" familiar with the concept of biodiversity.[20] The survey also suggested that there are still considerable differences of opinion between the public and biologists regarding the consequence of biodiversity loss and the steps that are necessary to prevent further loss. Focus group research using non-environmentalist voters, conducted for the Consultative Group on Biological Diversity (CGBD) in 1995, also suggested that Americans have a limited understanding of biodiversity, and that they were not convinced that biodiversity protection mattered directly to human life or outweighed the economic and social costs of saving habitats and species.[21]

Together, these studies suggest that Canadians are more aware of the significance of biodiversity and its links to ecosystem health. This is consistent with the results of a survey of 20 Western nations, in which Canadians scored highest in environmental and scientific knowledge, while Americans ranked seventh.[22]

More important than such comparisons, however, is evidence of room for greater awareness of biodiversity on both sides of the border. Canadians appear to have a general appreciation for the range of factors that can influence biodiversity, including habitat destruction and pollution. They also seem to value biological diversity both because of its relevance to human quality of life, and because of its intrinsic value. Americans' reluctance to associate biodiversity protection with human well-being is intriguing, and likely reflects how people in both countries place health, family, and economic concerns highest among their personal priorities.[23]

While surveys and focus group studies can help identify public views of biodiversity, other sources of data are available. In its most recent survey of the importance of wildlife to Canadians, the Canadian Wildlife Service found that almost 70 per cent of Canadians had participated in some wildlife-related activity close to home. Expenditures associated with wildlife-related activities were considerable. For example, $113.9 million were spent by the more than two-thirds of Canadians who encountered wildlife in the course of activities having some other purpose, while $2.4 billion in expenses were associated with the trips taken by the nearly one in five Canadians who intended specifically to participate in wildlife-related activities. With the exception of hunting, which appears to have declined in popularity over the last 15 years, involvement in other wildlife-related activities was stable or increased, keeping pace with overall population growth. This survey also confirmed strong support (over 83 per cent) for maintaining abundant and diverse wildlife, while more than half of the informants expressed a willingness to pay higher prices or taxes to ensure appropriate conservation and protection of wildlife.[24]

The Ontario Ministry of Natural Resources in Ontario reports that approximately 8 million people visit provincial parks each year. Direct revenue from parks amounts to about $14.5 million and the estimates of expenditures related to people's visits to parks are many times that amount.[25] Surveys of park visitors confirm that they are there for a variety of reasons. Enjoying nature is an important part of the value that people derive from their visits to provincial parks. This is reflected in the fact that they spend a significant amount of time viewing and photographing nature. Such indications of how important it is for people to spend time in natural areas indirectly indicate public appreciation of biodiversity.

Public Perspectives on Forest Biodiversity

Since 1970 there have been a number of studies of public perspectives on forests.[26] They consistently indicate that those characteristics with greatest appeal include green areas, big trees, open stands, ground vegetation, and species variety. Bare areas, sparse stands, or even-sized trees are commonly disliked by the public. Recognizing how natural landscape beauty and scenic quality are vital to the public, there have been efforts to modify the aesthetics of forest management practices. Evidence of roads, clear-cutting, prescribed burns, and the use of herbicides are generally perceived as unacceptable because it is believed they harm the environment and create unattractive landscapes. Overall, it appears that the public values biodiversity in forests particularly for its aesthetic appeal.

In Canada, a 1993 study of attitudes towards forests and forest management by the Ontario Forests Policy Panel indicated that Ontarians perceive forests as an essential resource, for the national economy, for recreational and leisure activities, and as a vital environmental and scenic component of the landscape. Forest diversity is viewed as worthy of protection, and most people see a connection between unacceptable methods of forest management, such as clear-cutting and monoculture, and a decline in biodiversity values.[27] This panel also emphasized that current provincial forest policy was out of step with the public view that forests should be managed for a range of ecological, social, and material values. It recommended, accordingly, that conservation of biological diversity become a cornerstone of the use and management of Ontario's forests.

The Public and Forest Biodiversity at Pinery Provincial Park

The status of forests as an imperiled stronghold of biodiversity implies a need to establish consensus regarding their preservation. One step in that direction would be to understand the values that motivate people to appreciate and protect forest biodiversity and to assess how these values differ from those of environmental scientists or forest managers.

This was the goal of a recent interdisciplinary project on "Forest Ecosystems and Human Values." Natural scientists from the University

Forest, and deer habitat, within Pinery Provincial Park.

photo: Dr. Aviva Patel

of Guelph (Eco-Research Chair Program in Ecosystem Health) and social scientists from McMaster University (Eco-Research Chair Program in Environmental Health) addressed the relationship between ecological indicators of human impact on forest biodiversity and public perceptions of forest health and biodiversity. The focus of the study was Pinery Provincial Park near Grand Bend, Ontario. It represents the largest expanse in Canada of the oak savanna ecosystem, a rare and endangered subtype of the Carolinian forest. Pinery Provincial Park is also used extensively by visitors who camp, hike, bike, and enjoy nature in its forest, beach, and sand dunes. Studying public attitudes towards biodiversity at this site offered an opportunity to uncover the conflicts between human needs and forest management, in an area that is both protected and that provides recreational services that can affect biodiversity.

The proximity of Pinery Provincial Park to London (population 326,000), a large urban centre that contributes much of its tourist traffic, gave the social scientists from McMaster University a ready sample population that could be used to help identify public perceptions and values regarding Pinery's biodiversity.

In our project we used focus groups, bringing together from six to ten individuals of similar background for two to three hours, during which we asked open-ended questions within a semi-structured discussion framework. This method encouraged the subjects to define the terms of the discussions themselves, thereby permitting thorough exploration of a given research question. Results from such an approach complements those obtained by quantitative methods, such as survey questionnaires. While large-scale surveys provide quantifiable data, they limit responses to the structure set by the researcher. Hence, only a narrow range of views may be expressed. In addition, the discussion format and group dynamic of the focus session promote a "stream of consciousness" that provides rich experiential data and can suggest ideas for future research strategies.

The project's researchers conducted six focused discussions in the summer and fall of 1996, recruiting participants from labour, business, health, and environmental groups in London, as well as Chamber of Commerce members from Grand Bend and residents of a local First Nations reserve. We selected these groups to represent not only different forest users but also people with a range of interests, opinions, levels of awareness, and experiences relating to biodiversity.

In the early stages of the project we also conducted a survey at Pinery Provincial Park itself, polling in July 1996 a sample of about 30 park visitors. While in hindsight this was mostly a pilot survey, useful for fine-tuning the focus group discussion framework, it nevertheless made possible some practical comparisons regarding perceptions of biodiversity. These comparisons are interesting in that they come from two very different methods of data collection (individual survey interview versus semi-structured focus group discussion) and from two distinct samples of the public (a sample of park visitors, versus participants chosen from specific interest groups).

The focus groups discussed forests and forest health. The discussion framework was able to draw out public perceptions of forest biodiversity in three different contexts. Participants described how they defined biodiversity; what threats to forest biodiversity they perceived; and what value it had for them.

Definitions of Biodiversity

Biodiversity was almost uniformly described as a fundamental and essential element of forest health. In our open-ended questions — "What does a forest mean for you?" and "What is a healthy forest?" — our informants described healthy forests as represented by a diversity of life-forms. Species were seen as interconnected and interdependent, as denoted by descriptive metaphors such as "the web of life" or "links in a chain." There was a belief that certain wildlife species are important as indicators, or sentinels of forest health.

> The words balance, infinite numbers of life-forms, from the most minute to the very large and how they're all depending on each other's health to remain healthy themselves. So how they're all linked.... And then the forest as a whole is linked in that same delicate balance with everything around it. So, it's a living being. (K., health professional)

> You find all the different levels in an ecosystem.... It's gotta go right down to the microbes in the ground, right up to the eagles, bears, wolves, or foxes, or whatever would be natural so that left on its own, with no human input at all, there's going to be a balance. (M., labour representative)

The notion of "balance" was frequently mentioned as a characteristic of biodiversity, while several also acknowledged that biodiversity is typified by imbalance, or cycles of change, including death and decay.

Biodiversity was also seen as vulnerable to human intervention, reflecting a view of humans and nature as essentially incompatible. Forest biodiversity was perceived to be greatest in the mythic "pristine" forest, while replanted forests of single tree species were viewed as contrived and not consistent with their images of forest biodiversity.

> Totally undisturbed. I mean, if we can use the word pristine, yeah, to me ... that's very much something I'd focus on. (Jm., labour representative)

> You can plant a multitude, but if they're all of the same type ... if

they're all lined up in nice rows, it just doesn't call to mind a forest. (W2, business person)

Some expressed a belief that species in an ecosystem are "self-regulating" and that humans alter that process. This idea was allied with
the concept of "balance" and is best exemplified by participants' views
of predator-prey relationships. The overpopulation of deer in Pinery's
forest was seen as a clear example of disruption of natural cycles, or of
an imbalance between deer and their predators. Our participants
understood that by habitat destruction humans have eliminated the
main deer predator, the wolf, which needs more forest to survive.
More recently, we have diminished our own role in controlling the
deer population through restrictions on hunting and a distaste for the
practice of culling.

A separate issue relating to the balance of species was encountered
in contrasting opinions concerning the gypsy moth infestations regularly seen in Pinery's forest. Most of the participants in our groups
knew that the infestations did not necessarily affect forest health, and
so could be left to follow their course without human intervention.
This conclusion was confirmed by the natural scientists involved on
our project.[18] During the recruitment phase for the Grand Bend focus
group, it also became clear that other members of the community had
great concern about gypsy moths "killing off" their trees and "coming
over with the wind" from the park's trees, and they blamed the park
for not spraying to control them. The focus group members
confirmed that there had been great pressure from some citizens to
deal aggressively with the gypsy moth "problem."

Focus group members were asked to discuss the importance of the
following list (written in lay terms) of forest health indicators that
stress biological diversity and are recognized by scientists as integral to
the health of any forest (see Table 1). During these discussions our participants expressed opinions that overlapped substantially with those
of scientists and were frequently in consensus with each other.

The focus group members agreed (with each other and with
scientific opinion) that a forest's health is reflected in its variety of flora
and fauna. They acknowledged that indicators A, C, E, and F are essential to assessing forest health. However, there were also points where
the public and science differed and where focus group discussions were

	Indicators	Agreement*	Disagreement†	Inconsistency‡
A.	Variety of trees	X		
B.	Condition of trees			X
C.	Variety of tree sizes	X		
D.	Number of trees			X
E.	Variety and condition of other plants	X		
F.	Variety and condition of other wildlife			X

Table 1: Public Opinion on Ecological Indicators of Forest Health from the Forest Ecosystems and Human Values Focus Groups

Agreement: Scientific views and public both agree that the indicator is an important measure.

†*Disagreement*: Scientific views and public disagree on the relevance of the indicator.

‡*Inconsistency*: Public presents inconsistent views on the relevance of the indicator.

inconsistent in their stated perceptions. Among these, "variety and condition of wildlife" is most relevant to our discussion, as noted below with regard to perceptions of deer. In addition, except for comments concerning planted pines, our participants did not comment on encroachment of native plant species by exotics at Pinery, although there was awareness that this is a problem in natural areas elsewhere.

The survey of park visitors provided similar comments regarding aspects of forest health such as tree and plant variety and the presence of wildlife. However, their emphasis was more general regarding how forest health is determined. They included remarks on visual aspects, especially colour and particularly "greenness."

It was also clear from this survey that park education efforts were helping visitors to recognize that healthy forests do have natural cycles of fire, pestilence, decay, and death, and that these are compatible with maintaining biodiversity. Park literature and interpretive programs are important sources of information for the public. The Ministry of Natural Resources pamphlet describes Pinery's unusual combination of oak savanna forest, sand dunes, and wet meadowlands as a "fragile ecosystem, highly sensitive to use and needing continuing careful management and protection."[29] It also informs people that there are more than 700 plant, 200 bird, and 29 mammal species inhabiting the park's forest, including many relatively rare indigenous forms. The Visitor Centre provides plant and bird checklists for guests and there are exhibits and a movie presentation on the park's natural history and management practices. For campers there is an outdoor amphitheatre where staff present slideshows, films, talks, and interpretive demonstrations on the wildlife and habitat at Pinery. The visitor information guide, published annually, includes feature articles that introduce park guests to some of the significant natural features of Pinery. The 1996 edition included a piece entitled "Oak Savanna – Our Most Precious Resource" that described the unique features of this ecosystem and the important role of brush fire in the past. Park managers have conducted several prescribed burns to restore the historic burn regime that has long shaped the oak-pine savanna,[10] and the visitors surveyed understood that this was necessary for the health of the forest. Finally, a non-profit organization, Friends of Pinery Park, helps fund projects and research relating to the natural environment at Pinery. Their newsletter is another source of educational information.

Threats to Biodiversity

Our informants perceived several major threats to forest biodiversity. Of these, the most frequently discussed was habitat destruction, as a result of both intentional and unintentional human activities. A few groups recognized that humans in many areas of the globe had reduced biodiversity by introducing exotic species that choked out native species. All were fairly well informed about current problems with the invasion of zebra mussels and purple loosestrife in Ontario.

In the case of Pinery's forest, the deer herd was of particular concern. Participants believed the deer to be having harmful effects on biodiversity, and yet their compassion was evident in the distaste expressed by a majority towards methods proposed to reduce the deer herd. They also recognized that public perception was hindering resolution of this dilemma: most people have a Disney-influenced view of deer as being like Bambi, and "natural" to the forest. This is reflected in the limited success of park officials in their campaigns to discourage the public from feeding deer, and to obtain permission for deer culling. Nevertheless, participants saw various levels of government as clearly responsible for this problem.

> ... To throw up your hands and say, you know, we can't do any-
> thing about this because the public might be upset 'cause we're
> shooting off Bambi or something like that.... That's deciding the
> future course of the forest ... through a relinquishing of respon-
> sibility. (B., Grand Bend businessman)

Ironically, it is the deer that draw visitors to the park, as focus group participants testified and as provincial Ministry of Natural Resources promotional brochures confirmed. But there has been an attempt to educate people otherwise. The spring 1996 issue of the Friends of Pinery newsletter included an article dealing at length with the problems of feeding deer in Pinery's forest during the wintertime. The article told how "artificial feeding," while well-intentioned, does more harm than good, by disturbing "a natural process and order."[31] The deer's natural winter response of metabolic slowdown is impeded, they become dependent on human food sources, and they are also brought into contact with areas of vehicular traffic, increasing the likelihood of acci-dents. This article reinforced the perception of an incompatibility of humans and nature within the context of the deer problem, while, however, failing to highlight the role of the deer in diminishing the forest's biodiversity. Nor did it present any alternative solutions except to suggest that the deer should, in essence, be left to fend for them-selves.

That forest biodiversity is acutely threatened by excessive deer browsing was confirmed by University of Guelph scientists. Browsing has altered the community structure of the forest, dramatically decreasing understorey vegetation, especially saplings representative of the endangered oak savanna ecosystem.[32] Another potential threat appears to be invasion of exotics and concomitant reduction in native species, particularly at trailsides – evidence of an impact (albeit a less critical one) of hikers using the forest trails. Interestingly, however, human presence on trails actually served to significantly reduce dam-age to understorey plants from deer grazing, and trails were also asso-ciated with greater plant cover because of higher nutrient input.[33]

Overall, therefore, our focus groups had a reasonably good appreciation of the range of established threats to forest biodiversity. They were particularly aware of the role of deer in Pinery's forest, and they appeared to articulate this understanding within the context of other values, such as ethical responsibility and aesthetic appreciation for living creatures. However, it is clear from the unexpected scientific results, such as those regarding trail impacts, that there also exist complex effects on Pinery's biodiversity that are likely not immediately apparent to the public.

The Value of Biodiversity

The values for biodiversity elicited from our focus groups can be categorized into two opposing views: anthropocentrism and biocentrism. The majority of participants had decidedly anthropocentric views: values for biodiversity were most often expressed in terms of how they relate to human health and well-being. Several utilitarian values from forest biodiversity were described. The ecosystem services of filtering air and water and maintaining soil were most often mentioned, but participants also noted known or potential biotechnological resources, such as foods, medicines or other products that could affect the quality of human life. The notion of a "cure" for cancer – a disease that functions allegorically to embody most people's concern regarding environmental health impacts – came up in several groups. The following excerpts typify these forest biodiversity values.

No bush, no air. Simple. (D., First Nations elder)

There's a natural tree in B.C., it's an old tree, everyone thought it was just a garbage tree, and it is used for curing breast cancer.... I can't even remember the name of the tree, but it's just some trashy tree that they've just been lobbing down. (Sv., self-employed business person)

Biodiversity was also seen to play a role in human appreciation of the aesthetics of natural spaces, as diversity (of colours, sounds, and smells) was correlated with the positive feelings that come from spending time in a forest. It was clear from the vast majority of our subjects that biodiversity embodies the physical, mental and spiritual benefits that are associated with forests.

> (I)f you go into a forest area the blast of oxygen you're getting in there, and the shade and the cooling effects and the colours and the diversity, I think ... physically does make you feel better, and probably mentally makes you feel more at ease and less distressed. (J., health professional)

> Places like this ... generate the peace you get in them, the relaxation you can't get anyplace else. (Rs., environmentalist)

> You go out in the morning after the rain and you smell that air coming from the bush.... Nice. It reminds you. It wakes up a sense in you that sort of sleeps.... It's a living, breathing sacred place for me.... If it wasn't for that bush we wouldn't be alive! (D., First nations elder)

Those communities closest to natural areas also see economic value in biodiversity. In Grand Bend, Chamber of Commerce members were acutely aware of the Pinery as a refuge of the rare oak savanna forest, home to many uncommon species of birds and insects, such as the pileated woodpecker and the Karner blue butterfly. They understood that while many come to Pinery for recreational activities, the beach and camping facilities, an increasing number come to appreciate these natural elements. Grand Bend obviously receives immediate economic benefits from this budding "ecotourism" that capitalizes on this unique biological diversity.

> [We have] always enjoyed the Pinery for camping reasons, and nature and the beach. We never really thought of it as being important tree-wise.... Pinery definitely brings [tourists and their] money into the area. (D., Grand Bend business person)

A more altruistic anthropocentric value for biodiversity was the concern that it be preserved for future generations. Many of our participants stressed the importance of family and relationships, and this is certainly consistent with the hope that their kin will be able to enjoy the same benefits of biodiversity that they do.

Biocentric values for biodiversity were discussed much less frequently by focus group participants. It can be surmised, therefore, that these values were not uppermost in their minds. One theme that did emerge from discussions of appropriate messages to promote preservation of forest biodiversity was the idea of advocacy: that forests and wildlife are not solely for human enjoyment or benefit.

While we did not ask respondents to comment on biodiversity values as expressed by scientists, it is worth considering this question. David Takacs's recent book, *The Idea of Biodiversity*, describes the broad range of values for biodiversity that many scientists now recognize. Scientists rank biocentric values much higher than does the general public, and note that they are personally motivated to protect biodiversity because of its aesthetic value, as well as because of a sense of ethical responsibility and an understanding of its importance for ecosystem health.[14] On the other hand, scientists also recognize that arguments expressed in terms of economics and human interests are required to make biodiversity a relevant issue for most people.

What Do Our Results Mean?

Do our participants' views reflect those of the general public? The breadth and depth of their comments suggest that the participants in this study are better informed than is the "average" person described by national survey results. This highlights a frustrating limitation of efforts to gauge public opinion. While the qualitative approach obtains richer information, in the voices of the subjects themselves, it is difficult to find even a small sample of people willing to devote several unpaid hours to a discussion of forests. For this reason, there is a tendency for respondents to be self-selected, most having an already well-formulated appreciation for forests and the natural environment. Nevertheless, our participants could be considered to represent the interested public, who serve as opinion leaders in their communities.

Overall, this study (and others of larger and smaller samples of Canadians) does suggest that the public shares with scientists some perceptions of biodiversity, while also differing in some respects.

Conceptual Models of Nature

Public perceptions of biodiversity are based on mental or cultural models that guide people as they interpret nature and their place within it. On the basis of numerous interviews, Kempton and his colleagues discerned three general types of mental models, that can help in interpreting public perceptions of biodiversity.[35] The first is the so-called "spaceship earth" scenario, in which humans are seen as part of a closed system, depending on it for vital physical and psychosocial needs, and harming themselves when the wastes they produce cycle back to them. The second model portrays nature as composed of interdependent parts, forming an entity that is both balanced and unpredictable. Kempton and his co-workers view this model as central to the public's understanding of nature. The interdependency of nature's parts implies an optimum balance in which all species have a purpose, and changes at any level create a chain reaction or ripple effect. This model also fuels a belief in nature as self-correcting, while its complexity precludes prediction of the effects of alterations. Many people believe, on the basis of this model, that the ideal relationship between society and nature is one of non-interference. The third model is derived from either nostalgic notions of the past, or utopian views of how traditional societies interact with their environment. According to this model, the ideal relationship between society and nature is not separation, but peaceful, gentle coexistence. Contemporary materialism, consumerism, and consumption are at odds with concern for the environment, and are the result of a physical separation from nature.

What models informed the perspectives expressed by our participants? They recognized that biodiversity is a vital foundation for healthy ecosystems, and viewed it as integral to their definitions of forests and forest health. There was an elementary appreciation for the intricacies of the concept, as reflected in references to biodiversity in terms of the web of life, or links in a chain. As others have suggested, both images are somewhat imprecise since they imply ecosystem fragility (rather than resilience): the web may easily be unravelled, or the chain may lose integrity when one link is removed.[36] The notion of "balance" as an attribute of biodiversity reflects a long-standing ecological view of nature. Such ideas, as expressed by the conservationist

Aldo Leopold, the ecologist Eugene Odum, or the writer and scientist Rachel Carson, have influenced public perspectives.[37] Current scientific opinion takes a more complex view of ecosystems as being rarely at any true equilibrium point, and having few universal rules to explain their functioning.[38] However, the notion of balance remains a reasonable simplification of ecological models.

Our study suggests that many (but not all) of our participants view ecosystems as self-regulating, and that since humans and nature are fundamentally incompatible nature should be left untouched. Such a view echoes the second model described by Kempton and his colleagues. However, the view that humans and nature are incompatible is an extrapolation beyond even Kempton's non-interventionist view. Not only did the participants view human modifications of nature as inadvisable, but they saw human impacts on nature as invariably destructive, and humans and nature, in effect, as irreconcilable. The notion of preserving biodiversity in unique ecosystems by restricting human access, described by one informant as creating "museum forests," reflects this non-interventionist, biocentric perspective.

This latter view of the human-nature dynamic is an extremely conservative interpretation of scientific models. It also contradicts the public's largely anthropocentric and utilitarian view of biodiversity. Our participants described, in effect, a "Catch-22" situation, in which human reliance on biodiversity is acknowledged, and yet human impacts on biodiversity imply only the most dire consequences. This theme of incompatibility also imposes a polarized world view that sees nature as "good" and humans as "evil" adversaries of nature. Such a strict moral perspective may restrict support for interventions to protect biodiversity. We do not advocate minimizing human responsibility for biodiversity loss. However, by defining human impact as uniformly negative, the scientific view of biodiversity loss as merely a biological fact, can be obscured.[39] As E.O. Wilson has noted, biodiversity loss is inherent in evolution: of all species that have ever lived, 99 per cent are extinct.[40] That said, of course it is the current rapidity of biodiversity loss that is most alarming.

Our focus groups had a general understanding of threats to biodiversity, expressing a fairly accurate understanding of a range of factors, such as urban and industrial development, habitat destruction, pollution, and other human activities. They also implied that many people are ignorant of how our lifestyles are directly responsible for biodiversity loss. This, according to our participants, is why others fail to appreciate the significance of this environmental issue. Such an explanation relies implicitly on the third model described by Kempton and his colleagues, according to which our social and economic systems are responsible for a devaluation of and separation from nature, fostering disregard for the environment.

Values

Understanding public biodiversity values is integral to achieving greater support for biodiversity preservation. In our study, as in other studies, these values have been most often expressed in terms of anthropocentric, utilitarian priorities, particularly human health and quality of life. Ecosystem services and biotechnology represented the most common justification for preservation of biodiversity.

Biocentric values for biodiversity do not receive as much support, although a significant proportion agree with the statement: "it's immoral to destroy other species."[41] In our focus groups biocentric values were mentioned, but they were not "top of mind," except for First Nations and environmentalist participants. The focus on individual species by environmental organizations such as the Canadian Nature Federation and the World Wildlife Fund may have significantly influenced public attitudes regarding biocentric values, by stressing the intrinsic rights of other species.[42] Yet even here, the public still tends to interpret species loss in terms of human aesthetics. Most people will get more passionate about the plight of "glamorous" endangered creatures, such as whales, pandas, tigers, or wolves, than about species of fish, insects, fungus, or other less exotic life-forms.[43] This orientation is also expressed in other instances. For example, several of our informants admitted to a romanticized view of white-tailed deer and provided this as an explanation for ambivalence towards solutions to deer overpopulation in Pinery.

Implications

Public values need to be addressed when planning biodiversity preservation strategies. Actions that contradict the public's stated values (such as "killing innocent deer") will be resisted. Ecologists and environmental managers must make the public aware of all relevant information regarding efforts to preserve ecosystem biodiversity. For example, the focus groups were inconsistent in their view of deer at Pinery. On the one hand, they understood that deer herds had surpassed the carrying capacity of the ecosystem, to the detriment of both the forest and the deer. One woman even expressed concern that the herd might spread disease, such as Lyme disease, to people.[44] Yet our informants also resolutely expressed their ethical opposition to culling deer.[45] Such contradictions support the idea that public ethics towards nature and wildlife are rooted in childhood, anthropomorphic perceptions "reflect(ing) emotions and memories of virtual, Disney-like worlds."[46] Our participants themselves recognized that a "Bambi syndrome" was influencing their views towards deer. This may reflect the ages of the people we sampled: the baby-boom generation, and their children or parents, for whom the Disney perspective has been particularly influential.[47] Such perceptions represent a considerable challenge to scientists and environmental managers. In this case, Pinery Provincial Park has made a concerted effort to provide information on all aspects of the problem. There has also been some media attention to this phenomenon in both Canada and the United States.[48]

Is it reasonable to expect the public to embrace biocentric values? As one business focus group participant suggested, the public's attachment to anthropocentric values indicates the most effective approach to obtaining public support for biodiversity preservation.

> To just talk about butterflies and native ways and so on, is not going to influence the bulk of the people.... We have to emphasize ... the economic importance, as well as the health importance. Not the health that we can walk through the forest, but the health that we can breathe the air.... My age and up is starting to think about our deteriorating health. (WI., London businessman)

The "average person," who places greatest importance on health, family, and jobs, will be most able to relate to biodiversity protection if the health and economic implications of its loss are stressed, although vivid accounts of threats to species that have particular appeal also remain powerful.

Values aside, there is much evidence that a majority of the public is not yet even aware of the urgency of the global biodiversity crisis. Indeed, the results of other surveys have led some to conclude that biodiversity "remains an enigma for many."[49] For example, recent research by the University of Stirling in Scotland indicates that biodiversity remains a poorly understood concept in that country. Their conclusion that a significant portion of the public is relatively unwilling to pay to help preserve biodiversity, despite agreeing that biotic rights should be protected irrespective of cost, casts doubt on the possibility of gaining public support by appealing solely to biocentric values.[50]

Others have agreed that biodiversity campaigns should focus on human quality of life,[51] while some have suggested a new term, such as "biocrisis" or "extinction crisis," would arouse public interest.[52] A World Wildlife Fund pamphlet presenting itself as a "battle report in the war to save biological diversity" reflects this organization's use of strong language to convey a sense of urgency.[53]

Such arguments suggest that scientists are now using biodiversity as a platform, acting as advocates for a new relationship between humans and the natural world.[54] It is interesting to note a recent exhibit on biodiversity at the American Museum of Natural History. Called simply "Endangered!" the exhibit was described as "speaking out" and "making the case for the value of biodiversity."[55]

Lessons from Our Findings

Biodiversity is only one part of the world, and competes with other domains for attention and action. The public "create[s] models by mixing parts of the scientists' models with parts that [they] construct themselves."[56] While scientists document and explain ecological phenomena, it is ultimately individual and societal values that determine which phenomena will receive significant attention. Are the public and scientists on common ground when it comes to strategies for biodiversity preservation? Our research suggests that these groups can be brought closer together. We have observed that there is no single "public" perception. Instead, there are a variety of complex and sometimes inconsistent value systems. We found that public opinion leaders were much better informed about forest biodiversity than were a sample of park tourists. Results from focus groups also indicated differences in perceptions of the value of biodiversity. This was to be expected, since how people frame their beliefs and values with regard to environmental issues is a product of individual social, cultural, economic, and political factors.[57] These results also suggested that distinct groups within the public can be placed in a linear sequence of differing views towards nature, science, and the human/environment connection: (a) First Nations, (b) environmental groups, (c) health unit workers, (d) labour council representatives, (e) Grand Bend Chamber of Commerce members, and (f) London area business people. The First Nations group was the most strongly oriented towards biocentric values and a spiritual relationship with forests and the environment, with humans seen as part of the environment. This contrasted with the business focus groups, which emphasized the economic value of forests and the separation of humans and the environment. However, differences between these groups were much less pronounced than one might have expected. This is consistent with other researchers' conclusions, which have suggested substantial similarities in opinions toward forest biodiversity protection among diverse stakeholders.[58]

Some authors have wondered if human values are truly consonant with biodiversity protection. Kempton and his colleagues suggest a need to bring things back to "basic values" (i.e., "guiding principles of what is moral, desirable, or just"). This could be achieved by highlighting the links between environmental views and core beliefs and values, such as spirituality, human utility, and responsibility to children and future generations, as well as the rights of nature.[59] Our focus group discussions suggest that these values are indeed fundamental to most people. In many cases, people already appreciate the links between human welfare and biodiversity.

Conclusions

Biodiversity protection requires partnerships and alliances. Its urgency and global nature demand approaches that are as inclusive as possible. The task is to ensure that diverse interests identify their common goals, and recognize and reconcile fairly their differences in values and perspectives.

We are not so far away from defining common goals. The Canadian public appears to have a reasonable, if somewhat conservative, understanding of many of the intricacies of biodiversity. As long as scientific concepts are conveyed in non-technical terms, the impact of biodiversity loss is likely to be interpretable by the public.

While many people recognize moral and ethical responsibilities toward other species, the vast majority most readily appreciate the anthropocentric and utilitarian values of biodiversity. As a result, broad public support for biodiversity preservation is most likely when the links between biodiversity and the physical and spiritual health and well-being of current and future generations of humans are emphasized.

This does not mean that people are materialistic automatons incapable of understanding issues beyond their own frame of reference. Nor is it only the public that might require further education. We must not rely too much on the cognitive authority of science or assume that science is entirely objective and value-free. Many scientists agree, and are now openly recognizing and acknowledging their personal spiritual motivation to argue for biodiversity.[60] With many scientists taking such a position, they and the public are more likely to discover that they share important values and perspectives regarding biodiversity. Perhaps the weakest links in the biodiversity alliance are policy-makers who are out of synch with both scientists and the public.[61] Few politicians have made the environment a key element of their platform, and recent years have seen cost-cutting decimate environment and natural resources ministries in both federal and provincial governments.

The most promising approach in education for biodiversity protection is to establish connections with the values most often expressed by people. A large segment of Canadian society may be open to learning more about human impacts on biodiversity and the effects of biodiversity loss on human health and welfare. These effects may be most real if they are explained in terms of the places that people value most (i.e., their local parks, forests, and nature and wildlife preserves). Ultimately, education may also be what can most effectively increase pressure on governments to maintain strong environmental policies. An appreciation for the diversity of human sensibilities towards nature – quasi-spiritual feelings, a Disney-influenced view, anthropocentric reasoning, or ethical biocentrism – obliges us to consider all perspectives, to "embrace both understanding and emotion, science and sentiment"[62] in formulating strategies to preserve biodiversity.

Notes

We gratefully thank Dr. Barbara Beardwood and Colin McMullan for their invaluable contributions to this project. We also thank our colleagues at University of Guelph, EcoResearch Chair Program in Ecosystem Health, Drs. David Rapport, Aviva Patel, and Sergei Yazvenko. This research was made possible by generous support from the Richard Ivey Foundation, London, Ontario. Dr. John Eyles is supported by the Tri-Council EcoResearch Chair Program in Environmental Health, McMaster University. We also thank our focus group participants and the staff at Pinery Provincial Park for their enthusiastic support.

1. Edward O. Wilson, *The Diversity of Life* (Cambridge, Mass.: Harvard University Press, 1992).
2. D.M.J.S. Bowman, "Biodiversity: much more than biological inventory," *Biodiversity Letters* 1 (1993): 163; Environment Canada, *State of the Environment Report*, Bulletin No. 97-1 (1997): 1.
3. Recommendations of the Fourth Global Biodiversity Forum, September 1996, 2; Statement to the second meeting of the Subsidiary Body on Scientific, Technical and Technological Advice (SBSTTA) to the Convention on Biological Diversity, Montreal; Environment Canada, *State of the Environment Report* (1997).
4. Sierra Club of Canada, *Biodiversity Fact Sheet* (1996): [http://www.sierraclub. org/canada/national/national/biodiv/biodiv.html]; T. Gray and N. Bayley,

"Ontario's Vanishing Old-Growth Forests: Old-growth Forests are a Logging Priority in Ontario," *Borealis* 4, 2 (1993): 32-37; Brad Cundiff, "Carolinian Canada," *Borealis* 4, 2 (1993): 17-23; J. Gordon Nelson and Rafal Serafin, "Assessing biodiversity: A human ecological approach," *Ambio* 21 (1992): 212-18.

5. See, for example, Paul Ehrlich and Anne H. Ehrlich, "The value of biodiversity," *Ambio* 21 (1992): 219-26; Richard Leakey and Roger Lewin, *The Sixth Extinction: Patterns of Life and the Future of Humankind* (New York: Doubleday, 1995), 124-44; N. Myers, "Environmental services of biodiversity," *Proceedings of the National Academy of Science* 93 (1996): 2764-69; Larry A. Neilson, "Biodiversity: Its meaning and its value," *Forum for Applied Research and Public Policy* (Spring 1995): 76-83; Otto T. Solbrig, "The origin and function of biodiversity," *Environment* 33, 5 (1991): 16-20, 34-38; David Takacs, *The Idea of Biodiversity* (Baltimore: Johns Hopkins University Press, 1996), devotes an entire chapter to scientists' views of the value of biodiversity.

6. *Idea of Biodiversity*, 220.

7. J.C. Avise, "Editorial: The real message from Biosphere 2," *Conservation Biology* 8 (1994): 327-29; Myers, "Environmental services."

8. D. Ehrenfeld, *The Arrogance of Humanism* (Oxford: Oxford University Press, 1978).

9. See, for example, E.O. Wilson, *Biophilia* (Cambridge, Mass.: Harvard University Press, 1984); S. Kaplan, "Aesthetics, affect and cognition: Environmental preference from an evolutionary perspective," *Environment and Behavior* 19, 1 (1987): 3-32.; S.R. Kellert and E.O. Wilson, eds., *The Biophilia Hypothesis* (Washington: Island Press, 1993); H.H. Iltis, O.L. Loucks, and P. Andrews, "Criteria for an optimum human nature," *Bulletin of Atomic Scientists* (January 1970): 2-6; Leakey and Lewin, *The Sixth Extinction.*

10. Talal Younès, "Ten years of Biodiversity: Gaps, traps and targets," *Ecodecision* 23 (Winter 1997): 24-27.

11. Karen D. Holl, Gretchen C. Daily, and Paul R. Ehrlich, "Knowledge and perceptions in Costa Rica regarding environment, population and biodiversity issues," *Conservation Biology* 9, 6 (1995): 1549; R. Costanza, "Social traps and environmental policy," *BioScience* 6 (1987): 1-10.

12. Willett Kempton, James S. Boster, and Jennifer A. Hartley, *Environmental Values in American Culture* (Cambridge, Mass.: MIT Press, 1995).

13. Ibid.

14. A 1998 Angus Reid poll of over 1,500 Canadians identified as their top

three concerns health care (36 per cent), unemployment (30 per cent), and national unity (28 per cent). Only 5 per cent mentioned environment as an important national issue. Angus Reid Group, "Healthcare overtakes all issues on public agenda," July 11, 1998. [http://www.angusreid.com/pressrel/pr110798.html; Belden & Russonello, Research & Communications, *Communicating Biodiversity: Focus Group Research Findings*, conducted for the Consultative Group on Biodiversity (Washington, 1995); G. Garin and D. Klingender (Peter D. Hart Research Associates), *Strategic Recommendations for a Communications Campaign on Biodiversity*, written for the Consultative Group on Biodiversity, (Washington, 1995); Consumer Inspiration Centre, *World Wildlife Fund: Biodiversity Project. Qualitative Report*, prepared for WWF (Toronto, 1996).

15. Environment Canada, Report on "Biodiversity Issues," 1994; Environment Canada, Report on "Attitudes Towards Issues Surrounding Biodiversity" (research conducted by Environics Research Group, presented in *Environmental Monitor*, 1997).

16. Data from December 1996 represent a slight improvement in the "means nothing" category over data from April-May of 1994, when 39 per cent fell in this category.

17. The data from 1996 represent a significant departure from the 1994 sample with responses to this question being: 75 per cent – the equity of future generations; 75 per cent – the importance of ecosystem services; 64 per cent – the possibility of loss of species that could provide cures for human diseases; and 58 per cent – the immorality of destroying other species.

18. Consumer Inspiration Centre, *World Wildlife Fund: Biodiversity Project*.

19. Reported by Elizabeth Pennisi, "What *is* biodiversity anyway?" *Science News* 143 (1993): 410.

20. Reported by Catherine Austen, "Biodiversity poll shows split," *Nature Alert* 8, 4 (1998): 4.

21. Pennisi, "What *is* biodiversity?"

22. National Opinion Research Center, *Environmental and Scientific Knowledge around the World* (Chicago: University of Chicago, 1995), cited in National Science Foundation, *Science and Environmental Indicators* (1996), ch. 7, available at: [http://www.nsf.gov/sbe/srs/seind96/. The Canadian mean score was 7.58 out of 12 marks versus an American mean score of 6.57.

23. See, for example, Charles Marwick, "Scientists stress biodiversity-human

health links," *Journal of the American Medical Association* 273 (1995): 1246; Walter V. Reid, "Biodiversity and health: prescription for progress," *Environment* 37 (1995): 12-15.

24. Environment Canada/Canadian Wildlife Service, *The Importance of Wildlife to Canadians: Highlights of the 1991 Survey*, prepared by F.L. Filion et al., Federal-Provincial Task Force on the Importance of Wildlife to Canadians, 1993.

25. [http://www.ontarioparks.com/parks/d44.htm#Survey Research.

26. J.C. Bliss et al., "Forestry community or Granfalloon? Do forest owners share the public's views?" *Journal of Forestry* 92, 9 (1994): 6-11; A.W. Magill, "What people see in managed and natural landscapes," *Journal of Forestry* 92, 9 (1994): 12-21; R.B. Ribe, "The aesthetics of forestry: What has empirical preference research taught us?" *Environmental Management* 13, 1 (1989): 55-74.

27. See, for example, Ontario Forests Policy Panel, *Diversity, Forests, People, Communities: The Report of the Ontario Forestry Panel to the Minister of Natural Resources* (Toronto: Queen's Printer, 1993); Jules Dufour, "Toward Sustainable Development of Canada's Forests," in Bruce Mitchell, ed., *Resource Management and Development* (Toronto: Oxford University Press, 1991); Thomas Dunk, "Talking About Trees: Environment and Society in Forest Workers' Culture," *Canadian Review of Sociology and Anthropology* 31, 1 (1994): 14-34.

28. A. Patel et al., "Forests and societal values: comparing scientific and public perception of forest health," *The Environmentalist* 19, 1 (1999); D. Rapport et al., *Forest Ecosystems and Human Values: Final Report* for Richard Ivey Foundation, Toronto, Ontario, November 20, 1997.

29. Ontario Ministry of Natural Resources, *Pinery Provincial Park* (Toronto: Queen's Printer, 1992).

30. J.R. Tester, "Effects of fire frequency on oak savanna in east-central Minnesota," *Bulletin of the Torrey Botanical Club* 116 (1989): 134-44; R.P. Guyette and B.E. Cutter, "Tree-ring analysis of fire history of a post oak savanna in the Missouri Ozarks," *Natural Areas Journal* 11 (1991): 93-99.

31. Tamara Herman, "Food for thought – The issue of feeding deer," *Friends of Pinery Park Newsletter* 7, 1 (Spring 1996): 3.

32. Their research indicated that very few saplings were above 10 cm in height. A. Patel et al., "Forests and societal values"; Rapport et al., *Forest Ecosystems*.

33. Patel and Rapport, "Assessing the impacts"; Rapport et al., *Forest Ecosystems*.

34. Takacs, *The Idea of Biodiversity*.

35. Kempton et al., *Environmental Values*.

36. Solbrig, "Origin and Function"; Canada, "Habitat Change: Spaces for Species," in *State of Canada's Environment* (Ottawa: Ministry of Supply and Services, 1991), 26.1-26.24.

37. Takacs, *The Idea of Biodiversity*, 204; Kempton et al., *Environmental Values*.

38. Ralph H. Lutts, *The Nature Fakers: Wildlife, Science and Sentiment* (Golden, Colo.: Fulcrum Publishing, 1990); Solbrig, "Origin and Function"; Kempton et al., *Environmental Values*; Takacs, *The Idea of Biodiversity*.

39. See, for example, Max W. McFadden and J. Kathy Parker, "Human values and biological diversity: Are we wasting *our* time?" *Canadian Entomologist* 126 (May-June 1994): 471-74.

40. Wilson, *Diversity of Life*.

41. Only 12 per cent agreed with this statement in the latest Environment Canada Biodiversity survey (Environment Canada, "Attitudes Towards Issues Surrounding Biodiversity"). However, in the 1994 survey, over half (58 per cent) of those surveyed agreed with it (Environment Canada, "Biodiversity Issues"). It is not clear whether this represents a real decline in the public's support for this particular idea or a subtle but important difference in the way the question was posed: i.e., "Canadians were asked to rate the relative importance of four arguments" (1994) versus "Canadians were asked to choose from a list of reasons, the most important one...." (1997).

42. An Environics survey for the World Wildlife Fund indicates that the most common first impression that Canadians have of the WWF's work in Canada is that relating to endangered species (32 per cent). Environmental Monitor, *Omnibus Report on Public Awareness and Attitudes to Biodiversity*, 1995, prepared for World Wildlife Fund, 10.

43. Stephen Kellert's study of attitudes towards invertebrates suggests that the general public is unanimous in viewing most of them, particularly arthropods, with aversion, fear, avoidance, and ignorance. Positive values were only expressed when invertebrate species had aesthetic, utilitarian, ecological, or recreational value. Stephen R. Kellert, "Values and Perceptions of Invertebrates," in David Ehrenfeld, ed., *To Preserve Biodiversity — An Overview* (Cambridge, Mass.: Blackwell Science, 1995), 118-28.

44. In Canada, Lyme disease is quite rare. Transmitted by deer ticks, there are no such ticks in most parts of the country. See Health Canada,

"Consensus Conference on Lyme Disease," *Canadian Medical Association Journal* 144 (1991): 1627-32. Available at: [http://www.cma.ca/cmaj/vol-144/1627e.htm].

45. Hunting was deemed an inappropriate solution by all, with the exception of First Nations participants, who saw harvesting deer as acceptable. However, they made an important distinction between hunting and culling, the latter being viewed as ethically suspect.

46. Younès, "Ten years of Biodiversity," 25. It will be interesting to assess the Disney influence on perceptions of nature in the current generation of children, since, notably, notions of death and interconnectedness of species are different in their recent films, such as *The Lion King*.

47. Walt Disney's animated feature, *Bambi* was first screened in 1942. See Richard Nelson, "The Bambi Syndrome," *Hamilton Spectator*, January 10, 1998, W3.

48. For example: the highly publicized problem with a deer herd that was relocated from around Pearson International Airport near Toronto; a recent *Hamilton Spectator* article (ibid.); and a CBS *60 Minutes* segment, "Public perceptions of White-tailed deer," November 24, 1996, and June 29, 1997.

49. Pennisi, "What *is* biodiversity?" 410.

50. Clive L. Spash and Nick Hanley, "Preferences, information and biodiversity preservation," *Ecological Economics* 12 (1995): 191-208.

51. Belden and Russonello, *Communicating Biodiversity*; Garin and Klingender, *Strategic Recommendations*; Consumer Inspiration Centre, *World Wildlife Fund*.

52. Rodger Schlickeisen, president of Defenders of Wildlife, as cited in Pennisi, "What *is* biodiversity?" 410.

53. World Wildlife Fund International, *Biological Diversity* (pamphlet, n.d.).

54. For example, see Takacs, *The Idea of Biodiversity;* Leakey and Lewin, *The Sixth Extinction*.

55. [http://www.sciam.com/explorations/041497biodiv/041497garcia.html].

56. Kempton et al., *Environmental Values*, 15.

57. Samuel Hays, "Human Choice in the Great Lakes Wildlands," in R.G. Lee, D.R. Field, and W.R. Burch Jr., eds., *Community and Forestry: Continuities in the Sociology of Natural Resources* (Boulder, Colo.: Westview Press, 1990), 41-51; Ronald Inglehart, *Culture Shift in Advanced Industrial Society* (Princeton, N.J.: Princeton University Press, 1990); John Cary, "The Nature of Symbolic Beliefs and Environmental Behavior in a Rural Setting," *Environment and*

Behavior 25 (1993): 555-76; Euel Elliott, James L. Regens, and Barry J. Sheldon, "Exploring Variation in Public Support for Environmental Protection," *Social Science Quarterly* 76 (1995): 41-52.

58. Bliss et al., "Forestry community or Granfalloon?"
59. Kempton et al., *Environmental Values*, 2.
60. Takacs, *The Idea of Biodiversity*.
61. Reports that the Alberta government is allowing logging in "protected" forests, while the federal government announces $9 million support for the University of Alberta's Sustainable Forest Management Network, testify to the problem of governments working at cross purposes. See: Alanna Mitchell, "Alberta to allow logging in 'protected' old-growth forest," *Globe and Mail*, July 24, 1998, A6; "Forest studies get $9 million," *Globe and Mail*, July 24, 1998, A7.
62. Lutts, *Nature Fakers*, 204.

Further Reading

Kellert, Stephen R. *The Value of Life: Biological Diversity and Human Society*. Washington: Island Press, 1996.
Kempton, Willett, James S. Boster, and Jennifer A. Hartley. *Environmental Values in American Culture*. Cambridge, Mass.: MIT Press, 1995.
Takacs, David. *The Idea of Biodiversity*. Baltimore: Johns Hopkins University Press, 1996.

Part Four: Taking Action

Robert Paehlke

Biodiversity:
The Policy Challenge

T HE POLICY CHALLENGES ASSOCIATED WITH THE PROTECTION OF biodiversity are daunting. Effective protection hinges on a transformation in societal values that is not yet complete, even among those in wealthier nations whose immediate economic interests are not threatened. Evidently, humans will rarely opt for the well-being of other species at their own expense. But there has nevertheless been a remarkable shift in the value we attach to wild species and spaces. Whether this shift is occurring rapidly enough, and is permanent, is unknown.

Changes in policy require more than just a transformation of values. This chapter considers four challenges facing biodiversity protection: (1) the fact that while biodiversity loss is often (mercifully) slow, governments tend to respond only to emergencies, and then only incrementally; (2) the need to protect habitat (and to make difficult political decisions) across political boundaries in order to protect many species; (3) the inadequacy of scientific knowledge regarding crucial aspects of biodiversity protection; and (4) the existence of unresolved value dilemmas at the heart of the concept of biodiversity. The third section of this chapter comments briefly on how we might measure biodiversity impacts and sort out some of the value conflicts involved.

Finally, the fourth section goes beyond these challenges facing biodiversity protection by examining some steps that either have been or might be initiated. These include endangered species legislation and habitat protection, on both the large and the small scale, the importance of materials and energy extraction, and particularly the production of construction materials, as well as some relevant policy options.

I conclude by turning from the direct protection of wilderness habitat to the importance of improving human (that is, urban) habitat as a means of assuring a future for wildlife and wilderness. At the heart of this argument is an irony: that much of the challenge of biodiversity can be met only within heavily populated urban agglomerations – in those places where biodiversity has been all but obliterated.

While this chapter does not directly discuss endangered species legislation in Canada or the United States, the policies it proposes – such as the restructuring of urban cores and the imposition of additional taxes on materials and energy extraction – take as a given that both endangered species and declining habitat will be protected directly. The United States has had effective legislation of this sort in place since the 1973 passage of its Endangered Species Act.[1] Canada has pointedly not followed suit in this regard, despite the 1992 Canadian signing of the United Nations Convention on Biodiversity and lengthy parliamentary committee hearings following introduction of a bill in 1996. Passage of this legislation has been repeatedly promised, but resistance from some provinces, from within the Liberal parliamentary majority, and from many economic interests has been systematic and effective. In this regard not just any legislation will do and, as the discussion below suggests, habitat and ecosystem protection may be even more important than the belated protection of individual species in isolation.

Biodiversity: Science, Values, and History

Given that biodiversity is now being very widely discussed, it is astonishing to realize that (as "biological diversity") the concept only entered the scientific literature about 1980, and really only entered broader public discourse with a noted 1986 scientific conference in Washington, D.C. This conference resulted in the 1988 book, *Biodiversity*, edited by Edward O. Wilson.[2] In the early 1990s much public attention was devoted to the concept in the run-up to the 1992 Rio Conference (the United Nations Conference on Environment and Development, also known as the Earth Summit), and to the refusal of U.S. President George Bush to sign the Biodiversity Convention associated with the conference.[3] This focus on biodiversity has developed in conjunction with now widespread fears that many major species may soon become extinct in the wild.

Biodiversity can be defined in terms of "the variety of life and its processes" – it is about both living entities and communities. As Noss put it, biodiversity "includes the variety of living things in an area, the genetic differences among them, the communities and ecosystems in which they occur, and the ecological and evolutionary processes that keep them functioning. Most definitions of biodiversity recognize variety at several different levels of biological organization. Four levels commonly considered are: genetic, species, community or ecosystem, and landscape or regional."[4] Understanding biodiversity as more than the existence of a maximum number of species is important to the establishment of effective and efficient biodiversity policies. We are only beginning to sort out the values, science, and definitions associated with this concept.

What is clear, though, is that human values regarding biodiversity are evolving profoundly. Human existence has always involved competition with and fear of other species. Humans compete with predator species on land and at sea for game, and protect domesticated species against predators and raptors. Unarmed humans can be themselves victims of predation in some situations. Humans have irrational fears of other species, such as snakes and spiders. These fears are probably rooted in risks that were perhaps more commonplace at some time in the past. Humans hunt and kill other species for food, for clothing, out of superstition (for seal penises, bear gall bladders, and tiger bones), by accident (as in by-catches at sea), and for fun. Moreover, agriculture is by definition the exclusion of some species of plants in favour of others, as is clear-cut/replant forestry. Excluding some plants more often than not narrows the diversity of both flora and fauna. Finally, human settlement and the noise and industrial character of most modern human activities set animals to flight and bury soil under now seemingly endless pavement.

Yet in this century and the last more and more humans have come to see other species differently, to value them for their own sake. Nineteenth-century figures, such as John James Audubon, Henry David Thoreau, George Perkins Marsh, and John Muir began the transformation of North American opinion.[5] In this century the most profound changes have taken place. In the early part of the twentieth century even conservation organizations, not to mention the public at large, were hostile to predators and raptors. Ranchers left poisoned meat for eagles and hawk hunting was widely popular. It was not until the 1930s that the National Audubon Society in the United States, under the challenge and leadership of Rosalie Edge and others, was prepared to see hawks as species to be valued, rather than species that fed on birds that bird watchers preferred. It was not until 1934 that the Hawk Mountain Sanctuary was established in eastern Pennsylvania and not until 1970 that the state of Pennsylvania passed the Model Hawk Law, while only in 1972 was the Canada-U.S. Migratory Bird Treaty amended to protect all migratory hawks.[6]

This shift is as yet far from universal, but other changes have been even more profound. Wetlands were only recently seen as useless and vile, "swamps" of little value other than as crude jokes. Deserts and the Arctic were regarded as worthless spaces or vast wastelands crying out for human modification, somehow hopelessly empty, their marvellously adapted plant and animal species all but ignored or hunted to be stuffed and placed in museum display cases. But the most vicious hunts were (and are yet) reserved for our fellow predatory mammals. Between 1947 and 1969, 5,400 cougars were killed in Arizona alone, for a $50 to $100 bounty. In California (between 1907, when the state was comparatively empty of humans, and 1963) the number was 12,452. Between 1937 and 1970 U.S. federal government employees slaughtered 477,104 bobcats.[7] In Canada wolves were frequently hunted from the air and forest and mining roads brought (and yet bring) hunters in vehicles deep within otherwise wild areas.

Though massive forest clear-cuts in British Columbia continue to deprive grizzly bears of their remaining habitat, some areas have been set aside to protect their space. Bears elsewhere in Canada and the United States are subject to hunts and to heavy poaching, but efforts are made to stop this practice. Predators are still hunted but the bounties are gone, and cougars and other species are no longer classified as dangerous predators but as game animals like deer, and thus are somewhat protected by hunting seasons and bag limits. In addition, in 1990 the passage of the California Wildlife Protection Act disallowed all sport hunting of cougars, following passage of a statewide referendum.[8] Attitudes have changed profoundly in North America regarding both spaces and species and these changes have taken place over the course of only several decades, a comparatively short period of time for a change in value perspective so broad and deep.

This is not to say that the change is either completed or sufficient. The influence of Peter and the Wolf and the Three Little Pigs run deep in our cultural consciousness. Moreover, changing perspectives on wolves and other creatures come very late for some species whose habitat in North America is now severely restricted (see, for example, the discussion of the Florida panther below). Another problem is that the change is far from universal; for example, according to Bildstein and Goodrich, cited above, protections for raptors in southern Europe are still insufficient and the quest for oriental "medicines" and "potency drugs" threaten various endangered species on most continents. However, attitudes continue to evolve and those oriented to the "deep ecology" and "animal rights" movements and others are pushing forward with philosophical perspectives that are again altering our perspective about the place of humans within the natural world and our relationship to other species of all kinds.

Science has played an important role in the changes which are taking place regarding the protection of species diversity and ecosystem health. Particularly important in the progress towards biodiversity protection has been work in taxonomy and genetics. We know much more about the diversity that exists than we did earlier in this century, though we have thus far only identified fewer than two million of the perhaps 10 to 100 million species of plants and animals on earth. Perhaps more important, we now better understand some of the myriad critical interconnections between species. We know that many fruit-bearing tropical plants are dependent on bats for propagation, just as temperate trees species may depend on small mammals that in turn require standing or fallen dead trees for survival. In the latter case the mammals and the propagation of new trees are severely reduced by clear-cutting followed by the burning of the forest floor prior to replanting. We also know that top predators, such as wolves, can reduce the number of coyotes in an ecosystem and thereby increase the number of rodents and therefore raptors in that ecosystem.

Only such knowledge allows us to understand the ways in which we humans often unintentionally alter ecosystems in profound ways. We also have learned painful lessons regarding exotic species introductions, as in the cases of the zebra mussel or purple loosestrife. Such introductions can simultaneously cost humans economically and cost nature in terms of biodiversity. We have also learned a great deal in recent decades about the vast scale of habitat necessary to sustain viable wild populations of large predators, and about the importance of corridors, pathways, fragmentation and patches to ecosystem health and viability.[9] Without such knowledge we humans would have little idea about how to enhance and protect biodiversity even if we were willing to do so and to pay the necessary economic price. Public knowledge of these often subtle and in some cases as yet uncertain factors is not widely disseminated. Even if experts in relevant government ministries are informed and on-side, others – including municipal officials, landowners, forest and mining companies, and farmers – may not be.

Policy Challenges I: Time, Space, and Uncertainty

Policies that result in the protection of existing biodiversity are not easily achieved for any number of reasons. These reasons include: (1) the disjuncture between the time horizon associated with species and habitat loss, on the one hand, and normal political processes, on the other; (2) the absence of spatial overlap between ecosystem boundaries and political jurisdictions; (3) gaps in scientific knowledge; (4) failures to resolve values issues and to set priorities; (5) the dominance of economic over all other values within the political processes of modern states; and (6) our limited capacity to measure in widely accepted and widely disseminated ways the several dimensions of biodiversity. Each of these challenges to effective biodiversity protection requires further discussion.

Governments face elections every four years or so. Those in political office are quick to blame current problems on past governments and to delay difficult decisions until after the next election. Biodiversity problems by their nature often develop very slowly: over decades if not centuries. Habitat loss may take many different forms and proceed in slow and even unobserved ways in some cases. The only biodiversity emergency that can grip public, and thereby political, attention is the imminent risk of species extinction; but not all species at risk have the characteristics which appeal to public concern sufficiently to provoke the level and kinds of action that frequently are necessary. Action may only be possible when things have proceeded past the point where conditions can be reversed.

Consider the case of the Florida panther as one example of how species loss can occur when political time frames are out of sync with ecological time frames. In 1800 the Florida panther, a distinct subspecies of cougar, lived in a habitat that stretched from Texas and Arkansas to Tennessee, South Carolina, and Florida. This species was hunted to extinction out of fear and economic interest (agriculture and deer hunting) in every state but Florida by the 1920s. Florida panthers were, as a matter of course, simply shot on sight. By the 1920s they survived only in the wilds of southern Florida (an area even in the 1940s all but unpopulated in comparison to today) and were, after 1928, subject to frequent accidents with cars and trucks on the then-new Tamiami Trail cross-state highway.

The 1930s brought another, more indirect, peril. Fever ticks were spreading from wild deer to domesticated cattle. To protect the cattle the deer in much of Florida were hunted to extinction, depriving the panther of its most important food source. Later problems for the panther included agricultural chemical run-off, including mercury, making its way up to the top of the food chain and making the declining numbers of the species less healthy. The small numbers in the wild also became increasingly inbred and subject to genetic weaknesses, bad news for a predator that needs every physical attribute at its disposal to survive in the best of situations. In the 1960s another cross-state highway (the so-called Alligator Alley) was constructed, bringing more accidents and hunter access.

By this time public attitudes had shifted (following important efforts by conservation-minded organizations and individuals). After decades upon decades of at best official indifference to the plight of the panther, a turn-around occurred. However, by this time there was a vast human population in and near the one small remaining patch of habitat of the Florida panther. Tourism and agriculture were and are big business in Florida. No endangered species could begin to outweigh rental car traffic and orange juice. The Florida panther has become the much loved mascot and namesake of sports teams, but with a total territory probably too small to assure long term survival in the wild. Hunting is banned. Millions of dollars have been spent on scientific research and on highway fencing and underpasses. It may well be that in 1900 vast national parks and wildlife refuges should have been established in several locations throughout the southern United States. But at the time there was little public or official will for such efforts, and now it would appear to be too late to turn back.

Biodiversity loss is part and parcel of the inexorable spread and increase in human populations and level of economic activity. Where we do not live in large numbers we farm or extract forest or mineral resources. The spread of human population over an area as vast as North America has taken centuries. We often do not see profound change in this regard in anything less than most of a human lifetime. We humans need to see a hundred or a thousand time-series maps or films of shifting maps showing the shrinking space that remains for any number of species, or types of relatively unaltered habitat. What remains of North America's ancient forests as a proportion of what once existed? A few per cent is the answer in this case. What of wetlands? What of the habitat of wild cats? Grizzly bears? Wolves? Bald eagles? The problem is that no single political, economic, or administrative decision seems to those who make it to be the crucial one. The buck can always be passed backwards or forwards in time; the process appears to be inexorable and no one feels that their particular removal or alteration of habitat was significant or decisive.

Jurisdictional boundaries are also problematic for biodiversity protection. What habitat now remains for the Florida panther may not be enough – the panther might well require additional spaces for healthy survival, spaces within more than one political jurisdiction. More than that, even large national parks should not remain islands. Ecological science suggests that some species must travel over vast spaces during their life cycles – outside of park jurisdictions and across state, provincial, and national borders. The initiative under way to attempt to establish a Y2Y (Yellowstone to Yukon) habitat corridor that would link Yellowstone National Park with Banff and Jasper National Parks is important, but will not easily be achieved. However, without corridors populations isolated in park islands are vulnerable to climate variability and change, fire, inbreeding, and human and other interventions. Mobile animal populations that have corridors through which they can from time to time move are safer, healthier, and more resilient.

Human political and administrative boundaries are almost never coterminous with ecosystem boundaries. As a result, decisions about ecosystems or bioregions or watersheds or rivers will almost always be multi-jurisdictional. Arrays of agencies can be assembled, but again opportunities for buck-passing abound. The buck can be passed, often to nowhere in particular, in any impasse with competing claims. More frequently a head of steam can be built for co-operation of municipalities, provinces and/or states, national governments, and international agencies in the face of a crisis, but long-term enforcement is difficult to sustain. That there has been any progress in a situation so jurisdictionally complex as the Great Lakes is a testament to the efforts of the International Joint Commission (IJC), but there may well remain as many problems as ever.[10] Even in less complex situations the challenges of tangled jurisdictions are frequently formidable.[11]

A third challenge to effective biodiversity policy is the fact that technological and economic developments are outstripping the capacity of ecological science to keep pace with change. Everywhere in the oceans the capacity to catch fish has overwhelmed measurement of the loss and the capacity to enact and enforce biodiversity protection measures. Fish sonar and factory ships are vacuuming the oceans clean of species faster than fisheries scientists can detect and understand the changes and propose new limits on fishing technology. But this is hardly the most complex case. Other situations where biodiversity is threatened involve threats that are simply not understood. Amphibian populations, for example, are in wide decline, but there is no consensus about why. One obvious partial cause is the loss of wetland habitat, but losses also occur within surviving wetlands. Two other prime candidates for causing population declines are run-off of agricultural chemicals and damage to the earth's ozone layer. Achieving policy solutions when problems are fully understood is politically difficult enough, given the problems outlined above and others. Without scientific consensus the forces on the side of biodiversity protection are generally insufficient in the face of bureaucratic and political complexity and hesitancy, not to mention economic power.

Two other biodiversity policy challenges are notable in this regard: multigenerational forest harvesting and coral reefs. In the latter case die-offs of coral reefs are occurring widely, but have not been explained. This is crucial because coral reefs are among the most biologically rich locales on the planet, rivalling wetlands and rain forests. Possible scientific explanations have run from human ecological disruptions (involving the crown-of-thorns starfish) to (in some cases) ocean pollution to climate warming. Uncertainty at this level almost guarantees inaction, perhaps rightly so in some cases.[12] Finally, despite extensive study we simply do not understand enough about the complex ecological interactions of ecosystems such as the coastal rain forests of the Pacific Northwest. We do not know what will be lost ecologically in those forests which are recreated through replanting following clear-cutting. A few examples in the form of questions should suffice.

If few trees of cone-bearing age exist over a wide area of replanted forest, how long will it take for populations of seed-eating mammals and birds to return to former levels? If there are few if any standing dead trees remaining what proportion of the woodpecker population is lost? How well can the various species involved withstand such losses? Which insect, animal, and bird species are affected by the reduction or loss of certain tree or brush species or trees of particular ages? Which reductions in insect populations reduce the numbers of which bird species? What are the ecological effects of microclimate alterations and will those changes ever be recovered? Can there be a viable third- or fourth-generation forest of a single species of the same age grown on the same land and at a comparable rate and quality (or is something lost within the soils)? Which pests will thrive to excess within uniform-age and uniform-species forests of various types and what will be the ecological effects associated with controlling those pests? There is a great deal that we do not know about one of the most ecologically and economically important ecosystems in the world and yet we have already lost all but a small proportion in such crucial locations as Vancouver Island.

Fourth and finally, effective biodiversity protection may require that we make some very difficult value choices. Priorities must be set.

Is the top priority the avoidance of particular extinctions, or the avoidance of particular extinctions in the wild? That is, if a species has insufficient habitat remaining is its preservation at great cost more worthwhile than the preservation of other functioning ecosystems? Or recall the case of the Florida panther. Is the panther a higher priority than the declining waterflows in the everglades ecosystem as a whole? Is the higher priority amelioration, such as animal overpasses on wilderness highways (as in Banff), or the protection of remaining intact large wilderness regions or ecosystems (including the denial of any road or motorized access whatever)? Or should restoration of damaged areas near to or within human settlements be seen as more important? Clearly, all these options are important, but one must assume limited resources and especially limited political resources, including the ability to command public attention and public funds. Biodiversity protection requires at the least that political strategists, ethicists, and ecological scientists work closely together.

Policy Challenges II:
Measurement and the Dominance of Economic Values

Underlying all of the above concerns regarding the challenges facing biodiversity protection is one overarching reality. Economic values still dominate human societies, remaining critical even when opinion polls show that most citizens are genuinely concerned about the environment.[13] Few will make significant economic sacrifices to better the environment, even if they would they might well not have that option. One cannot opt for public transportation if it is not already in place or is utterly inconvenient, and few think about environmental impacts when considering whether to add another room to their house. Few citizens have the option of not working, even if the job they can get is environmentally doubtful and they know it. Since there clearly is not anything like a one-to-one relationship between economic growth and biodiversity loss, few will be inclined to favour the former in the name of the latter. Further, the domination of economics in our society is not likely to decline in the future given the transformation widely known as globalization.[14]

In this context it is critical for biodiversity defenders to demonstrate with clarity and in detail what particular economic activities threaten which environmental values. It is necessary to show how much damage occurs and what economic activity, if any, must be altered or restrained. It is necessary to show how the damage occurs and why its negative effects cannot be sufficiently ameliorated without curtailment of some sort. Even still there will be strong opponents to any protection which implies any restraint on economic activity. So long as there is another of the species or the ecosystem somewhere else it is difficult to make the case that any particular habitat must be preserved. Moreover, a preservation battle can be lost only once, while a loss of the opportunity to extract resources, or to otherwise damage or remove habitat, can be accepted for the moment and revisited another day when the political and economic equations are more "favourable."

Economic gains are always easily and quite precisely measured – a given proportion of GDP, employment, and tax revenue derives from any given industry. Any particular undertaking or project will bring or leave in place so much investment and create or preserve so many jobs. In contrast, biodiversity losses can be much more ambiguous. Some species thrive in disturbed landscapes, others do not. Biodiversity is reduced within a given area, but the species lost to that area are imagined to have just moved on to another locale, perhaps to return at some later date. Cowbirds in, woodpeckers out. Deer and grouse in, grizzly bears and eagles out. What is not seen within the appraisal of one activity and one proposal at a time is the march of history and the reality that the process of habitat removal is worldwide, accelerating, and not far short of complete obliteration for many types of ecosystem.

Biodiversity loss needs first of all to be seen in the widest possible perspective. Norman Myers has documented in overview the worldwide loss of tropical rain forest habitat: approximately 150,000 square kilometres per year, having increased by 89 per cent in per year losses between 1980 and 1990.[15] Worldwide, 2 per cent of the remaining tropical forest is being removed every year. The rate is much faster in many countries, including virtually all of the nations of Southeast Asia. Tropical rain forests cover 6 per cent of the earth's surface but provide habitat for fully half of the earth's species of plants and animals. A significant proportion of the loss is not harvested so much as destroyed in slash and burn agriculture or in order to create plantations to produce palm oil or other tropical export crops. Palm oil is decidedly unhealthy and is used primarily in junk food. How are decisions made in these particular economy-environment equations? What is the basis for calculating the rationality of the outcome? Who decides what and on what basis? Again, it is clear that habitat changes must be measured, understood and communicated in terms of historic patterns and future projections, thus using past history to justify interventions on behalf of the future.

Taken to an even higher level of generality and converted into spatial terms the non-viability of the present course of events becomes even more clear. Wackernagel and Rees have calculated the ecological footprint of various nations, cities, and industries.[16] The ecological footprint is the amount of land area necessary to sustain the total resource consumption and waste disposal of a given collectivity. The ecological bottom line emerges when it is calculated that if the present population of the world lived as North Americans do now the land area needed to sustain the economy would be equal to three earths. This suggests both that with continued human population and economic growth there soon will be little space on earth for wild species, and that North American levels of resource consumption cannot be universalized (nor sustained in any case).

It is necessary to make and to refine such data and calculations as offered by Myers and by Wackernagel and Rees to put aside the commonly held view that there is always somewhere else where preservation can occur, or that islands of "wilderness" are sufficient. Seen in this light biodiversity policy is about nothing less than the biological character of the planet and the moral worth of humans as a species. Biodiversity protection will determine, and its absence on a global scale is now determining, the fundamental character of the future planet earth. Is this earth to be a space for humans alone – and one dimension of humans at that? Is every space and every species that exists to exist only as and when it serves our immediate material needs? Clearly not. The questions then become where and how and on what basis are lines to be drawn? What is to be preserved and protected? How are such decisions to be made? And how can the economy be urged or directed away from the present course – from the long, slow (and now accelerating) centuries-long slide towards an ever more marginalized nature – a future that few humans would consciously choose other than out of utter desperation.

Given that human desperation is not uncommon, on what basis might choices be made that take into account the limited economic resources available for such objectives? The Specialist Group Reports and Action Plans of the IUCN are one such initiative.[17] The *World Conservation Strategy* and related recent national and regional initiatives also are crucial.[18] So, too, are both the deep ecology movement and the efforts to attach dollar values to wilderness and to identify the "services" wilderness areas such as ancient forests provide to surrounding lands and waters, even if such approaches exhibit some contradictions.[19] Also needed, however, is a means to integrate all such efforts and perspectives and to apply them to particular decisions.

How valuable in ecological terms is a given segment of habitat and how greatly will it be affected by a proposed undertaking? At the least such an assessment must measure four dimensions of ecological and biodiversity impacts: extensiveness, intensity, duration, and significance. Significance in turn involves measures of both ecosystem uniqueness and richness. Recent studies by the author of this article and others have found that each of the three principal construction materials (wood, iron ore, and the components of concrete) involves significant ecological and environmental impacts both in extraction and in manufacture (wood being especially problematic at the point of extraction and the other materials at the point of production, especially in terms of energy use and pollution).[20]

Needless to say, rarely, if ever, are comprehensive ecological impact calculations used as the basis for private decision-making. Almost as infrequently are they a significant factor in public land-use decisions. Sometimes calculations in this spirit are part of the decision to create a new national or provincial park, and sometimes related issues and understandings are part of environmental assessment decisions. But parks are rarely imposed where there is a significant alternative economic use available, and environmental assessments have turned back few resource extraction opportunities anywhere in Canada. In addition, many of the impositions and rules imposed on, for example, mining in Canada have in recent years been withdrawn both federally and in Ontario. In Ontario, one of the first acts of the Harris government upon its election in 1995 was to remove the requirement that mining firms must deposit money for clean-up before the fact lest they simply walk away and the province end up with an environmental mess like the Moira River, about which nothing has been done for decades. Only in British Columbia, under intense national and international scrutiny from conservation organizations, has there been any significant restraint of forest extraction and that is, thus far, more in terms of how extraction is to take place than where. The upper slopes in Clayoquot Sound and the new large segment in the northern interior mentioned elsewhere are exceptions rather than a new norm.

It can be concluded that the extraction of resources is an important factor in biodiversity loss and is certainly a source of significant habitat deterioration in Canada and throughout the world. In an era of economic globalization it is also more difficult to establish or to maintain effective protection at the point of extraction or to resist the desire to extract in the first place. Efforts to maintain and improve the direct protection of wilderness must continue and are discussed elsewhere in this volume. As much or more, however, can be done on another front where fewer citizens depend directly on resource extraction to earn their livelihoods: in our cities.

Towards More Comprehensive Biodiversity Protection Policies

I begin this concluding section with a counter-intuitive assertion: the first and most important steps in biodiversity protection can and should be taken within our urban cores. This is not to say that parks and endangered species policies are not also crucial, but it is to say that such policies will not be easily achieved if other urban-centred initiatives are not also forthcoming. The logic of this view is as follows: the greatest threats to biodiversity are associated with the high volume extraction of raw materials and, probably to a lesser extent, agricultural extensiveness and practices. The largest amount of raw materials extraction by far goes into building materials (including gravel, cement, steel, and other materials for highways, bridges, sewers, and water pipes).[21] Next in terms of total volume of extraction and hectares impacted are the metals for transportation vehicles, food, and fibre (especially pulp and paper). The biodiversity impacts of all of the above (except pulp and paper) materials extraction are significantly affected by urban density and urban sprawl.

The first source of building materials should be existing buildings. Conversion of function is, environmentally, far and away the best option. This is not so much because of the significant contribution of building materials to landfill sites (though that, too, adds to sprawl), but because of the lost environmental opportunity cost of not extracting the equivalent materials otherwise lost to demolition or abandonment. The greatest source of such convertible buildings is within existing urban cores, or in smaller, now economically marginalized, communities. These buildings and nearby underutilized building sites are crucial for two other sets of factors related to biodiversity protection. First, urban core infrastructure already exists and, even if some of it must be repaired or replaced, the volume of materials involved in updating will be less per capita, both because repair is less materials-intensive than is building new infrastructure and because urban core use-densities are higher and distances shorter than in the suburbs. Second, there is a startlingly consistent and strong correlation between urban residential density and the character, and, most important, the energy and materials intensity of transportation systems.

This latter point requires some corroborating detail. Newman and Kenworthy studied transportation and density in 32 world cities and demonstrated a direct relationship between density, viability of public transit systems, and automotive fuel usage.[22] For example, Metro Toronto's population density is about twice that of Chicago and its per capita gasoline use is two-thirds of the level in Chicago. Chicago, in turn, is twice as dense as Houston and this results in 76 per cent as against 94 per cent commuting to work by auto. European population densities are typically one-third higher than Toronto and public transportation, cycling, and walking are all more frequently used. Private car travel per capita is less than one half of the levels of Metro Toronto.

Transit has had a 20+ per cent share in total peak-period round trips in the Greater Toronto Area. This is considerably higher that in most smaller urban centres in Ontario. Shifting just 5 per cent of the remaining peak period car trips to transit in the GTA would save more than 150,000 trips and more than 1,570,000 vehicle kilometres per working day. Emissions on each workday would be reduced by more than 3.6 tonnes of volatile organic compounds (VOCS), 3.1 tonnes of nitrogen oxide (NOx) and 4,226 tonnes of CO_2. On a yearly basis, assuming 250 working days, this 5 per cent peak period shift would eliminate more than 900 tonnes of VOCS, 775 tonnes of NOx, and one million tonnes of CO_2. The energy savings and effect on climate change associated with alternative transportation systems are significant, but the effects on biodiversity may be even more important.

Automobile transportation and use is land-intensive in itself and it spurs land-use configurations that encroach in many ways upon the agricultural and wilderness landscape. Suburban land-use configurations can devote up to 50 per cent of all land directly to automobiles in parking lots, highways, gas stations, drive-in food windows, car dealerships, driveways, local streets, bridges, scrap yards, tire stores, and home garages. The curvy streets, large lots, and cul-de-sacs of suburbs everywhere would not be possible without universal automobile ownership. Nor would the location of shopping and entertainment that is all but inaccessible other than by automobile. Public transportation is uneconomic within suburban configurations and sprawling suburbs are almost impossible to inhabit without automobiles. In combination the effect is the use of three to four times the land per capita that would otherwise be either necessary or desirable. The bottom line is that where there is full residential and commercial occupancy by humans all but a few wild species are excluded, whether that occupancy is urban or suburban.

The combination of materials extraction (especially forest and mining), energy extraction and urban and suburban sprawl are an important cause of biodiversity losses. The only rival is agricultural practice and those on-going impositions would often be even harder to resolve without putting human lives and well-being at risk. Moreover, there is the possibility that much of the loss attributable to agriculture could be lessened through three changes: (1) a shift to a less meat-based (and thereby more land-efficient) human diet; (2) reduced dependence on slash-and-burn agriculture; and (3) direct attempts to harmonize agriculture and wildlife habitat for their mutual benefit. In any case, given the now all but inevitable future rise in human numbers, transformation of both urban and agricultural spaces are necessary to avoid the decimation of most wild species and spaces over the coming century.[23]

Increasingly, there are calls for management of land uses that is sensitive to nature. As Turner and Rylander put it regarding the United States: "In a little more than a generation this nation has been transformed — 80 per cent of everything built in the United States was built in the last 50 years." And again: "Environmental progress in the next generation will increasingly depend on stemming the environmental cost of current land use patterns." They note that "Large-lot-exclusionary zoning can be extremely costly, but many planners and citizens cling to the notion that such practices are inherently profitable."[24] The economic profit excludes the cost of highways and the accelerating decay of inner cities as taxpayers take their income and property values into new municipal jurisdictions, which nevertheless still have a tough time breaking even once new sewers, roads, schools, and all other amenities are factored into the equation. Excluded, of course, are the environmental impacts of nearby gravel pits and the impacts on and within far-away forests subject to clear-cut to build wraparound decks on the large house on the exclusionary large lot.

Biodiversity policies, then, must focus on both wilderness and cities. A safe, clean, lively, affordable, and interesting urban core lures home buyers downtown and slows urban sprawl. Homelessness, drug use, weak urban schools, and shifts from income taxes to property taxes urge people to the suburbs. Policies fostering urban intensification, public transportation, and mixed use create more compact cities and save one more piece of habitat for some creature at the urban fringe (as well as forests filled with life deep in the wilderness). The three policies that would do the most to protect wilderness, then, are: (1) a tough endangered species act in Canada to directly protect all wild species most at risk and their habitat; (2) an energy and materials throughput tax (EMTT); and (3) a combination of policies that promote urban core residential density and quality urban public transportation. The first of these is crucial, of course, and is discussed more extensively elsewhere in this volume. Variations on the other two policies are often advanced, but are rarely, if ever, seen to have much to do with biodiversity protection and, as such, need elaboration here.[25]

An EMTT would apply an additional tax to any and all newly extracted raw materials from mines, wells, or forests, but would not apply to materials derived from recycled sources. Some products would thus become more expensive, but there would be a strong incentive to produce goods from re-used materials. How strong an incentive would depend on how high the tax rate was set. Such a tax would not necessarily slow the global economy as a whole. The balanced budget in Canada would, for example, open an opportunity to simultaneously make other products less expensive by reducing other forms of taxation or by lowering the cost of public (or for that matter privately delivered) services. Thus, gravel, cement, lumber, metal other than that produced from scrap, and all forms of energy would be more costly, but the cost of university tuition or public transportation might be reduced. Alternately, payroll taxes, and/or property taxes (perhaps selectively), and/or income taxes could be reduced by an amount equivalent to the EMTT, lowering the price of a basket of privately produced goods.

The principal real economic problem (when seen from the perspective of the nation as a whole as distinct from the balance sheets of individual firms) would be the effect on the exports of Canadian raw materials. Mining in Canada represents more than 4 per cent of GDP, while forestry and energy are even larger sectors of the economy. All are heavily export-oriented. Political leaders tread with care in these corridors and any sensible policy analyst is mindful of power. An EMTT is not a policy that would be seen in the corridors of power as a good idea – its passage, even at a modest scale with an extended phase-in, would require massive political demand and the co-operation of other nations bringing in similar measures concurrently.

As a policy related to biodiversity protection the rate of tax could be determined in relation to the combined environmental effects of materials extraction with biodiversity impacts featured prominently in the equation. If possible the tax should be introduced and the environmental effects calculated on a global basis. Otherwise, jobs and impacts on biodiversity would be exported from one nation's or continent's ecosystems to those of another. The policy precedents for such calculations (wherein environmental factors are quantified and embedded into financial calculations and regulated payments) are experience ratings in occupational safety as a basis for contributions for worker's compensation, and life-cycle energy impacts as a basis for calculating demand side management (DSM) expenditures by regulated U.S. utilities.[26] Experience ratings are calculations of the safety performance (number and seriousness of accidents per thousand person days) of a given industry group. DSM expenditure levels have been mandated by some U.S. (state) utility regulators to a level equal to the cost of new supply capacities and are accordingly added to the capitalized base of the utility (the base on which regulated rates to all customers are calculated).

Policies promoting more compact urban cores and improved public transportation (as well as walking and cycling as transportation options) are best treated as mutually supportive and virtually inseparable goals. One effort without the other is unlikely to succeed, as Newman and Kenworthy's findings demonstrate (that is, without at least moderately compact urban arrays public transportation will not likely be either heavily used or anything like economic). Any number of policies are relevant including: (1) zoning (mandating minimum densities, encouraging adaptation of use toward urban core residential conversions and in-filling, promoting mixed use, etc.); (2) property taxes (keeping levels at least even as between the suburbs and the city core and/or between multiple dwelling units and single family housing); (3) social policy (maintaining and promoting quality public schools and community life and low crime rates within urban cores); (4) subsidies and subsidy removal (creating cost structures which favour public transportation over private automobiles within large metropolitan areas). This latter balance is presently skewed strongly in favour of automobiles: urban road construction and maintenance, related low-density infrastructure provision, as well as traffic policing and perhaps the cost of health care related to automobile accidents (or the equivalent), should be paid for by urban automobile users (through toll roads, gasoline taxes, and parking charges), not by all taxpayers.

Policies such as these, as well as a return to, and/or an increase in, the active direct improvement of urban cores by government, would result in cities different from what would otherwise come about. There would be a reduced human settlement of land and, in combination with an EMTT, a reduced need to extract virgin raw materials in distant wilderness locations. There is a very small difference in biodiversity (if any) between a suburb and a medium density urban formation with pockets of greenspace and a very large difference between either of those and the extensive field or forest that would remain somewhere if we humans arrayed ourselves a bit differently. Given that the human population is all but certain to double again within the next century, only a reversal of the settlement trends and patterns of the past 50 years will leave much space for nature anywhere. Without changes in this direction it will be exceedingly difficult to directly protect either near-urban natural areas or many of the remaining wilderness locales.

Conclusion

Biodiversity protection is crucial for reasons that we all know well and also for reasons that we do not fully understand and cannot anticipate. Ecological science suggests the wide applicability of the precautionary principle and a general need for prudence, through protection of both individual species and whole ecosystems. Politically, such preservation is not easily achieved given problems such as the non-continuity of ecological and political boundaries. Perhaps most damaging in this regard is the increasing dominance of economic values over all other values associated with the globalization of economic institutions and political processes. Four initiatives that could help to advance biodiversity protection are: (1) improved quantitative measures of habitat and biodiversity impacts; (2) the obvious: stringent endangered species protective legislation and enforcement, including habitat maintenance; (3) establishment of more compact urban cores and ongoing utilization of existing buildings of all kinds; and (4) introduction of an energy and materials throughput tax. These latter two measures are highly indirect with regard to biodiversity protection, but would have a significant positive effect on this and other important environmental values.

Notes

1. See, for example, Richard Littell, *Endangered and Other Protected Species: Federal Law and Regulation* (Washington: Bureau of National Affairs, 1992).
2. Edward O. Wilson, ed., *Biodiversity: Proceedings of National Forum on Biodiversity, 1986* (Washington: National Academy Press, 1988).
3. Marvin S. Soroos, "Rio Conference (1992)," in Robert Paehlke, ed., *Conservation and Environmentalism: An Encyclopedia* (New York: Garland Publishers, 1995), 570-72.
4. Reed F. Noss, "Biodiversity," in Paehlke, ed., *Conservation and Environmentalism*, 80-81.
5. Robert Paehlke, *Environmentalism and the Future of Progressive Politics* (New Haven: Yale University Press, 1989), ch. 2.
6. Keith L. Bildstein and Laurie J. Goodrich, "Hawk Shooting," in Paehlke, ed., *Conservation and Environmentalism*, 343.
7. Kevin Hansen, *Cougar: The American Lion* (Flagstaff, Ariz.: Northland Publishing, 1992), 57.
8. Ibid., ix.
9. Gray Merriam, "Habitat Fragmentation, Patches, and Corridors," in Paehlke, ed., *Conservation and Environmentalism*, 337-39.
10. John H. Hartig, *Under RAPs: Toward Grassroots Ecological Democracy in the Great Lakes Basin* (Ann Arbor: University of Michigan Press, 1992).
11. Robert Paehlke, "Environmental Challenges to Democratic Practice," in William M. Lafferty and James Meadowcroft, eds., *Democracy and the Environment: Problems and Prospects* (Cheltenham: Edward Elgar, 1996), 18-38.
12. Robert Paehlke, "Coral Reefs," in Paehlke, ed., *Conservation and Environmentalism*.
13. See, for example, Willett Kempton, James S. Boster, and Jennifer A. Hartley, *Environmental Values in American Culture* (Cambridge, Mass.: MIT Press, 1995); Alan Frizzell and Jon H. Pammett, *Shades of Green: Environmental Attitudes in Canada and Around the World* (Ottawa: Carleton University Press, 1997).
14. See the discussions in William Greider, *One World, Ready or Not* (New York: Simon & Schuster, 1997); Joshua Karliner, *The Corporate Planet* (San Francisco: Sierra Club Books, 1997).
15. Norman Myers, "Biodepletion," "Tropical Deforestation," and "Tropical Rainforests," in Paehlke, ed., *Conservation and Environmentalism*, 77-80, 642-47;

Norman Myers, *The Primary Source: Tropical Forests and Our Future* (New York: Norton, 1992).

16. Mathis Wackernagel and William Rees, *Our Ecological Footprint: Reducing Human Impact on the Earth* (Gabriola Island, B.C.: New Society Publishers, 1996).

17. See, for example, the reports cited by Roderic B. Mast and Russell A. Mittermeier in Paehlke, ed., *Conservation and Environmentalism*, 533-35.

18. *World Conservation Strategy: Living Resource Conservation for Sustainable Development* (Gland, Switzerland: IUCN, 1980).

19. Regarding nature's services, see Janet N. Abramovitz, "Valuing Nature's Services," in Lester R. Brown et al., *State of the World 1997* (New York: Norton, 1997), 95-114.

20. Robert Paehlke, *Building Materials in the Context of Sustainable Development* (Ottawa: Forintek Canada Corporation, 1994).

21. Marina Fischer-Kowalski and Helmut Haberl, "Metabolism and Colonization: Modes of Production and Physical Exchange between Societies and Nature," *Innovation in Social Science Research* 6 (1993): 415-42.

22. Peter Newman and Jeffrey Kenworthy, *Cities and Automobile Dependence: An International Sourcebook* (Hants, England: Gower Publishing, 1989); Peter Newman, "Greening the City: The Ecological and Human Dimension of the City Can Be Part of Town Planning," *Alternatives Journal* 22, (1996): 10-16.

23. Joel E. Cohen, *How Many People Can the Earth Support?* (New York: Norton, 1995).

24. John Turner and Jason Rylander, "Land Use: The Forgotten Agenda," in Marian R. Chertow and Daniel C. Esty, eds., *Thinking Ecologically: The Next Generation of Environmental Policy* (New Haven: Yale University Press, 1997). Quotations at pages 50, 51, 75.

25. An excellent discussion of environmental taxes generally can be found in Timothy O'Riordan, ed., *Ecotaxation* (London: Earthscan, 1997).

26. For a detailed discussion of utility conservation policies, see Richard Ottinger et al., *Environmental Costs of Electricity* (New York: Oceana Publications, 1991); David Moskovitz et al., *Increasing the Efficiency of Electricity Production and Use* (Washington: American Council for an Energy Efficient Economy, 1991).

Further Reading

Audubon, John James. *Audubon and His Journals*. New York: Dover Publications, 1960.

Cohen, Joel E. *How Many People Can the Earth Support?* New York: Norton, 1995.

Fischer-Kowalski, Marina, and Helmut Haberl. "Metabolism and Colonization: Modes of Production and the Physical Exchange between Societies and Nature," *Innovation in Social Science Research* 6 (1993): 415-42.

Myers, Norman. *The Primary Source: Tropical Forests and Our Future*. New York: Norton, 1985 and 1992.

Newman, Peter, and Jeffrey Kenworthy. *Winning Back the Cities*. Marrickville, N.S.W.: Australian Consumers' Association, 1992.

Paehlke, Robert, ed. *Conservation and Environmentalism: An Encyclopedia*. New York: Garland Publishers, 1995.

Wackernagel, Mathis, and William Rees. *Our Ecological Footprint: Reducing Human Impact on the Earth*. Gabriola Island, B.C.: New Society Publishers, 1996.

Wilson, Edward O., ed. *Biodiversity: Proceedings of National Forum on Biodiversity, 1986*. Washington: National Academy Press, 1988.

Ian Attridge

Canadian Biodiversity and the Law

P EOPLE ARE OFTEN SURPRISED TO LEARN THAT CANADA HAS NO national endangered species legislation. Its absence exemplifies the challenge of conserving biodiversity in Canada. In 1996, after a series of consultations and reports, the Canadian Endangered Species Protection Act (Bill C-65, or CESPA) was introduced. It legally established the already existing Committee on the Status of Endangered Wildlife in Canada (COSEWIC), and provided some protection for aquatic species, migratory birds, species on federal lands, or (in consultation with the provinces) that cross international boundaries. Prohibitions against harming or taking listed species, damaging their "residences," emergency orders, citizen enforcement, and measures to stop declines and restore populations all were part of the package. However, CESPA was never passed. The task force's consensus broke down, there were misconceptions and fears about the bill's scope, and strong lobbying for and against habitat protection. Provinces had concerns about interference with their jurisdiction over habitat, and many people felt the bill focused too much on regulatory approaches and not enough on voluntary, or "stewardship," approaches to conservation. The outcome of this failure has been further consultation, and a national accord among senior governments. A new bill is to be introduced in 1999, but whether it is passed and actually protects anything remains to be seen.

This is the quintessential biodiversity legal scenario, including a general direction from the International Biodiversity Convention to protect species at risk; a constitutional dispute between the federal government and provinces as to who should do it and how; industry resistance to regulation yet inadequate government support for voluntary stewardship; and environmentalists' concerns that decisions be based on science, and about the extent of governmental discretion given past inaction and reduced funds and staff.

Law has many implications for how Canadians interact with other life forms. Biodiversity law can be grouped into four main areas: protection of species; landscape issues, such as protected areas and planning; genetics; and sustainable use. Each area will be discussed below. However, we begin with some background on our Canadian legal system.

Law is usually seen as the familiar rules and regulations that tell us what we can or cannot do, but it is much more than that. Law can assist in nature conservation, sustainable use, and fair sharing. For example, law can: establish organizations, their composition, mandate, and activities; recognize or authorize individuals and organizations; help settle disputes and determine rights and responsibilities; set out principles, goals, and priorities to guide decision-making; declare or reflect publicly held social and ethical values; provide for funding mechanisms; alter the marketplace and create financial incentives for action; and educate people about the law, by making cross-references and clarifying relationships among legislation.

Law derives from many sources. It can arise from international agreements or customary practices in the world community, such as the Convention on Biological Diversity and Agenda 21, two products of the 1992 Earth Summit. A key component of Canada's response to the Convention is the 1995 Canadian Biodiversity Strategy. The Strategy is general in nature and avoids strong commitments.[1] Nonetheless, the document does lay out a context and range of measures by which Canada might address biodiversity issues.

Within Canada, the Constitution is made up of a number of separate documents, including the various Constitution Acts and the Charter of Rights and Freedoms. These provide the framework within which governments' authority to pass legislation and to act must be exercised. Courts interpret and adjudicate these laws, creating a pattern of decisions called the "common law."

Laws and associated policies are grounded in moral values, and the choices and actions we take based on them. While such values may vary among cultures, all of us, and particularly indigenous peoples and young people, feel a sense of wonder and care for the natural world, and for our non-human companions on the planet. We can hope such values will carry more influence than any law.

Governments play a large role in managing biodiversity. Individual citizens, companies, and especially non-government organizations also have been active, through education, research, management and restoration, and advocacy at every level. Many organizations propose and comment on legislation and policy, and increasingly assert their concerns through court cases, several of which have substantially altered Canada's environmental and biodiversity law.[2] They are supported by regional law centres and organizations that conduct research, education, analyses and advocacy, or bring, defend, and support such court actions. In recent landmark cases, the Supreme Court of Canada upheld the rights of citizens to go to court as representatives of a public interest to ensure that governments follow legal procedures and give full consideration to public, including environmental, concerns.[3] Such actions often foster changes in legislation, in policy, as well as wider awareness and new approaches to biodiversity concerns.

Constitutional Law and Government Structure

The international context of biodiversity law and policy is formed by a number of international treaties, conventions, and declarations. These include, for example, the 1971 (Ramsar) Convention on Wetlands of International Importance Especially as Waterfowl Habitat, the 1972 UNESCO Convention for the Protection of the World Cultural and Natural Heritage, the 1973 Convention on the International Trade in Endangered Species of Wild Fauna and Flora (CITES), and the 1992 Convention on Biological Diversity.

Canada has entered into several regional and bilateral treaties, such as the 1909 Boundary Waters Treaty (with the United States), the 1916 Migratory Birds Protection Convention (with the United States and Mexico), the 1973 Agreement on the Conservation of Polar Bears (with other circumpolar nations), and the 1978 Great Lakes Water Quality Agreement and 1987 Protocol (with the United States). Canada has ratified numerous fisheries and pollution conventions and agreements.

When it comes to nature, Canada's constitution is particularly complicated. It does not consider biodiversity *per se* and is often silent or unspecific on how it distributes responsibilities. National, provincial, territorial, Aboriginal, and municipal governments all have some authority over biodiversity, often through Departments of Natural Resources and Departments of the Environment.

The federal government has exclusive jurisdiction over international and interprovincial trade and facilities, navigation and shipping, fisheries, "Indians and Lands reserved for the Indians," criminal law, federally declared public works, and treaty-making.[4] It thus has considerable environmental authority, recently confirmed by the Supreme Court of Canada.[5] Further, the federal government may impose taxation and spend funds, as well as use its "peace, order, and good government" clause to address issues that have achieved a "national dimension" or concern.[6]

The broad, sweeping powers of federal authority encompass but are constrained by provincial jurisdiction. Provincial governments have exclusive control over natural resources, lands belonging to the province and the timber located on these lands, municipalities and any other local and private matters, and broad property and civil rights (including the right to carry on businesses and make contracts).[7] This gives the provinces the lead in conserving wildlife and habitat, and in managing biodiversity, translated into legislation for provincial parks, wildlife management, public and private land use planning, and a host of land management agencies and programs.

Provinces share jurisdiction with the federal government over some areas, such as agriculture. While the federal government has constitutional jurisdiction over fisheries, the provinces have responsibility for much land-based activities that directly affect fish, fish habitat, and fisheries. Aboriginal rights may also be involved. Territorial, Indian band, and municipal governments are established on the basis of powers delegated from the federal or provincial governments; they do not have their own constitutional mandate (however, Aboriginal rights are protected at the constitutional level). While territorial and municipal governments operate at the discretion of their parent governments, they nonetheless are well-entrenched, and exercise substantial powers and influence. Besides band councils under the federal Indian Act,[8] traditional Aboriginal systems of governance have existed for at least hundreds of years, and in many locations remain relatively intact with a considerable following and important responsibilities; traditionally, this authority is believed to come from the Creator.

Wild Animals and Plants

Traditionally, law and policy relating to wild animals and plants dealt with rights of ownership and use of such species, either by individuals or by commercial enterprises. Thus, there has been a long evolution of rules to govern hunting, trapping, and fishing of game animals and fish, and the cutting of timber for various purposes. As the value and extent of these activities increased, population numbers and quality were affected. Law and policy changes were made to more closely regulate these activities and to protect or restore certain species that had declined. An initial focus on individual plants or animals has been broadened in some cases to consider the ecosystems or landscapes of which they are a part.

Recognizing animals' tendencies to move around, the courts have long considered them to be owned by the Crown (i.e., the government) until either lawfully captured or killed, and thus brought into possession by someone. Plants, on the other hand, do not move around much and thus are deemed owned by the owner of the land where they are rooted. Especially in central and western Canada, much of the land is owned by the Crown (through the provincial governments) and thus the Crown owns the trees and other plants as well. While the different legal systems developed by humans reflect these fundamental differences in behaviour, common ownership, controls or agreements can create a blending of approaches for both animals and plants.

The rules governing hunting, trapping, and fishing tend to be some of the oldest and most familiar biodiversity laws in Canada. All provinces and territories have "wildlife" or "fish and game" Acts, generally consolidating this authority from various statutes and sources over the last century or so. Many of these jurisdictions include fish through provincial authority over property, although the federal Fisheries Act remains the primary authority. The prairie provinces have important wildlife responsibilities, especially to respect Aboriginal treaty rights to hunt and fish, entrenched in the constitution when they joined Confederation in the 1930s. These provinces also have established government ownership of (but not liability for damage by) wild animals in such laws, rather than relying solely on the common law.

Some wildlife legislation recognizes the full spectrum of wild animal species, while many retain their historical legacy by focusing on game and fur-bearing species and others listed in the regulations. Such definitions often include just mammals and birds, and overlook invertebrate species and plants as well as some body parts and juvenile stages of animals. Wildlife management and conservation is achieved through prohibitions or restrictions on various aspects of the use of wildlife, such as particular species (e.g., migratory birds or fur-bearing animals), certain characteristics of animals (e.g., sex, size, accompanying young, or nesting), closed seasons, quotas, or methods of taking wildlife.

Most jurisdictions require protection during breeding and rearing periods. Regulations prohibiting the taking of females and some males at juvenile and peak breeding ages or in vulnerable locations, areas, or habitat also are common. Provincial and territorial governments use a combination of regulations that set out broad practices and associated permits issued for specific areas, species, numbers, seasons, methods of taking animals, or types of users. Licences or permits are usually required for hunting large game species or for trapping fur-bearers, and a tagging procedure is usually necessary to correlate the carcass of an animal with the person licensed to take it. Non-residents may be required to follow somewhat different rules from residents in order to ensure appropriate conservation practices and support a local economy. Efficient use of the meat or pelt of an animal is usually required to reduce wastage and overharvesting, while dealing with animals that damage or destroy property (such as beaver or fox) may be subject to fewer restrictions or to government compensation to people affected by their activities.

Penalties for wildlife offences can be substantial, and include fines, confiscation of equipment, and loss of future use privileges. Many jurisdictions are adopting a comprehensive penalty system to address growing concerns about commercial poaching and species at risk. Wildlife enforcement powers tend to be broad, with designated wildlife officers and other enforcement officials able to inspect, search, confiscate or seize equipment and vehicles, and to make arrests. However, enforcement capability is often overextended: typically a few officers with dwindling resources patrol a large area, in the face of mounting commercial and recreational pressures on wildlife.[9]

Movement, Trade, and Captivity of Animals

Individual animals or plants introduced into an area from other jurisdictions may carry diseases or parasites, be less adapted to a new area, or out-compete local populations or species. Accordingly, the export and introduction of wildlife may be controlled by both federal and provincial wildlife legislation. Procedures under the federal Health of Animals Act, Fish Health Protection Regulations, and Migratory Bird Regulations provide opportunities to monitor and control the introduction of non-native species,[10] while provincial permits to release animals into the wild or move domestic species may also be required. A patchwork of federal, provincial, and municipal laws also governs the conditions under which wildlife is held in captivity (as in zoos, botanical gardens, laboratories, game ranches, and museum collections).

International trade in wildlife is a growing concern. This is especially so when harvesting for export causes declines in wildlife, such as bear parts taken illicitly for Asian pharmaceutical markets. The federal Wild Animal and Plant Protection and Regulation in International and Interprovincial Trade Act (WAPPRIITA) consolidates federal authority over the import, export, transport, and possession of wild animals, plants, and their parts and products.[11] It implements the trade permit system of the international Convention on the International Trade in Endangered Species of Wild Fauna and Flora (CITES). Listed animals, plants, their parts and derivatives may not be imported into Canada if they were taken, possessed, distributed, or transported in contravention of any law of a foreign state. They also may not be imported or transported interprovincially, out of a province, or in contravention of provincial law, without appropriate federal or provincial permits or other authorization.

Endangered, Migratory, and Other Species

Some species require specific measures to conserve them, either because their population is declining (e.g., endangered species) or because of their particular behaviour (e.g., migratory birds or butterflies). Species that are becoming rare or endangered can be protected at both federal and provincial levels. Besides general Canada Wildlife Act powers, there is, since CESPA's demise, still little federal law to protect endangered species. The federal and provincial governments have signed a National Accord for the Protection of Species at Risk and under this framework, and with a renewed interest in stewardship, new national programs and legislation may emerge from CESPA's ashes.

Four provinces have endangered species protection legislation,[12] while several others recognize species at risk within general wildlife legislation. Species usually are listed by regulation, and such species are protected from killing and other forms of taking or disturbance. The designations may only recognize endangered species at the most critical stage before becoming extinct, or acknowledge other levels of risk, such as threatened or vulnerable. However, governments across the country have been reluctant to list more than a few species at risk, because of resulting impacts on land users. Further, key powers for habitat protection accompanies only a few of these laws, and appear in practice to be less frequently applied. As recovery plans are developed for particular species or landscapes, territorial or provincial governments may provide support and funding or invoke other land management powers to assist in conservation efforts. Yet these often seem too little, too late, with enforcement of such laws for species at risk achieving limited success.

Beyond species at risk, other provisions in wildlife legislation may conserve non-game wildlife. Among the most important is the federal Migratory Birds Convention Act, first enacted in 1917 to implement a Canada-U.S. treaty, which now includes Mexico. The Act regulates hunting seasons, methods, and limits for the possession, transfer, and sale of migratory game birds, and prohibits hunting of migratory insectivorous birds and other migratory non-game birds. The eggs and nests of these types of birds are protected, except in the case of collecting for scientific or propagation purposes. The Act also provides authority to establish migratory bird sanctuaries. Besides this Act, other international treaty obligations protect migratory species of wildlife, such as the 1976 Agreement on the Conservation of Polar Bears, and the 1987 Canada-U.S. Agreement on the Conservation of the Porcupine Caribou Herd.

The Canada Wildlife Act enables the federal Minister of the Environment to co-ordinate, encourage, develop, and implement wildlife education, research, and conservation programs and policies. The minister may enter into agreements to carry out wildlife programs, and the Act's promotion of public education and awareness of biodiversity has given support to National Wildlife Week and other community projects.

Both federal and provincial governments adopt policies and programs that help implement their wildlife legislation, and also set a context for legislative developments. Nationally, A Wildlife Policy for Canada defines wildlife broadly within an ecosystem approach and was adopted by the Wildlife Ministers' Council of Canada in 1990. The 1991 Federal Policy on Wetland Conservation has the objective to "promote the conservation of Canada's wetlands to sustain their ecological and socio-economic functions, now and in the future." Other federal policies that may relate to wildlife and especially their habitat include the 1987 Federal Water Policy, the Environmental Quality Policy Framework, the Arctic Marine Conservation Strategy, and the Federal Policy on Land Use. Provincial and territorial governments have also adopted their own strategic documents or policies relating to some aspects of biodiversity, but few have comprehensively addressed the subject through a strategy or action plan.

Wild Plants

Less legal attention has been paid to wild plants, except as they may be affected by forestry and other commercial applications. Given their status as private property, governments have been more reluctant to regulate plants than wild animals.

Besides the important regulation of forestry on public lands, provinces may enable municipal restrictions on tree-cutting, or may support private land forestry or tree-planting (e.g., by providing trees, grants, or advice). Rarely does such consideration of plants encompass non-woody species, except the control of weed species, or the commercial harvest of wild rice and sea plants (e.g., kelp and Irish moss). Conservation practices are rarely prescribed for non-woody species, although protected areas or planning legislation may conserve significant areas and habitat of sensitive species.

The fact that plants do not migrate has generally precluded them from federal coverage, except as they are addressed in international agreements or are transported by human activity (and thus governed by statutes such as WAPPRIITA). This can limit the effectiveness of measures for conservation of animals since they are dependent upon plants for food, cover, nesting, and the like. Plants are included in the Fisheries Act, National Parks Act, Canada Wildlife Act, and in discussions of new federal endangered species legislation.

Aboriginal Rights to Wildlife

Many aspects of wildlife conservation relate to Aboriginal peoples and their rights to use wildlife and plants. These rights fall into three broad categories: treaties, land claim settlements, and unnegotiated Aboriginal rights. Section 35 of the Constitution Act, 1982 gives these constitutional protection by declaring "the existing aboriginal and treaty rights of the aboriginal peoples of Canada are hereby recognized and affirmed," while treaty rights are given precedence over provincial legislation in the federal Indian Act.

In treaties between Aboriginal communities and the Crown over the last few centuries, generally Aboriginal people *retained* (as opposed to being *granted*) rights to use wildlife, sole use of reserves, and other benefits in exchange for allowing the expansion of European settlement. Where wildlife uses were not described or transferred in treaties, separate Aboriginal rights may still survive today (such as the right to gather plants).

Unfortunately, most court interpretations of treaty and Aboriginal rights have occurred as part of prosecutions for wildlife offences, which do not provide the forum for wider-ranging discussion of the issues. A landmark prosecution of Aboriginal rights, the *Sparrow* case, identified conservation as a legitimate area for government regulation of Aboriginal (and likely treaty) rights, and that conservation takes precedence over these rights.[13] However, the case also decided that governments must carefully justify, consult on, and possibly compensate for any restrictions on these rights.

Treaty rights to wildlife are made subject to federal laws (e.g., concerning fisheries or migratory birds); in the case of the prairie province Resource Transfer Agreements of the 1930s, these rights were also made subject to provincial wildlife legislation. Other wildlife legislation and policies also explicitly reflect and respect Aboriginal and treaty rights. This may involve a general acknowledgement of these rights, or provide certain exceptions to hunting restrictions, such as in the Migratory Birds Convention Act and its 1995 Protocol. The specific wordings and context of individual Treaties are often interpreted by governments and the courts to extend only so far as subsistence use; this may reduce pressures on wildlife populations from commercial harvesting levels but may not have been the original understanding or be currently practical in a global economy.

Northern land claim settlements tend to be both more recent and more comprehensive. Conservation principles are stated in all agreements, and such principles guide the interpretation of rights and wildlife management decisions. As in much provincial and territorial wildlife legislation, there are restrictions on who may hunt, trap, and fish; for what purposes (e.g., meeting basic needs or for commerce); where; for what quotas; at what time of year; and in what manner. Such conditions are typically determined by a wildlife management board that comprises representatives from interested groups, usually the federal and provincial/territorial governments, and First Nations people. Agreements may include other mechanisms for conservation. Wildlife research, traditional knowledge, and sensitive sites are regularly identified as priorities, and lands may be allocated to various purposes, such as protected areas. Approval processes for resource developments are also increasingly included in land claim settlements.

Ecosystems and Landscapes

A variety of legal mechanisms define and allow management of specified areas of the landscape. Such areas include protected areas (or "parks," as most people know them), private stewardship, land-use planning, and restoration.

Protected Areas

Protected areas are managed primarily for conservation, usually by government. They include national, provincial, and territorial parks, as well as ecological reserves, wilderness areas, wildlife areas, and similar locations. Parks tend to focus on larger, spectacularly scenic sites and on making them accessible for recreation, whereas ecological reserves are usually smaller with a mandate to protect and support research in unique environments. Wilderness areas enable ecological processes (like fire and pest cycles) to function, and provide expansive landscapes for backcountry recreation. Wildlife areas conserve habitat while sometimes allowing hunting, fishing, and trapping along with passive recreational activities.

Most provinces and territories have some form of these designations established by a specific statute, such as a Parks Act, Ecological Reserves Act, or Wildlife Act. The federal designations are primarily national parks (National Parks Act), migratory bird sanctuaries (Migratory Birds Convention Act), and national wildlife areas (Canada Wildlife Act). Other federal lands may be protected under the Territorial Lands Act, the National Capital Act, or by other legislation.

The allocation of land into protected areas is usually conducted through a land-use planning exercise by a senior government. Boundaries are then described in the Act or more usually in regulations. Many governments have developed frameworks and targets, for completing their protected areas systems. Generally, the goal has been to adequately represent within one or more protected areas each type of ecosystem existing in the jurisdiction, as promoted by the "Endangered Spaces Campaign" of the World Wildlife Fund (Canada) and other non-government organizations. Most of these frameworks, targets, and land use allocations are established in policy, with few principles or targets set in legislation itself (British Columbia's Provincial Parks Act and Ecological Reserves Act have provided notable exceptions).

Water may be incorporated into a protected area, either adjoining a land-based area, or with its own aquatic focus. The federal government has several ways to establish aquatic protected areas: representative national marine conservation areas (National Parks Act), the Oceans Act's marine protected areas to be used for various conservation purposes, or marine or national wildlife Areas under the broad scope of the Canada Wildlife Act. Provinces may have waterway parks or extend terrestrial protected area boundaries, and all jurisdictions participate in the Canadian Heritage Rivers program that recognizes important rivers.

Establishment of protected areas means little without specifying what management and activities are allowed. Several approaches address this. First, the governing statute will set out general rules for what can take place (e.g., no mining or forestry) with the details described in the regulations and policies (e.g., only camp in certain locations at specified times). Second, areas are grouped into classifications (e.g., natural or historic), and within each area, further specific zones may be established (e.g., protection, wilderness, or access). Some classes or zones have specific purposes specified or uses prohibited. Third, the Act will assign the minister and usually a park superintendent or warden certain responsibilities to manage the area within these rules and additional policies.

A park management plan pulls together the public's wishes, professional advice, and these laws and policies. It will determine the important features and themes for a site, prohibited and permitted uses (perhaps with restrictions), and any plans to develop access roads, trails, interpretation centres, campgrounds, viewing platforms, and the like. Given their importance, it is surprising that many provinces do not have requirements in their park or ecological reserve acts to prepare, consult on, and approve management plans.

The National Parks Act has perhaps the best management plan provisions in Canada. Section 5 requires a plan within five years of establishing a park, a review every five years, public involvement, and communication of the plan and a report on the state of the parks system in the House of Commons. It also states that "[m]aintenance of ecological integrity through the protection of natural resources shall be the first priority." This means, first, that protection takes priority over recreation, and second, that the park must be seen in the larger landscape context, perhaps involving activities outside the park to maintain ecological functions within. Specifying these important principles in law ensures that they receive attention.

It is difficult for the public to ensure that governments establish protected areas and determine their appropriate type and management, because most protected areas laws have very general administrative and procedural requirements, and much is left to policy. Consequently, governments have substantial latitude in their decisions, without specific directions that the public could enforce through the courts.

Private Land Stewardship

Parks and other protected areas conserve only a small percentage of the country, thus other approaches are needed. Regulatory means such as land-use planning and wildlife laws have been tried, but often encounter resistance. In contrast, voluntary approaches enable individuals to select the methods, timing, and partnerships most appropriate to their needs, permitting wider and more positive possibilities for management and conservation. Voluntary "stewardship" of lands by private owners is critical, particularly in southern Canada where the country's population, private property, agriculture, biodiversity, and associated conflicts are concentrated. The law can enable this voluntary potential in a variety of ways by creating organizations, defining mandates, providing incentives, and enabling tools (such as through real estate and contract law) to accomplish particular tasks. Yet improvements are necessary to ensure that these various aspects work more smoothly together to protect biodiversity on private lands.

Many conservation organizations across Canada are making great efforts to protect a remnant woodlot, a patch of prairie, an agricultural landscape, or a historic trail. These organizations are established under corporations and charity laws, and exist in several forms:

- sophisticated national or provincial non-government organizations;

- quasi-governmental organizations active at the provincial scale;

- community-based "land trusts" that focus on acquiring, managing, and encouraging private landowners' stewardship of lands;

- local naturalist, trail, or game and fish associations which have acquired and manage lands, often as a secondary aspect of their activities.

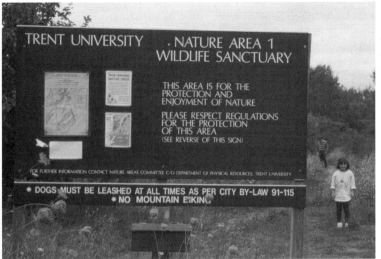

photo: Stephen Bocking

With limited resources but much energy and creativity, such groups (especially land trusts) use a whole range of private conservation methods. These include land acquisition and management techniques as well as federal and provincial tax incentives. They enable landowners to achieve long-term conservation and financial planning goals, while enhancing the conservation of lands in partnership with private organizations.

Many older landowners are now considering the future ownership and possible transfer of their properties, thus, the opportunity to move private properties into conservation ownership is larger than ever. This has traditionally involved donation to or purchase of the property by a conservation organization. Management agreements, licences, or long-term leases also may be used to set out conservation practices and responsibilities.

A new type of agreement, the "conservation easement" (or "covenant"), allows landowners to place restrictions on land use, which are then registered on their land title. This makes the agreement binding against the current and any future landowners, with the restrictions enforced by an agency or conservation organization that also signs the agreement. The owner still retains control of and the ability to sell the property, within the terms of the agreement. Easements can be more creatively applied, such as to "dedicate" private lands to long-term conservation or to further protect certain features on public lands (for example, when land is donated to public agencies, or is sold by them).

Ordinary covenants and easements require someone to own nearby land, and their use for conservation is somewhat uncertain. Accordingly, since 1990 most provinces and territories have passed new or revised conservation easement laws, to tailor this tool to a broader spectrum of purposes and to non-government players.[14] With such reforms in place, a growing number of private conservation easements have now been negotiated across the country.

Tax incentives can encourage land conservation. Where any property is given to a charity, the charity can issue a tax receipt for the money or land's value, which can be used to reduce the donor's income tax. Changes proposed for the Income Tax Act between 1995 and 1997 allow donors to claim the value of their gifts against a larger portion of their income, increasing from 20 per cent to 75 per cent generally, and to 100 per cent for certified donations of "ecologically sensitive lands." Donations of land usually still trigger a capital gains tax on the property's increase in value, but with tax credits or deductions a donor will get the benefit of about half of the gift's value.

At the provincial level, property taxes can affect the ability of landowners to manage their property for conservation. For example, owners may be forced to pursue revenue-generating activities (e.g., forestry or housing development), in order to pay high property taxes. To counter this, some provinces provide exemptions, reductions or rebates on taxes to particular kinds of landowners (e.g., farmers or non-profit organizations) or for certain types of lands (e.g., farms, forests or those with conservation value). These benefits reflect the fact that these lands provide valuable public amenities, require little if any public services, reduce costly sprawl, and would be converted from such uses if they were taxed at higher rates.

Land-Use Planning

Planning has many dimensions in Canada. It determines what activities are permitted in certain locations, may (or may not) ensure that activities are compatible with biodiversity, and specifies who has the right to participate and decide on permitted uses. It is not only a matter for governments: planning also involves many private decisions as to where and when changes in land use may occur.

Land use planning usually involves research, study, consultation, and then preparation of a plan, with associated maps, policies, and rules that elaborate and carry out the plan. Most often, areas of land are assigned to categories of use, such as housing, industrial and commercial development, roads, farming, and "open space," or preferably natural or ecological areas. These categories will permit, limit, or prohibit certain activities. Other planning tools include information requirements and permits for certain types of development.

Laws and policies for planning can be divided into two types: those governing private lands and those for public lands. Typically, planning for private lands occurs through a general provincial framework, such as a Planning Act, that sets out the types of planning tools that can be used, and any provincial goals or role. It also establishes the process that must be followed in developing, amending or reviewing a plan, and in dealing with development applications. Generally, this process is administered by the local government within this provincial framework. Other rules concerning building and fire codes, sewage treatment, flood plain development, tree cutting, and the like also are considered during this process.

Provincial, territorial, or federal governments may take a more direct approach in special areas, such as Ontario's Niagara Escarpment, Saskatchewan's Meewasin Valley, British Columbia's Creston Valley and Capital District, and the National Capital. Typically, special legislation establishes agencies to develop a plan for these areas and to administer a variety of planning controls within a specified mandate (usually in co-operation or partnership with local authorities).

Senior governments have responsibility for extensive public lands, totalling about 90 per cent of Canada's land base. While some public lands are near settled regions, much is located in more sparsely populated areas north of where agriculture is practised. Many activities occur on or may be proposed for public lands, and thus senior governments must determine what should happen where. Such exercises may cover a huge area and involve the allocation of diverse uses, or may be specific to a certain project, like a pipeline or mine.

Processes for these lands have been established in many jurisdictions. General public lands statutes provide for wide discretion by government to plan and allocate uses, and to lease or sell off public lands. Sometimes conditions, steps, and approvals are specified, but environmental conditions may only be mentioned in general terms, if at all.

Forestry laws and plans are the key means for planning most land uses in public forest regions. Mining, oil and gas development, and wildlife management all have their own planning processes, many of which overlap and must be integrated over both space and time. For certain projects environmental assessment procedures under separate legislation will guide the gathering and consideration of information and appropriate approvals.

The public is usually invited to participate in providing information, shaping the plan, and commenting on its implementation. This may occur through sitting on planning boards or advisory committees, or by having access to information, notification of proposals, public meetings, and rights of appeal to independent bodies. Public interest is usually at its most intense when there are proposals to change the plan to accommodate new development, and is critical to ensuring that biodiversity concerns are reflected in the final result. To be most effective, such interest needs to be organized and involved early in the process.

A variety of approaches in land-use planning can be used to conserve biodiversity. These include having: separate land use categories for natural and restoration areas, buffer areas around and corridors between natural areas, impact study requirements for developments, additional approval steps for site-specific details and plans, land and lot subdivision controls, controls on development densities and timing, and local environmental and planning advisory committees to provide ongoing expert and community review of plans and projects. Information on the economic benefits of conservation can also be very helpful, especially since many studies show that people and businesses prefer to live, work, and play near greenways and natural areas. Open space is less costly to service than is sprawled development, and thus produces a net tax (as well as environmental) benefit for the community.

An emerging issue affecting planning is the notion of "property rights" and a related resistance to regulating land uses. The concept, exported most recently from the United States, is based on the notion that anyone can do what they want on their own land, and that regulations constitute government interference in private lives. However, such arguments fail to acknowledge the need to balance other environmental, social, or economic values within communities. It is worth noting several points about restrictions for environmental purposes:

- planning is a public process that allows people to raise concerns, and that protects the entire community from inappropriate activities;

- planning gives individuals and organizations who do not own property a means to participate in decisions affecting them;

- similar limits based on public safety concerns on others' property (e.g., building or fire codes that protect visitors) are widely accepted;

- many regulations are based upon past experience with problems, and can prevent bigger and more costly problems later;

- governments do not receive compensation for decisions that benefit some landowners (e.g., roads), and thus are not obliged to pay for negative effects;

- if governments were to compensate people for all restrictions, the bureaucracy and taxes to administer this would be overwhelming;

- restrictions do not constitute expropriation, since government has not taken anything unto itself, and thus "compensation for expropriation" is not appropriate.

We need to balance individual and community needs. This requires a planning process based on good information, public participation, and a long-term vision. Most planning frameworks attempt to achieve this in various ways. If everyone gives a little, we all can achieve a lot more — both for ourselves and for our communities.

Case Study: Ontario's Lands for Life

Planning for public lands on a large scale took place in Ontario during 1997 and 1998. The middle half of the province that is Crown land is to

Algoma Highlands, Ontario — an area to be protected as a result of the Lands for Life process

photo: Jerry Valen DeMarco

be allocated to one of several uses: protected, tourism, and multiple use (i.e., forestry and mining) areas. The provincial government established round tables representing local sectoral interests, held public consultation events, and then let the round tables deliver their recommendations. The round tables did not constrain themselves to the government's existing policy nor direction to establish a representative system of protected areas, and industry voices were able to largely veto protected areas and tourism proposals while claiming potential job losses. Despite strong public support for protection of natural areas, the result was recommendations for only a minimal increase in protected areas, confusing designations with weaker protections, and much greater access of industrial interests to public lands.

With long-term land allocation by the government at stake, the process exposed tensions between northern rural and southern urban residents, between environmental and industry interests, and between a resource extraction (and increasingly mechanized) tradition on the one hand and a vision of a more diversified economy (including more ecotourism) on the other. As elsewhere in Canada, Lands for Life highlighted the need for confidence in secure access to and management of resources, and exemplified how managed consultations can go awry and become very contentious if they lack a clear and balanced direction.

photo: Stephen Bocking

Restoration and Genetic Diversity

Restoration and rehabilitation of damaged ecosystems is often needed to re-establish or enhance biodiversity in an area. Law and policy can assist this process by setting out principles and standards, enabling research, authorizing demonstration projects, establishing restoration areas, removing legal barriers (e.g., controls on "weeds"), and authorizing courts to order restoration measures where biodiversity has been damaged. Unfortunately, the treatment of restoration is not well elaborated in federal or provincial law, and tends to be confined to pollution, environmental assessment, and resource-use statutes (fisheries, forestry, and mining). Much of the practical direction comes from more regional or local programs and their implementing partnerships and plans.

Genetic diversity tends to be subsumed within measures for species or ecosystems. Yet this is not sufficient to deal with particular concerns about genetic diversity or with practices focused on the use of genetic material. We thus need to consider three areas of interest: genetic conservation, biotechnology and associated hazards, and the legal protection of genetic creations. The legal and policy regime in Canada is generally scattered and weak for these topics, and each deserves more concerted attention as the commercial collection, use, and transformation of genetic material expands.

Sustainable Use

Resource industries, including fisheries, forestry, and agriculture, all have substantial effects on Canadian biodiversity. Yet there are also unique dimensions to each: the elusive, migratory and international nature of fish, which only become property once caught; the long-term, extensive management of public land for forestry; and the choice of species and genetic properties by private landowners in agriculture. Federal jurisdiction is shared with the provinces for each sector, particularly in forestry and agriculture.

Fisheries

The federal Fisheries Act is the key statute governing Canadian fisheries. The Act defines "fish" broadly, to include not only fish themselves, but "shellfish, crustaceans, marine animals [e.g., whales] and [their] eggs, spawn, spat, and juvenile stages." The Act's provisions are used to regulate quotas (the total allowable catch) and the location, manner, and times in which fish may be sought and caught. These rules are set out in lengthy regulations for the commercial and recreational fisheries of the country.[15]

For non-coastal provinces, administration and enforcement of fisheries concerns have been largely delegated to provincial wildlife agencies, although lack of funding has led Ontario to refuse to assume this role. The legislation remains the responsibility of the federal government, and serves to establish some national standards, co-ordination among provinces, allocations for Aboriginal people (another federal jurisdiction), and as a trigger for other federal responsibilities such as environmental assessment.

In addition to fisheries management, the Fisheries Act seeks to sustain stocks through prohibitions on work causing "harmful alteration, disruption or destruction of fish habitat," and the deposit of any "deleterious substance" into waters frequented by fish.[16] These prohibitions may be overridden by the Minister of Fisheries and Oceans, by authorization of plans that will prevent or mitigate effects on fish habitat, or by regulations that authorize deleterious discharges.[17] The minister's authorizations are guided by the 1986 Policy for the Management of

Fish Habitat and its objective of net gain of fish habitat and sustainability of fish populations and associated fisheries.[18] The Policy is to be implemented by the Department of Fisheries and Oceans, and through agreements and protocols with provincial agencies where these organizations have been delegated the lead management role.

The Fisheries Act contains many strong provisions, backed by penalties of up to $1 million, three years' imprisonment for the worst, repeat offenders, a variety of court order powers, and incentives for citizen enforcement.[19] However, these enforcement measures are limited because they only apply after damage is done, and the scope of its habitat protection provisions is considerably constrained by provincial jurisdiction over surrounding land and property. With such constitutional and administrative division of responsibilities, it is not surprising that the fisheries enforcement track record (especially for habitat) has been mixed.

Canada's role in expanding coastal states' jurisdiction in international law has been principally oriented to fisheries management, although access to continental shelf riches has undoubtedly played a factor. Canada signed the United Nations Convention on the Law of the Sea (UNCLOS) in 1982. It contains extensive provisions regarding fisheries, marine pollution, and shipping and navigation, among other subjects.[20] UNCLOS came into force on November 16, 1994, and all relevant aspects of UNCLOS that pertain to fisheries are already considered customary international law. Canada has signed other international agreements related to fisheries and the oceans (such as the Pacific Salmon Treaty with the U.S.), and has implemented these through a variety of other legislation, such as the new Oceans Act. The 1994 amendments to the Coastal Fisheries Protection Act allowed Canada to arrest a Spanish trawler for contravening conservation measures for turbot on the Grand Bank. This focused international attention on the case, and led to negotiation of the 1995 United Nations' Agreement on Straddling and Highly Migratory Fish Stocks. While such international initiatives strengthen management capabilities and co-ordination, Canada's east and west coast fisheries remain in serious trouble and will require further attention.

Forestry

Extensive provincial laws and policies govern forestry.[21] Most concern commercial cutting on public lands. Systems of tenures and licences have evolved over the years, with increased corporate responsibilities for gathering information, planning, harvesting, wood processing, regeneration, and making payments to the Crown for the right to cut wood. Certain measures are intended to conserve biodiversity during forestry activities. These include: goals and legislative standards, an annual allowable cut set according to prescribed criteria, identification and protection of sensitive areas (e.g., rare species, wetlands, steep slopes, and vegetation along water courses), policies or guidelines on how to manage for certain habitats or species, reforestation requirements and funding commitments, local advisory committees and opportunities for public review of forest management plans, and approvals by a professional forester and by senior government officials once general criteria are met.

New forestry legislation in British Columbia and Ontario and developments elsewhere are moving these practices towards considering entire forest ecosystems and their social goods, rather than the traditional focus on commercial extraction of trees.[22] However, implementation of these schemes has been less than ideal. For example, the Ontario Court of Appeal has found that several plans under the new Act were not sustainable, thereby raising similar questions about other plans and practices (as well as an illegal road built in Temagami). In B.C., the Sierra Legal Defence Fund has released its critical reports, *The Clearcut Code* and *Stream Protection Under the Code: The Destruction Continues*, and has challenged before the Forest Appeals Commission the forest industry's technical arguments used to avoid responsibility for damaging activities.

While the provinces have primary responsibility for forestry, the federal government plays some role. This includes the territories, which are largely under its jurisdiction. Other federal authority relating to forestry can be found in the Forestry Act and the Department of Natural Resources Act, the latter enabling the "development and application of codes and standards," such as certification programs for forestry products. Federal jurisdiction indirectly influences forestry through legislation such as Fisheries Act provisions protecting fish habitat, and controls on mill effluents in the Fisheries Act and Canadian Environmental Protection Act. Other important federal roles include: promoting national-level policies and strategic directions (e.g., the National Forest Strategy); entering federal-provincial agreements guiding research and other activities; the international promotion of Canadian forestry products; membership in international organizations such as the International Tropical Timber Organization; and the supply of technical advice to other countries.

Agriculture

With international trade, farm income and debt, weather and daily business concerns, it is not surprising that the agricultural community feels overwhelmed and prefers voluntary approaches to achieving biodiversity goals. Economic incentives often support farm businesses, and these often have significant effects on both agricultural decisions and biodiversity.

The federal role in agriculture is similar, but possibly more complex, to that for forestry, and includes, among other activities, research, pilot projects, transport and export policy, and income support. Agriculture and Agri-Food Canada has a significant public role in the approval and grading of foods, seeds, and crops, and their promotion within and beyond the country. The provinces' principal roles are in agricultural technology transfer, extension and land policy. Many income support programs are cost-shared; some provinces (e.g., Ontario) support research and inspect and grade produce. Funding encompasses federal, provincial, and, increasingly, private sources.

Objectives for the conservation or sustainable use of biodiversity are rarely included within agricultural legislation, thus, programs have been oriented towards encouraging marketable, but not necessarily sustainably produced, commodities. Subsidies in the past acted as incentives to convert natural ecosystems, such as wetlands, to farm purposes. Particularly at the provincial level, drainage and weed control laws have focused on production, with substantial negative impacts on wetlands and restoration efforts.

However, there are numerous examples of how biodiversity and production objectives have converged, often within voluntary programs.[23] Examples include watercourse conservation practices, environmental farm plans, integrated pest management techniques, preservation of economically-important plant genetic material through the Plant Gene Resources of Canada, and sustainable management of significant western lands through the federal Prairie Farm Rehabilitation Administration. The 1990 Report to Ministers of Agriculture, Federal-Provincial Committee on Environmental Sustainability has been followed by Agriculture and Agri-Food Canada's 1995 National Environmental Strategy for Agriculture and Agri-Food and its 1997 Agriculture in Harmony with Nature strategy. With the new focus on understanding, stewardship, innovations, and market opportunities, such documents give new impetus to integrating environmental and social concerns into agriculture.

Conclusion

Responsibilities for the conservation and sustainable use of biodiversity are distributed across the length and breadth of Canadian society, reflecting how Canadians' prospects are tied to the destiny of the natural world. As this chapter has demonstrated, biodiversity law and policy have many dimensions, extending beyond regulation to include an array of enabling, voluntary, and private opportunities.

Internationally, the Biodiversity Convention has focused attention on conservation, sustainable use, and equitable sharing. While Canadian governments have made commitments concerning biodiversity by signing the Convention and preparing the Canadian Biodiversity Strategy, implementation has lagged well behind,[24] in spite of consistent public interest demonstrated by opinion polls, consumer preferences, and volunteer involvement in related activities.

Much of biodiversity law and policy is established by governments, whether to regulate wildlife use or forestry, or to manage protected areas. Except for a few prominent areas, such as hunting, fishing, or land-stewardship incentives, much of this is apparent only to experts, not to the general public. In this context, governments have usually been able to retain broad discretion in how they administer their legislation and programs. In consequence, clear directions, criteria, and procedures are less common for biodiversity (especially conservation) interests than for other fields, such as development planning or civil rights.

Commercial uses of biodiversity have understandably drawn the most attention throughout Canada's history. Such an emphasis is now increasingly framed by international trade rules established and arbitrated by economic specialists, with such rules taking precedence over and making only passing reference to biodiversity concerns and existing agreements. Yet a comprehensive domestic framework for biodiversity issues remains largely undeveloped or unimplemented in most Canadian jurisdictions. Certain subjects typically have limited or no recognition in senior governments' approaches to biodiversity (including non-game, rare and invertebrate wildlife; herbaceous plants; non-commercial species' genetics; aquatic ecosystems; restoration; and Aboriginal uses and management).

This uneven treatment of biodiversity must change if Canadians are to address our "ecological debt." This can occur through leadership, awareness, clear principles and criteria, and public processes; by assuming responsibilities within the Constitutional tangle; and by undertaking concerted implementation of various strategies. There also remains a large need for interdisciplinary environmental research, as well as public education and professional training, in order to support better policy and legal decision-making.[25]

Public interest in biodiversity is high, but enhanced awareness of law and policy is necessary if this interest is to be translated into fuller involvement in and support of the roles of non-governmental agencies. Involvement will also keep governments aware of their responsibilities. To foster this public role, provisions for environmental democracy must be maintained, and in some cases developed. This involves monitoring and reporting on the state of the environment, freedom to obtain information collected by governments, watchdog and advisory roles, funding of participation, and environmental assessment of decision-making.

Ultimately, it is personal actions — influenced by values, leadership, information, incentives, and regulations — that will determine the future of biodiversity in Canada. Working to their full potential, law and policy can contribute to shaping the pattern of human behaviour that is so intertwined with the biodiversity around us.

Notes

1. See the comments that most of Canada's environmental law centres provided on a later draft in *A Legal and Policy Response to the Draft Canadian
   Biodiversity Strategy* (Toronto: Canadian Institute for Environmental Law
   and Policy, 1994).
2. See, for example, *Friends of the Oldman River Society v. Canada* (1992), 88 DLR
   (4th) 1, 7 CELR (N.S.) 1 (SCC.) concerning federal environmental assessment responsibilities; *Canadian Parks and Wilderness Society v. Canada (Minister of
   Environment)* (1992), 55 FTR 286 (FCTD) regarding logging in national parks.
3. See *Canadian Wildlife Federation v. Canada (Minister of Environment)* (1989), 3 CELR
   (N.S.) 287 (FCTD), aff'd (1989), 4 CELR (N.S.) 1 (FCA); *Friends of the Oldman
   River Society v. Canada* (1992).
4. Constitution Act, 1867, 30 & 31 Vict., c.3 (formerly, the British North
   America Act, 1867, Sections 91(2), (10), (12), (24), (27), 92 (10)(c), 132, respectively. If the subject of a treaty is within provincial jurisdiction, then generally the province must pass legislation to give effect to the treaty.
5. *R. v. Hydro-Québec*, unreported, 18 September 1997, Supreme Court of
   Canada.
6. The leading case is *R. v. Crown Zellerbach Ltd.* (1988), [1988] 1 SCR 401.
7. Constitution Act, 1867, Sections 92(5), 92(13), 92A, 109.
8. Indian Act, RSC 1985, c.I-5.
9. L.J. Gregorich, *Poaching and the Illegal Trade in Wildlife and Wildlife Parts in
   Canada* (Ottawa: Canadian Wildlife Federation, 1992).
10. Health of Animals Act, SC 1990, c.21 (RS, C.h-3.3); Fish Health Protection
    Regulations, CRC 1978, vol. VII, c.812; Migratory Bird Regulations, CRC
    1978, vol. XI, c.1035.
11. Wild Animal and Plant Protection and Regulation of International and
    Interprovincial Trade Act, SC 1992, c.52, brought into force in 1996.
12. Endangered Species Act, SM 1989-90, c.39 (c.EIII); Endangered Species Act,
    RSO 1990, c.E.15; La Loi sur les espèces menacées ou vulnérables, LRQ, c.E-
    12.01; Endangered Species Act, SNB 1996, c.E-9.101. See also Newfoundland's
    1997 proposal.
13. *R. v. Sparrow* (1990), [1990] 1 SCR 1075, 3 CNLR 16.
14. For a fuller discussion of conservation easement legislation, see Thea M.
    Silver, Ian C. Attridge, Maria MacRae, and Kenneth W. Cox, *Canadian
    Legislation for Conservation Covenants, Easements and Servitudes: The Current Situation*,
    Report No.95-1 (Ottawa: North American Wetlands Conservation

Council [Canada], 1995).

15. For a comprehensive treatment of the protection of Canada's marine biodiversity and environment, see David VanderZwaag, *Canada and Marine Environmental Protection: Charting a Legal Course Towards Sustainable Development* (London: Kluwer Law International, 1995); David VanderZwaag, ed., *Canadian Ocean Law and Policy* (Markham, Ont.: Butterworths, 1992).

16. Sections 35(1) and 36(3), respectively.

17. Section 35(2). A variety of these regulations have been passed to date.

18. Canada, Department of Fisheries and Oceans, *Policy for the Management of Fish Habitat* (Ottawa: Department of Fisheries and Oceans, 1986). The 1990 *Wildlife Policy for Canada* also includes fish within its scope.

19. See Sections 40 to 42, and 63 to 83 (especially 78.1 and 79.2), among others.

20. *United Nations Convention on the Law of the Sea* (1982), UN Doc. A/CONF.62/122; 21 I.L.M. 1261. See Part XII (Environment), Articles 192-237, and for fisheries, Part V, Articles 55-75, and Part VII, Articles 116-20.

21. See Monique Ross, *Forest Management in Canada* (Calgary: Canadian Institute of Resources Law, 1995).

22. Forest Practices Code of British Columbia Act, SBC 1994, c.41, and Crown Forest Sustainability Act, SO 1994, c.25.

23. Joyce Greenfield and Nicole Richer, *Biodiversity Initiatives Involving Canadian Agricultural Producers* (Ottawa: Agriculture and Agri-Food Canada, National Agriculture Environment Committee, and Canadian Cattlemen's Association, 1996).

24. Auditor-General of Canada, *Report to the House of Commons* (Ottawa: Auditor-General, 1998).

25. Nina-Marie Lister, personal communication, May 8, 1996.

Further Reading

Attridge, Ian, ed. *Biodiversity Law and Policy in Canada: Review and Recommendations.* Toronto: Canadian Institute for Environmental Law and Policy, 1996.

Attridge, Ian. *Conservation Easement Valuation and Taxation in Canada.* Ottawa: North American Wetlands Conservation Council, Canada, 1997.

Biodiversity Working Group. *Canadian Biodiversity Strategy: Canada's Response to the Convention on Biological Diversity.* Ottawa: Environment Canada, 1995.

Canadian Bar Association. *Sustainable Development in Canada: Options for Law Reform.* Ottawa: Canadian Bar Association, 1990.

Caza, C. *Saving Species: Building Habitat into Endangered Species Conservation in Canada.* Ottawa: Wildlife Habitat Canada, 1995.

Clark, Karen, and Ian Attridge. *Legal and Policy Mechanisms Concerning Genetic Resources in Canada.* Toronto: Canadian Institute for Environmental Law and Policy, 1997.

Estrin, David, and John Swaigen, eds. *Environment on Trial: A Guide to Environmental Law and Policy,* 3rd ed. Toronto: Canadian Institute for Environmental Law and Policy, and Emond Montgomery Publications, 1993.

Findlay, Barbara, and Ann Hillyer. *Here Today, Here Tomorrow: Legal Tools for the Voluntary Protection of Private Land in British Columbia.* Vancouver: West Coast Environmental Law Research Foundation, 1994.

Geist, Valerius, and Ian McTaggart-Cowan, eds. *Wildlife Conservation Policy.* Calgary: Detselig, 1995.

Locke, Harvey, and Stewart Elgie. "Using the Law to Protect Wild Places," in Monte Hummel, ed., *Protecting Canada's Endangered Spaces: An Owner's Manual.* Toronto: Key Porter, 1995.

Rankin, Colin, and Michael M'Gonigle. "Legislation for Biological Diversity: A Review and Proposal for British Columbia," *University of British Columbia Law Review* 277 (1991).

Sandborn, Calvin, ed. *Law Reform for Sustainable Development in British Columbia.* Vancouver: Canadian Bar Association, British Columbia Branch, 1990.

Sandborn, Calvin. *Green Space and Growth: Conserving Natural Areas in B.C. Communities.* Victoria: Ministry of Environment, Lands and Parks, 1996.

Jacques Prescott,

Benoît Gauthier,

& Léopold Gaudreau

Implementing a Biodiversity Strategy and Action Plan in Quebec

QUEBEC CONTAINS A REMARKABLE DIVERSITY OF LAND-scapes, from the boreal and mixed forests and streams and lakes of the St. Lawrence region to the tundra and taiga of northern Quebec. The effects of centuries of human activity also are evident. In the south, farms have been carved from the forests that covered much of the St. Lawrence River valley, and forests, fields and wetlands continue to be consumed as Montreal and other urban areas expand. Further north, the boreal forests feed the mills of Quebec's pulp and paper industry. There, and in the tundra and taiga of northern Quebec, rivers have been reshaped for hydroelectric power generation.

Historically, Quebec has had relatively few parks or other protected areas. However, the provincial government, with its partners, is now acting more decisively to conserve, and to ensure sustainable use and equitable sharing of Quebec's biodiversity.[1] Across Canada's largest province, this interaction between natural heritage and human activities is being played out, reproducing many of the conflicts and complexities that, on a global scale, led the United Nations to adopt, at the 1992 Earth Summit in Rio de Janeiro, an international Convention on Biological Diversity to protect and sustainably use biological resources.[2]

A biodiversity strategy is essential to implementing the commitment of each party to this Convention. In Canada, the federal government has ratified the Convention and has prepared a national strategy in collaboration with the provinces and territories and with the contribution of stakeholders.[3] Resource management in Canada being for the most part under provincial jurisdiction, provincial and territorial governments were expected to lead in implementing the national strategy. Accordingly, since 1992 the Quebec government has developed a strategy and action plan, and a supporting ecological framework with which to do so. The process demonstrates how, despite the recognized failure of the United Nations to meet the Earth Summit commitments, the Biodiversity Convention can be implemented if efforts are co-ordinated effectively. An effective process requires participation by a wide array of agencies and partners, both within and outside the provincial government, co-ordinated by a central office and task force.

Implementing the Biodiversity Convention in Quebec

In crafting its strategy and action plan the Quebec government followed a seven-step process.[4]

Step 1: Getting Organized: Mandate and Work Plan

Once signed by Canada at the Earth Summit in June 1992, the Convention on Biological Diversity was endorsed by Québec and the other provincial and territorial governments. In December 1992 the Convention was formally ratified by the Canadian government.

The Québec government mandated the Ministère de l'Environnement et de la Faune (Department of Environment and Wildlife) to implement the Convention. In March 1993 an Interdepartmental Biodiversity Task Force was appointed, with participation by numerous departments (agriculture, municipal affairs, international relations, environment and wildlife, education, transport, health and social care, natural resources, industry, commerce, science and technology), as well as the interdepartmental committee on environmental education and two semi-private organizations (Fondation de la Faune du Québec and Hydro-Québec). While implementing the Convention at the provincial level, this task force also participated actively in developing the Canadian biodiversity strategy. A strong communication link between the task force and the ministerial directorates in charge of protected areas and endangered species in Quebec was established.

Step 2: Gathering Information and Assessing Biological Diversity

The task force prepared an assessment of existing biodiversity laws, regulations, policies, programs and activities in Quebec related to the Convention, with special reference to protected areas, and vulnerable and endangered species.[5] The outcomes of numerous public consultations on sustainable development and related issues were sifted for considerations related to biodiversity.[6]

A general assessment of biodiversity in Quebec was also prepared. From north to south, Quebec comprises five biogeographical zones — tundra, taiga, the spruce belt, the balsam fir belt, and the hardwood forest. Quebec possesses at least 9,044 of the world's plant and animal species, including 740 introduced plant species and 18 introduced animal species, as well as 100 plant species and 17 animal species that are cultivated or domesticated. There are also 653 native animal species, including 199 fish, 326 bird, and 91 mammal species, and over 30,000 invertebrate species. Likely to be designated threatened or vulnerable

Salmon fishing on the Matapedia River — one element of the economic value of biodiversity in Quebec

are 374 native vascular plants and more than 50 invertebrate and 72 vertebrate species. Forests cover 40 per cent of the territory, agricultural land accounts for 2 per cent and urban land 1.4 per cent. Protected areas now cover 3.15 per cent of the province.[7]

Our assessment emphasized the economic value of biodiversity. Each year biodiversity generates more than $15.5 billion within the primary and secondary economic sectors, and provides direct employment to 225,000 workers. The contribution of national and provincial parks alone is substantial: Quebecers and non-residents spend about $590 million annually on non-consumptive activities such as hiking, outing, and nature observation. By emphasizing these economic val-

---

Box 1 | **A Biodiversity Strategy for Sustainable Development**

Biodiversity information was organized according to a sustainable development framework[1] taking into account the different sectors of activities coupled with an ecological approach. This ecosystemic framework was used as a foundation for the Biodiversity Strategy and Action Plan adopted by the government in May 1996.[2] It involves several steps.

First, the framework *determines the geographical entity* or territory concerned: in this case the Quebec territory.

Second, it classifies the different uses and activities according to the type of resources considered:

- Energy resources (energy development, transportation, and use)
- Conservation of natural resources (protected areas, endangered species, *ex situ* conservation)
- Wildlife resources (fisheries, angling, trapping, hunting)
- Forest resources (logging, reforestation, forest management)
- Agriculture resources (cultivation, animal production, aquaculture)
- Mineral resources (mining, site restoration)
- Industry, technology, and services (biotechnology)
- Urban environment (pollution, population issues, transport, urban land use)

All these activities have some impact on the territory, whether it is defined in terms of political divisions, or as a terrestrial watershed or atmospheric basin. In Quebec, by monitoring the St. Lawrence River watershed the environmental quality of this territory can be verified. Information related to the St. Lawrence watershed will thus be filed under a distinct heading. Similarly, information concerning northern Quebec, a region that is less populated and

---

ues to senior levels of government, a higher priority came to be attached to biodiversity.

Reflecting the commitment of the Quebec government to sustainable development, the biodiversity strategy was built on a framework incorporating this commitment (Box 1). This approach strengthened the interest of the various government departments in biodiversity.

Step 3: Formulation of an Implementation Strategy

Formulating a strategy to implement the Biodiversity Convention itself involved several steps:

---

that is governed by specific conventions with indigenous peoples, is gathered under another category.

Environmental emergencies constitute another heading where information is collected on emergency plans.

Two other headings concern individual (*ecocivism*: public, NGO, and private-sector participation) and collective (*societal*: public education and awareness) values. These headings address ethical values, awareness and education. The next to the last heading concerns *quality of life* — the ultimate goal of sustainable development. This heading provides an integrated portrait of the contribution of biodiversity to the well-being of Quebec society (GNP, employment, revenues, etc.). A final heading concerns *spiritual values* and integrates the contribution of traditional knowledge, rituals, and religious beliefs to nature conservation.

Within each heading, information can be classed according to the three categories proposed by the Organization of Economic Co-operation and Development for environmental indicators: knowledge of the situation or the state of the resources, impacts or pressure of human activities on the environment, and activities in response to these impacts.

One will thus find under each heading information on the state of the resources, species, ecosystems, research and monitoring activities, exploitation and management activities, conservation and mitigation measures, as well as a series of objectives, targets, and measures concerning each domain of interest (Table 1).

---

1   See B. Gauthier. "Cadre de référence théorique pour le développement durable et al biodiversite au Québec," Ministère de l'Environnement et de la Faune, Direction de la conservation et du patrimoine écologique, 1997.

2   Quebec, *Québec Biodiversity Action Plan* (Ministère de l'Environnement et de la Faune, 1996).

First, a gap analysis was conducted. That is, the current government activities were compared with the Biodiversity Convention's requirements. This involved analysis of the principles and objectives of the Convention, existing policy objectives within each government sector, and biodiversity related recommendations made in previous public consultations. A draft strategy was then prepared, setting out the main objectives, aims, and measures concerning each sector. Finally, there was extensive public consultation, with open sessions, and more than 300 organizations, institutions, and selected individuals being invited to comment on the draft. Many responded to the invitation, including the Quebec Mining Association, the Forestry Industry Association, Hydro-Québec, the Union of Agricultural Producers, the Quebec Zoo Association, the Fédération québécoise de la faune (Quebec Wildlife Federation), the Quebec Union for the Conservation of Nature (UQCN), and the Fondation de la faune du Québec (Quebec Wildlife Foundation). Recommendations made by the public were integrated within the document.

The outcome of this process was the Quebec Biodiversity Strategy. It suggests 30 general objectives and identifies 189 measures to be implemented in response to the Convention. These cover the major sectors related to biological diversity, such as wildlife, forestry, agriculture, mineral resources, aquatic environment, energy, northern resources, urban environment, biotechnology, and education. More specifically, they encompass the conservation of ecosystems, sustainable use of renewable resources, conservation and sustainable use of northern resources, land use planning, and the active participation of the partners in defining and following up international agreements (Box 2).

Based on analysis of the Parks Act, the Ecological Reserve Act, and the Vulnerable and Endangered Species Act, as well as analysis of the Biodiversity Convention itself, the following five objectives were targeted for conserving natural resources:

- Increase the ecological knowledge needed to establish a quality system of protected areas and to safeguard vulnerable or threatened components of natural biological diversity (this will be achieved, among other things, through government initiatives encouraging research into ecosystems in protected areas, by identifying and expanding our knowledge of exceptional forests, and by consolidating and expanding existing natural heritage databases).

- Establish and maintain an integrated, representative system of protected areas that will ensure preservation of biodiversity.

- Consolidate our system of management areas in order to protect biodiversity in a larger proportion of the territory (for example, by adopting and enforcing regulations respecting the protection of wildlife; by drafting consolidation plans for wildlife sanctuaries; by supporting urban communities in developing regional parks; and by amending current legislation and tax measures to facilitate the conservation of natural environments on lands in the private domain).

- Conserve *ex situ* vulnerable or threatened components of natural biological diversity.

- Adopt and implement measures to safeguard species and ecosystems outside conservation areas, for example, by regulating the use of all-terrain vehicles in sensitive areas; determining the legal framework required to manage native plants other than commercial species; determining the littoral limit for wetlands (peat bogs, marshes, swamps); and establishing and implementing recovery plans for threatened or vulnerable species.

During public consultation on the draft strategy special attention was given to inviting groups and institutions active in the field of protected areas, endangered species, and *ex situ* conservation.

Step 4: Formulation of an Action Plan

The Action Plan began in May 1996 with 429 activities and programs to be carried out by government agencies and their partners between 1996 and 2000. These actions included 344 existing activities and programs directly related to biodiversity conservation and sustainable use. There were also 63 new initiatives or activities developed to comply with the Biodiversity Convention articles, including 18 added during the first year. For each of these, the Action Plan provides a short description and year of completion, and identifies the responsible agency and/or partner. Some examples include:

- production of a status report on forest biodiversity.

- definition of criteria and indicators for measuring biodiversity.

- taking ecosystem and biodiversity conservation into account when assessing the environmental impacts of agricultural programs.

- financial support for the Convention on Biological Diversity secretariat in Montreal.

- identification and prioritization of *ex situ* conservation needs.

- review of forestry practices regarding their impacts on biodiversity.

Box 2

Implementing the Convention on Biological Diversity in Quebec

Two key components of the Quebec Biodiversity Strategy are:

1. *Strategy for the conservation and sustainable use of biological diversity*

This includes objectives for each sector of activity covered in the sustainable development framework. Some examples of these objectives are:

- improve our knowledge and management of biological diversity through an ecosystem-based approach;

- establish and maintain an integrated, representative system of protected areas that will ensure the preservation of biodiversity;

- meet demand while ensuring maintenance and sustainable use of wildlife resources;

- promote forest management that is consistent with the objectives of sustainable ecosystem use, integrated resource management, and environmental protection;

- ensure the sustainable use of agricultural resources;

- promote biotechnology that contributes to the protection and maintenance of biological diversity;

- preserve and enhance biological diversity in urban and near-urban areas;

- support mineral resource development activities that have minimal impact on biological diversity;

In addition, 40 existing activities were modified to include biodiversity considerations.

The Action Plan is continually evolving, and activities are closely monitored and evaluated each year. In the process, complementary actions may be merged, some activities may be deleted for lack of funding or lack of pertinence and others may be added. The Action Plan should be completely revised at the end of the four-year period and emerge as a new plan to be submitted for government approval. In the meantime, all foreseen measures of the Strategy will be integrated into governmental programs. Regional and municipal authorities, as well as all provincial institutions, NGOs, and businesses, have been invited to implement the Strategy and incorporate its objectives into their own development and conservation programs.

In the first published version of the Biodiversity Action Plan 70 actions were listed under the five general objectives relating to conservation of natural resources. The majority of these actions involve the Department of Environment and Wildlife, and the Department of

---

- support measures apt to minimize the impact of energy-related activities on biological diversity and that favour the rehabilitation of ecosystems;
- adopt measures aimed at eliminating or reducing the adverse effects of certain human activities on biodiversity (species and ecosystems) in northern Quebec;
- ensure maximum protection of the physical environment of protected areas and sensitive and *ex situ* conservation sites during environmental emergencies;
- broaden awareness regarding the importance of conserving and using sustainably biological diversity.

2. *Main government measures to be implemented*

These measures have been prioritized according to the following criteria:

- geographical impact (provincial impact supersedes local impact);
- consistency with Convention objectives (action that indirectly affects biological diversity is deemed less relevant than action that directly affects it);
- urgency (the current state of biodiversity makes certain actions, such as safeguarding threatened species, more urgent than others);
- sequence (certain measures, often related to knowledge acquisition, ought to be implemented before taking other action).

Natural Resources. Some also involve the Department of Agriculture, Fisheries and Food; Municipal Affairs; and Transport. During the first year of the plan, three new actions were added to this list by the Department of Environment and the Fondation de la faune du Québec.[8] Examples of these actions include:

- Action 103. Develop methodology enabling parks to serve as yardsticks for measuring changes in natural ecological processes.

- Action 106. Produce a guide to mossy spruce stands.

- Action 109. Collect and enter data on rare wildlife species.

- Action 111. Establish the provincial park action plan for 1998-2002.

- Action 142. Prepare and table a draft bill on off-road vehicles to regulate the use of off-road vehicles in sensitive areas.

Step 5: Implementation

As we have noted the provincial cabinet delegated in 1992 to the Minister of Environment and Wildlife responsibility for implementing the Convention. Following the adoption of the provincial strategy and action plan in May 1996, the existing Interdepartmental Committee on Sustainable Development received the mandate to implement the Biodiversity Strategy and Action plan. This interdepartmental committee is assisted by the Interdepartmental Biodiversity Task Force that was created in 1993 to prepare the strategy. The task force is supported by a Biodiversity Co-ordination Centre, which acts as a secretariat for biodiversity issues. This Centre is staffed with three people and has a small yet adequate budget.

The four-year implementation program thus involves nine departments and two public corporations. It must be noted that this program does not involve new funds. Rather, the Strategy and Action Plan provides specific direction for existing or redesigned activities that are then funded through regular departmental budgets. These agencies and corporations deal with provincial programs and activities that are implemented in the different administrative regions of the province. However, given the importance of the local efforts in implementing the Convention, steps were also taken in the spring of 1997 to establish a pilot implementation program in the Mauricie-Bois-Francs region. A local NGO already involved in biodiversity issues, the Centre de la diversité biologique du Québec, organized a workshop involving a number of agencies and local organizations interested in biodiversity conservation and sustainable use. This NGO was designated by the workshop participants as a local focal point and clearing house with the mandate of preparing and orchestrating a biodiversity action plan for this area. This initiative could eventually lead to similar activities in other regions.

Implementation being critical to the success or failure of any strategy or action plan, the co-ordination team has to face the challenge of continually informing and educating their counterparts in the various agencies about biodiversity. Often, this is a matter of explaining the relation between local initiatives and global agreements. Also, new partners are actively sought.

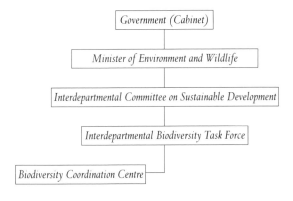

Figure 1:
Implementing
the Convention
on biological
diversity in
Quebec

Step 6: Evaluation and Follow-up

The monitoring and follow-up of this ambitious program of activities has been entrusted to the Interdepartmental Committee on Sustainable Development, steered by the Ministère de l'Environnement et de la Faune. This committee, composed of representatives from all government departments and agencies involved in the Biodiversity Action Plan, is supported by a Co-ordination Centre that maintains communication between the members of the Inter-departmental Biodiversity Task Force. The Co-ordination Centre is at the heart of a biodiversity information network involving other key players on the international and national scenes. Information from the Convention Secretariat or the Canadian Biodiversity Office is relayed by the Centre to the concerned agencies and organizations. When needed, the Co-ordination Centre produces analyses or summaries of priority issues and documents and may suggest some activity. The general orientation of the positions and actions suggested by the Co-ordination Centre is directly inspired by the Quebec Biodiversity Strategy and Action Plan objectives. The Centre also produces progress reports on the Action Plan, and agencies are asked to produce an update of their actions twice a year.

The Quebec Biodiversity Strategy and Action Plan is related to a number of other sectoral government initiatives concerned with the sustainable use of renewable resources: energy, conservation, wildlife, forestry, and agriculture. Together they constitute a strong commitment towards sustainable development.

Step 7: Report on Conservation, Sustainable Use, and Equitable Sharing

During the first year of implementation (1996-97), 366 actions were monitored by the Co-ordination Centre. Forty-one of these actions were completed, 19 were inactive, and nine were abandoned or merged with complementary activities. The other actions were either partially completed or considered as part of a recurrent program. Another 18 new actions were added to the list.[9]

Following the publication of the first annual report, positive comments were made by several individuals and non-governmental organizations on the co-ordination efforts underlying the action plan and on the quality of the information presented. It was noted nevertheless that an evaluation of the progress made in the field was needed and that future efforts should be oriented towards identifying and monitoring biodiversity indicators.

After the Strategy and Action Plan is completed, the Co-ordination Centre plans to evaluate its impact on biodiversity with the use of such indicators. At the provincial level, biodiversity indicators could include, for example, percentage of area in strictly protected status, proportion of actual versus potential timber harvesting, total cultivated area, freshwater (bacteriological and physico-chemical) quality index, total forest area affected by natural or human-induced disasters (forest fires, ice storms, insect plagues), investments related to biotechnology research and development, or total production value and number of jobs associated with primary and secondary exploitation of biodiversity.

Examples of completed actions include:

Action 112 - In September 1996, the Quebec government officially created the Mont-Valin Conservation Park with a total surface area of 153.6 km². In December of the same year, the Ministère de l'Environnement et de la Faune tabled before the National Assembly the draft bill on the Saguenay-St. Lawrence Marine park.

Action 131 — The Ministère des Affaires Municipales helped set up eight regional committees with a mandate to analyse plans to create regional parks in the vicinity of the Bonaventure River, the Seignory of Matapedia Lake, Mont Grand-Fonds, the Massif du Sud, the Kekeko Hills, Opemican, Kenogami Lake, and the Pays-d'en-Haut.

By the year 2000, and the end of this four-year process, a revised Strategy and Action Plan should emerge, laying the basis for renewed progress.

Lessons Learned

Several elements characterize this co-ordination exercise and illustrate how biodiversity planning can improve management of natural resources:

Understanding the problems in a larger context. The Strategy and Action Plan provide both a local and a global perspective to the managers and administrators. These documents also provide a common framework for every policy and program concerning the different aspects of biodiversity. Before the adoption of the strategy, one could envisage a different framework for each department. The adoption of a common framework unites the sectoral views and contributes to establishing a sense of unity and co-operation around common objectives.

Better identification of responsibilities. As a result of the Action Plan and the efforts of the ministerial co-ordinators, the global commitments of the government towards biodiversity are better known and understood within each department and outside the government. This leads to greater cohesion between the different stakeholders and guarantees continuity especially in the implementation of priority actions. One may also argue that the financial effort associated with this planning exercise more than pays for itself with the money saved by avoiding duplication of efforts.

Obliging civil servants to report to partners and helping identify new opportunities for partnership. Civil servants normally report only to their hierarchical authority. The collegial system established in the Strategy and Action Plan obliges them to report annually to the Co-ordination Centre, to the other partners and agencies, and ultimately to the general public. This new approach is more transparent and leads to a more democratic appraisal of government work. At the same time, it helps in identifying new opportunities for partnership.

Contributing to establish an ongoing multi-stakeholder planning process. A biannual appraisal of the Action Plan demands a continual updating of the different programs and actions. This updating may in turn fuel a proactive approach to the issues.

Promoting decentralization of the Convention implementation process. Dissemination of information regarding the Strategy and Action Plan gives rise to new initiatives particularly related to local implementation of the Convention objectives. It also facilitates the association and integration of new partners into the Action Plan at the provincial or the local level. For example, in the weeks following publication of the first annual report, two provincial NGOs responded to the invitation of the government and announced their willingness to develop their own biodiversity action plan. One of them, the Quebec Wildlife Federation, launched an educational campaign to promote biodiversity conservation among its membership.

Win-win approach. This approach builds on existing programs and activities related to biodiversity conservation and sustainable use. The information shared in the process helps identify gaps and future commitments.

Promoting innovative programs. Development of the Strategy and Action Plan fostered the elaboration and implementation of innovative actions for biodiversity conservation. It also induced the integration of biodiversity considerations into a number of existing programs. As a matter of fact, of the 429 actions listed in the action plan, 63 are considered new activities and 40 concern existing programs that were modified to comply with the convention.

Putting a concrete face on sustainable development. The three objectives of the Biodiversity Convention cover all aspects of sustainable development: preserving the environment (biodiversity conservation), developing the economy (sustainable use of biological resources), and preserving and developing social equity (equitable sharing of the benefits). In this regard, the Biodiversity Strategy and Action Plan may be seen as a major contribution to sustainable development.

Key to success. To be successful, the approach must be based on the commitment of a handful of skilled individuals, be interdisciplinary, multisectoral, and ensure the active participation of relevant stakeholders.

Conclusion

More than six years after Rio, the global environment has continued to deteriorate. However, the implementation of the Convention on Biological Diversity provides for some encouragement. The Convention can be seen as a catalyst for sustainable development. In Quebec, the following ingredients facilitated a rapid and efficient implementation of the Convention:

Table 1: Biodiversity Action Plan Framework	THEMES	1. Energy resources	2. Conservation of Natural resources	3. Wildlife resources	4. Forest resources	5. Agriculture resources	6. Agriculture resources	7. Mineral resources	8. Industry, technology and services	9. Urban environment	10. Oceanographic & atmospheric basin (St Lawrence Watershed)	11. Environmental emergencies	12. Ecocivism	13. Societal values	14. Quality of life
DECISION PROCESS															
IMPLEMENTATION — Indicators															
Expected results 1-5-10 years															
$ 1 yr, 5 yr, 10 yr															
Scientific & technological requirements															
ACTIONS — Cooperation & coordination															
Related to Management															
Data & information															
OBJECTIVES — General & specific															
BASE FOR ACTION — Litigation															
Impacts															
Data															
Context (international, national, provincial)															

- strong political will from the government;

- active participation of all ministerial partners and natural resources managers;

- consultation of the public at an appropriate time;

- availability of adequate information on the status of our natural resources;

- the very large economic importance of our biodiversity;

- and, most importantly the adoption of an appropriate ecological framework.

Of all the difficulties we encountered in developing and implementing our Biodiversity Strategy and Action Plan, most important has been the determination of the topics to be covered. Although Miller and Lanou have published a useful biodiversity planning guide and the IUCN has produced a well documented guide to the Convention,[10] one major planning tool was lacking: a *clear ecosystemic framework for biodiversity planning*. Biodiversity planners and decision-makers need a global framework to delineate their ballpark and describe in simple terms the innumerable relations that exist between human activities and the living world.

Biodiversity is a vast domain that may be interpreted or viewed differently depending on point of view or expertise. How does biodiversity planning fit with sustainable development planning or with existing nature conservation, forestry, agriculture, urban planning, or pollution prevention policies and programs? Where does biodiversity planning start and where does it end? Which topics, department, agencies, or sectors of activity should be involved or included in the planning? We solved this difficulty by adapting to our needs the framework developed by Gauthier (Table 1).[11] This simple ecosystemic framework helped guide and unify the thoughts of the stakeholders around common issues and helped them better understand their role in the process. The real challenge facing the Biodiversity Convention signatory parties in the coming years will be to adopt a global ecosystemic framework of this kind to facilitate implementation of the Convention objectives in all sectors of society and everywhere in the world.

Notes

1. L. Gaudreau, "The Québec Action Plan on Biological Diversity: The importance of protected areas in a conservation strategy," *Ecodecision* 23 (1997): 53-55.
2. United Nations Environment Program, *Convention on Biological Diversity* (Nairobi: UNEP, 1992).
3. Canada, *Canadian Biodiversity Strategy* (Ottawa: Ministry of Supply and Services, 1995).
4. This process was similar to the seven-step approach suggested by K. Miller and S.M. Lanou, *Biodiversity Planning: Guidelines Based on Early Experiences around the World* (Washington, Gland, Switzerland, Nairobi: World Resources Institute in co-operation with the United Nations Environment Program and the World Conservation Union (IUCN), 1995).
5. Québec, *Bilan des lois, règlements, politiques, programmes et activités au Québec reliés aux dispositions de la Convention sur la diversité biologique* (Groupe de travail inter-ministériel sur la diversité biologique, 1993).
6. B. Gauthier, *Compilation et classification des principaux énoncés sur la diversité biologique* (Québec: Environnement et Faune, 1994).
7. G. Boisseau and B. Gauthier, *Répertoire des aires naturelles protégées au Québec* (Direction de la conservation et du patrimoine écologique, Ministère de l'Environnement et de la Faune, 1997).
8. Québec, *Suivi du plan d'action québécois sur la diversité biologique: Rapport annuel 1996-1997* (Ministère de l'Environnement et de la Faune, 1997).
9. Ibid.
10. Miller and Lanou, *Biodiversity Planning*; L. Glowka, et al., *A Guide to the Convention on Biological Diversity* (Gland and Cambridge: IUCN, Environmental Policy and Law Paper No. 30, 1994).
11. B. Gauthier, "Cadre de référence théorique pour le développement durable et la biodiversité au Québec," Ministère de l'Environnement et de la Faune, Direction de la conservation et du patrimaine écologique, 1997.

Further Reading

Boisseau, G., and B. Gauthier. *Répertoire des aires naturelles protégées au Québec.* Québec: Direction de la conservation et du patrimoine écologique, Ministère de l'Environnement et de la Faune, 1997.

Dansereau, P. "Ecology and the escalation of human impact," *International Social Science Journal* 22, 4 (1970): 628-47.

Dansereau, P. "Biodiversity, ecodiversity, sociodiversity: three aspects of diversity. Part 1: Biodiversity. Part 2. Ecodiversity. Part 3: Sociodiversity," *La biodiversité mondiale/Global biodiversity* 6, 4 (1996): 2-9; 7, 1 (1997): 2-8; 7, 3 (1997): 44-53.

Gauthier, J. *Les oiseaux nicheurs du Québec: atlas des oiseaux nicheurs du Québec méridional.* Association québécoise des groupes ornithologiques, Société québécoise de protection des oiseaux, Service canadien de la faune, Environnement Canada, Région du Québec, 1995.

Lauzon, L., H. Dion, and C.E. Delisle, eds. *Le Saint-Laurent pour la vie.* Actes du 21e Congrès de l'Association des biologistes du Québec, Collection Environnement de l'Université de Montréal, vol. 23, 1997.

Lauzon, L., I. Tousignant, and C.E. Delisle, eds. *Biodiversité et développement: Mariage possible?* Actes du 19e Congrès de l'Association des biologistes du Québec, Collection Environnement de l'Université de Montréal, vol. 19, 1995.

Marie-Victorin, F. *Flore laurentienne,* 3e édition mise au jour et annotée par L. Brouillet et I. Goulet. Montréal: Presses de l'Université de Montréal, 1995.

Ministère du Loisir, de la Chasse et de la Pêche. *Bilan de la faune 1992.* Direction générale de la ressource faunique, 1992.

Ordre des ingénieurs forestiers du Québec. *Manuel de foresterie.* Ouvrage en collaboration. Québec: Presses de l'Université Laval, 1996.

Prescott, J., and P. Richard. *Mammifères du Québec et de l'est du Canada.* Waterloo: Éditions Michel Quintin, 1997.

Québec, Ministère de l'Environnement. *État de l'environnement au Québec, 1992.* Montréal: Guérin, 1993.

Québec. *Convention on Biological Diversity Québec's Implementation Strategy.* Ministère de l'Environnement et de la Faune, 1996.

Rousseau, C. *Géographie floristique du Québec-Labrador: Distribution des principales espèces vasculaires.* Québec: Presses de l'Université Laval, 1974.

Jerry V. DeMarco and

Anne C. Bell

The Role of Non-Government Organizations in Biodiversity Conservation

T HE Red River Valley of south-central Manitoba was once a wide expanse of tall-grass prairie, a rich and intricate weave of grasses, flowers, and wildlife. Early in the nineteenth century, however, the valley's deep, fertile soils proved irresistible to settlers from Europe and eastern Canada who set to work taming and transforming nature's complex design. Today, a sea of cereal and forage crops blankets the land, and less than 1 per cent of the original tall-grass prairie remains.

The surviving prairie remnants have been the focus of conservation efforts since 1987, when the Manitoba Naturalists Society launched a two-year survey to locate the remaining sites and then spearheaded efforts to preserve some of the largest remaining tracts. The Critical Wildlife Habitat Program, involving both government and non-government conservation organizations, was established in 1989 with the aim of identifying and preserving critical wildlife habitat, with particular emphasis on the prairie landscape.[1]

Since that time, the groups involved have engaged in extensive fund-raising, research, and public education and outreach efforts. In addition to purchasing and leasing properties for the preserve, they have inventoried and monitored them and experimented with active management techniques such as prescribed burns, rotational grazing, mowing, and girdling of invasive trees and shrubs. They have paid special attention to species at risk, such as the western prairie fringed orchid, only known to be located in Canada in this prairie preserve.[2] Since much of the remaining prairie is outside the preserve, on private land, they have also contacted hundreds of landowners to raise awareness about the importance of prairie and good stewardship.[3]

Like many environmental non-government organizations (ENGOS), the Manitoba naturalists have adopted a variety of approaches to protecting biodiversity. Key to their success have been partnerships with government agencies (e.g., Canadian Wildlife Service, Manitoba Department of Natural Resources) and national ENGOS (e.g., World Wildlife Fund Canada, Nature Conservancy of Canada, Wildlife Habitat Canada). Such co-operative efforts, which result in a sharing of resources and expertise, have long been typical of ENGO involvement in conservation. Unfortunately, however, not all political climates favour such collaboration between government and non-government sectors.

Watchdogs for Biodiversity

As the twentieth century draws to a close, many governments in Canada are imposing severe budget and staff cuts to environment and natural resource departments at the same time as they are weakening and even eliminating protective laws and policies. In fact, despite strong public support for environmental protection,[4] government action has been not only inadequate, but declining since its zenith in the late 1980s and early 1990s. Reasons for this abdication of responsibility are varied and include an unwillingness to interfere with the interests of extractive industries, a reluctance to intrude on areas of responsibility perceived to be assigned to or shared with other levels of government, a trend towards tighter government budgets, and a general political disinclination to stray too far from the status quo. Many nature advocates fear that limitations on government authority resulting from international trade agreements may further exacerbate the problem.

This backsliding on environmental protection is regarded as a betrayal of the public trust by many ENGOs who have had to assume an increasingly proactive, watchdog role.[5] While nature conservation groups have existed in Canada for many decades, their original focus was to promote nature appreciation, and rarely to advocate for legal or political protection.[6] Growing concern over environmental problems in the 1960s, however, led to the formation of a number of advocacy groups, including the Nature Conservancy of Canada (1962), the Canadian Parks and Wilderness Society (1963 as the National and Provincial Parks Association of Canada), World Wildlife Fund Canada (1967), and the Canadian Nature Federation (evolved in 1971 from the Canadian Audubon Society, which was originally founded in 1948). By 1973 there were over 300 environmental organizations across the country.[7] That number is now approximately 2,000, including naturalist clubs, citizens' groups, recreation associations, Public Interest Research Groups, observatories, provincial and national environmental organizations, and coalitions. Many of these groups focus directly on the protection of biodiversity while others address the issue indirectly through their efforts to tackle such problems as pollution, climate change, ozone depletion, pesticide use, resource consumption, and related social justice matters.[8]

Greenpeace's anti-whaling activities in the mid-1970s illustrate the rise of ENGO biodiversity protection activity in Canada. With its bold tactics and simple messages, Greenpeace was able to bring the urgent need to protect marine mammals to newspapers and television screens across the country, and thus to the forefront of public concern. Whales proved to be an ideal focal point through which to draw attention to the plight of non-human beings. Large and charismatic, they had been vastly reduced in number, meeting violent deaths at the hands of a readily identifiable adversary, the whaling industry. The efforts of Greenpeace on their behalf helped turn many who appreciated nature into defenders of nature. At the same time, in terms of the organization itself, a small but dedicated group of concerned individuals with ample energy and courage developed by 1976 into an organization that included 10,000 supporters, office systems, a board of directors and a newspaper.[9]

Protecting Species

Defending nature, or in more recent times "biodiversity," has proven to be a complex task. Greenpeace's early anti-whaling, direct-action campaigns were prototypical species-centred efforts. A group of organisms under threat of extinction was identified as a special concern and significant energy was put into ensuring its survival. Direct confrontation is not for every nature advocate, however, and understandably ENGOS employ a wide range of methods depending on political and cultural contexts and on the opportunities that present themselves (Table 1). Most large ENGOS (e.g., World Wildlife Fund Canada, Canadian Nature Federation) use a variety of strategies to achieve their goals while others focus primarily on a particular area of expertise

Table 1: Examples of ENGO Activity

Working with Government and the Private Sector

- public/private/ENGO partnerships (e.g., to protect sensitive habitats)
- exchanging information, including the development and management of databases
- improving landowner stewardship
- promoting environmentally preferable consumer products and industry standards
- participating in land-use and park management planning processes
- participating in environmental assessments and other administrative hearings and processes
- advising government bodies on biodiversity agreements at national and international levels
- making presentations to government committees, panels, etc.
- lobbying governments for human and financial resources

Generating Public Awareness and Involvement

- community outreach/education initiatives (e.g., public meetings, workshops, apprenticeship programs, conferences, rallies, contact with private landowners)
- production and distribution of pamphlets, newsletters, reports, educational packages
- using the media to reach the general public

such as land acquisition (e.g., Nature Conservancy of Canada), seed collection and exchange (e.g., Seeds of Diversity Canada), ecological restoration (e.g., Evergreen Foundation), or litigation (e.g., Sierra Legal Defence Fund).

ENGO efforts to protect endangered species illustrate how a variety of approaches may be called upon to work towards a common goal. In the United States, such endeavours have long involved the use of the Endangered Species Act. This strong piece of legislation is aimed at conserving endangered species and the habitats upon which they depend as well as implementing international conventions respecting such species. American ENGOs frequently conduct multifaceted campaigns involving research, lobbying and litigation to help get a species listed under the Act and to ensure that the protective measures

---

- organizing hands-on volunteer projects (e.g., monitoring of species and habitats, bird surveys, habitat restoration initiatives, clean-ups)
- development of citizens' guides to facilitate public involvement (e.g., guides to land-use planning, forestry, park management, wildlife gardens)
- organizing petitions or letter-writing campaigns

On-the-Ground Conservation Efforts

- land acquisition and management (especially of rare, sensitive, threatened, or biologically diverse habitats)
- habitat restoration projects
- funding or undertaking research and monitoring
- providing technical support or advice
- seed collection and exchange
- propagation and sale of native plant species

Advocating for Institutional Change

- lobbying government for policy and regulatory reform
- exerting pressure on domestic governments through international forums
- litigation (public interest environmental lawsuits)
- civil disobedience

---

afforded it are enforced. This has the effect of protecting not only the listed species itself, but often countless others occupying the same habitat.

In Canada, efforts to protect species at risk have been much more diffuse. Only recently has the call for legislative protection been strong. Prior to Canada's signing of the Biodiversity Convention in 1992, much ENGO attention focused on non-legislative undertakings concerning the protection of endangered species. This work, often involving the World Wildlife Fund (WWF) and the Canadian Nature Federation (CNF), generally consisted of joint ENGO-government programs such as COSEWIC (Committee on the Status of Endangered Wildlife in Canada) and RENEW (Recovery of Nationally Endangered Wildlife). While the programs exemplify long-standing cooperation between ENGOs and governments, these policy-driven efforts have met with mixed success, hampered by limited funding, insufficient political support and the lack of a legislative foundation for their work. COSEWIC was established to identify species at risk, but given no role in ensuring that listed species were protected or recovered.[10] RENEW was given a mandate that permitted it to develop recovery plans for only a small fraction of the species identified through COSEWIC.[11] Its terms of reference address only terrestrial vertebrates and exclude species designated as "vulnerable," thereby ignoring over 80 per cent of Canada's species at risk, including all plants, molluscs, fish, marine mammals, and marine reptiles.

A recognition of COSEWIC's and RENEW's limitations led to increased attention to ensuring that species at risk received legislative protection. ENGOs participated in the parliamentary consultation process that followed Canada's ratification of the Biodiversity Convention and convinced the Parliamentary Standing Committee on Environment to recommend to the federal government that it pass endangered species legislation.[12] Subsequent commitments by the federal government to pass such legislation help show that efforts to bring about strong international treaties (however unenforceable by ENGOs) can pay dividends on the domestic policy front. Equally, the Standing Committee Report demonstrated that responsible participation in government hearings and other public processes can also bring about change (though not always).

Some ENGOS, like Bird Studies Canada (BSC), stress on-the-ground research and monitoring in their approach to species protection. Located on the north shore of Lake Erie, within the United Nations-designated Long Point World Biosphere Reserve, BSC is committed to involving Canadians in research directed towards the conservation of wild birds and their habitats. Through its bird-banding and breeding-bird census plots work at the Long Point Bird Observatory and volunteer-based surveys elsewhere, BSC draws on the skills, enthusiasm, and support of its members, volunteers, staff, and the interested public to advance and encourage wider understanding and appreciation of the species studied. Participants in Project FeederWatch, for example, keep track of the birds at their feeders during designated periods throughout the winter. The collected data become part of a continental survey that helps track long-term population trends in winter birds so that declines may be documented before a species is in serious trouble. Responsible for identifying Canada's Important Bird Areas, at Long Point BSC is also involved in developing a conservation plan that includes land-use planning strategies, conservation easements, co-operative agreements with local landowners, the creation or purchase of reserves and environmental education initiatives.[13]

Protecting Habitats

In recent years, there has been a widespread recognition that traditional approaches to saving species cannot succeed unless the ecological processes and natural systems upon which they depend are conserved. In the long-term, conserving biodiversity involves protecting the full range of genes, species, communities, ecological functions, and evolutionary processes. Necessary to accomplishing this goal is the *in situ* conservation of natural communities through a network of protected areas free from industrial exploitation.[14]

Perhaps Canada's most ambitious ENGO biodiversity conservation campaign embarked upon to date is WWF's Endangered Spaces Campaign. This campaign is a comprehensive proposal to establish protected areas across the country's lands and waters to preserve natural diversity.[15] Though it is led by ENGOS, it is premised on significant government co-operation and implementation. In fact the campaign is largely an effort to influence public policy. Launched in a "spirit of cooperation," the campaign seeks "to identify science-based action steps and to build sufficient consensus behind them, both within and outside government, to ensure that they are taken."[16]

Shortly after its inception in 1989, the campaign received widespread backing from organizations, citizens, and governments in favour of establishing representative protected areas in all of Canada's natural regions. One of the campaign's strengths has been its ability to marry scientific research with political accountability. The "report cards" used to monitor progress in each jurisdiction call governments to task with regular reminders of their progress (or lack thereof) and become a sure-fire mechanism to draw attention to the campaign's goals (see

	Jurisdiction	1992	1993	94-95	95-96	96-97	97-98	98-99	% protected (1999)
	Marine								
	Fed.-Marine	C-	D	D-	C	D	D+	n/a	n/a
	Atlantic	n/a	n/a	n/a	D+	D-	D+	n/a	n/a
	Pacific	n/a	n/a	n/a	C	C-	D+	n/a	n/a
	Great Lakes	n/a	n/a	n/a	D	D	D	n/a	n/a
	Arctic	n/a	n/a	n/a	D-	D-	D-	n/a	n/a
	Terrestrial								
	Fed.-Terr.	A-	B	C-	C	A-	D	C	2.3
	Yukon	C	D+	D	D	C-	C+	C-	9.0
	N.W.T.	B-	C	D	D	C-	C	C-	4.6
	B.C.	B-	B+	A-	A	C	C+	C	11.2
	Alberta	D	C	F	B	D+	F	F	9.8
	Sask.	C	B-	D+	C	F	B-	C	6.0
	Manitoba	D	B	C-	D-	B+	C	B-	8.1
	Ontario	C+	B	D+	F	C-	D+	B+	8.8
	Quebec	C+	B-	D+	C-	D-	F	F	4.2
	N.B.	D-	B-	D-	F	F	D	D	1.3
	N.S.	C	C	C+	A	C-	C+	C+	8.2
	P.E.I.	A-	B+	B-	C+	B	B	C	4.1
	Nfld./Lab.	C	C+	C-	D	C-	D	D+	1.8
	TOTAL								6.4

Table 2: Endangered Spaces Campaign Report Cards: Yearly Grades Assigned by WWF for Progress in Establishing a Comprehensive System of Protected Areas

Source: WWF, *1992, 1993, 1994-95, 1995-96, 1996-97, 1997-98 1998-99 Endangered Spaces Progress Reports* (Toronto: WWF).

Table 2). The grades are based on criteria such as: the degree to which ecological factors are used in selecting new protected areas; how close a jurisdiction is to completing a representative system of protected areas; how much progress was made in a given year; and the adequacy of standards put in place to maintain the ecological integrity of existing protected areas. The criteria are assessed and weighted annually to track the degree to which jurisdictions have taken the necessary steps towards achieving the Spaces goal.[17] For example, a year of "minimal progress towards completing a protected areas system" coupled with an existing protected areas system which protected very few of the province's natural regions contributed to New Brunswick's "F" grade in 1995-96. That same year, British Columbia got an "A" for its progress, which included improved legislative protection for parks and the designation of several new protected areas.[18]

Whether or not the Spaces campaign ever succeeds in achieving a comprehensive marine and terrestrial protected areas system in Canada, it has established ENGO benchmarks on a number of fronts. For instance, the campaign has been noteworthy for its use of a "federal" approach to campaigning. While the major decisions regarding the direction of the campaign have emanated from WWF's head office, regional co-ordinators stationed across the country have been responsible for implementing the campaign in each jurisdiction. This often has involved establishing partnerships with existing provincial ENGOs with previous experience in biodiversity conservation at the provincial level.

Spaces campaigners also have demonstrated a degree of adaptability in slowly de-emphasizing the campaign's objective of protecting a minimum of 12 per cent of the country's lands and waters in favour of the more defensible objective of establishing a comprehensive network of protected areas in all natural regions. The 12 per cent figure had political significance by virtue of its association with the Brundtland Report,[19] and as a "finishable agenda" it was attractive to politicians. Nevertheless, it had little scientific credibility, and met with criticism from some ENGOs who pointed out that protecting 12 per cent of Canada would be unlikely to result in significant gains for biodiversity unless it adequately incorporated such key considerations as representation and ecological integrity accompanied by sound land-use

Tatshenshini-Alsek an area protected as a result of pressure by environmental organizations

photo: Jerry Valen DeMarco

decisions outside protected areas. For example, in order to maintain natural disturbance regimes (e.g., wildfire) and viable populations of large carnivores, far more than 12 per cent of the landscape would have to be managed with the objective of protecting biodiversity.[20] (WWF itself has made a point of reinforcing the need for ecologically sound decision-making and management over the entire landscape.)[21]

Also evident from an analysis of the Spaces campaign is the fact that gains made over the course of the campaign may be unravelled some day by future government actions. The on-again, off-again protection of Nova Scotia's Jim Campbell's Barren is a case in point. The Nova Scotia cabinet decision to protect the Barren and thirty other sites in 1995 led to a rare "A" grade in the Spaces campaign. The decision to protect this unique boreal forest, bog and lichen complex on the Cape Breton Highland plateau was short-lived, however, when mining interests convinced the presiding Nova Scotia premier that the Barren was of more "use" for mines than nature.[22] The premier's November 1996 move to overturn the decision to protect the Barren, despite it being supported in a comprehensive public consultation program, spawned the formation of a coalition of over 40 organizations. Coalition members included not only ENGOs, such as WWF and the Canadian Parks and Wilderness Society, but other interest groups such as the Nova Scotia Salmon Association, the Union of Nova Scotia Indians and the province's wildlife federation and tourism association.[23] All were bent on ensuring that a further reversal – this time in favour of protection – came about. Nearly one year of grassroots campaigning later, protection for the Barren was regained. In the meantime, the Premier who rescinded the protection decision had resigned. While it cannot be said that the ill-advised decision to revoke the Barren's protected status was the only cause for the Premier's downfall, it can be hoped at least that obvious efforts to cater to narrow economic interests in the face of widespread public support for protection will not be tolerated by the citizenry. The Barren saga also illustrates, however, the unfortunate reality that ENGOs face when opposing the forces of industrial development: they may have to win a campaign not only once, but over and over again.

Legal Recourse and Civil Disobedience

While governments frequently ignore political commitments to environmental protection, when they fail to abide by their legal obligations ENGOs now have some recourse. With the Supreme Court of Canada's expansion of the law of standing (establishing the right to sue in the "public interest" rather than simply to protect personal or economic interests) in 1986 came the removal of one of the most significant legal barriers to ENGO use of the courts.[24] Some of the financial barriers to public interest environmental lawsuits also fell with the formation of specialized ENGOs, such as the Canadian Environmental Law Association (1972) and the Sierra Legal Defence Fund (1990). Since that time, Canadian ENGOs frequently have used the courts to ensure that governments act within the law in matters affecting the environment. Among the most significant court decisions for biodiversity was a Supreme Court of Canada case requiring mandatory environmental assessment for many federal projects affecting the environment, and a Federal Court case ending clear-cut logging in Wood Buffalo National Park, thus making it clear that industrial development had no place in national parks.

There are situations, however, where institutional barriers to change spawn much more radical approaches to biodiversity conservation. When reasoned arguments fail, some groups resort to civil dis-

Entrance to
Clayoquot Peace
Camp,
Summer 1993.

photo: Anne Bell

obedience as the court of last resort. In recent years, Canada has witnessed large-scale civil disobedience actions focused on protecting old-
growth forest ecosystems threatened by imminent logging plans.

For instance, demonstrations and blockades in British Columbia's
Clayoquot Sound in 1993 brought civil disobedience in Canada to new
heights. The action was one of North America's largest non-violent
demonstrations ever. Over the course of the summer, 12,000 people of
all ages and backgrounds participated in a "peace camp" that garnered
international attention. According to one campaigner, participants felt
that democracy had failed them and that this failure explained their
presence.[25] As author Irshad Manji notes, the action "resurrected civil
disobedience as a valid, indeed ethically compelling, response to corporate irresponsibility and government complacency."[26] The demonstration's emphasis on non-violence helped to garner public support
and enabled the action to build momentum as the summer went on.
While the provincial government never capitulated to the tactics of
the blockaders – indeed many were arrested and jailed – plans for massive clear-cuts in the Sound were eventually shelved following the recommendations of a government-appointed scientific panel examining
management options for the area. The Panel's report helped vindicate
the claims made by the protesters.

Obviously, actions of this sort cannot be undertaken with any frequency. They require a coming-together of resources, people, energy and public concern over a specific issue, often a manifestation of a more widespread problem (in the case of Clayoquot, the systematic "liquidation" of British Columbia's old-growth rain forests). They can also exact a great personal toll from participants, the majority of whom prefer to regard themselves as otherwise law-abiding citizens who coexist amicably with their neighbours. Some of the key campaigners in the Clayoquot demonstration, for example, expressed deep regret at the hostilities that arose between nearby communities as a result of the blockades.[27] Nevertheless, these lodestones of public sentiment serve as crucial reference points in the evolution of environmental debate and often catalyse change within government and public opinion. It is this sort of fundamental change that many regard as necessary if ENGOS are to succeed in protecting biodiversity where governments have failed.

Restoring Relationships

But change, even fundamental change, does not result solely from confrontation. Environmental education, legislative and policy reform, and other approaches can challenge long-standing societal patterns and are crucial to protecting biodiversity. For instance, "protecting" in the sense of "preserving" biodiversity is not an option in many parts of the country where forests, rivers, wetlands, prairies, and other natural systems have been destroyed or degraded over large regions by agriculture, urbanization, and industrial activities. In areas that have been subject to intensive development, such as southwestern Ontario, the southern prairies, and the dry lowland valleys of interior southern British Columbia,[28] one promising ENGO approach to biodiversity conservation has been through ecological restoration. Restoration projects aim to repair "damage caused by humans to the diversity and dynamics of indigenous ecosystems"[29] through the reintroduction of native species and the re-creation of native habitats, ideally taking into account both genetic and broader landscape diversity.[30] These efforts aim to support the insects, birds, amphibians, and other animals that have evolved to depend on native species and to bring back a diversity of wildlife to urban and rural areas. In some cases, they

Box 1 | **Youth Activism**

Various student groups play an important role in furthering biodiversity conservation. These groups typically have broad environmental/social justice mandates enabling them to focus their efforts on specific current issues and interests within the student community. They contribute to biodiversity conservation through their general environmental advocacy work and occasional specific biodiversity campaigns. For example, the Youth Caucus of the Canadian Environmental Network (CEN) exists "to support, facilitate and promote member youth groups in their work to protect the earth and encourage socially just, ecologically sustainable and holistic ways of life." Member groups include student organizations in universities, high schools, and communities across Canada.

The mandate of the CEN Youth Caucus is to:

- ensure networking, communication, and outreach to groups;

- share skills, solutions, tools, concepts, vision, and actions;

- facilitate a strong, accountable youth eco-voice for policy change;

- ensure a youth-friendly CEN;

- promote global solidarity and partnership within the members' eco-regions.

In addition to creating networking opportunities for youth, the Youth Caucus has established a number of working groups focused on issues common among members. One project undertaken, for example, was Youth Habitat II Canada, which resulted in Canadian youth participation at the United Nations conference on Human Settlements in Istanbul, Turkey, in 1996.[31] Another is the Youth Sustainability Project, which involves a partnership with the Youth Network for Sustainable Development of Latin America. It aims to raise awareness about the impacts of consumptive Western lifestyles and includes such concrete local initiatives as urban agriculture and sustainable forestry campaigns.[32]

Contact Information: CEN, #300-945 Wellington St., Ottawa, ON, K1Y 2X5, Tel: (613) 728-9810, Fax: (613) 728-2963, e-mail: cenyouth@web.net

represent a means of linking and expanding upon isolated fragments of natural areas.

Restoration projects occur where most of the Canadian population lives and since they often involve volunteers and local residents, they provide a prime opportunity to educate the public about biodiversity through hands-on experience. Through school-ground naturalization projects, for instance, children, their parents, and other community members can participate in long-term efforts to reintroduce native species, restore their habitats and rekindle a nurturing awareness of other life. According to restoration advocates such as the Evergreen

Gathering seed for restoration project near Long Point Ontario

Foundation, this direct involvement in planning for, planting, and tending local places offers hope for a fundamental shift in human relationships with the rest of nature.[31] Playing a small but beneficial role in the larger web of life can lay the basis for cultural as well as ecological renewal.

Future Directions

As Canadian ENGOs develop and mature, attention to relationships is bound to be crucial in sustaining the diversity of life. While certainly ENGOs can take a great deal of credit for raising awareness of and taking steps to address threats to biodiversity, they have often been hampered in their efforts by their isolation and limited constituency. Even though nature protection generally is supported by the public, translating heartfelt visions into comprehensible, workable, widely acceptable strategies has proven a daunting task. Consequently, notwithstanding the many hard-won success stories, the overall outlook for biodiversity conservation in Canada is alarming. As naturalist John Livingston contends, nature advocates seem to be "stamping at tiny smoulders in the carpet, rushing from hot spot to hot spot, when all the while the roof is racing to a fire-storm and the walls are creaking toward collapse."[34]

Part of the problem, it seems, is that conservationists traditionally have made the mistake of separating discussions of biodiversity from the cultures in which they are embedded. Increasingly, however, ENGOS are recognizing the inaccessibility of scientific jargon and argument and the weakness of "management" approaches to conservation which fail to factor in human lifestyles and livelihoods. Working from an understanding of the interdependence of cultural and biological diversity, they are beginning to reach out to First Nations and others, hoping to establish some common ground. They know that, in addition to advocating new protected areas and recovery plans for endangered species, they must meet the challenge of finding the words and images that appeal to gardeners, farmers, cottagers, loggers, and the rest of us. The hope is that we will be reminded of and thus ready to stand up for the many ways that life's infinite variety enriches us all.[35]

Notes

The authors wish to thank the following individuals for their assistance: Catherine Austen, Stephen Bocking, Janis Bogart, Michael Bradstreet, Jennifer Good, Marc Johnson, Kevin Kavanagh, Marilyn Latta, Kevin McNamee, Colin Stewart, and Ron Ridout.

1. Marilyn Latta, "Five Years of Prairie Conservation," *Manitoba Naturalists Society Bulletin* 17, 5 (May 1992): 1, 15.
2. Critical Wildlife Habitat Program (CWHP), *Manitoba's Tall-grass Prairie Preserve* (Winnipeg: CWHP, undated pamphlet).
3. Marilyn Latta, "Progress on the Prairie," *Manitoba Naturalists Society Bulletin* 14, 2 (February 1989): 1.

4. See Chapter 12, by Vanderlinden and Eyles, in this volume. Also see Angus Reid Group, *Public Support for Endangered Species Legislation* (June 1995), showing that over 90 per cent of Canadians support federal endangered species legislation; Monte Hummel and Arlin Hackman, "Introduction," in Monte Hummel, ed., *Protecting Canada's Endangered Spaces: An Owner's Manual* (Toronto: Key Porter Books, 1995), xi, regarding the fact that more than 600,000 Canadians and nearly 300 organizations have endorsed the Endangered Spaces campaign to protect representative examples of each of Canada's natural regions.

5. In its analysis of the B.C. government's performance, for example, the Sierra Legal Defence Fund (SLDF) reports that: "environmental laws have been rolled back, important decisions reversed, critical promises broken, national and international commitments violated and enforcement has dropped off." SLDF, *Betraying Our Trust* (Vancouver: SLDF, 1998), 2-3.

6. The Federation of Ontario Naturalists, for example, formed in 1931. Stewart A.G. Elgie, "Environmental Groups and the Courts: 1970-1992," in Geoffrey Thompson, Moira L. McConnell, and Lynne B. Huestis, eds., *Environmental Law and Business in Canada* (Aurora, Ont.: Canada Law Book, 1993), 213-14 n. 9.

7. Ibid.

8. Canadian Environmental Network, *The Green List: A Guide to Canadian Environmental Organizations and Agencies*, 2nd ed. (Ottawa: Canadian Environmental Network, 1994).

9. Michael Brown and John May, *The Greenpeace Story*, 2nd ed. (London: Dorling Kindersley, 1991), 40.

10. COSEWIC uses the most reliable data available to assign species at risk to one of five categories (extinct, extirpated, endangered, threatened, and vulnerable). Each designation reflects a particular level of risk. For example, endangered species face imminent extinction or extirpation while vulnerable species are of special concern because of characteristics that make them particularly sensitive to human activities or natural events.

11. See Jacques Prescott and B. Theresa Aniskowicz, "Helping Endangered Species: COSEWIC and RENEW: Is This the Best We Can Do?" *Canadian Biodiversity* 2, 1 (Spring 1992): 23-30.

12. Standing Committee on Environment, *A Global Partnership: Canada and the Conventions of the United Nations Conference on Environment and Development (UNCED)* (Ottawa: House of Commons, Canada, April 1993), p. 30.

13. Long Point Bird Observatory (LPBO), LPBO/James L. Baillie Memorial

Fund/Bird Studies Canada 1996 Annual Report (Port Rowan, Ont.: LPBO, 1997), 3, 6.

14. Hummel and Hackman, "Introduction," xviii-xix.

15. Ibid., xi.

16. Arlin Hackman, "Working with Government," in Hummel, ed., *Protecting Canada's Endangered Spaces*, 34-37.

17. WWF, *1997-98 Guide to the Grades: A Companion to World Wildlife Fund's Endangered Spaces Progress Report* (Toronto: WWF, 1998), 7-10.

18. WWF, *1995-96 Endangered Spaces Progress Repor* (Toronto: WWF, 1996), 38, 50.

19. The Report recommended tripling the total expanse of protected areas worldwide, which was nearly 4 per cent at that time. See World Commission on Environment and Development, *Our Common Future* (New York: Oxford University Press, 1987), 147, 166.

20. See Edward O. Wilson, *The Diversity of Life* (New York: Norton, 1993), 337; Reed Noss, "Science Editor's Note," *Wild Earth* 1, 4 (Winter 1991-92): 37.

21. WWF, *Making Choices: A Submission to the Government of British Columbia Regarding Protected Areas and Forest Land Use* (Toronto: WWF, November 1993), 2-6.

22. Colin Stewart, "31 Steps Forward, 1 Big Step Back," *The Wilderness Activist: CPAWS National Newsletter* (Spring 1997): 5.

23. Neal Burnham, "Protected Area Goes to Miners," *Alternatives Journal* 23, 4 (Fall 1997): 2.

24. Elgie, "Environmental Groups," 202.

25. Jill Thomas, Friends of Clayoquot Sound, as quoted in "Community Perspectives: Clayoquot," in Sabine Jessen, ed., *The Wilderness Vision for British Columbia: Proceedings from a Colloquium on Completing British Columbia's Protected Area System* (Vancouver: Canadian Parks and Wilderness Society, 1996), 205.

26. Irshad Manji, *Risking Utopia: On the Edge of a New Democracy* (Vancouver: Douglas & McIntyre, 1997), 60.

27. Jessen, *Wilderness Vision*, 204-05.

28. Ted Mosquin, Peter G. Whiting, Don E. McAllister, *Canada's Biodiversity* (Ottawa: Canadian Museum of Nature, 1995), 57-58.

29. Laura L. Jackson, Nikita Lopoukhine, and Deborah Hillyard, "Ecological Restoration: A Definition and Comments," *Restoration Ecology* 3, 2 (June 1995): 71.

30. See Kenneth Towle, *The Role of Ecological Restoration in Biodiversity Conservation: Basic Issues and Guidelines* (Toronto: Evergreen Foundation, 1996), 3-4.

31. Canadian Environmental Network, *The Canadian Environmental Network: Youth*

Caucus! (Ottawa: Canadian Environmental Network, undated pamphlet).

32. Linda Geggie and Jacinda Fairholm, "Times They are a Changin': A New Wave of Youth Activism Promises a Broader Approach to Social Change," *Alternatives Journal* 24, 3 (Summer 1998): 12.

33. Geoff Cape, "Foreword," in Towle, *Role of Ecological Restoration.*

34. John A. Livingston, *The Fallacy of Wildlife Conservation* (Toronto: McClelland & Stewart, 1981), 13.

35. See Gary Paul Nabhan, *Cultures of Habitat: On Nature, Culture and Story* (Washington: Counterpoint, 1997), 17-29.

Further Reading

Alternatives Journal (special issue on youth activism, including a directory of Youth Environmental Groups and Related Resources) 24, 3 (Summer 1998).

Canadian Environmental Network. *The Green List: A Guide to Canadian Environmental Organizations and Agencies,* 2nd ed. Ottawa: Canadian Environmental Network, 1994.

Careless, Ric. *To Save the Wild Earth.* Vancouver: Raincoast Books, 1997.

Hummel, Monte, ed. *Endangered Spaces: The Future for Canada's Wilderness.* Toronto: Key Porter Books, 1989.

Hummel, Monte, ed. *Protecting Canada's Endangered Spaces: An Owner's Manual.* Toronto: Key Porter Books, 1995.

May, Elizabeth. *Paradise Won: The Struggle for South Moresby.* Toronto: McClelland & Stewart, 1990.

Mowat, Farley. *Rescue the Earth! Conversations with the Green Crusaders.* Toronto: McClelland & Stewart, 1990.

Snow, Donald. *Inside the Environmental Movement: Meeting the Leadership Challenge.* Washington: Island Press, 1992.

Lorna Stefanick
and Kathleen Wells

Alberta's Special Places 2000: Conservation, Conflict, and the Castle-Crown Wilderness

IN NOVEMBER 1992, THE ALBERTA GOVERNMENT TABLED A DRAFT policy document entitled *Special Places 2000: Alberta's Natural Heritage*. The Alberta Special Places program was described as "a bold, new direction" for environmental conservation decision-making and was seen as a statement of Alberta's commitment to the World Wildlife Fund's Endangered Spaces campaign. The draft document was widely distributed, open houses and group meetings solicited public input, and a public advisory committee gathered public responses and recommended a course of action. In 1995, the final draft of the *Special Places 2000* document was released, and industry, conservation groups, and citizens were invited to begin submitting nominating sites to be considered for preservation. Provincial leaders claimed that this "made in Alberta" process would balance the needs of various stakeholders with respect to economics and the environment, and be a model of how public consultation processes could be designed to serve the unique needs of a particular jurisdiction. These same leaders, however, were undoubtedly also motivated by a desire to avoid the bitter conflict between environmentalists and industry that was drawing international attention to the province's neighbour to the west, British Columbia.

But the reaction of the environmental community to the 1995 Special Places final document was not particularly positive. A coalition of 21 Alberta environmental groups angrily denounced it, with some predicting that confrontational B.C.-style tactics would soon be a reality in Alberta.[1] By 1996 the situation had deteriorated to such an extent that one environmental group in Alberta actually withdrew its nomination for special place designation of the Castle wilderness area in southwestern Alberta. The process was so flawed, it claimed, that this area could be better protected outside the Special Places program.[2]

This chapter examines the birth and growing pains of Alberta's protected areas strategy; it assesses the prospects for public consultation processes in Alberta and the implications of the Special Places experience for other jurisdictions. It begins with an analysis of public consultation in Canadian environmental decision-making and then examines the evolution and structure of the Special Places program as a method of public consultation, particularly with respect to how this process actually played out in the Castle area – a particularly contentious conservation "hot spot." The Castle wilderness is of particular salience because the composition and mandate of the committee created to make recommendations with respect to its nomination as a "special place" are so contentious that the ensuing furore could precipitate the unravelling of the Special Places process province-wide. The Castle experience illustrates some of the pitfalls of public participation, and provides important lessons for policy-makers contemplating using consultative mechanisms.

In order for public participatory processes to be successful, they must be perceived to legitimately represent all affected interests. Accordingly, the processes must be open to all interested members of the public or, at the very least, be representative of all important stakeholders; be facilitated by a neutral party; have local input; be based on a consensual decision-making model; and be autonomous from government to some degree. Anything less will encourage political manipulation by affected stakeholders, ultimately resulting in the breakdown of the process. If the Special Places experiment does break down, the failure may inflame a comparatively conservative Alberta environmental community that has not traditionally relied on confrontational and media-driven tactics. Should this community decide to capitalize on the fact that Alberta is home to four UNESCO World Heritage sites[3] and aggressively seek political support from the international conservation lobby, the prospects for Albertans resolving conservation disputes without outside interference will be very dim indeed.

Consultation, Decision-making, and the Environment

The 1990s have seen unprecedented shifts in how environmental and resource decisions are made. Two major factors have caused these changes. First, there is no longer a consensus over what is the "public's best interest." Second, there is increased public scepticism toward the soundness of decisions made behind closed doors. This has been seen in all sectors in Canada, from constitutional issues to health care. Years ago governments could credibly claim that society was united behind economic development as a key societal goal. For most citizens (particularly in Canada), the activities of government were not a concern so long as the economy was strong and the general standard of living was high.

This acquiescence and consensus, in Alberta as elsewhere, began to break down in the 1960s. The post-war generation demanded input into how their "best interest" was defined, beyond simply casting a ballot every few years.[4] As Cleaveland has observed "for the most part individuals and corporations and governments don't have a choice about this; it is the ineluctable consequence of creating – through education – societies with millions of knowledgeable people."[5]

In the Alberta of the 1960s, there was no comprehensive environmental legislation, nor was the public given much opportunity for input into political decision-making. But the province was changing quickly. With the discovery of oil near Edmonton in 1947, the economy experienced unprecedented growth. Albertans were feeling self-confident and, after decades of Social Credit rule, were becoming increasingly assertive with respect to how they were being governed. Western Canadians have traditionally harboured a distrust of "eastern élites" who, it is argued, have systematically exploited the prairie hinterland to fuel the industrial machine of central Canada. This distrust of élites provides a natural home for prairie populism as a style of political discourse, and by extension, support for the idea that individual citizens should have some input into public decision-making processes. As two observers of western Canadian politics write, "populism is designed to loosen the control of political élites, and to vest legislative power in the hands of the people."[6]

In response to fears regarding the health of Alberta's environment and the desire of citizens to have input into decision-making, the provincial government established the Advisory Committee on Pollution Control in 1967 to study how to deal with pollution problems in the province. While the committee was made up primarily of government representatives, it also had a significant number of industry and public representatives, as well as a few academics. The Advisory Committee can be seen as a pioneer both in Alberta and, for that matter, in Canada in its attempt to shape environmental legislation using extra-legislative methods. Three years later, the Environmental Conservation Authority (ECA) was created to review all government procedures in the broad area of pollution; it reported to the Minister of the Environment. The lifeblood of the ECA was its public advisory committees: semi-independent bodies comprised of volunteers who chose to study any issue they deemed important, passing resolutions accordingly. During its most productive years the ECA (through its advisory committees) provided a communication link between the government of Alberta and the public.

By 1980, however, it had become apparent that there was a significant difference of opinion between the government of Alberta and the ECA with respect to plans to build a major dam on the Oldman River.[7] This resulted in a waning of the government's commitment to support the ECA's work, and, compounded with the dramatic economic downturn experienced by Alberta in the early 1980s and the formation of the Alberta Environmental Network,[8] led to the decline of the ECA's effectiveness as the "voice" of the public with respect to the environment.

Driven by changing public opinion and a number of costly lawsuits launched by environmental groups (including litigation launched to halt the construction of the Oldman Dam), federal and provincial governments began to develop decision-making processes acceptable to all stakeholders and the general public. The most popular innovation, the multi-stakeholder forum, has been touted as the most significant innovation in the Canadian policy process in the past decade, and as Canada's "principal institutional response to the challenge of sustainable development"[9] presented by the Brundtland Commission.[10]

In 1986 Canada established the National Task Force on Environment and Economy, which recommended the creation of round tables at the national and provincial levels of government. Their purpose was to bring together senior decision-makers from government, industry, environmental organizations, labour, academe, and the Aboriginal community to begin a dialogue on the relationship between the environment and the economy, and to develop an integrated sustainable development strategy. A major goal was reorienting existing institutional arrangements that were seen as a major impediment to the development of this strategy. The underlying assumption was that:

> progress toward sustainability requires new kinds of lateral thinking if we are to overcome the vertically organized bureaucratic systems, the reductionism of science, and the compartmentalization of information. Round tables were founded to overcome the constraints of the bureaucratic system and to analyze problems from a perspective that is cross-disciplinary, cross-jurisdictional, and cross-temporal.[11]

A key implication of the concept of sustainable development is recognition that environmental problems are complex, and effective problem-solving must consider the multifaceted nature of each issue. Not only is a multipartite forum useful in this regard, it is also thought to be more "ecological" than traditional processes, because it considers many viewpoints and thus is more democratic. For many environmental thinkers, ecological solutions can only be found if the processes used consider the perspectives and needs of a vast array of humans and, more importantly, allow affected individuals some say regarding issues that directly affect them.[12]

Although the multi-stakeholder concept has generated great enthusiasm, its biggest drawback is the time that it takes to reach a decision. The underlying assumption is that ongoing discussion will reveal common values that can be built upon, producing a result that is at least minimally agreeable to all. Clearly, this can be both complicated and time-consuming, particularly when stakeholders are polarized. This process meshes well with the liberal democratic principle that citizens should have some degree of control over issues that affect them. Complex consultations are also problematic, however, in that politicians in liberal democracies have difficulty adopting a long-term policy perspective. Those who do take such a perspective may be punished in the next election, if they have not "produced" immediate short-term results. And in the end, there is always the possibility that the perspectives of the various stakeholders may not be reconcilable. As Glen Toner points out:

> While the decisions which emanate from multi-stakeholder forums ought to be superior, given that they contain the collective wisdom and consent of a range of stakeholders, there is also no question that the process of achieving them can be complicated and difficult. In other words, the strength of the multi-stakeholder process is that it can develop better decisions with broader "buy-in;" its weakness is that the complexity implicit to such processes may diminish the chances for success.[13]

A second, but equally important problem for advocates of the multipartite forum is the selection of participants. Who exactly should be involved? And how should these people be selected? Critics point out that the act of selecting individuals to represent various interests frequently remains hierarchical and closed, and thus the process will still be antithetical to environmental values. As Michael Howlett has noted:

> in many cases decisions as to the structure of the Round Tables, their composition, and membership were made through a closed nomination and appointment procedure in which only a few individuals, carefully selected by senior officials or responsible ministers, were actually invited to participate. While the qualifications of many of these individuals in terms of expertise may be unimpeachable, the closed method of recruitment and selection does not approximate the model of open interest rep-

resentation advocated by many critics of the existing environmental policy process.[14]

In the final analysis, if all important societal stakeholders are not represented (or perceived to be represented) in the multipartite forum, the final outcome (regardless of what it looks like) will be considered illegitimate.

These problems aside, the multipartite forum is by far the most popular method of obtaining resolution to environmental controversies; it has been used with varying success at both the federal and provincial levels of government. In Alberta, the designation and establishment of a "special place" is to be derived after consultation with a committee representing various sectors of the local community. Thus, the Special Places program is itself based on the multipartite model.

The Evolution of Alberta's Special Places 2000 Program

The Special Places program was a direct response to the World Wildlife Fund Canada's Endangered Spaces campaign. Alberta's support for the goals of this campaign was affirmed at the 1992 meeting of federal and provincial ministers of parks, environment, and wildlife when its Minister of Environmental Protection signed a national conservation contract to create a network of protected areas. At this meeting Alberta unveiled its plan for completion of a protected areas system, entitled "Special Places 2000: Alberta's Natural Heritage."

The aim of the program as outlined in the original draft document was to complete a conservation system that would "represent the environmental diversity of the province's six Natural Regions (20 subregions) by the end of 1998."[15] The plan had four overall goals: (1) preservation; (2) outdoor recreation; (3) heritage appreciation; and (4) tourism.[16] In addition, the document stated that the province would provide the public, local communities, industrial sectors, and environmental groups the opportunity to participate in the site-selection process, and promised a systematic and scientific approach to evaluating sites.

Significant effort was made to attain public input into the draft document, through press releases and advertisements in area newspapers, open house information sessions, the establishment of a toll-free information line, and focus group interviews. A public advisory committee was appointed by the Minister of Environmental Protection, Ty Lund, to formulate recommendations based on public responses. As a result of this committee's deliberations, 37 recommendations were submitted to the Minister in 1993, and released to the public in February 1994. The first and most important recommendation was that the primary goal of Special Places should be protection of the environment.

After more than two years of consideration, Ty Lund released the final version of the government's Special Places program in 1995. The product of this lengthy consultation process could have been more aptly described as a multiple-use policy for public lands than a conservation policy. The new program spoke of balancing environmental concerns with the reality of economic development. In addition to the goal of preservation and the parallel goals of outdoor recreation, heritage appreciation, and tourism, economic development was identified as an important goal of the protected areas program. This represented a new, and in environmental quarters, unwelcome theme in the Special Places repertoire.

As outlined in the 1995 Special Places program, the designation of any region as a special place is a six-step process. The first step allows any Albertan, including individuals or interest groups, to nominate an area for Special Place designation. Once received, the nomination moves to step two, where the Provincial Co-ordinating Committee (PCC) reviews the nomination. The PCC is a representative body of various stakeholders (including local governments, industry, business, conservation, recreation, tourism, academic and scientific groups), appointed by the Minister of Environmental Protection. Its role is to

> review nominated sites against Special Places policy, objectives and criteria; review management plans; ensure Special Places is part of, and consistent with, an improved integrated resource planning ... system; make recommendations to the Minister regarding establishment of sites; prepare annual progress reports. The committee will provide consistent overall direction for the program, and help increase general awareness and understanding of Special Places.[17]

Once the nomination is approved by the PCC, it moves to the Interdepartmental Committee (IC), which has 45 days to submit a report on the consistency of the nomination with approved integrated resource plans, legislation, and other government policies. This procedure is designed to allow a number of government departments to provide feedback into the nature and scope of actual or potential alternate land uses in a nominated area, such as agriculture, mining, oil and gas exploration, forestry, fish and game, tourism, and recreational developments. The IC is composed of cabinet ministers from the departments of Environmental Protection; Economic Development and Tourism; Agriculture; Food, and Rural Development; Energy; Community Development; and Municipal Affairs.[18] The role of the IC is thus one of co-ordination and communication among government departments.

Step three of the Special Places process returns the nomination to a local committee. This committee is to be "established by Ministers, based on recommendation from municipality" and is to include two

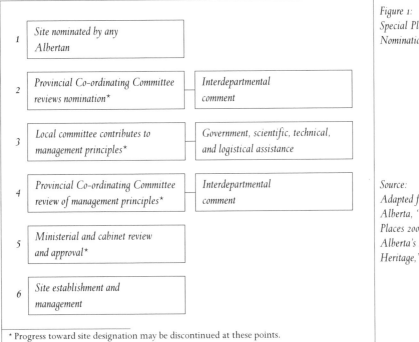

Figure 1:
Special Place Site
Nomination Process

Source:
Adapted from
Alberta, "Special
Places 2000:
Alberta's Natural
Heritage," 1995, 8

1 | Site nominated by any Albertan

2 | Provincial Co-ordinating Committee reviews nomination* | Interdepartmental comment

3 | Local committee contributes to management principles* | Government, scientific, technical, and logistical assistance

4 | Provincial Co-ordinating Committee review of management principles* | Interdepartmental comment

5 | Ministerial and cabinet review and approval*

6 | Site establishment and management

* Progress toward site designation may be discontinued at these points.

local municipal government officials; tenure holders such as grazing, forestry, and oil and gas lessees; industry; interest groups, such as environmental and recreation groups; the local Chamber of Commerce; local economic development committees; and the public.[19] The local committee's role is to identify regional issues, set boundaries, options for designation, and guidelines for ongoing activities. The committee is provided with scientific, technical, and logistical support from the government.

Step four sees the report of the local committee forwarded to the PCC, which then reviews the committee's management principles for consistency with Special Places policy and principles. As in step two, another 45 days is allotted for the IC to comment on the management principles as they relate to approved integrated resource plans, legislation, and other governmental policies. Step five sees the successful sites referred for ministerial and cabinet approval, and the sixth and final step is site establishment and management. A site may be rejected at any point between steps two and five.

With respect to public participation and local input into decision-making, step three is the most critical stage in the process. It is here that the local community and the general public can influence decisions that will have a direct impact on a local community. As will be illustrated in the next section, however, step three is also the stage that can cause the most difficulty for the public consultation process, and thus has the most potential for bitter conflict.

Conservation of the Castle Wilderness Area

The Castle wilderness area in southwestern Alberta is part of the "Crown of the Continent Ecosystem" that extends from the Crowsnest Pass in Alberta and B.C. to the Bob Marshall Wilderness south of Glacier National Park in Montana. Because of its unique climatic conditions, the Crown is home to many species of rare plants. This region was also identified at the 1997 Yellowstone to Yukon Conference in Waterton National Park as critical habitat for the conservation of large carnivores in North America. These animals need an enormous range to survive, and the Crown provides a connective corridor from Yellowstone National Park in Wyoming to Yukon, the so-called "Serengeti" of North America. The Castle-Crown Wilderness Coalition was formed in 1990 to represent the concerns of a number of local citizens over the development of this region. It now claims 350 active members.[20] A major impetus for the formation of this coalition was Vacation Alberta Corporation's proposal to construct recreational and tourism facilities in the Castle valley. While the Special Places program was still being developed, the Natural Resources Conservation Board in 1993 approved Vacation Alberta's development application. This approval was conditional; the Board allowed for a ski development, but only if an 800-square kilometre wild land area (approximately 12 per cent of the total area) was established. No construction could begin until this area had been set aside to mitigate the environmental impact of the project. According to Vacation Alberta, the development plan had the potential to generate $72 million in employment revenue.[21]

The following year, the Alberta cabinet approved the Conservation Board's decision, and in December 1993 Ty Lund announced the formation of a multi-stakeholder committee, the Castle River Consultation Group, which was to develop a plan for the wild land area. The group was comprised of 12 members representing area stakeholders – agriculture, oil and gas, tourism, recreation, and environmental interests. The consultation group's mandate was to make consensus-based recommendations as to what the wild land area would look like. The committee managed to reach consensus on all but one issue, and was in the process of moving towards agreement on the last item when, in May 1995, the provincial government made a stunning reversal. Ty Lund announced that the provincial government was withdrawing its conditional authorization of the proposed development, saying that "[t]he decision to discontinue the group was an extremely difficult one," and was the result of serious disagreements among the group's members, who, "despite their best intentions ... have not been able to achieve consensus on land use."[22] It was widely believed, however, that this process was overturned largely as a result of back-room lobbying by four of the committee members, who protested against the creation of the wild land reserve directly to Lund.[23] These four did not accept the compromises relating to recreational development; their subsequent mass resignation from the local committee provided Lund with justification to nullify the entire committee's recommendations.

This action was taken without consulting the other members of the committee, and attempts by the Canadian Parks and Wilderness Society (one of Alberta's most prominent environmental groups) to appeal failed.[24] While inflaming the environmental community in Alberta, this outcome also soured relations between stakeholders in the Castle-Crown region.[25]

Undeterred, the Castle-Crown Wilderness Coalition began another conservation initiative: the nomination of the Castle as a Special Place. This nomination was reviewed and approved by both the PCC and IC, which set the stage for step three of the Special Places process: the establishment of a local committee. In October of 1996, the PCC recommended that the Municipal District of Pincher Creek establish a "local committee to develop management principles for the creation of a protected area to preserve the unique and significant features of the Castle Area for designation under the Special Places program." The recommendation went on to state that "it is anticipated that the recommended site will contribute to the Special Places goal of protection, but also contribute significantly to the other three Special Places goals."[26]

The PCC's terms of reference for the Castle Special Place candidate area outlined the mandate of the local committee: it was to "review the Castle in the Rocky Mountain natural region and make recommendations on the level of protection required for preserving its unique and significant features."[27] The committee was to make specific recommendations on boundaries, permitted activities or uses, guidelines for ongoing activities, and mechanisms for ongoing management. It was also to identify the traditional and current uses of the Castle area, as well as any contentious local issues affecting the site.

Many dispositions are in effect in the Castle region. The PCC recognized these commitments and emphasized the need for those persons holding dispositions to be included in decisions relating to the area. In total, 28 groups whose interests should be represented on the local committee were identified. Since this large number would prove unmanageable given the time constraint imposed by the PCC, it suggested the "interests should be lumped into sectors" and that between 12 and 15 participants should represent these sectors. Selecting stakeholders would not be easy; it was recommended that the local committee use an outside facilitator to monitor the selection process.[28] Once the membership was established, participants were instructed to "develop their operating ground rules."[29] Despite this seeming *carte blanche* to create its own rule book, it should be noted that the PCC did provide clear directions as to both the committee's mandate and membership, and offered it the necessary resources to support the whole process. Moreover, the PCC clearly stated that participants "will be appointed to ensure that all interests impacted by a potential nomination will be represented on the local committee," and that it "will function by consensus."[30]

Because of the long history of local animosity with respect to land use in the Castle Crown area, the Municipal District of Pincher Creek was initially reluctant to accept the PCC's request for leadership. It eventually did so, however, and set up a local committee, which submitted detailed terms of reference for the minister's approval. These terms of reference stated that the Rocky Mountain Natural region was fully represented, that is, that 12 per cent of this region was already protected within existing protected areas. The terms went on to state that the boundaries of the nominated area could be "reduced or minimally expanded by the Local Committee to meet the program goals."[31] This document also stated that the Municipal District of Pincher Creek "will appoint two councillors to the local committee, one of which will chair the local committee and the other as a member of the local committee and alternate chair. There will be no more than seven members from the greater Southern Alberta community." Members of the local committee were not to be replaced if members resigned for any reason; the final report of the committee would thus be the product of members of the original committee. The local committee's terms of reference gave the chair voting privileges and directed the chair to obtain decisions by consensus where possible. They also allowed the chair to call for simple majority votes on issues that cannot be decided by consensus. These terms of reference were approved in January 1997, and six months later the local committee for the Castle candidate area completed its work, making public its conservation recommendations in July 1997. While this committee was successful in coming to consensus on what should be done with respect to the conservation of the Castle wilderness area, its activities and final report did nothing to decrease animosity among local stakeholders. Indeed, the

Special Places processes may have even increased polarization of local citizens over conservation issues.

The Castle Conflict: Lessons To Be Learned

The notion of conserving certain places in perpetuity is very popular in Alberta. A 1994 poll commissioned by the World Wildlife Fund found that 80 per cent of Albertans felt the government should immediately approve the Special Places program and begin designating areas, while 93 per cent favoured setting aside protected areas where no logging, mining, or other industrial activity was allowed.[32] After releasing the 1992 Special Places draft document, public opinion was solicited by an advisory committee. This committee reported that the "vast majority supported the vision outlined in the draft document."[33] In the intervening three years between the draft and the final version of the Special Places program document, however, interests opposed to conservation mobilized. Leading the charge was the Minister of Environmental Protection, Ty Lund, along with backbench MLAS Gary Friedel and Lorne Taylor. They questioned why Albertans should give in to the demands of "eco-terrorists" by "sterilizing" large tracts of land, making them off limits to economic development and recreational use.[34] Significant opposition mounted against the original 1992 Special Places draft document, primarily from ranchers, farmers, and recreational interests, such as all-terrain-vehicle enthusiasts.[35] As a result of this pressure, the revised 1995 document saw the inclusion of economic development as one of the goals of the Special Places program. Environmental groups were enraged by the dilution of the 1992 conservation program; all of Alberta's major groups chose to boycott any further participation in the Special Places program.[36] Although initially a powerful statement and show of force, the boycott proved ineffective when three of Alberta's most influential environmental groups, the Canadian Parks and Wilderness Society, the Federation of Alberta Naturalists, and World Wildlife Fund Canada, decided to continue their participation. While many environmentalists were unhappy with this decision by the "big three," others drifted back to their local Special Places process. But in 1997, the controversy over the composition and terms of reference of the Castle local committee again caused an uproar in Alberta's environmental community, with activists threatening boycotts and protests.

There were a number of serious flaws in the structure of the Castle local committee as a multipartite consultative forum. As a result, the outcome of this particular process lacked legitimacy. The most contentious issue was the terms of reference created by the Municipal District of Pincher Creek, and subsequently approved by the minister. The PCC had originally recommended that "all interests that would be affected by the nomination should be represented."[37] Accordingly, the Municipal District of Pincher Creek ran ads in area newspapers inviting the participation of "individuals with an interest in becoming actively involved on this committee."[38] The local committee's terms of reference state, however, that "[i]ndividuals who have participated actively as representatives of a particular perspective in previous processes will not be given preference in the selection process."[39] According to the chair of the local committee, this decision was taken to "get the politics out" of the decision-making process.[40] While 28 key stakeholders had been initially identified by the PCC, the local committee's terms of reference stated that two seats on the committee would be reserved for local government, and only seven other representatives would be appointed. No facilitator was used in the process: participants were selected by the Municipal District of Pincher Creek. In the end, participants were chosen more by chance than by design. Aside from the two participants from the Municipal Districts of Pincher Creek and Crowsnest Pass, and one participant representing an "outside" perspective (that is, someone who did not live or work in the local area), the other participants were selected by drawing names from a jar. As luck would have it, no one representing an environmental group, including the original nominator of the Castle site, the Castle-Crown Wilderness Coalition, was invited to participate.

The Municipal District's rationale for changing the terms of reference of the local committee was past experience with public consultation in the area, and was inspired by the "citizen's jury" approach to decision-making. Given the entrenched positions that many locals held and the resulting "burn-out" from disputes over land management issues, it was felt that a smaller committee would function more effectively and that the chair needed the discretion to call a vote in order to break a deadlock on any particular issue. According to the chair, however, the committee ultimately achieved all its decisions by consensus, and thus this power was never exercised. The decision to draw participants by lot was to ensure that individuals would not come to the table as representatives of a particular sector. It was hoped that participants would be perceived as interested individuals making decisions based on submissions from concerned citizens and organized interests.

Incensed at the exclusion of organized environmental interests from the local committee, in March 1997 the Castle-Crown Wilderness Coalition dramatically demonstrated its displeasure at simultaneous press conferences in Lethbridge, Calgary, and Edmonton where it was announced that they were withdrawing their nomination of the Castle as a Special Place. According to Coalition president Klaus Jericho, "[t]he government has given Albertans one process for protecting land, but it is so flawed that environmental groups like ours have decided that we can't be part of it. The local procedures of Special Places 2000 are such that we think it might actually harm our efforts to protect the Castle Wilderness, not help them."[41]

The problems with the Castle Special Places process occurred at step three, where the nomination is returned to a local committee after it has been approved by the PCC and the IC. The terms of reference for each local committee include very specific directives as to how the committee should be established, as well as its fundamental rules of order. The recommendations of the PCC/IC, however, were in large part disregarded by the Castle committee, which developed its own terms of reference. Even though these new terms were significantly different from the original (particularly with respect to how participants would be chosen), they were accepted by the PCC/IC and became the operating principles of the Castle committee. This third step in a process designed to encourage public consultation may have thus become untenable from the start. The statement that the need for protection of the Castle was not shared by everyone within the PCC, and the government's commitment to honour all existing dispositions (such as logging leases), may have inadvertently biased the local committee by encouraging dissent regarding the principle of conservation in the Castle region. Given that conservation issues had previously created profound divisions within the community the local committee's task of making land use recommendations in six months was virtually impossible within a consensual-based, multi-stakeholder process. The particular history of the Castle-Crown region may have swayed the minister and the PCC to accept modified terms of reference for the Castle committee. Special Places is, however, a consultative process; the purpose of the local committees is to represent area stakeholders, and to come to a decision that is at least minimally accepted by all those affected. Since the local committee in this case did not represent all stakeholders, it could not complete its mandate as originally outlined by the PCC.

Whither Special Places?

The inherent difficulty in meeting government (and presumably societal) objectives while responding to local public input is clearly demonstrated in the case of the Castle candidate nomination. Meaningful public input will only be attained if a decision-making process has a degree of autonomy from the government. Autonomy, however, necessitates a system of checks and balances so that the local process is both accountable to the public, and compatible with larger societal objectives. While decentralized decision-making and local empowerment are often seen as desirable, as both the Canadian Parks and Wilderness Society and World Wildlife Fund Canada point out, local communities may not "fully appreciate" the importance of areas that may be of national or international significance.[42] Moreover, at the local level the power differential between competing stakeholders may in fact be much greater than at the regional or national level, and thus some interests may be greatly disadvantaged.

In the case of the Castle nomination, the modification of the terms of reference by the local committee and the subsequent acceptance of these terms by the provincial government irreparably damaged the credibility of its final report. First, critical stakeholders were excluded from the local process. Second, those stakeholders that were included were picked by another stakeholder, in this case a representative of the local government. Third, this same stakeholder was also the facilitator and chair of the local committee, in addition to having voting privileges. Fourth, the terms of reference of the committee allowed for the possibility that its deliberations be conducted by majority vote rather than by consensus.

In a stakeholder process, it is critically important that there be at least the *perception* that the composition of the group is balanced and representative, that the process is neutral, and that there is some degree of autonomy from government. Consensus is a useful tool for claiming process neutrality, as long as stakeholders know that an impasse will result in a higher authority making the decision for them. In a 50 per cent + 1 majority-vote process, or in a consensus process where an impasse means the status quo, stakeholders have little incentive to compromise. In the case of the Castle candidate area, the changes in the terms of reference left the perception among those excluded that the local committee had been hijacked by the Municipal District, which manipulated the process for its own purposes. This result is ironic, given that the committee's chair claims that the Municipal District changed the terms to depoliticize the process and encourage compromise. Given that consensual processes that include participants with very different viewpoints are notoriously slow, the speed with which the Municipal District completed its mandate reflected the committee's lack of internal polarization, and the ability of the chair to invoke a majority decision-making model in case of an impasse. Despite the success of the Castle committee in producing a set of recommendations, other Special Places participants fear that the acrimony over the altered Castle terms of reference will jeopardize the credibility of other Special Place processes throughout the province, regardless of the process used, or the outcomes achieved.

The Special Places program in Alberta clearly demonstrates that multipartite environmental decision-making processes will be perceived as legitimate and meaningful only if public participation is seen to be balanced. Anything less, and the process will be seen as simply a thinly disguised method used by particular interests to manipulate the public agenda to achieve their own goals. Whether or not the final report of a local committee makes sound recommendations is not the critical issue; the point is that in a multipartite process, participants are supposed to be stakeholders representing a particular sectoral interest. If critical stakeholders are excluded, if some stakeholders are allowed to act as both participant and facilitator, and if there is the possibility that the consensual decision-making model can be abandoned at the discretion of a stakeholder, the local committee's final report will be perceived to be biased (and therefore illegitimate) even if its recommendations are balanced and well thought out.

The Special Places program will be perceived to be a legitimate method of addressing land-use conflicts if, and only if, the weak points of the process are addressed. First, the PCC/IC must establish (and adhere to) a standard terms of reference for all nominations. Stakeholders will vary from nomination to nomination, but this standard format would provide a thread of continuity throughout the province, rather than allowing for the possibility that the terms of reference could be reinvented by each local committee at the whim of local interests. It would also give the committee a degree of autonomy from political interference. All stakeholders identified by the PCC/IC should be represented, and chosen by a neutral facilitator, preferably someone with professional qualifications who is not from the local area. Again, perception of impartiality is critical; a facilitator who has no "history" in the local community would enhance the legitimacy of the process. And finally, consensus decision-making is critical to a stakeholder process, particularly one which is attempting to solve a contentious issue. A consensus requirement where impasse does not mean the status quo, but rather passes the decision-making on to another body forces stakeholders to strive for common ground, while a straight majority vote gives the advantage to the status quo over the minority viewpoint. Finally, there must be a provision for the PCC/IC to overrule local committees that are unable to achieve consensus in order to promote broader provincial and national interests. This is critical in the event that the local processes become mired down in irresolvable issues. In any event, difficult decisions must be made regarding the environment, and processes that favour the status quo will do nothing to help resolve complex problems. In the case of the Castle-Crown, the Special Places mechanism may have been inappropriate from the start, given the divisions about its suitability within the PCC, and the bitter history of the area. Local interests, and indeed the interests of the Special Places program itself, may well have been better served by using something other than a multipartite process in this situation.

Like any new decision-making process, the multipartite forum will experience growing pains. There are important lessons that can be learned from the Castle Special Places process, and in that sense, this process cannot be described as a complete failure. What would be a failure is to learn nothing from this case, blindly continuing to make the same blunders again and again, exacerbating the already strained relations between various stakeholders in places like the Castle area. Without proper care and attention, what is now a dispute that has been contained within provincial boundaries may erupt into a vicious battle involving those living beyond Alberta's borders. Alberta contains some of the world's last great wilderness areas, and the Germans, Japanese, and in particular, the Americans who have discovered the province's natural charms provide a ready constituency to be drawn into conservation battles. This is particularly critical with respect to the Castle-Crown wilderness area, which is located adjacent to the Waterton Lakes/Glacier International Peace Park, a UNESCO World Heritage Site. This point was illustrated at an October 1997 international conference in Waterton Park attended by over 300 conservationists. The Castle wilderness was identified by conservation biologists as the "Black Hole" of a conservation initiative that would see the establishment of almost 3,000 kilometres of protected land running from Yellowstone National Park to the Yukon. Biologists argue that because large carnivores need a large range, the lack of species protection in the Castle area is threatening the viability of the more limited number of the same species in the U.S. Alberta would be well advised to consider the experience her neighbour to the west has had when international attention is focused on domestic conservation disputes. It is notable that the year the final draft of the Special Places Program was announced, World Wildlife Fund Canada gave Alberta the dubious distinction of being the first province in Canada to receive a grade of "F" for its conservation efforts. Anything less than a concerted effort to resolve Alberta's conservation disputes through careful attention to the mechanics of the Special Places process may result in further unwanted notoriety.

Notes

1. "It's a 'recipe for conflict,'" *Calgary Herald*, March 21, 1995, A12.
2. The Castle region is an area of 795 km², located north of Glacier and Waterton Lakes National Parks. It is southwest of the municipality of Pincher Creek, on the eastern slopes of the Rocky Mountains, and takes in the west and south Castle Rivers. Between 1914 and 1921, the Castle wilderness area was a part of Waterton Lakes National Park and until 1954 was a game preserve.
3. Banff National Park, Dinosaur Provincial Park, Head Smashed in Buffalo Jump, and Waterton Lakes/Glacier International Peace Park.
4. Ronald Inglehart, *The Silent Revolution* (Princeton, N.J.: Princeton University Press, 1977).
5. H. Cleveland, "The twilight of hierarchy: Speculations on the global information society," *Public Administration Review* 45 (1985): 192.
6. Roger Gibbins and Sonia Arrison, *Western Visions: Perspective on the West in Canada* (Peterborough, Ont.: Broadview Press, 1995), 66.
7. The Oldman Dam site is, coincidentally, in the same region as the Castle wilderness area. The construction of this dam vaulted Alberta onto the national stage in 1991 when a coalition of environmental groups took the federal government to court, claiming that the federal and provincial governments had failed to conduct a proper environmental assessment of the Oldman Dam construction project before a licence to proceed had been issued. While the environmental groups ultimately failed to stop the construction of the dam, the Supreme Court agreed that the federal government has an obligation to conduct environmental assessments on the impact of dam construction because of its constitutional responsibilities for navigable waters and fisheries.
8. The Alberta Environmental Network is comprised of over 200 environmental groups in Alberta. Its mandate is to facilitate communication among Albertans who are concerned about the environment.
9. Ronald L. Doering, "Canadian Round Tables on the Environment and the Economy: Their History, Form and Function," *Working Paper Number 14, National Round Table on the Environment and the Economy*, 2. According to Glen Toner, the 1987 Canadian Environmental Protection Act signalled the first step towards a multimedia ecosystem approach to resource management. That is, it was recognized that a single-sector, single-discipline

approach to environmental problems would not achieve integrated solutions. Round table processes were an attempt to integrate economic and social goals in the development of public policy. See Glen Toner, "The Green Plan: From Great Expectations to Eco-Backtracking ... to Revitalization?" in *How Ottawa Spends, 1994-95: Making Change* (Ottawa: Carleton University Press, 1994).

10. World Commission on Environment and Development, Gro Harlem Brundtland, chair, *Our Common Future* (New York: Oxford University Press, 1987).

11. Doering, "Canadian Round Tables," 3.

12. Murray Bookchin, *Remaking Society: Pathways to a Green Future* (Boston: South End Press, 1990), 155.

13. Glen Toner, "ENGOs and the Policy Process," *National Round Table Review* (Spring 1993), 4.

14. Michael Howlett, "The Round Table Experience: Representation and Legitimacy in Canadian Environmental Policy-Making," *Queen's Quarterly* 97 (1990): 585.

15. Alberta, Environmental Protection, *Special Places 2000: Alberta's Natural Heritage* (November 1992) 5.

16. Ibid., 1.

17. Alberta, Environmental Protection, *Fact Sheet: Special Places 2000: Alberta's Natural Heritage*, n.p., n.d., question and answer ¢18.

18. Ibid.

19. Ibid.

20. Castle-Crown Wilderness Coalition, *The Castle Wilderness*, n.d., 4.

21. Alberta, Natural Resources Conservation Board, *Application No. 9201, Application to Construct Recreational and Tourism Facilities in the West Castle Valley, near Pincher Creek, Alberta*, December 1993.

22. Alberta, Office of the Minister of Environmental Protection, News Release, "Government Withdraws Conditional Authorization of West Castle Resort," May 11, 1995.

23. "Lund Loose Cannon: Albertans have a right to know when debacles like Westcastle will end," *Calgary Herald*, May 17, 1995.

24. Ibid.

25. Ironically, the entire debate over this development may well have been moot, since some degree of provincial government financial participation was requested. In the wake of a string of provincial government disasters

in supporting private-sector ventures, such development assistance was unlikely.

26. Alberta, Special Places Provincial Co-ordinating Committee, "Rocky Mountains Recommendation, Castle Subregion Local Committee," 1.

27. Ibid.

28. Ibid., 4.

29. Ibid., 3.

30. Ibid.

31. Municipal District of Pincher Creek, "Castle Nomination – Special Places Local Committee Terms of Reference."

32. The random telephone survey of 502 Albertans was conducted June 2-12 by the Dunvegan Group of Calgary. See "Klein warned by Environmental Activists," *Calgary Herald*, July 3, 1994, A2.

33. The Advisory Committee reported that 1,600 people phoned and received copies of the 1992 *Special Places 2000: Alberta's Natural Heritage*, and 500 wrote letters to comment on the report. In addition, open houses were conducted in six locations and focus group interviews were conducted at another six centres. Alberta, *Special Places 2000: Alberta's Natural Heritage, Report of the Advisory Committee*, November 1993.

34. "A Kick in their Special Places," *Alberta Report*, April 19, 1995, 19.

35. It should be noted that the Canadian Association of Petroleum Producers unanimously voted in favour of supporting the 1992 Special Places 2000 program, a phenomenon that can be attributed to the Whaleback debacle. After five years of preparatory work, Amoco Canada's 1994 application to sink an exploratory well in the Whaleback region was denied on environmental grounds, sending shock waves through the industry. It was felt that supporting Special Places 2000 was in the industry's best interests, as it would create a stable, predictable regulatory structure. According to the Association's vice president in charge of the environment, "we want to help identify where the protected areas are so that our members don't get mired down in confrontational hearings every time they apply for a drilling license." Quoted in *Alberta Report*, February 6, 1995, 7.

36. "Environmentalists ask public to circumvent Special Places process," *Calgary Herald*, June 21, 1995, A15.

37. Alberta, PCC, "Rocky Mountains Recommendation, " 3.

38. *Pincher Creek Echo*, January 14, 1997, 30.

39. Municipal District of Pincher Creek, "Castle Nomination – Special Places Local Committee Terms of Reference."
40. Interview with the chair of the Castle local committee, September 15, 1997.
41. Castle-Crown Wilderness Coalition, *News Release*, March 20, 1997.
42. Interview with World Wildlife Fund Alberta Special Places co-ordinator, July 1997. See also a letter written by the Canadian Parks and Wilderness Society to Ty Lund, dated February 19, 1997, posted at http://www.rockies.ca/cpaws/sp2000_ff/htm

Further Reading

Mitchell, Dawn, and Dianne Pachal. "Alberta," in Monte Hummel, ed., *Protecting Canada's Endangered Spaces: An Owner's Manual.* Toronto: Key Porter Books, 1995.

Pratt, Larry, and Ian Urquhart. *The Last Great Forest: Japanese Multinationals and Alberta's Northern Forests.* Edmonton: NeWest Press, 1994.

Van Tighem, Kevin, and Stephen Hutchings. *Coming West: A Natural History of Home.* Canmore, Alta.: Altitude Publishing, 1997.

R. Michael M'Gonigle   The Political Ecology of

Biodiversity: A View from the

Western Woods

O N October 21, 1996, the British Columbia Land Use
Co-ordination Office issued a press release under the headline
"Kootenay Land Use Plan Implementation Unveiled." Trumpeting the
government's "historic progress towards sustainability" in the region,
including the designation of 16 new provincial parks, the release also
revealed that cutting permits in the domestic watershed for the town
of New Denver had been issued to Slocan Forest Products, now the
province's largest forest company. Logging, it was stated, would be
according to the highest standards "for management of special values,
including biodiversity."[1]

To those who had followed debates about wilderness protection and
"alternative" forestry in unprotected lands – the twin pillars of biological conservation for forested regions – the irony in this announcement was bitter. The Slocan Valley has long represented perhaps the
world's leading opportunity to do forestry differently and, in doing so,
to create a new model of both ecological and economic sustainability.
This is the home of the Valhalla Society, one of the premiere environmental organizations in the province, and the Silva Foundation, whose
principal, Herb Hammond, is known worldwide for his ecoforestry
scholarship and practice. Despite intensive lobbying to undertake a
pilot ecoforestry project, the shrinking resources in the West
Kootenays instead led the provincial government to assign the timber
resources to the region's main industrial corporation.

In 1996, Silva completed a comprehensive ecosystem-based plan for the valley, including a detailed inventory, a forest development plan, and the beginnings of an economic transition strategy. The plan calls for a reduction of 83 per cent in the allowable annual cut, a dramatic reduction that clearly requires broad support to be workable.[2] Instead, following the provincial announcement, in the summer of 1997, large numbers of protesters were arrested at blockades against industrial development on the proposed logging roads, and sent to jail. Many of these people were local residents trying to protect the watersheds on which they depend for their rural water supply.

Ten years ago, when biodiversity was in its conceptual infancy, the phrase "sustainable development" was making the rounds of the planet's national capitals and conference halls. In the globalized world of the 1990s, however, there has been a surfeit of development, but precious little sustainability. As the forces of production and growth put ever more pressure on the planet's resources, a similar fate awaits the growing concern for maintaining biodiversity. In this situation, one would do well to pay heed to B.C.'s recent history of environmental reform.

Between Theory and Practice

Biodiversity conservation, like other environmental initiatives, will not take place in a vacuum but within the confines of a political and economic "system" that has its own dynamics of adaptation and survival. This brings the discussion into the field of political economy, a field that looks at the operation of a range of social processes – such as markets, legal rights (including property rights), corporations, bureaucracies, and the state – not just on their own but as institutions integrated within a social whole, an important part of which are the various values and forms of knowledge that are embedded within, or marginalized by, these structures.

The literature on the dynamics of these structures is well established, from Adam Smith to Karl Marx to the recent writings of more ecologically oriented scholars. Indeed, where earlier political economists have focused on the sorts of institutions just listed, the new perspective offered by an *ecological* political economy uncovers aspects of economic production and political regulation unconsidered in the past. In particular, only recently have the role of nature in wealth creation and the "spatial" imbalance in the power relations between urbanized industries/agencies and rural resource suppliers been addressed. These new perspectives are, for example, clearly articulated in the writings both of regional geographers, such as John Friedmann, Edward Soya, and Ralph Matthews, and of "common property" theorists such as Elinor Ostrom.[3] This literature is an important foundation for ecological political economy, an awareness of which is essential for any strategy that seeks to put the forest industry — or any other resource industry, for that matter — onto a sustainable path that will protect biodiversity. Unfortunately, such an awareness has not pervaded the NDP's actions in British Columbia throughout the 1990s.

In 1991, an NDP government, elected with the support of the environmental community, began an ambitious program of wilderness protection and forestry regulation, an agenda explicitly directed at maintaining biodiversity. Environmentalists enthusiastically embraced this agenda. For example, a new co-ordinating body, BC Wild, was established in Victoria, to ensure full, province-wide participation in the negotiations. Its board has included a representative of almost every major group in the province (Sierra Club, Sierra Legal Defence Fund, Valhalla Wilderness Society, Greenpeace, and so on). In undertaking this program, the government was confronted by an industry that directly employed almost 100,000 people and, as importantly, contributed several billion dollars a year in export earnings. Despite the shrinkage of the workforce since the 1970s as a result of modernization, the industry remained a prime economic generator. Nevertheless, the Harcourt government created over 200 new protected areas, enacted a comprehensive *Forest Practices Code*,[4] established a $400 million annual program for "forest renewal,"[5] put in place innovative management regimes (including a community-based "co-management" authority in Clayoquot Sound), and initiated treaty negotiations with the province's First Nations.

There have been gains, particularly in the formal protection of many long-contentious wilderness areas. Overall, however, the program has failed. And, in one important respect, the reforms have actually left the environmental movement to protect biodiversity worse off than before. Because the environmental movement accepted incremental reforms within the dominant paradigm of continued industrial forestry, rather than insisting on structural reforms to the whole model of production and regulation, the movement is now tangled within a model of forestry that is clearly unecological, and is disempowered as a force for piercing the curtain of green rhetoric.

Despite the *Forest Practices Code* and other legislative interventions, the industrial model continues to erode the prospects for maintaining biological diversity. Two government research scientists made this point at a 1998 joint Canadian Forest Service/B.C. Ministry of Forests workshop held in Victoria on the "Structure, Processes and Diversity in Successional Forests of Coastal British Columbia." They wrote, "B.C. is conducting a vast, province-wide experiment with its forests, converting them from wild, idiosyncratic, resilient ecosystems to less variable, more predictable (maybe), managed ecosystems".[6] Behind the rhetoric of sustainability, this B.C. experiment demonstrates that biodiversity cannot be protected within the prevailing industrial paradigm but can only be hoped for by building a new, ecosystem-based alternative to industrial exploitation.

The Current Regime

The current B.C. forestry regime has three basic components – a land zonation system that attempts to balance environmental interests with continued industrial timber utilization, a comprehensive regulatory regime of locally specific forestry standards, and a financing mechanism to facilitate economic adjustments to those affected by the new system. This regime seems comprehensive, and was certainly heralded as a new approach, yet it remains firmly entrenched within the unsustainable assumptions of "sustained yield management" (Box 1).[7]

Forest Zoning

For biodiversity preservation, the core provision of the new regime is a comprehensive protected area system that was created through a province-wide Protected Areas Strategy, a series of regional Land and Resource Management Plans, and two-year-long negotiations under the independent Commission on Resources and the Environment (CORE). Dating back to the beginning of the Harcourt government, these initiatives were propelled forward by the 1993 Clayoquot Sound blockades. In an effort to reach consensus and foster support, almost all protected area designations occurred after a process of negotiations between various "stakeholders" including the forest industry and environmentalists, and against a background of ecological assessments. Protected areas constitute one form of forest zone. Other zones were contemplated to allow for varying degrees of intensity in forestry operations, from low-intensity zones (where innovative ecoforestry might be practised) to high-intensity zones (where high-impact plantation forestry would be encouraged).

Forest Practices

Based on these zonations, the government produced a comprehensive set of forest practices regulations. The vehicle for these is the mammoth *Forest Practices Code Act*, a huge legislative instrument that, when combined with all the regulations, proposed standards, and guidebooks, runs to some 1800 pages. While a range of guidelines and planning rules had existed for some time in B.C., the Code sets out a new, comprehensive framework for the conduct of forestry operations, detailing the strategic and operational planning required, the objectives of planning, and the standards that forest managers should apply for each type of zone. Just as the Clayoquot blockades stimulated action on protected areas, so, too, the international environmental campaign against B.C. forestry practices provoked this legislative initiative.

Forest Renewal

Accompanying the commitment to these new set-asides and stricter standards was a concern that employment levels in the forest industry would be negatively affected. While environmentalists had blockaded logging roads in Clayoquot Sound, some 20,000 forest workers showed up on the steps of the provincial legislature to protest CORE's announcement of the Vancouver Island Land Use Plan. In response,

Conventional Forest Management Policy in B.C.

Forest management in B.C. is based on a number of policies established by the Ministry of Forests. Sustained-yield forest management (SYFM) is the dominant policy. Adopted in the late 1940s, SYFM has since provided the framework for maximizing timber production, while encouraging concentration of production within relatively few companies.

SYFM was introduced to North America at the turn of the century and adopted as policy in B.C. in 1947 following the 1945 Sloan Royal Commission.[8] SYFM was designed to maximize timber yield and reorder the forest on the basis of long-term crop rotations.[9] Based on plantation forestry in Europe, the objective of SYFM is to "normalize" the forest, replacing old growth with even-aged managed stands of preferred commercial species.

Fundamental to SYFM is the allowable annual cut (AAC) calculation, which is supposed to ensure a perpetual forest yield by setting an annual cut volume equal to annual forest growth within a given area. The long-term harvest level (LTHL) determines the sustainable rate of cut over the long term to ensure future timber supply. Currently, the AAC exceeds the LTHL by nearly 30 million cubic metres.[10] Despite the fact that the available timber supply has apparently been reduced as a result of initiatives such as the FPC, CORE, and the Protected Areas Strategy, the AAC remains relatively unchanged. At the conclusion of the Timber Supply Review process in 1996, the overall rate of cut for the entire province had been reduced by less than 1 per cent and the Chief Forester had increased the AAC for 37 of the province's 71 timber supply areas and tree farm licences.[11] For example, in the Nass Valley, the AAC has been set at more than triple the LTHL. Areas to the far north, for example, the Cassiar TSA, have had their AACs increased to make up for a lack of timber supply in the south.

Sustained yield policy determines the AAC based on *projected* future timber yields. Consequently, investments in intensive silviculture, which increase the likelihood of higher future timber yields, are factored in to maintain or increase the AAC today. This renders future cut levels vulnerable to changes in the conditions and assumptions that underpin the growth model, such as: the extent of forest land available; the growth rate of second growth forests; the health and persistence of new forests in the face of a range of pests, diseases, and environmental changes; and the utilization and future markets for commercial timber of different species. Furthermore, the AAC calculation has been based on a German formula designed for even-aged forests,[12] which, when applied to the diverse forests of B.C., can lead to inaccuracies. Marginal and unproductive lands have been included in calculations, whether or not they contained commercial timber. This has enabled tenure holders to increase the size of their total allowable cut, affecting timber supply and the accuracy of long-term planning.[13] Recently, the AAC has increased in certain areas because of newly accessible or acceptable timber not included in earlier AAC calculations, thus impacting the long-run sustained yield calculated by previous inventories.

With B.C. currently in its first rotation, over 95 per cent of logging continues to take place in old growth. The inevitable transition to second growth entails what is known as the "falldown effect," which involves a reduction in timber volume. With cutting rates higher than the LTHL for many years, the onset of the falldown effect has been accelerated, resulting in the prospect of transition to a second-growth forest resource that is commercially immature.

Beyond maximizing timber production, sustained-yield forest management, as envisaged by the Sloan Commission, involved granting access by private companies to publicly owned forests, placing responsibility on the tenure holder to access remote forests, develop a stable timber processing industry, create jobs and permanent rural communities, and generate more revenue for the province in the form of stumpage fees. In return, licensees were assured a continuous, non-competitive supply of timber that would justify the huge capital investments needed to purchase logging equipment and construct appurtenant mills. They were also offered rights to substantial areas of Crown forest in exchange for committing private lands and existing tenure holdings to sustained-yield management.[14]

The 1947 Forest Act encoded two types of tenures. Forest management licences (now TFLs) were areas of public timber granted to private companies to manage in accordance with SYFM. These were issued primarily to large firms as vast areas of timberland surrounding their new or existing mills. Thus large multinational firms who could finance the mills or were already in operation were granted most of the new tenures. Public sustained yield units (PSYU, now timber supply areas) were established for the allocation of volume-based timber sales on public timber land, managed by the Forest Service. These smaller licences were to be reserved for independent operators.

In the 1950s and 1960s, a quota system divided the AAC for PSYUs among licence holders in proportion to the amount of timber they had originally been allocated, resulting in large firms obtaining the largest quotas. These companies were guaranteed a certain quota of timber each year, and competitive bidding became a formality. As quotas were sold and traded, only companies capable of raising the requisite capital could participate. Today, these quotas — now forest licences — are controlled mainly by large corporations. By the 1960s all TFLs were required to allocate 30 per cent to 50 per cent of their cut to contract loggers. In turn, small loggers sold their quotas to large firms in exchange for guaranteed logging contracts. By 1975, 15 companies controlled over half of the timber in the PSYUs, held rights to virtually all the TFLs in the province, and owned most of the private land, in total controlling 85 per cent of the timber in the province.[15] This concentration continues today.

Right: Clearcut in Clayquot Sound, British Columbia

photo: Jerry Valen DeMarco

the government created Forest Renewal B.C., a Crown corporation funded out of increased royalty rates on timber ("stumpage") to the tune of some $400 million per year. These monies were designated to support environmental restoration, silviculture, community development, value-added manufacturing, and so on. Workers laid off as a result of the new measures were assured of meaningful employment in new government-supported areas of the forestry sector.

Old Wine in New Bottles

There is certainly a rounded logic to this package of environmental protection, industrial regulation, and economic redeployment. Nevertheless, the environmental objective has run up against two contrary objectives – ensuring the survival of a corporate-based, industrial forest industry (rather than seeking to replace or, at least, redefine it), and continuing the pre-eminent role of the forest ministry (rather than devising alternatives to bureaucratic management). The result is a classic instance of repackaging a stale product.

Forest Zoning

The protected area negotiations were extremely rancorous. The CORE process failed to reach consensus in its four regions and, as a result, protected area designations were established by the CORE staff, and further modified by the provincial government. Many of the most highly sought-after wilderness areas were either excluded from protection (such as the Klashkish on Vancouver Island) or so compromised (such as Vancouver Island's upper Walbran Valley, the Interior's Cariboo Mountains, the White Grizzly area in Kootenays) as to be ecologically and aesthetically unrecognizable.

Overall, the province set a target of protecting 12 per cent of the landscape, an artificial figure that does not ensure the maintenance of biodiversity. At present, more than 12 per cent of B.C. is de facto wilderness already. The target merely represents the portion of this existing wilderness that is officially designated as exempt from future industrial exploitation. But, as industrial logging continues, thousands of kilometres of new roads and some 200,000 hectares of new clear-cuts every year continue to fragment wild areas, undermine ecosystem integrity, and shrink the amount of natural habitat to support wildlife and biodiversity across the province. Under the protectionist approach, designated wilderness areas are destined to become islands of refuge in an otherwise highly disturbed landscape, islands that will, over time, generally be too small to maintain their biodiversity. In addition, as the areas of prime forest land continue to diminish, there is nothing to guarantee that the park areas won't themselves eventually be "opened up" to industrial exploitation at some time in the future.

Moreover, those areas that contain the best habitat, such as lowland valley bottoms, are underrepresented because they also contain the most easily accessible and most valuable timber. Where the goal is to "balance" environmental interests with economic realities, biologically rich, protected areas are reduced. On Vancouver Island, they amount to 6 per cent, not 12 per cent, of their original area. As a recent report by the province's Land Use Co-ordination Office reveals, 61.2 per cent of the total protected areas in B.C. are located in alpine and subalpine areas ("rock and ice") with less than 10 per cent in biologically rich areas.[16] Predictably, this has led to new environmental campaigns, such as that of the Canadian Rainforest Network and Greenpeace in B.C.'s mid-coast region (the area now known as the "Great Bear Rainforest").

At least equally serious problems affect the remaining 88 per cent of the land base. What happens here is crucial for biodiversity and for the 12 per cent of lands "locked up" in islands of protection. Outside these protected areas, buffer zones and wildlife corridors are necessary, as are zones of differing levels of industrial activity, including the "special management zones" (smz) for *low-intensity* forestry. Such special zones were to be a significant part of the new regime and were critical to the overall planning compromises made by environmentalists. The environmentalists believed the special management zones would provide additional areas serving both ecological protection and economic development. This would help offset the 12 per cent limit.[17] In reality, quite a contrary process is taking place.

Huge areas of the land base are being designated for *high-intensity* (i.e., plantation) forestry to "make up" for the removal of some of the land base into protected status. For example, on Vancouver Island, the government led a largely closed-door process known as Vancouver Island Resource Targets (or VIRT), which is moving to designate over 50 per cent of the land base as *high-intensity* areas.[18] While there have been some successes in regional Land and Resource Management Planning (LRMP) exercises, a great deal of dissatisfaction exists that the LRMP can achieve its promise of "balanced" land use.[19] This has certainly been the case for the Kootenays (where the Slocan Valley is found) where environmentalists complain that the plan will lead to a high risk of exterminating endangered species unless there is a major reduction in cut levels, and the termination of all old-growth logging. Similarly, most of the remaining forests in the headwaters of the upper Fraser River (the Robson Valley) are to be logged under a recent LRMP despite threats to the spawning habitat of chinook salmon, and despite the nearly unanimous opposition of local members of the planning process. On the mid-coast, environmentalists are boycotting the negotiations. Meanwhile, implementation of the anticipated *low-intensity* development is stalled across the province, especially in sparsely populated areas that have fewer public interest groups to oversee the process.

Forest Practices

The new *Forest Practices Code*, surely one of the largest and most unwieldy pieces of state regulation ever created, has proven to be even less successful. To the corporate forester, it is massively bureaucratic. To the small woodlot owner, it is impossibly expensive and unnecessary.[20] To the environmentalist, the Code's size, complexity, technicalities, and cumbersome administrative procedures make it very difficult to enforce, even with a special review and appeals process.[21]

The Code's problems are legion. For example, until new standards for environmentally sensitive, low-intensity areas are developed, regular Code practices are to apply. Indeed, identifying an area for a "special management" designation often has the opposite of its intended effect, tipping off industry to start logging in the area while the old regulatory regime still applies.[22]

While the Code articulates the need for sustainable forestry that conserves "biological diversity, soil, water, fish, wildlife, scenic diversity, and other forest resources,"[23] it does not translate this into meaningful practice. After intense lobbying by organized labour as the Code was being developed, the government implemented a 6 per cent cap on the amount that the Code's provisions could affect the annual cut level.[24] Furthermore, a high biodiversity designation is not to apply to more than 10 per cent of the area covered by the Code.[25]

Moreover, the Code stipulates that higher standards will only apply to logging plans in "landscape units," which are not designated by the legislation, but are left to the discretion of forest ministry district managers.[26] As of this writing, almost three years after the proclamation of the Code, not one landscape unit has been designated to protect biodiversity. Nor has there been a single designation of "old growth management areas," "identified wildlife species," "wildlife habitat areas," or "sensitive areas." In 1998, the province's draft identified Wildlife Management Strategy under the Code was released. The Strategy is intended to protect species at risk, but now made subject to a mandated cap of no more than 1 per cent impact on overall cut levels! As a result of such constraints, the Code's on-the-ground impact has been the subject of alarming charges. For example, in various reports the Sierra Legal Defence Fund reveals that clear-cutting was approved for 92 per cent of the over 10,000 cutblocks authorized since the Code came into effect, and that 83 per cent of all streams in a surveyed sample of four forest districts were clear-cut to the banks, eliminating the entire riparian area.[27]

The problem here is obvious. The overall legislative package seeks to protect biodiversity but within the "sustained yield" paradigm that still assigns priority to maintaining timber production. Indeed, the official policy is the "liquidation" of old growth forests, and their "conversion" to managed, even-aged plantations of "normal forests." Imposed constraints are a constant irritant to a fibre-hungry forest industry that is able to exert significant political and economic pressures on government. Thus, when new parks are designated, the level of the allowable annual cut (AAC) is often not reduced to account for the resulting timber withdrawals in the parks but, at cabinet's insistence, is kept high to reflect the Crown's "socio-economic objectives."[28] Furthermore, a provision in the Code's *Biodiversity Guidebook* explicitly allows the biodiversity requirements to be relaxed where there will be a significant impact on the AAC.[29]

So long as corporate-based industrial exploitation continued to set the context for legislative reform to protect biodiversity, it was inevitable that pressure to repeal these measures would continue. For an industry that has long been able to externalize a range of environmental costs (and, indeed, for whom such externalization represents the basis of profits), pressure to avoid or remove any imposed restraints will actually increase as logging costs inevitably rise to reflect the decreasing quality and accessibility of the timber remaining.[30] In B.C., this problem was exacerbated by a jobs-conscious government that created a "Jobs and Timber Accord" imposing another cost on the industry by requiring it to hire more workers, a cost that has to be offset by relaxation of environmental protection or other obligations. As a result, the ongoing industry campaign to "streamline" many of the Code's operational provisions was finally successful in the spring of 1998 when a host of amendments to the Code were implemented.

The changes to the Code were touted as "administrative streamlining" aimed at improving efficiency without undermining environmental standards. In fact, they include a host of substantive rollbacks, including relaxed road-building standards, removal of the requirement to identify fish-bearing streams, elimination of requirements to address management of endangered species, and so on. Indeed, the government's own agency, the Forest Practices Board went to the unusual length of publicly criticizing the severe reductions which the changes entail, explaining that the ability of the public to gain planning information and engage in public consultations was being undercut. Reflecting on the impacts of curtailing public participation on substantive outcomes, the Board was "very concerned that the net result of these changes will be to remove any incentive for improved forest management through meaningful public involvement and proactive planning at the landscape, rather than the cutblock level."[31]

The pursuit of a reformist strategy has had another effect: it has made more basic challenges to the corporate/bureaucratic structure of power exceedingly difficult. After the years of debate generated by the CORE process, who is going to pay attention to the details about how the 12 per cent is allocated? How is one to translate to the public what a technocratic exercise like "VIRT" implies for real sustainability? How are European purchasers of B.C.'s supposedly "sustainable" forest products to be convinced that an 1,800-page forestry code is really a paper tiger that doesn't begin to achieve its biodiversity objectives?

Forest Renewal

The Forest Renewal Act was enacted in 1994 to help rejuvenate the forest sector in B.C. Through an increase in stumpage rates, the objective of the Act is to invest these funds in the enhancement of the productive capacity and environmental values of forest lands, job creation, worker retraining, and community stability.[12] This Act established a Crown corporation, Forest Renewal B.C. (FRBC), to distribute funds for a range of projects and programs to enhance B.C.'s forests and forest products industry. FRBC's budget of over $400 million per annum funds project proposals put forward by government, industry, labour, First Nations, environmental organizations, communities, and research institutions. The majority of the funds have been recirculated back to industry and government. According to the most recent, publicly available information, as of October 1996, industry and government received 41 per cent and 35 per cent of FRBC funding respectively. Academia received 6 per cent, communities 5 per cent, First Nations 3 per cent, and the environmental sector approximately 2 per cent.[13]

The funds are intended to target investment in forest research, job creation, community economic development, value-added manufacturing, and technical improvements in forestry. The majority of FRBC investments will go to enhanced silviculture, to improve the productivity of forests and increase the capacity of the land base to grow trees.[14] The purpose of FRBC is not to facilitate the transition towards an ecosystem-based economy with lower volume production. In fact, as is set out in the original 1994 Forest Renewal Plan document, intensive silviculture is projected to maintain and increase the AAC in years to come.[15] Useful in specific areas, FRBC is generally a mitigative approach to forest renewal, redirecting funds collected from timber companies both to partially restore ecosystems damaged by industrial timber production, and to reinvest in continued high-volume industrial timber production by means of intensive silviculture.

What is the Alternative?

Having shifted from a powerful social movement outside the control of government into a willing participant in the CORE/Code/Forest Renewal processes of reform and management, environmental groups now find themselves with much reduced influence. They can be and are treated as just another interest to be "managed." To reclaim its lost power, this movement must develop a fuller understanding of the dynamics of the political/economic system, and embrace a larger agenda.

Ecosystem-based Management

The basic lesson of political ecology is clear: the continuing crisis of biodiversity cannot be resolved within the existing models of economic development and bureaucratic regulation. Today, our overbuilt economic and political institutions are overwhelmingly dependent on linear systems of extraction, production, and disposal that have long been underwritten by the twin subsidies of environmental erosion and social inequity. Whether it is the large fisheries corporations plundering Canada's east and west coasts (and decimating the communities there), or the forestry multinationals clear-cutting all the forests in between, the lesson of the B.C. reform project is clear: biodiversity and corporatism do not mix, and bureaucratic intervention is clearly on the side of continued corporatist extractions.

In contrast, as I have explained in greater detail elsewhere, ecological and community-based processes are *circular* systems that:

> maintain themselves, living on the stock of natural and social capital with which they have been endowed, so that they can return long-term stability to the forest and long-term value to the community....
>
> Just as healthy ecosystems recirculate nutrients and water locally, so too a healthy community is internally dynamic, recirculating wealth locally, in a diversified economy that is only partly dependent on outside employers and outside markets.[16]

But shifting to circular systems is not just a matter of economic accounting, of getting the calculus right. It is a matter of power, of political economy. The corporate/bureaucratic hierarchy of the B.C. forest economy is characterized by a pervasive anti-ecological centralism, and reforms that leave this pattern in place are bound to be undone. To preserve biological diversity, we must build new institutions that can exist *within* natural systems.[37]

In the late 1980s, a new school of "ecosystem-based management" emerged among resource managers seeking to constrain human activity within the limits of ecosystem functioning. This approach identifies the issue not as *forest* management but as *forestry* management, that is, not managing forests for economic functions, but designing human institutions to operate within the limits of ecosystem sustainability.[38] This was the central thrust of the report of the Scientific Panel for Sustainable Practices in Clayoquot Sound, which proposed replacing the economically driven AAC with an ecologically based approach where cut levels and logging methods were determined by what a particular watershed area could yield without endangering its overall ecological integrity.[39] This was also the thrust of the now-rejected Silva plan for the Slocan Valley.

Beyond Zonation: Land Reform

In B.C., implementing an ecosystem-based process demands, above all, the reformation of control over forest lands by shifting from large corporate tenures towards new ecosystem based tenures. The essential element of tenure reform is to remove the inside/outside dichotomy between ecological protection in parks and economically based annihilation everywhere else, by progressively moving the whole regional economy onto a sustainable base.

Land tenure reform is certainly radical, although it is an omnipresent objective of Aboriginals, peasants, and environmental activists worldwide. Ironically, with the legislative changes of the past five years, tenure reform in B.C. is now officially seen as irrelevant because the protected areas system, special management zones, and *Forest Practices Code* are claimed as protecting all the appropriate values. In contrast, restructuring forestry away from high-volume corporate tenures to new forms of tenure and production is exactly what has been envisioned by the people in the Slocan Valley, and articulated by them for over 20 years.[40]

The B.C. government, despite its ostensible social democratic ideology, has refused to entertain any such alternatives. No provision for community-based tenure is included in the Forest Act. Any municipality seeking a local tenure is forced, therefore, to work within the productionist constraints of the tree farm licence system.[41] In the draft Agreement-in-Principle with the Nisga'a First Nation, no new tenures are envisioned either. On the contrary, the agreement is riddled with restrictions that require the Nisga'a to maintain existing cut levels, and to continue supplying existing mills. Meanwhile, the renewal in 1996 of the Interim Measures Agreement for the Nuu-Chah-Nulth First Nation of Clayoquot Sound (a pre-treaty agreement) was predicated on this group's agreeing to create joint ventures in the sound with MacMillan Bloedel. By not allowing a new form of tenure under provincial legislation, the government has historically precluded even the possibility of doing things differently on Crown land. Although not available at the time of writing, a new Community Tenure is being proposed by the government, but it promises to be of extremely limited scope, for example, allowing only three "pilot projects" in its initial operation, and being restricted to those very few areas where unused AAC exists.

Beyond Forest Practices – Community Management

Concurrent with changes to the tenure system would be a shift from a rules-based form of bureaucratic management to a goals-oriented form of community empowerment and self-management. How an authoritative "community forest board" might operate has been well described by many commentators over the years.[42] Overall, however, such boards would have a clear mandate to implement ecosystem-based approaches; possess real standard-setting and enforcement authority for local forest operations; embody a structure that is both representative of community interests and, at least in part, democratically accountable; and be entitled to a funding base that is independent of the provincial government.[43] These boards would replace many of the functions of the existing forest service, and would do so under criteria that were more oriented to environmental health, regional economic stability, and local public participation.

Support for community-based management alternatives does not imply that one is blind to the possibility of abuses at that level where vested economic and political interests can also dominate. The issue is simply the proper democratic design of alternative management processes that draw on the central government (the "state") in a transformative mode that both creates *decentralized* institutions outside the big agencies, and then supports their operations to ensure that they truly foster a reinvigorated, *territorial* culture of ecological self-development. This entails a profound re-ordering of the centralist state from its historical role of exploiting such areas for centralist growth to a progressive role of supporting their economic transition to greater regional self-sufficiency.⁴⁴ The success of forest-dependent communities in the United States that have made the transition from logging to amenities-based economies demonstrates the potential of this approach.⁴⁵

Overall, comprehensive reforms must do two things: devolve to the community level the powers and responsibilities necessary to pursue a new ecosystem-based future and, simultaneously, begin the transformation of larger state structures. An innovative vehicle for this (proposed collaboratively by the author) is a Community Forest Trust Act that would redefine Crown forest land onto an ecologically based foundation by placing it into a "trust" for those regions that sought it, accompanied by a host of supportive transition mechanisms for the management of the lands in that trust.⁴⁶ The conditions of the trust would require all activities taking place therein to embody two basic premises of sustainability – the maintenance of ecosystem integrity, and the application of community management.

The trust for forest lands is a simple concept, but its implications as a vehicle for an ecologically based transition are dramatic. It calls for the repeal of no existing tenures – so long as existing tenure holders update their operations to respect the latest scientific knowledge in ecosystem science. It calls for a dramatically new attitude to the forest land base – but asks us to implement that new attitude one community at a time, as each community is ready to make the move. It calls for a decentralization of authority to the local level ("community control"), but all within a protective and supportive framework maintained by the provincial government.

The creative implications of the proposal are wide-ranging. It doesn't just try to add on a new constraint to business-as-usual but sets a new context for communities to create something new for themselves – new local tenures, new local businesses, a new stewardship relationship to their local forests. By opening up the "political space" it would enable the local logger to sit down and talk to the environmentalist and band member and manufacturer, and talk about the real roots of the environmental conflict, and the continuing loss of biodiversity – the absence of ecologically based alternatives. In other words, it changes the focus from just imposing constraints on existing practices to creating opportunities for new ones.

Put another way, this proposal moves policy from *sustainable development* to *developing sustainability*. This distinction sums up the argument of this paper. As environmentalists commented on *sustainable development* in the 1980s, "they got the noun and we got the adjective." In contrast, with *developing sustainability*, "they get the verb, but we get the noun." This means growth into no-growth, and economic development but of transformative, new institutions.[47]

The process envisioned here is also gradual. While the eventual outcome would be transformative in our approach to the forest land base, this transformation occurs only as communities look at their futures, and decide to take the plunge. Indeed, if the government passed the Community Forest Trust Act tomorrow, nothing would change – until a community put up its collective hand and said, "Me first." While the proposal doesn't merely tinker with the status quo, neither does it pose a radical change overnight. Instead, it proposes a radical change, but it proposes getting there incrementally. It allows this to occur one place, one precedent, at a time.

This is precisely the lesson that British Columbia's experience with forestry reform has to offer those seeking to maintain biological diversity – a new model of government intervention is needed, one that is not just *restrictive* of an industry that inherently resists constraints but is *facilitative* of new forms of industry and economy that are, by their nature, supportive of values of environmental sustainability and biological diversity. The approach must move from "managing the unmanageable" to "unmanaging the manageable." We must find the solutions – and set them free.

Building an Ecological State

We come back to the Slocan Valley – and Clayoquot Sound and the Nass Valley of the Nisga'a – places where the communities have done their ecological homework and where a new approach to the land and its people could come together. The new potential that these places represent cannot be achieved by tinkering. Unfortunately, even social democratic governments fail to understand the necessity, and the promise, of such a transition to an ecological state. As a result, they lose their vision, and their only prospect for success. If the provincial, national, and even international movement to preserve biodiversity is to save itself from the frustrations of those who have gone before, it must not be equally short-sighted. The only solution is to bypass incrementalism by embracing bold new measures to build our economic and political foundations anew.

Notes

1. Land Use Co-ordination Office, Government of British Columbia, Victoria, October 21, 1996.
2. Silva Forest Foundation, *An Ecosystem-Based Landscape Plan for the Slocan River Watershed: Part 1- Report of Findings* (Winlaw, B.C.: Silva Forest Foundation, June 1996). For a critical analysis of the implications for the region's forests of status quo industrial forestry, see *What the Kootenay-Boundary Land Use Plan Means to the Environment and Communities: Economic and Ecological Implications of the Government's Draft Strategy to Implement the Land Use Plan* (New Denver, B.C.: Valhalla Wilderness Society, February 28, 1997).
3. See John Friedmann and Clyde Weaver, *Territory and Function: The Evolution of Regional Planning* (Berkeley: University of California Press, 1979); John Friedmann, *Life Space and Economic Space* (New Brunswick, N.J.: Transaction Books, 1988); Edward Soya, *Postmodern Geographies* (London: Verso, 1989); Ralph Matthews, *The Creation of Regional Dependency* (Toronto: University of Toronto Press, 1983); Elinor Ostrom, *Governing the Common: The Evolution of*

Institutions for Collective Action (Cambridge: Cambridge University Press, 1990).

4. *Forest Practices Code of British Columbia Ac* (1994, Statutes of B.C.), c.41.
5. See *Forest Renewal BC Business Plan 1995-2000* (Victoria: Forest Renewal BC, June 1995).
6. A summary of this workshop is provided in "Science Confirms Activists' Warnings," *BC Environmental Report* (Spring 1998): 28-29. The *Report* is available from BCEN, 1672 East Tenth Avenue, Vancouver, B.C., V5N 1X5.
7. For a detailed critique of this regime, and comprehensive comparison with an ecosystem-based approach, see Cheri Burda et al., *Forests in Trust*, Research Report 97-2 (Victoria: Eco-Research Chair of Environmental Law and Policy, July 1997).
8. Gordon Sloan, *Report of the Commissioner relating to the Forest Resources of British Columbia* (Victoria, B.C.: King's Printer, 1945).
9. Lois Dellert, "Sustained Yield Forestry in British Columbia: The Making and Breaking of a Policy (1900-1993)," Master's thesis, York University, 1994.
10. B.C. Ministry of Forests, *Regional Long Term Harvest Projections and Associated Employment Opportunities* (Victoria: Fibre Targets Task Group, 1997).
11. Greenpeace, *Broken Promises* (Vancouver: Greenpeace Canada, April 1997).
12. Peter H. Pearse, "Conflicting Objectives in Forest Policy: The Case of British Columbia," *Forestry Chronicle* (August 1970).
13. B.C. Ministry of Forests, "Review of the Timber Supply Analysis Process," 1991.
14. Sloan, *Report of the Commissioner*.
15. Ken Drushka, *Stumped* (Vancouver: Douglas & McIntyre, 1986).
16. See Karen Lewis, *A Protected Areas Strategy for BC: Provincial Overview and Status Report, Version One* (Victoria: Land Use Co-ordination Office, April 1996), 74.
17. For an analysis of what has happened in the United States where a fragmented (i.e., parks-based) approach to biodiversity conservation was taken, see Reed Noss and Allen Cooperrider, *Saving Nature's Legacy: Protecting and Restoring Biodiversity* (Washington: Island Press, 1994). A more recent study reiterates these concerns, noting that "current management practices seldom meet the SMZ goals. Of most concern, timber extraction volume targets frequently override other land use objectives...." From the Executive Summary, Jim Cooperman, *Keeping the Special in Special Management Zones: A Citizens' Guide* (Gibsons, B.C.: BC Spaces for Nature, May 1998).

18. VIRT Technical Team, *Resource Management Zones for Vancouver Island: VIRT Project Report* (Victoria: Land Use Co-ordination Office, 1998).

19. For example, on March 7 and 26, 1997, two large-scale LRMP processes were concluded in the Fort Nelson and Fort St. John areas of northern B.C., with the promise of designating over 1,000,000 hectares as protected areas in the Northern Rockies. However, the failure to achieve practical implementation of the protective zonations within these agreements continues to undermine their effectiveness outside protected areas.

20. Fred Marshall told the annual general meeting of the Boundary Woodlot Association in July 1996 that many experienced woodlot owners are now turning their licences back to the government because they cannot afford to comply with the paperwork or because they oppose the industrial standards now being applied to them (e.g.. requirements to "upgrade" their horse-logging trail to accommodate a motorized skidder).

21. In the ongoing Klaskish Valley case, Sierra Legal Defence Fund (SLDF), the informal watchdog of the Code's implementation, brought the inadequacy of MacMillan Bloedel's 1996-97 Forest Development Plan for the Klaskish area to the attention of the Forest Practices Board. The Board subsequently recommended cancellation of the plan; however, a review panel reversed the Board's decision. The Board has appealed the matter to the Forest Appeals Commission and SLDF has been granted intervenor status, but by the time the case is decided by the Commission, the development plan and the logging will have largely been completed.

22. For example, the SLDF report, *Business As Usual: The Failure to Implement the Cariboo-Chilcotin Land Use Plan* (Vancouver: SLDF, April 1996), shows that although low-intensity zones account for only 18 per cent of the productive forest land base in this area, forest companies with approved logging plans expect to extract over 30 per cent of their cut from them, using almost exclusively traditional clear-cutting methods with virtually no consideration for non-forest values.

23. *Forest Practices Code*, preamble.

24. See Gordon Hamilton, "Forest Code Change Allows More Logging," *Vancouver Sun*, March 2, 1996.

25. *Biodiversity Guidebook, 1995* (Victoria: B.C. Ministries of Forests and Environment, 1995), 9.

26. *Forest Practices Code*, s.4 (4).

27. See *British Columbia's Clear Cut Code* (Vancouver: SLDF, November 1996) and *Stream Protection Under the Code: The Destruction Continues* (Vancouver: SLDF, February 1997).

28. Overall, the provincial AAC remained at 71 million cubic metres after the conclusion of the Timber Supply Review in December 1996. See *Summary of Timber Supply Review Results 1992-96* (Victoria: Ministry of Forests, January 1997).

29. *Biodiversity Guidebook*, 9.

30. See Greenpeace, *Broken Promises*; Patricia Lush, "Cheaper Logs Not a Clear-cut Issue," *Globe and Mail*, April 9, 1997; Gordon Hamilton, "Forest Industry Makes Less, Blames Government Costs," *Vancouver Sun*, May 7, 1997.

31. The Board's letter to the Minister of Forests, David Zirnhelt, dated March 5, 1998, provoked an extensive public debate with the minister. In the letter, the Board noted that the changes would lead to: "the very significant reduction in the public's ability to have adequate opportunity to review, and comment on, forestry plans"; "the significant reduction in the level of information, particularly the results of assessments of forest resources"; and "important information not being available to decision-makers at the appropriate time." To access this correspondence, see http://www.Fpb.gov.bc.ca/events/letterl.htm

32. Forest Renewal British Columbia (FRBC), *Our Forest Future: Working in Partnership*, (Victoria: Queen's Printer, 1995).

33. BCEN, *Forest Renewal Outreach* 2, 1 (Spring 1997).

34. FRBC, *Our Forest Future*.

35. British Columbia, *British Columbia's Forest Renewal Plan*, (Victoria: Queen's Printer, 1994).

36. Michael M'Gonigle and Ben Parfitt, *Forestopia: A Practical Guide to the New Forest Economy* (Madeira Park, B.C.: Harbour Publishing, 1994), 54-55.

37. See Michael M'Gonigle, *Between Centre and Territory: Toward a Political Ecology of Ecological Economics*, Discussion Paper 95-2 (Victoria: Eco-Research Chair of Environmental Law and Policy, August 1996).

38. For example, R.E. Grumbine, "What Is Ecosystem Management?" *Conservation Biology* 8 (1994): 27. Grumbine observes that, "in the academic and popular literature there is general agreement that maintaining ecosystem integrity should take precedence over any other management goal.... This may be due partially to the fact that, given the rate and scale of environmental deterioration along with our profound scientific igno-

rance of ecological patterns and processes, we are in no position to make judgments about what ecosystem elements to favor in our management efforts."

39. See *Sustainable Ecosystem Management in Clayoquot Sound: Planning and Practice*, Report 5 (Victoria: Scientific Panel for Sustainable Forest Practices in Clayoquot Sound, 1995).

40. See *The Slocan Valley Community Forest Management Project: Final Report* (Winlaw, B.C.: Slocan Community, 1975).

41. See Cheri Burda and Michael M'Gonigle, "Tree Farm or Community Forest?: Reflections on the Revelstoke Experience," *Making Waves: Canada's Community Economic Development Quarterly* 7, 4 (Winter 1996): 16-21. Innovative proposals stymied by this situation include *Malcolm Island Community Forest Feasibility Study* (Vancouver: Robin Clark Inc., 1996) and *Feasibility Study: Prince George Community Forest* (Victoria: Cortex Consultants, May 1996).

42. See *The Slocan Valley Community Forest Management Project: Final Report*; *Village of Hazelton's Framework for Watershed Managemen* (Hazelton, B.C.: Village of Hazelton, 1991); and the Tin Wis Coalition's Forestry Working Group, Draft Model Legislation, *The Tin Wis Forest Stewardship Act* (Vancouver: Tin Wis Coalition, 1991).

43. See *From Compromise to Consensus: A Blueprint for Building Sustainable Communities and Protecting Ecosystems in Clayoquot Sound* (Tofino, B.C.: Central Region Board, September 20, 1996).

44. For details, see M'Gonigle and Parfitt, *Forestopia*.

45. For example, the writings of the Montana-based economist, Thomas Power, including "The Wealth of Nature," *Issues in Science and Technology* (Spring 1996): 48-54; and *Lost Landscapes and Failed Economies* (Washington: Island Press, 1996).

46. See Burda et al., *Forests in Trust*.

47. For the original source of this inversion of sustainable development, see Michael M'Gonigle, "Designing for Sustainability: A Native/Environmentalist Prescription for Third Level Government," *BC Studies* 84 (Winter 1989-1990): 65-99.

Further Reading

Burda, Cheri, Deborah Curran, Fred Gale, and Michael M'Gonigle. *Forests in Trust: Reforming British Columbia's Forest Tenure System for Ecosystem and Community*

Health. Research Report 97-2. Victoria: Eco-Research Chair of Environmental Law and Policy, July 1997.

Drushka, Ken, Bob Nixon, and Ray Travers, eds. *Touch Wood: BC Forests at the Crossroads.* Madeira Park, B.C.: Harbour Publishing, 1993.

Hammond, Herb. *Seeing the Forest Among the Trees: The Case for Wholistic Forest Use.* Vancouver: Polestar, 1991.

May, Elizabeth. *At the Cutting Edge: The Crisis in Canada's Forests.* Toronto: Key Porter, 1998.

M'Gonigle, Michael, and Ben Parfitt. *Forestopia: A Practical Guide to the New Forest Economy.* Madeira Park, B.C.: Harbour Publishing, 1994.

Rajala, Richard. *Clearcutting the Pacific Rainforest: Production, Science, and Regulation.* Vancouver: University of British Columbia Press, 1998.

Tollefson, Chris, ed. *The Wealth of Forests: Markets, Regulation and Sustainable Forestry.* Vancouver: University of British Columbia Press, 1998.

Wilson, Jeremy. *Talk and Log: Wilderness Politics in British Columbia.* Vancouver: University of British Columbia Press, 1998.

Contributors

Ian Attridge is an environmental lawyer in Peterborough, Ontario, and a Research Associate of the Canadian Institute for Environmental Law and Policy (CIELAP) and Trent University's Frost Centre for Canadian Heritage and Development Studies. He advises landowners, organizations, and agencies on biodiversity conservation measures, particularly private land stewardship. Before entering private practice, he was a legal and policy adviser to the Ontario Ministry of Natural Resources. He has researched, written, and presented extensively on biodiversity law and policy in Canada.

Russel Barsh teaches courses on indigenous science and community development at the University of Lethbridge, and co-ordinates a number of grassroots research projects in the Blackfoot Confederacy. He has worked as a consultant for United Nations agencies on strategies for development grounded in indigenous peoples' own knowledge systems, and on the protection of indigenous science.

Richard K. Baydack is Associate Director of the Natural Resources Institute at the University of Manitoba. He is an editor of *Practical Approaches to the Conservation of Biological Diversity* (1999).

Anne C. Bell is a Ph.D. candidate in Environmental Studies at York University. Her current areas of research include biological conservation, environmental education, and ecological restoration. She is a board member of the Wildlands League.

Stephen Bocking is an Associate Professor in the Environmental and Resource Studies Program at Trent University. His research interests include environmental history and the role of science in environmental politics. He is the author of *Ecologists and Environmental Politics: A History of Contemporary Ecology* (1997).

JY CHIPERZAK is founder and former director of Rare Breeds Canada and of the Canadian Coalition for Biodiversity.

JERRY V. DEMARCO is a Staff Lawyer with the Sierra Legal Defence Fund and is a board member of the Wildlands League and the Canadian Parks and Wilderness Society. He holds degrees in geography (Windsor), environmental studies (York), and law (Toronto).

JOHN EYLES is Director of the McMaster Institute of Environment and Health and Professor of Geography at McMaster University. He has published widely in the fields of environmental health, health care, social theory, and methodology. His research interests include the interface of human values and the environment, claims-making in environmental policy and the role of evidence in decision-making and evaluation.

LÉOPOLD GAUDREAU is director of conservation and ecological heritage for the Ministère de l'Environnement et de la Faune du Québec. His field of expertise includes botany, protected areas and endangered species.

BENOÎT GAUTHIER is a Ph.D. ecologist working for the Ministère de l'Environnement et de la Faune du Québec. He is co-ordinating the implementation of the Quebec biodiversity strategy and action plan.

JAMES KAY is an Associate Professor of Environment and Resource Studies (with a cross-appointment in Systems Design Engineering) at the University of Waterloo. His principal research is on the development of the ecosystem approach to ecological management and planning. His research activities include the theoretical and epistemological basis for an ecosystem approach, the formulation of ecosystem-based environmental policy, the development of ecosystem monitoring programs, and on-the-ground planning in the context of both urban and natural ecosystems and the greening of institutions.

NINA-MARIE E. LISTER is an ecological planner specializing in environmental and landscape planning and design. She is an instructor in the Environmental Studies program at the University of Toronto, and her research interests and publications focus on biodiversity conservation, adaptive management, ecosystem ecology, and landscape design/planning. She is an Associate of the Canadian Biodiversity Institute and the Network for Ecosystem Sustainability and Health.

DON MCALLISTER is President of Ocean Voice International, a Canadian marine environmental organization. He was Curator of Fishes at the Canadian Museum of Nature for 30 years; there he originated and edited the *Global Biodiversity* bulletin for eight years. He is currently co-chair of the IUCN Species Survival Commission's Coral Reef Fish Specialist Group. He is the author of over 200 scientific papers, chapters, and books on fish taxonomy, ecology, zoogeography, and other topics, and he is co-author of *Canada's Biodiversity: The Variety of Life, Its Status, Economic Benefits, Conservation Costs, and Unmet Needs* (1995).

R. MICHAEL M'GONIGLE is Professor of Law and holds the Eco-Research Chair of Environmental Law and Policy at the University of Victoria, B.C. He is a co-founder of Greenpeace International, a former chairperson of Greenpeace Canada (during which time he initiated the organization's National Forests campaign), and a founding director of the Sierra Legal Defence Fund.

TED MOSQUIN is a naturalist, botanist, and consultant with extensive knowledge of the flora, fauna, and natural ecosystems of Canada and the United States. He is a former researcher with Agriculture Canada, specializing in the evolution and pollination of Canadian flora. He has served as Executive Director of the Canadian Nature Federation and as president of the Ottawa Field-Naturalists Club, the Canadian Audubon Society, and most recently, the Canadian Parks and Wilderness Society. Ted created and edited *Nature Canada* for its first five years, and edited the *Canadian Field-Naturalist* for four years. He co-wrote *Legacy: A Natural History of Ontario* (1988) and *On the Brink: Endangered Species in Canada* (1989), and was principal author of *Canada's Biodiversity: The Variety of Life, Its Status, Economic Benefits, Conservation Costs, and Unmet Needs* (1995).

ROBERT PAEHLKE is a Professor in the Environmental and Resource Studies Program and the Political Studies Department at Trent

University. He is the author of *Environmentalism and the Future of Progressive Politics* (1989) and edited the *Encyclopedia of Environmentalism and Conservation* (1995).

Bob Page was until 1997 Dean of the Faculty of Environmental Design at the University of Calgary. Between 1994 and 1996 he chaired the Banff-Bow Valley Study, which assessed the prospects for ecological sustainability in Banff National Park. He is currently Vice-President, Sustainable Development, at the TransAlta Corporation in Calgary.

Jacques Prescott is a conservation biologist in charge of the endangered species conservation service for the Ministère de l'Environnement et de la Faune du Québec. He is the co-author of a field guide on the mammals of eastern Canada and a United Nations Development Program consultant for biodiversity planning.

Lorna Stefanick is a visiting Assistant Professor in the Department of Political Science at the University of Alberta. Her research interests include the environmental movement, environmental policy, and participatory decision making processes.

Loren Vanderlinden is a physical anthropologist with interests in human population biology, environmental health, and health, well-being, and values. She teaches in the Department of Anthropology, University of Toronto, and was recently a postdoctoral fellow of the McMaster Institute of Environment and Health. She is currently a collaborator on research projects concerning children's health, contaminants, and standard setting in Ontario, as well as environmental health issues among First Nations communities.

Kathleen Wells is a law student at the University of Alberta in Edmonton.

Peter Whiting, a natural resource economist for over 25 years, has been a consultant concentrating on the economics of natural resources and the environment for the past 15 years. His interests and projects have been in a wide range of fields in Canada and abroad, including biodiversity, parks and protected areas, wildlife, endangered species, sport fisheries, and ecotourism. He is co-author of *Canada's Biodiversity: The Variety of Life, Its Status, Economic Benefits, Conservation Costs, and Unmet Needs* (1995).

BOB WILDFONG is the president of Seeds of Diversity Canada, a non-profit network of gardeners from coast-to-coast who grow and share the seeds of rare plants for the purpose of preserving them.

Index

acid rain, 64
adaptive planning and management,
    xvi, 182-84, 196-98, 202, 203, 206, 210-12
Advisory Committee on Pollution
    Control (Alberta), 370
Agreement on Straddling and Highly
    Migratory Fish Stocks (1995), 319
Agreement on the Conservation of Polar
    Bears (1973), 299, 305
agriculture, xii, xiv, 61, 64, 67, 70-72, 76, 87-
    89, 137-49, 230, 275, 289, 321-22
Agriculture and Agri-Food Canada, 70-
    72, 73, 321-22
Agriculture Canada Plant Gene
    Resources, 142
Alberta, ix, xxii-xxiii, 31, 46, 67, 72, 85, 87,
    168, 270, 354, 367-70, 373-87
Alberta Environmental Network, 370
Alberta Wilderness Association, 18
Algonquin Park, 3, 8, 12, 13, 14, 19, 20
Algonquin Wildlands League, 19
American Museum of Natural History,
    244, 261
animal rights, 277
aquaculture, 90-91
aquatic ecosystems, xiii, 45, 81-105
Arctic, 3, 21-22, 69, 99, 276
Arctic Biological Research Station, 73
Atlantic salmon, 9
attitudes, towards biodiversity, 24-25, 241-
    46, 249-64; and environmentalism, 15-
    16; and predators, xvii, 10, 14, 19, 275-
    276; and values, xvii-xix, 108, 131, 197,
    202, 226-29, 237-38, 240-241, 268, 273, 275-77,
    282-84; as expressed in parks, 13, 18-19,
    33, 36-38, 41; in nineteenth century, 4-
    7, 10; indigenous, xvi, 12, 158-61, 165-67,
    269
Audubon, John James, 275
auk, 10, 95

automobiles, 288-89, 292

Banff-Bow Valley Study, xi, 37, 39, 40;
    report of, 42-55
Banff National Park, xi, 7, 10, 11, 31-56, 85,
    128, 280, 283
BC Wild, 393
bears, xv, 16, 53, 81, 99, 160, 192, 276, 280, 284,
    303
Berger, Thomas, 22
biodiversity: and cultural diversity, xii,
    xiv; at ecosystem level, xii, xiii, 66-67,
    84, 180, 191, 257-58, 275, 353; at genetic
    level, xii, xiii, xiv, 61-62, 89, 139-42, 180,
    275, 317; at species level, xii, 62-66, 84-
    86, 94-95, 180, 191, 192, 275, 277, 329; con-
    ceptual models of, 257-59, 261;
    definitions of, 177, 249-250; ecological
    functions of, xiii, 111-30; economic
    value of, 109, 219, 222-34, 240, 245, 254-55,
    259, 260, 262, 263, 286, 329-31; in agricul-
    ture, 137-49; intrinsic value of, 108, 110-
    11, 129-30, 131-32, 241, 256, 259, 260, 262, 263-
    64; origin of term, 23, 274; political
    challenges in conserving, xx, 278-81,
    297, 314-21, 323, 348, 352, 371-73; restora-
    tion of, 317, 359-61; scientific percep-
    tions of, 263, 277, 281-82; status of, 59-69
biogeochemical cycles, 124-25
Biological Board of Canada, 11
biophilia, 241
Biosphere Reserves, 189
birds, 63-65, 175-84, 284
Bird Studies Canada, 353
Blais-Grenier, Suzanne, 23
Bouchard, Lucien, 24
Boundary Waters Treaty (1909), 299
Bousfield, Edward, 95
Briggs, J.C., 92

Quebec Union of Agricultural
  Producers, 332
Quebec Vulnerable and Endangered
  Species Act, 332
Quebec Zoo Association, 332
Quetico Park, 12, 20, 232-33

Ramsar Convention (1971), 23, 299
Rare Breeds Canada, 145, 146
Recovery of Nationally Endangered
  Wildlife program (RENEW), 65, 352
Rees, William, 285
Rolston, Holmes, 130

Saskatchewan, 354
Saskatchewan Plains Research Centre, 67
Schindler, David, 75
science: and biodiversity conservation,
  xiii, xvi-xviii, xix, 47, 191, 175-84, 197-205,
  210, 332-33; and perceptions of biodi-
  versity, 5, 25, 256, 258, 263; communica-
  tion of, xvi, 183, 243-44; declining
  funding for, xv, 73-76, 208
Scott, Duncan Campbell, 9
Seed Savers Exchange, 144, 148
Seeds of Diversity Canada, xiv, 144, 148, 351
Seeds of Survival program, 143
Seton, Ernest Thompson, 7
Sierra Club, 393
Sierra Legal Defence Fund, 320, 351, 357,
  363, 393, 401, 411
Sifton, Clifford, 9
Silva Foundation, 391, 392, 405
Sloan Royal Commission (B.C.), 15, 396-
  97
Slocan Forest Products, 391
Slocan Valley (B.C.), 391-92, 400, 409
South Moresby National Park, 24
Soya, Edward, 393
Special Places 2000 program, ix, xxii-xxiii,
  31, 72, 367-68, 373-76, 380-86
State of the Environment Reporting, 75
Statistics Canada, 68
stewardship, of land, xx, 209, 310-12
Stirling, Ian, 99
Supreme Court of Canada, 299, 300, 357
sustained-yield forest management, 396-
  97

Takacs, David, 256
Tatshenshini-Alsek, 356
taxes, 290-93, 312
Temagami region, 8
Territorial Lands Act, 308
Thoreau, Henry David, xvii, 275
Toner, Glen, 372, 387
Toronto, 288-89
tourism and recreation, 7, 13, 17, 18, 20, 24,
  245, 255, 279-80, 377; economic value of,
  231-33, 240; in Banff Park, 32-36, 43, 47-51
Tourism Destination Model (in Banff
  Park), 47-50, 53
trade agreements, 76
traditional ecological knowledge. See
  indigenous knowledge
Traill, Catherine Parr, 6
Trent University, 311, 317
Trout Unlimited, 35

Union of Nova Scotia Indians, 357
United Nations Conference on
  Environment and Development
  (1992), ix, 23, 219, 274, 298, 327
United Nations Convention on the Law
  of the Sea, 319
United Nations Environment Program,
  226
University of Alberta, 270
University of British Columbia, 182
University of Guelph, 246-47
University of Stirling (Scotland), 261
University of Toronto, 8, 19

Vacation Alberta Corporation, 377
Valhalla Wilderness Society, 391, 393
Vancouver Island Land Use Plan, 395
Van Horne, Cornelius, 32
Vavilov, N.I., 138

Wackernagel, Mathis, 285
water export, 91
Waterton Lakes National Park, 7, 386, 387
Western Canada Wilderness Committee,
  18
western yew, 233, 254
wetlands, 276, 321
Whaleback region (Alberta), 389